Introduction
to
Handwriting
Examination
and
Identification

Introduction
to
Handwriting Examination
and
Identification

Russell R. Bradford

and

Ralph B. Bradford

Nelson-Hall Publishers
Chicago

Library of Congress Cataloging-in-Publication Data

Bradford, Russell R.
    Introduction to handwriting examination and identification /
Russell R. Bradford and Ralph Bradford.
        p.   cm.
    Includes bibliographical references and indexes.
    ISBN 0-8304-1241-7
    1. Writing—Identification.   I. Bradford, Ralph. II. Title.
HV8074.B68 1992
363.2'565—dc20

92-1234
CIP

Manufactured in the United States of America

10 9 8 7 6 5 4 3 2 1

™ The paper used in this book meets the
minimum requirements of American
National Standard for Information
Sciences—Permanence of Paper for
Printed Library Materials, ANSI
Z39.48-1984.

Dedicated to
Marianne Bradford
and
Margaret Bradford

Contents

Preface

Russell R. Bradford

I n 1953, almost every law enforcement agency in Southern California purchased a new publication, the *Bradford System of Classification* by Ralph Bradford, and set up the system this booklet introduced. Forgery detail detectives who
began using the system quickly discovered that they knew little or nothing about
handwriting comparison.

The monthly meeting of the Southern California Check Investigators
Association turned into a question-and-answer session, with check investigators
firing questions at Ralph about the comparison of handwriting when using the
Bradford System. He was also called on to speak at the California State Division
of the International Association for Identification Conference, the State Check
Investigators Conference, the Retail Clerks Association, the Special Agents Association, and the FBI Law Enforcement Conference in Los Angeles.

In 1957, Ralph Bradford advised the members of the various agencies in
Southern California that he would teach a handwriting course at the Long Beach
Police Honor Farm. Two-hour classes were scheduled, one night a week for
twelve weeks. There was no charge for the course, and it was open to all who
wished to attend. On March 4, 1957, 104 students were present, including
twelve San Diego investigators who drove a hundred miles to attend the session.
Members of police and sheriff departments, representatives of the Secret Service,
the Army, the Air Force, and many banks, and also special investigators from
private industry attended the course.

Ralph opened the class by asking all the students to fill out handwriting
exemplars. Blank checks were then passed out, and each person was asked to fill
out one check in his or her normal handwriting and another in disguised writing.
Copies of all 104 exemplars and 208 checks were made for each student. Since
there was no beginner's handwriting book on the market, Ralph typed new
material for each class, making copies for each student. He also told the class about
many excellent advanced texts they could access for further study after completing
the beginner's class.

For each subsequent class Ralph retyped and expanded on the handout material. This proved to be such a massive job, in the days before fast copying machines, that Ralph decided he would write a beginner's book on handwriting comparison.

On January 7, 1963, he began a new twelve-week course with two innovations. He taped the class and asked the students to fill out the handwriting exemplars using special fictitious names.

Work on the book went slowly, as Ralph continued to teach his course at California State University at Long Beach. The last course he taught was in Las Vegas, Nevada, on May 7, 1968, with eighty law enforcement officers from Clark County, Nevada, graduating. Diplomas were presented by District Attorney George Franklin. Ralph and his son, Russell, continued working on the new book, and both agreed the book would follow the class curriculum as closely as possible. There would be twelve chapters corresponding to the twelve classes. But when Ralph Bradford died on October 26, 1971, the actual writing had scarcely started.

A while after my father's death, I took leave from the Long Beach Police Department to complete a few of my father's cases for the Clark County District Attorney's Office in Las Vegas, Nevada. During this time, Robert Burgess, a good friend of Ralph's, asked me how the book was coming. It was at that time I decided to gather all my father's material and organize it into the twelve chapters of the book. I also started to do further research for the book.

Whenever I could find appropriate material in the work of my father, or in cases he worked on, I have used it. I have included many photographs of his cases and all are authentic.

The purpose of this book is to teach beginning handwriting examination. Like our handwriting course, it is primarily intended for investigators seeking information to help them to do a better job. Every investigator should know enough about handwriting to enable him or her to do preliminary work and to know when to contact an examiner.

This text is intended to teach only the fundamentals of handwriting examination. Advanced subjects, such as the comparison of inks and paper, indented writing, erased writing, charred documents, or ultraviolet photography, are not covered in detail. If you wish to continue in this field, there are many excellent books and materials to assist in advanced study. At least seventeen students did go on with their study and have testified as experts. Since this book uses, to a great extent, the materials and knowledge of my late father, Ralph Bradford, he is listed as coauthor.

I would like to thank the many persons who helped make this book a reality. First, I want to thank Letty James, secretary in the Long Beach Forgery Detail for five years with Ralph and nine years with me, and who attended two of the handwriting classes. She transcribed the tapes of the 1963 class and typed the first draft of this book. Also, thanks to Lt. George Workman, a close friend of the Bradfords, who attended two handwriting classes and who worked as an investigator and later as a lieutenant in command of the Forgery Detail. With George's editing and great assistance, this work was completed. I also want to acknowledge the help and encouragement I received from the late Sgt. Stanley White, my superior in the Forgery Detail. Stan attended the first class and rates special thanks for the assistance he gave me as a "new" examiner. I would like to thank the officers of the Long Beach Police Department, including Richard Coleman, William Corson, Deo Gemignani, Barbara Summers, and all the members of the Forgery Detail for their assistance and support.

Special thanks also to document examiners Arthur Blenski, Richard Clason, Donald Doud, Marilyn Gooch, Martin Tytell, and the late Albert Somerford. I would also like to thank the examiners who read the sections of the book that related to them: Robert Cabanne, Alwyn Cole, Jack J. Harris, Wilson R. Harrison, Ordway Hilton, and Charles C. Scott.

I am grateful to the 590 students who helped demonstrate the value of the handwriting classes and the need for this book. A great deal of assistance was received from the personnel of California State University of Long Beach (especially Vicky Pearlson), and the Long Beach Public Library.

I extend very special thanks to the two women to whom this book is dedicated, my wife, Marianne, and my mother, Margaret Bradford, who accompanied Ralph and me to numerous California State Division meetings and to conferences of the International Association for Identification throughout California and the United States. Their presence, patience, and understanding encouraged my father and me, and enabled us to work toward our goals.

Finally, I must say a few words about my father. When I was ten years old, during an illness which required me to remain in bed, my father gave me the book *Forgeries*, by George H. Zinnel. Since that day, I have been interested in the science of handwriting examination. During the succeeding years, he gave me information and copies of cases only as I requested that help. In 1954, when I decided to pursue a career in law enforcement, he began to assemble information for me, which led to his first class in 1957.

In 1961, I was chosen to replace my father as the Long Beach Police Handwriting Examiner. After training me intensively for two years, he retired. So I had nine years' experience as a handwriting examiner at the time he was employed in the Howard Hughes v. Maheu case in 1970. I saw his tremendous ability at work in each opinion he reached. He solved some cases that I considered beyond solution. His ability was demonstrated to the members of the 1970 International Association for Identification Conference in Pittsburgh. Members still speak of his questioning of Dr. Vassislis C. Morfopoulos regarding the Kent murder case. Walter G. Hoetzer, secretary-treasuer of the IAI wrote my father after that conference: "You have saved the day for us and helped to overcome a most embarrassing situation." (This case is discussed in chapter 11.)

Ralph B. Bradford would have written a truly great beginner's book. I regret that he was not able to complete his work. I hope that this book reflects to a small degree the success he achieved in his work and in his classes.

Preface

Ralph B. Bradford

The adage "A little knowledge is a dangerous thing" applies as well to handwriting examination and identification as to any other field. A cursory reading of a standard text on the subject is not "quite enough" to make one a qualified expert.

In designing this book, I have employed an approach adapted from standard textbooks. The resulting basic study should enable a beginner to acquire the fundamentals that will assist him or her in doing a better job and eventually develop into a qualified examiner.

Virtually every security agent, and especially those in the fields of food marketing and department stores, can use such training. It is equally useful to bankers, attorneys, and credit men and women, and an important tool of the trade for security people in the armed forces and defense industries. In the field of law enforcement, a knowledge of basic handwriting examination and identification principles is vital in obtaining exemplars and evidence for successful prosecution.

This book will also assist in the development of handwriting examiners who are called upon to identify the writers of extortion letters; malicious, threatening, or lewd letters; fictitious-name checks; betting markers; forged medical prescriptions; hold-up notes; and so forth.

Where forgery is suspected, the handwriting examiner must be able to identify the authenticity or spuriousness of signatures on checks, pawn tickets, credit card invoices, charge slips, and signatures on all types of legal documents, such as bills of sale, powers of attorney, or ownership (pink) slips for automobiles and boats.

The first chapter contains an in-depth study of the history of handwriting comparison. It lists some famous cases and the experts who testified in them. Next is an introduction that will tell you everything you want to know about handwriting comparison. It lists the books, equipment, and information necessary to get started as a handwriting trainee.

The book includes a classification system of checks based on the modus operandi in which the spurious check is written, instead of the handwriting itself. Next, the numbering system of the American Bankers Association is explained, plus a detailed vocabulary for the profession of Document Examiner. The vocabulary will be used to describe every letter in detail. The letters of the handwriting systems taught in the United States are listed for your study.

The "Five Basic Types" of handwriting are introduced and explained. To obtain exemplars or to make a comparison, knowledge of the basic types of handwriting is needed. The actual methods of handwriting comparison and identification are analyzed in detail, by the numbers. You will learn to recognize proportion, arrangement, slant, curves, and all the other elements involved in the comparison of handwriting, hand printing, and numbers.

Other important phases of modern identification methods are examined in the study of typewriter and check protector comparison. Identification of an individual typewriter and the typist, and identification of the brands of typewriters, history, vocabulary, and step-by-step identification are studied.

Fingerprints can be found on many documents and are explained in detail from a to z. You will learn the history of fingerprints, their vocabulary, and the need for information by a document examiner. A simplified method of classifying individual fingerprints and their identification will be taught.

The last chapter describes the final opinion, preparation of exhibits, and the steps leading up to the final court testimony. Each of these subjects is described in detail, especially the court testimony.

I started each of my handwriting classes by telling the students that there is only one way, my way. Later, when you have finished, you may change the methods if you wish. If I knew of a better way, I would be doing it that way. Many think handwriting comparison is too difficult to learn; it is not. I have no secrets and, therefore, this book will teach you everything I know. It will be done by the numbers, with all the shortcuts I know.

—1—

A History of Handwriting Examination

A lbert Sherman Osborn, "The Dean of Document Examiners," wrote in 1940 that during the previous sixty to seventy years (1870–1940) there developed in this country a distinctly new profession, "The Scientific Examination and Proof of Handwriting and other Facts relating to Documents."[1]

This chapter is divided into seven periods in the history of this new profession, which is called Document Examination.

1. Origins of Handwriting Examination, ?–1869
2. Pioneering Period, 1870–1931
3. The Lindbergh Kidnap Case, 1932–35
4. A New Profession, 1936–41
5. Modern Period, 1942–69
6. Howard Hughes Period, 1970–78
7. The 1980s, 1990s, and Beyond

Origins of Handwriting Examination, ?–1869

Forgery has been practiced from earliest times, in every country. In ancient Rome, Marc Antony forged decrees and other documents, and the Emperor Titus was regarded as the greatest and most skillful forger of his time.

The rule for the identification and comparison of handwriting was clearly expressed in the *Code of Justinian*, Order 49, *Title* IV, chapter II, enacted in A.D. 539:

> Comparison of handwriting shall only be made in the case of public documents, and in the case of private instruments where the adverse party can use them to his own advantage. . . . For we entertain hatred for the crime

1

of forgery. We order that experts charged with the comparison of the handwriting of public documents shall be sworn before any private instruments are placed in their hands for this purpose. Wherefore this law, as well as the present modification of the same, shall remain in full force, and experts aforesaid shall by all means be sworn.[2]

In early English law, expert testimony was unknown. For many years, "comparison of hands" was not allowed, and only a witness who had knowledge or had witnessed the writing was allowed to testify. The Colonel Algeron Sidney trial, reported in nine Howell's State Trials 818 (1683), was one of the early reasons for these objections to the comparison of hands. The writing was compared by the jury, and Sidney was convicted and executed in 1684. The evidence consisted of proving the book was produced to be Colonel Sidney's writing, because "the hand was like what some of the witnesses had seen him write." The conviction was declared null and void in 1689, because the mere "similitude of handwriting" in the two papers shown to the jury, without concurrent testimony, was not evidence that both were written by the same person.

In 1854, England changed an old statute to allow properly proven exemplars in court. Massachusetts, Connecticut, and Maine followed suit. It was amazing to the average person that he could not fill out an exemplar to prove that he did not write a questioned document. New York joined them in 1880, and the United States followed with the statute of 1913, fifty-nine years after England.

The case of Sylvia Ann Howland in New Bedford, Massachusetts in 1867 was the first important handwriting case tried in America. It was possible because Massachusetts had accepted the English statute of 1854, thirteen years earlier. As usual for this time, the "experts" were bankers, tellers, professors of penmanship, photographers who offered enlarged photographs, engravers who discussed tracing, chemists who gave testimony on ink, and microscopists. They all testified that the signature "Sylvia Ann Howland" on a $2 million codicil was a forgery. The questioned signature entirely covered the genuine will signature. The codicil signature was therefore a forgery by tracing. The line quality was very bad, and this fact assisted in proving the forgery.

The most interesting part of the case concerns the testimony of Professor Benjamin Pierce, a celebrated mathematician from Harvard, who said:

> The relative frequency of coincidence expresses how often there is a coincidence in either of the characteristic lines such as in line one, for example. The product of the relative frequency into itself expresses how the coincidence of a characteristic line one is combined with that of line two; the cube of the relative frequency of coincidence shows how often there will be the simultaneous combination of the coincidences of the three first lines, and so on. Finally, the relative frequency must be multiplied into itself as many times as there are characteristic lines to express how often there can be a complete coincidence in position of all the lines of the signature.

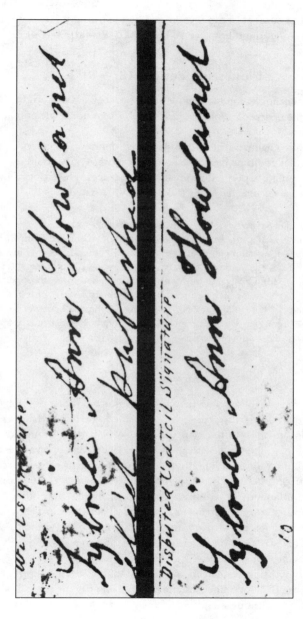

Figure 1–1: Howland case. The lower signature is of questioned codicil. (*Albert S. Osborn*)

In other words, the identical coincidence of thirty downward strokes with the same strokes of the second signature of Sylvia Ann Howland could occur only once in the number of times expressed by the thirtieth power of five (nine hundred thirty-one quintillions, or 931,000,000,000,000,000,000).[3]

Pioneering Period, 1870–1931

In 1870, handwriting comparison emerged from its dark ages. In the next sixty-two years, the new profession would achieve recognition as a legitimate science in courts of law.

Testimony changed from unsubstantiated opinion to evidence presented with exhibits that could be described so clearly that the jury could see what the examiner saw, unlike expert testimony in other sciences. The Honorable Edward Twistleton in *Handwriting of Junius* (London, 1871) stated:

> One skilled in handwriting may point out coincidences in documents which a volunteer would not have observed, if the document had been in his possession during a long series of years; but those coincidences are outward objective facts, the common property of experts and of volunteers. If the expert has skill in analyzing his own impressions, he can go through the proofs of everything which he asserts and can make others see what he sees. Hence the case with which he deals, however complicated, becomes merely one of reasoning, in which the internal circumstantial evidence is applied to demonstrate a disputed fact.[4]

Dreyfus Case

One case that did not follow Twistleton was the notorious case of Captain Alfred Dreyfus. In 1894, Count Esterhazy, commander of a French battalion, delivered confidential information to the German embassy in Paris. On one occasion, he left a note in the mailbox of Lieutenant Colonel Schwarzkoppen at the embassy. This note and other information intended for the Germans were intercepted by counterespionage officials. The handwritten note, which became known as the *bordereau* (memorandum, schedule, or list) was examined with other espionage items, including a message referring to a "scoundrel" by the initial D. The officials consulted a personnel list for names beginning with *D*, and came to the name "Dreyfus." This was a period of anti-Semitism, and they immediately stopped at Dreyfus, saying, "It was a Jew!"

The handwriting was given to Alfred Gobert, a handwriting examiner employed by the Bank of France, but he failed to identify the suspect. They then went to the world-famous scientist, Alphonse Bertillon. (Bertillon had taken the ideas of Quetelet, Stevens, and Renault, and in 1879 developed a new anthropometry identification system. In 1888 the French Government adopted the "Bertil-

4

lon System" as their national system.) The famed Bertillon, man of science, was asked to identify the traitor. Bertillon, who was not a handwriting expert, did what he thought would be popular with the people of France—he identified the specimen as the handwriting of Dreyfus.[5] In the trial, Bertillon used the handwriting system of Persifor Frazer in his testimony. (Frazer was to write *Bibliotics* in 1901. Albert S. Osborn reviewed the book in 1929 and said "Its ideas are impractical and almost valueless. . . . It can now be positively stated that these theories have no practical or scientific standing."[6]) Dreyfus was found guilty and sent to Devil's Island. Esterhazy later confessed to writing the *bordereau*, and Dreyfus received a second trial in 1899. Because of political considerations, Dreyfus was again found guilty, but ten days later was pardoned.

The Botkin and Molineux Poisoning Cases

The days of amateur experts like Bertillon and the "bank experts" were coming to an end, but two additional famous cases were tried before the turn of the century. Cordelia Botkin was tried in California in 1898. Botkin was arrested for mailing poisoned candy, which killed a Mrs. Dunning, but was encouraged when she learned that fingerprint evidence was not allowed in California. Handwriting examiners Daniel Ames, Carl Eisenschimel, and Theodore Kytke identified Botkin. She was found guilty and sentenced to life imprisonment. She died ten years later.

A more notorious case involved Roland B. Molineux, a distinguished member of the New York Knickerbocker Athletic Club, who accidentally killed an innocent person instead of his intended victim when he sent a poisoned bottle of Bromo Seltzer through the mail. Club officials examined the writing on the envelope and saw a resemblance to Molineux's writing. Yellow journalism was flourishing, and Molineux was named the poisoner by the press. Two months later he was arrested for murder, and five hundred persons were questioned before an impartial jury could be found. At least seventeen handwriting experts were involved in the case, six of them amateurs, employed as tellers and clerks in banks. The defense attorneys regarded the amateurs as unqualified and did not cross-examine most of them. (Amateurs would be a factor in very few cases in the future.)

The professional handwriting experts were led by Daniel T. Ames of New York. Ames was a flamboyant witness who gestured wildly and talked at the rate of 175 words a minute (the average is 80 words per minute).

When Ames testified, he called particular attention to the word "oblige." He pointed out the two coincident methods of making the *ge* and the forms of the ampersand. He also pointed out the break between the *i* and the *g* in most of the writing.

Thomas W. Cantwell, Dr. Persifor Frazer, William F. Hagen, Edwin D. Hay, B. F. Kelly, William J. Kinsley, Albert S. Osborn, Henry L. Tolman, and John F. Tyrrell also testified. Tyrrell's testimony was so outstanding that the

Document Examiner Hall of Fame

Daniel T. Ames

Ames was born December 19, 1835, in Vershire, Vermont. He was educated at Chelsea Academy and was a handwriting examiner in private practice from 1861 to 1909 (associated with William J. Kinsley). His major cases were Botkin and Molineux murders and the Samuel Davis will. He wrote *Ames on Forgery* and was editor and founder of *The Penman's Art Journal of New York*. He was an instructor at Ames National Business College and founder of Ames and Rollinson, Publishers. Ames died August 9, 1909, at the age of seventy-three in Mountain View, California.

defense referred to him as the "Wizard of the Pen." It was said that while the other witnesses were sightseeing in New York, Tyrrell remained in his room, using a drawing board, copying the disputed writing over and over until he became familiar with every detail. During testimony, he would draw the characteristics on a large piece of paper as he explained them. This was all from memory.[7]

The suspect was found guilty, but after a period in Sing Sing Death House, received a second trial. Time had obscured the details of the case and he was found not guilty. Eleven years later, he was committed for insanity and died a short time later.

An interesting sidelight to the first Molineux trial is that it lasted three months and cost the State of New York $200,000. The experts in this case were

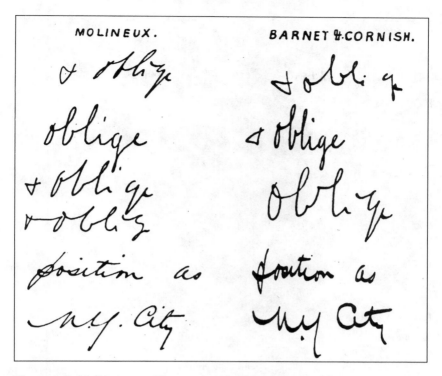

Figure 1–2: Molineux case. The questioned writing is on the right.

paid $50 a day and expenses, except those from New York, who received only $25 a day. The *New York Times* of August 10, 1900, reported the still-unpaid claims of Daniel T. Ames, $1,700; Thomas W. Cantwell, $450; Persifor Frazer, $2,181; William F. Hagen, $1,289.15; R. DeWitt Mann, $1,100; Albert S. Osborn, $1,268.87; Henry L. Tolman, $1,150; and John F. Tyrrell, $1,600.

Rice Will Case

The Rice-Patrick case (174 N.Y. 570 1903) was important not only to document examiners but also to Rice University. In 1891, millionaire William Marsh Rice caused to be incorporated under Texas law "The Rice Institute," dedicated to the advancement of literature, science, and art. Albert T. Patrick and an accomplice, murdered Rice and forged his name on several checks and a will dated June 30, 1900. The forged will changed the beneficiary from Rice Institute (fifteen-sixteenths of the estate) to Patrick (nine-tenths of Rice's property). The Patrick-Rice Will trial was held in January 1902. Handwriting experts Albert S. Osborn and David N. Carvalho met with Assistant District Attorney Garvan. They decided that photographic exhibits could best explain their opinion, so they con-

Document Examiner Hall of Fame

John F. Tyrrell

Tyrrell was born January 18, 1861, in Melbourne, Australia, and educated in Milwaukee, Wisconsin schools. He was a Document Examiner with Northwestern Mutual Life Insurance Company for forty-five years and in private practice from 1896–1955 (associated with Donald Doud). Major cases were Lindbergh kidnapping, Molineux murder, Rice will, and Leopold-Loeb murder. He was the author of many articles and engrosser of fine penmanship, and pioneered questioned document photography. He was one of the founders of the American Society of Questioned Document Examiners. Tyrrell died November 11, 1955, at the age of ninety-four in Shorewood, Wisconsin. (*Donald Doud*).

tacted Ernst J. Lederly of the Health Commission, who prepared the exhibit for court. Osborn was the first expert to testify, and the defense immediately argued that by common law, he could not testify unless he had seen Rice write. It was ruled that the 1880 law prescribed that experts might testify by comparing writing, so Osborn, John F. Tyrrell, and Carvalho all testified. The examiners used photographic reproductions transferred to thin, transparent paper to show that the four signatures were identical. The law of chance, as determined by mathematical science, is wholly against such a possibility. Osborn testified that the documents were probably copied by placing a light beneath the document.[8]

Some of the traced signatures in this case were better than others, due to the translucent quality of the paper. It is interesting to note that at least seven amateur experts also testified. When one of them, William E. Hartford, was asked for an opinion, he said, "Tellers have no opinion, they [the handwriting] are either good or bad."[9] Interesting sidelights to this case are that the William Marsh Rice will was a forgery, and Rice's grand-niece was Ella Rice, the first wife of Howard Robard Hughes, Jr., whose will was also to be declared a forgery after a handwriting battle.

Handwriting experts throughout this period were confronted with all types of obstacles preventing them from expressing an opinion in court. At the turn of the century, only a few states had passed laws allowing handwriting exemplars to be introduced into court. The Rice-Patrick case, the 1859 *Luce v. United States* case, and the 1874 *Frank v. Chemical National Banks* case allowed photographs in court and emphasized their importance. Testimony by the experts, however, was frequently objected to. References to past testimony, which were quoted in arguments by lawyers, were presented against the experts. The tools of the trade, such as microscopes and measuring instruments, were excluded. Also, experts had only three reference books: William F. Hagen's *Disputed Handwriting*, Persifor Frazer's *Bibliotics or the Study of Documents*, and Daniel T. Ames's *Ames on Forgery*. Ames's book was the best of the three, but it had only limited value.

The Wigmore and Osborn Books

The two principal books in the history of handwriting were published in 1904 and 1910. They are *The Law of Evidence*, by John H. Wigmore, and *Questioned Documents*, by Albert S. Osborn (first edition in 1910 and second in 1929). Wigmore's book revolutionized the legal profession regarding expert document testimony.

The book, when published, was opposed by the courts because of its constructive criticism of the restrictive rules of evidence. Progressive judges and the books of Wigmore and Osborn began to break down the old rules. Wigmore was a successful crusader for document examiners in these early days. In the second edition, published in 1925, he stated:

> On direct examination, the witness may, and if required must, point out his grounds for belief in the identity of the handwriting, on the principle already considered. Without such a reenforcement of testimony, the opinion of experts would usually involve little more than a counting of the numbers on either side. The progress of modern chirographic science makes it all the more possible, as well as desirable, to discriminate between witnesses according to the convincingness of the reasons that may be given by them for their conclusions.

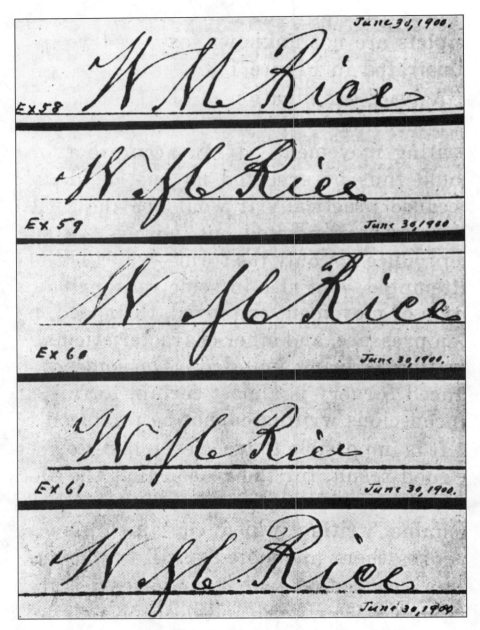

Figure 1–3: Rice Will case. Exemplars showing normal shading (left) and questioned traced signatures.

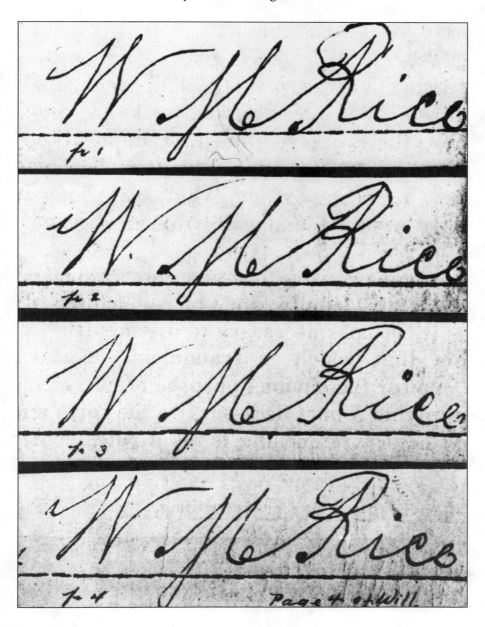

Document Examiner Hall of Fame

John H. Wigmore

Wigmore was born on March 4, 1863, in San Francisco, California. He was educated at the University of Wisconsin, Harvard, Louvain, Lyon, and Northwestern
(LL.D). He served as Professor of Law at Northwestern University from 1884 to
1943. He was author of *Law of Evidence* (10 volumes), forty-six other volumes,
including casebooks, thirty-eight edited volumes, articles, comments, and editori-
als—a total of nine-hundred titles. He organized the National Conference on
Criminal Law and Criminology, and the Scientific Crime Detection Laboratory.
He was president of the American Institute of Criminal Law and Criminology, and
American Association of University Professors. Wigmore died April 20, 1943, at
the age of eighty in Chicago, Illinois. (*Albert S. Osborn*).

These great works of evidence carried scientific and convincing discussions
of questioned documents throughout the nation. The message published in the
books can be stated in four words: *measured by its convincingness.*

Questioned Documents by Albert Osborn, often referred to as the "Bible
of Questioned Documents," completely overshadowed the three previous
handwriting books by Hagen, Frazer, and Ames. His was the first to scientifically
demonstrate that an opinion is no stronger than the reasons given to support

Document Examiner Hall of Fame

Albert S. Osborn

Osborn was born on March 26, 1858, in Sharon, Michigan. He was educated at Colby College (D.Sc.). An Examiner of Questioned Documents in private practice, 1887–1946 (associated with his son Albert D. Osborn), his major cases were the Lindbergh kidnapping (investigation and trial), Rice will, and Molineux murder. He was the author of *Questioned Documents* (the bible of the questioned document profession), *The Problem of Proof, The Mind of the Juror, Questioned Document Problems*, and many articles. Osborn was president and one of the founders of the American Society of Questioned Document Examiners. He died April 10, 1946, at the age of eighty-eight, in Montclair, New Jersey. (*Donald Doud*)

it. He advocated the need for full explanation of an opinion on direct testimony. Osborn was concerned in this book with all aspects of questioned documents: examination, techniques, court testimony, and the legal application.

Seventy years later, his books are still of great value to the document examiner. In this book, I frequently quote from *Questioned Documents* and refer to it a great deal. Osborn also wrote *Problem of Proof* in 1922, *The Mind of the Juror* in 1937, and *Questioned Document Problems* in 1944.

Law Regarding Exemplars

A few years after the publication of the Wigmore and Osborn books, the problem of introducing handwriting exemplars in court was resolved. President William Howard Taft, through the influence of George Wickersham, U.S. Attorney General, persuaded the Sixty-second Congress to enact the United States Statute of 1913, Chapter 77, stating that "any admitted or proved handwriting of such person shall be competent evidence." North Dakota did not adopt this new procedure until 1924, and Texas accepted it for civil cases in 1928.

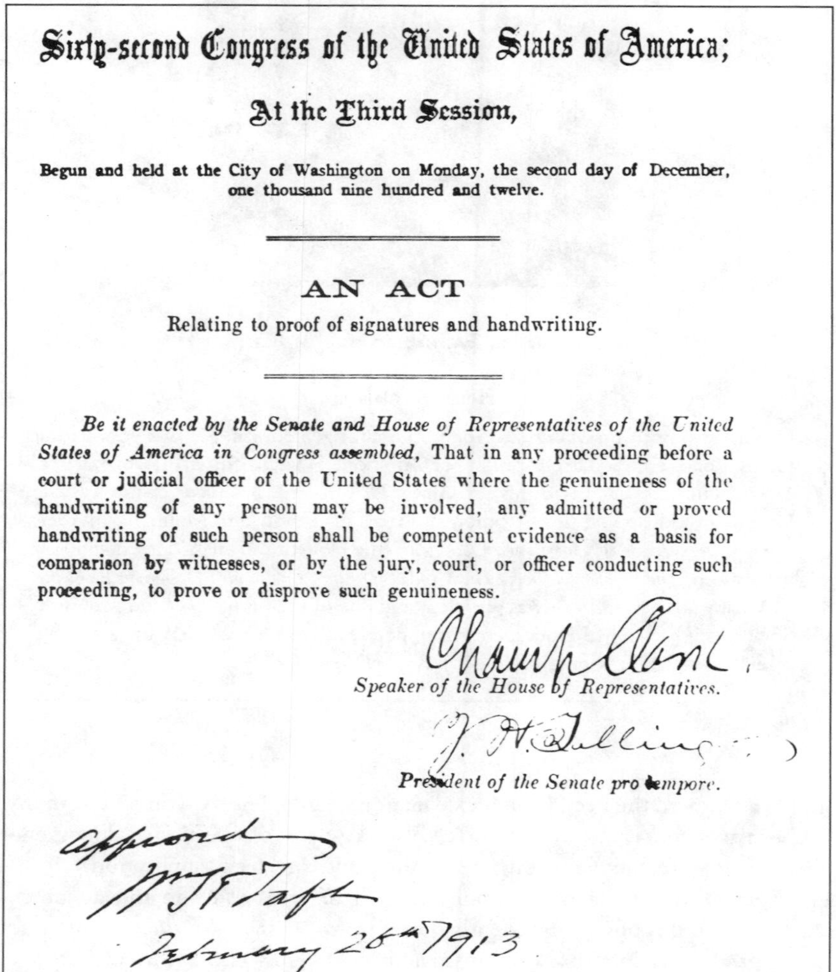

Sixty-second Congress of the United States of America;

At the Third Session,

Begun and held at the City of Washington on Monday, the second day of December, one thousand nine hundred and twelve.

AN ACT

Relating to proof of signatures and handwriting.

Be it enacted by the Senate and House of Representatives of the United States of America in Congress assembled, That in any proceeding before a court or judicial officer of the United States where the genuineness of the handwriting of any person may be involved, any admitted or proved handwriting of such person shall be competent evidence as a basis for comparison by witnesses, or by the jury, court, or officer conducting such proceeding, to prove or disprove such genuineness.

Speaker of the House of Representatives.

President of the Senate pro tempore.

Figure 1–4: United States Statute of 1913. (*National Archives*).

Court rulings were handed down, as in *Kansas–Baird v. Shaffer*, 168 Pac 836 (1917), in which three eyewitnesses testified that the signature to a will was genuine and was signed in their presence. Expert testimony was introduced showing the signature to be a forgery. The Supreme Court upheld the jury's decision that the will was a forgery. The expanded acceptance of expert testimony involving document matters was expressed in *State v. Gummer*, 51 N.D. 445, 200 N.W. 20 (1924). The court stated:

> The study of handwriting has become a scientific matter and, with modern theories as to individual characteristics as expressed in handwriting and the scientific means for measurement and demonstration that have been devised, the status of handwriting evidence has wholly changed. That being the case, the rules of evidence with respect to handwriting have had to be enlarged accordingly. It is another case of the growth and progress of the law to meet modern requirements.

Series of Articles on Document Examination

Chauncey McGovern, handwriting expert in San Francisco, California, created a sensation in 1922 by writing an article, "Indistinct Pen-Writing Made Clear by the Camera," for *Camera Craft Magazine*. This article was followed by a speech to the California Division of the IAI at Martinez, California, in 1922. McGovern stated: "No matter what the handwriting expert sees, or imagines he sees in disputed writings, it is not of the least value (as legal evidence) unless he can make photographs— contact prints or bromide enlargements—which the judge and jury can see clearly and understand distinctly." From April 1923 through January 1925, McGovern wrote monthly articles describing how photography solved many handwriting problems. In an October 1923 article, he credited "the late William J. Kinsley, Handwriting Expert of New York, who did Trojan work in bringing about the use of the photographic plate in court work." Undoubtedly, this series of articles also had a great effect on the acceptance of photographs in court. Photography took another leap forward with the work of Clark Sellers, Albert D. Osborn, and Elbridge Stein.[10] Almost simultaneously these examiners made scientific advances in the use of ultraviolet light in the examination of questioned documents.

On February 8, 1947, Alva Johnson wrote a series of four articles entitled "Hot Documents," which ran in the *Saturday Evening Post*. The series described how Clark Sellers, a Los Angeles document examiner, had solved many handwriting cases. In one case, five thousand "heirs" filed claims to the Strickland Oil millions. Sellers was able, in this one case, to detect spurious evidence in wills, in family Bibles, on tombstones, and even on oak trees. With this series, the *Saturday Evening Post* introduced the nation to the "Document Examiner."

In 1964, Raymond C. Farber decided to publish a new magazine, *Security World*. To lead off the premier issue in July 1964, he needed a series of articles that would draw subscribers. Ralph Bradford was asked by Farber to write a continuing "Handwriting Notebook" for the magazine. The series of articles appeared monthly through November 1975 and served two purposes. First, much of the series was incorporated into this book; and second, the magazine survived and is an important element in today's security profession.

Law Enforcement Document Examiners

In the early years, professional handwriting examiners came strictly from the private sector. Dr. Wilmer Souder of the National Bureau of Standards, Department of Commerce, and Bert C. Farrar, Treasury Department, were two of the earliest government experts. As Farrar's reputation grew his office expanded, and in 1929, Alwyn Cole was hired. Souder was one of the first experts to examine the handwriting in the Lindbergh kidnapping case, in which he later testified. Farrar also examined the evidence and was prepared to be a rebuttal witness.

In 1930, John H. Wigmore organized and founded the first comprehensive scientific police laboratory in the United States. The laboratory was set up as a division of Northwestern University Law School, and Colonel Calvin Hooker Goddard was named its first director. Techniques and methods of document examination were researched at the laboratory. The crime laboratory was transferred to the Chicago Police Department in 1938.

On November 24, 1932, the Federal Bureau of Investigation Laboratory was officially established. The document office was opened with one microscope and one examiner. The office quickly added various reference and standard files to facilitate its work. One of these files was the National Fraudulent Check File set up in 1936.

In 1940, the Post Office Department founded an identification laboratory with an initial staff of three document examiner trainees. They immediately realized the importance of the availability of examiners for court, and set up a regional laboratory in Cincinnati in 1940. In 1943, laboratories were added in San Francisco, in Atlanta (transferred to St. Louis that same year), and later in Chicago.

Scottsboro Boys Case

In 1924, the Leopold–Loeb murder of Bobby Franks hit the headlines. Examiners John F. Tyrrell and Jay Fordyce Wood testified in the case. A couple of years later, one of the most notorious cases in American history brought out "old-fashioned Southern lynch justice." The Scottsboro Boys case involved Communists, Socialists, civil liberty defenders, and others. The case began in 1931, when a large number of poor people became hobos riding the freight trains. On one such freight train, a group of blacks got into a fist fight with some white boys. The blacks, who outnumbered the whites, threw the white boys from the train. The

Document Examiner Hall of Fame

J. Vreeland Haring

Haring was born March 13, 1868, in New York City and educated at the New
Jersey Business College. He was an Examiner of Questioned Documents in private
practice, 1900–1954 (associated with his son J. Howard Haring). His major cases
were the Lindbergh kidnapping, Hall–Mills trial, and Scottsboro Boys case. He was
the author of *Hand of Hauptman* and numerous articles, and founder of Engrossing
Studio, New York, N.Y. Haring died October 1, 1954, at the age of eighty-six
in Westfield, Massachusetts (*Walter Nilsson*).

whites went to the sheriff, who telephoned ahead to the sheriff of Point Rock,
Alabama. Nine blacks were arrested, the oldest nineteen years old and the youn-
gest, thirteen. Two white girls, found at the arrest site, claimed they had been
raped. The girls and the blacks were taken to Scottsboro, the county seat. In a
city of 1,500, a crowd of 10,000 gathered. A band played "There'll Be a Hot
Time in the Old Town Tonight." The blacks were tried, found guilty, and
sentenced to death. Communists and others came to their defense, and the U.S.
Supreme Court granted a new trial. By the time the second trial began, the two
girls admitted they had not been raped, but the blacks were again found guilty.
This time, Trial Judge James Horton overturned the verdict. A third trial began
on November 20, 1933. Defense Counsel Samuel Leibowitz announced a motion

to quash the "Morgan County Jury" on the grounds that blacks had been systematically excluded. Judge Callahan called for a jury list and asked that it be read. After reading several pages, the clerk read several names of blacks. Leibowitz called Document Examiner John Vreeland Haring.

Haring gave detailed testimony on his examination of the documents using a twenty-power microscope. His conclusion was simple and straight-forward: the majority of the blacks' names were written on top of red lines and, therefore, were fraudulent.[11] Judge Callahan concluded that he could not presume fraud because members of the jury board were sworn officers, and it would reflect on them. The blacks were found guilty for the third time, and the case was appealed to the Alabama Supreme Court and then to the U.S. Supreme Court.

On February 15, 1935, Leibowitz argued the fraudulent jury list and the exclusion of blacks. Chief Justice Hughes asked, "Can you prove this forgery?" One by one, the eight Justices examined the names under a magnification glass, while Leibowitz explained the forgery as Haring had done. After the hearing, it was learned that the Supreme Court had never allowed this procedure before. The function of the Court was to decide questions of law, not to decide whether or not names had been forged on a document. In the Supreme Court decision, which is frequently cited to this day, the Court ruled for the first time that the systematic exclusion of blacks from juries was grounds for reversal. A fourth trial was held and through plea-bargaining, an agreement was reached: four boys were freed and five found guilty: the latter were released within one year.

The Lindbergh Kidnap Case, 1932–35

The pioneer period of document examination came to an end, and the new profession was established during one of the world's great trials. Handwriting experts throughout the United States point to this case, widely publicized as "The Lindbergh Case," as the most important in the history of document examinations.

Charles Augustus Lindbergh was born on February 4, 1902, in Detroit, Michigan. Twenty-five years later, this man made aviation history and became a national hero. On May 20, 1927, Lindbergh took off from Roosevelt field, Long Island in the *Spirit of St. Louis*. Thirty-three-and-one-half hours later, he landed in Paris after a nonstop solo flight of more than 3,500 miles. Lindbergh returned home a national hero and was given a ticker tape parade witnessed by between three and four million persons, far exceeding the Armistice Day celebration.

On May 27, 1929, Lindbergh married Anne Spencer Morrow and on June 22, 1930, a son, Charles Augustus Lindbergh, Jr., was born. The family rented a farmhouse near Princeton, New Jersey. Because of their national-celebrity status, they purchased four hundred acres and built a home in the quiet area of Hopewell, New Jersey.

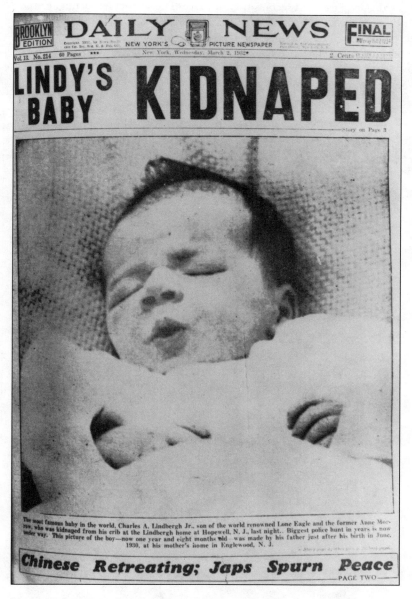

Figure 1–5: *New York Daily News*, March 2, 1932.

On March 1, 1932, between 7:30 P.M. and 10 P.M., the Lindbergh baby was kidnapped from his second-floor nursery. The suspect left behind a crudely written note (with three holes) demanding $50,000 ransom. Lindbergh notified the police, and their examination of the home revealed a ladder, footprints, and other evidence. The police broadcast an alarm, and on every highway officers searched for a blue-eyed, blond infant in a gray sleeping suit. The next day, the world read the newspaper headlines "Lindbergh's Baby Kidnapped."

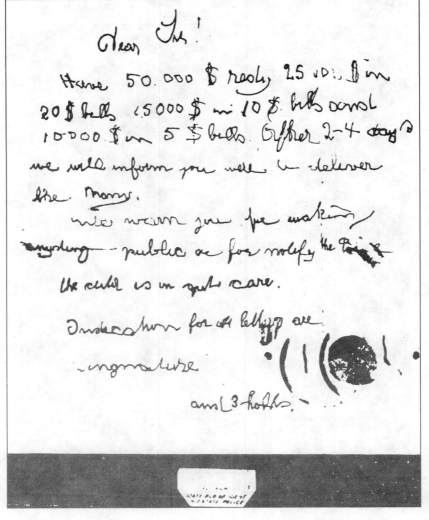

Figure 1–6: Nursery note demanding $50,000 ransom. (*J. Vreeland Haring*)

An examination of the nursery note discloses that (1) it was disguised, and (2) it was written by a foreigner, probably a German. The irregularity of the writing and the exaggerated size of the letters in the first three lines leads to the first conclusion. Throughout the letter, there is confusion of forehand and backhand. The writer started with a backhand disguise, then forgot. On the second line, "Have" is backhand and "ready" is in a different slant.

The second conclusion, that the writer was a foreigner, probably a German, is indicated by several facts:

1. The use of the dollar sign after the numerals—not an English or American custom even among the illiterate.
2. The peculiar formation of some of the letters—the "D" and "S" in "Dear Sir!" for example.
3. The phrasing of the letter: "We warn you for making anyding public or for notify the Police." The preposition *for* is never used in this manner in English—but it is in German.
4. The words "gute," "anyding," and "singnature." "Gute" is taken directly from the German; "anyding" indicates an unfamiliarity with the English "th," always difficult for foreigners. But the word "singnature"! What a struggle for the writer in this word! Here is a word he does not use often, the pronunciation of which he is not certain. Does the "n" follow the "g" or precede it? He puts it in both positions.
5. The exclamation mark after the salutation (Dear Sir!) is not usually used in English, except by persons of foreign extraction.[12]

Fourteen subsequent letters were sent by the kidnapper. Dr. Wilmer T. Souder of the U.S. Bureau of Standards, Department of Commerce and C. C. Farrar of the Treasury Department were contacted, and both men made a great number of examinations in an attempt to identify the writer of the notes. Colonel Schwarzkopf then directed Captain Snook (the custodian of the notes) to submit the kidnap notes to the nation's best known examiner, Albert S. Osborn. Osborn examined and photographed the documents and then devised a test paragraph that contained key words, syllables, and letters that could be submitted to possible suspects. In the next two years, Osborn examined handwriting of one-hundred suspects and did not identify anyone.[13]

On September 17, 1934, a man purchased gasoline with a $10 gold note. An attendant wrote his license number on the note in accordance with circulars that had been put out by the authorities, and this led to the arrest of Bruno Richard Hauptman. The suspect was taken to the police department, interrogated, and then asked to submit to a handwriting test. Hauptman replied, "I would be glad to write because it will get me out of this thing." From 9:00 P.M. to 10:00 A.M. the next day, request writing was dictated and written. Osborn identified the suspect and so testified at a grand jury hearing.

On January 2, 1935, the "Trial of the Century" began in Flemington, New Jersey (the Hunterdon County seat). The national furor was such that three hundred reporters came to cover the trial, including Walter Winchell, Edna Ferber, Damon Runyon, and Fanny Hurst. Judge Thomas W. Trenchard presided, with the prosecution handled by Attorney General David Wilentz, and Edward J. Reilly as Hauptman's chief defense counsel.

On January 10, 1935, a promissory note, insurance application, and nine automobile registration applications were introduced as known writing of Hauptman, as were the exemplars obtained after the arrest. The prosecution had prepared the handwriting part of the case by calling the top twelve handwriting experts in the country to examine the documents independently and then testify.

Albert S. Osborn of New York opened the handwriting testimony on Friday, January 11, 1935. After he took the stand for a brief period, his testimony was suspended until the next Monday. When asked how a comparison was made, he said:

> Now, this handwriting is identified by comparison of the characteristics. A characteristic in handwriting is that by which it may be described, just the same as the characteristic of anything else. They are the things by which it may be described. And in handwriting, characteristics of varying degrees of force as a means of identification are not all alike. They are like the description of an individual. Handwriting is identified exactly as a man is identified, as an automobile is identified, as a horse is identified; by general description and then by individual marks and scars and characteristics which, in combination, and that is the significant part of this matter of comparison, is the combination of characteristics so that it is not responsible to say that they would accidentally coincide. That is the question.
>
> Now, we have this writing, certain characteristics, which are characteristic merely of a class of writing. When pupils learn the same system of writing, if they learn to write perfectly, you couldn't distinguish one writing from another, because it would be merely the copybooks of writing; they would be just alike, but that does not occur.
>
> In the first place, handwriting from the same system and the same teacher with a different pupil produces a different result in certain particulars, so that some of the handwriting characteristics given at the beginning, given at the time that writing is learned, and then as soon as writing is employed— and what I am saying, when writing is employed, it may be assumed that all the time I am referring to this writing, this writing (ransom note exhibits). In my opinion, this writing in this case, both classes, is what may be described as developed writing.
>
> Now, developed writing is that which differs from copybook, differs from the model that one follows, or differs from the copies that were set for them to learn.
>
> Writing, of course, begins, it is an acquired qualification, it is an acquired habit, first imitating the forms, and then the forms become easily

22

made, until finally writing is a succession of habitual motions; the signature part of writing are the motions which are made with the pen, with the ink on, it records the motions.[14]

The State had Osborn testify regarding various handwriting exhibits that had been displayed. Testimony was also given regarding a new letter exemplar signed by "Richard Hauptman." Osborn testified that the likeness between Bruno's hand and that of the ransom note is "irresistible, unanswerable, and overwhelming." Defense counsel pointed out a dissimilarity in the two letters, but Osborn said that while they were not very much alike, his opinion was not based on any one comparison anywhere.

Elbridge W. Stein of New York was the second expert to testify; he discussed in detail the errors in spelling in the documents. Stein said "There are many misspellings in this case. Standing alone not so important, as when considered together."

John F. Tyrrell of Wisconsin was the third expert to testify. As he had done in the Molineux trial, Tyrrell had memorized the writing on the "wrapper" of the sleeping suit. The "Wizard of the Pen" then proceeded to draw every characteristic on a piece of paper, simultaneously explaining them to the jury.

Testimony was also offered by Herbert J. Walter of Illinois, consultant to the Scientific Crime Detection Laboratory at Northwestern University and examiner in the income tax evasion case of Al Capone; Wilmer T. Souder, Washington D.C., employed by the U.S. Bureau of Standards, Department of Commerce, Harry M. Cassidy of Virginia, handwriting examiner for the Chesapeake Railroad and Albert D. Osborn of New York, who, with his father Albert S. Osborn, examined the documents early in the Lindbergh case.

J. Clark Sellers of California was a famous West Coast examiner who had been involved in many Hollywood cases, such as the Ruldoph Valentino estate dispute. He was also the examiner in the *Arizona v. Winnie Ruth Judd* murder case. Called to testify in the Lindbergh case, he summed up the opinions of the previous examiners.

On January 13, 1935, the *New York Times* published a photo of eight experts for the defense, including Frau Hilda Braunlich of Germany, president of the Handwriting Experts Association of Europe. To confront this battery of experts, the prosecution decided to reserve its final four examiners for rebuttal testimony. They were C. C. Farrar, chief handwriting expert of the Treasury Department; Joseph Schulfhofer, German expert from Birmingham, Alabama; J. Vreeland Haring; and his son, J. Howard Haring. But the defense called only one expert to the stand, and on cross-examination, his credibility was badly damaged. The rebuttal experts were therefore not called.

Prosecuting Attorney David Wilentz stated in closing arguments to the jury, "I didn't want to take my chances. I sent to the best men in the country and said tell me what you think about it. Did you hear what one of the witnesses

Document Examiner Hall of Fame

Elbridge W. Stein

Stein was born October 24, 1879, in Emmaville, Pennsylvania, and educated at Zanerian College in Columbus, Ohio. He was a Document Examiner in private practice, 1913–1970 (associated with Ordway Hilton). His major cases were the Lindbergh kidnapping, Hall–Mills murder, and Starr Faithfull dead girl letters. He was the author of many articles and an instructor at a business college in Pittsburgh, Pennsylvania. He pioneered the development of ultraviolet photographic reactions in questioned documents, and he was first secretary of the American Society of Questioned Document Examiners. Stein died September 17, 1970, at the age of ninety in Sarasota, Florida. (*Donald Doud*)

said? The Attorney General says he won't stand for any conference between handwriting experts. He wants their opinions separately."

The jury returned a unanimous verdict of "guilty." Their opinion stated: "Our conclusion is that the verdict is not only not contrary to the weight of the evidence, but one to which the evidence inescapably led. From three different and, in the main unrelated sources, the proofs point unerringly to guilt, viz: (a) possession and use of the ransom money; (b) handwriting of the ransom notes; and (c) the wood used in the construction of the ladder."

Figure 1–7: Albert D. Osborn during the Lindbergh case.

Document Examiner Hall of Fame

J. Clark Sellers

Sellers was born October 16, 1891, in Heber, Utah. He was educated at the University of Salt Lake City and the University of Southern California. He was an Examiner of Questioned Documents in private practice, 1924–1973 (associated with David A. Black). His major cases were the Lindbergh kidnapping, Overall yacht murder, and Hickman kidnapping. He was the author of *Handwriting Identification and Expert Testimony* and other books and articles. Sellers was president of the American Society of Questioned Document Examiners and the Southern Academy of Criminology. He died April 10, 1973, at the age of eighty-one in San Marino, California. (*Donald Doud*).

One of the jurors later said, "The most brilliant performances in the witness chair should be credited to the handwriting experts and the wood specialist. Their testimony was a treat to the jury. The question as to which side of the case they were on disappeared. The perfection of their work submerged both prosecution and defense. Eight handwriting experts of national reputation were introduced and all were interesting. The way they testified showed they were masters of their craft.[15] It was reported on February 20, 1935, that Hauptman said, "Dot handwriting is the worst thing against me."

Hauptman was electrocuted at Trenton State Prison on April 3, 1936, four years after the Lindbergh baby was kidnapped. Between these two events, the "Trial of the Century" saw the rise of a new profession: the Document Examiner.

A New Profession, 1936–41

"This is the age of the specialist. The leader and recognized authority in any line of human endeavor is, inevitably, one whose concentrated thought and observation have enabled him to hew his way to the light of Truth through darkening walls that to the mutable many are impenetrable, inscrutable." So wrote Daniel T. Ames.[16]

Police and Handwriting Examination Schools

In the late 1920s and the 1930s, schools organized programs to teach police personnel subjects that would help them in the performance of their jobs. The first of these programs was offered by the University of Wisconsin in 1927, when Dr. A. G. Barry inaugurated the system in Kenosha. Dr. Barry expanded the system to other police departments until he resigned from the university and the instruction was abandoned. In 1929, the University of Chicago employed August Vollmer to teach a college course in police procedure, including criminal investigation and identification. The following year, Vollmer left Chicago to work for the Police Department in Berkeley and to teach at the University of California, where he set up a course and brought in outstanding teachers like Oscar Heinrich.[17]

Northwestern University set up the first scientific laboratory in 1930 and established a course called "Methods of Scientific Crime Detection" the same year. The University of Southern California, with the backing of the Los Angeles Police and Sheriff's Department, also established a program. In about 1938 John L. Harris, a prominent document examiner for the Los Angeles Sheriff's Department, started to teach a handwriting class at the university and this class helped develop most of the area's examiners.

San Jose State College (California) inaugurated a two-year course in police training in about 1930. Professor George J. Brereton, who began his career in 1920 under Vollmer's tutelage, organized the first formal college-degree program in police science at San Jose. Brereton later became director of the California State Bureau in Sacramento.

The most ambitious school of all was organized in 1916 by T. G. Cooke and Capt. W. K. Evans. The Institute of Applied Science offered such a wide range of identification studies that it opened a new era. Fingerprint identification was the cornerstone of IAS correspondence training, which also included police photography, firearms identification, investigative work, and modus operandi

Document Examiner Hall of Fame

Clarence D. Lee

Lee was born February 20, 1878, in Grand Rapids, Iowa, and educated in Grand Rapids, Iowa, schools. He was captain and scientific specialist with the Berkeley Police for thirty years, and in private practice (1909–1976). His major cases were the Folsom escape plot and Schwartz murder. He is the author of *Classification and Identification of Handwriting* (coauthor R. A. Abbey), Handwriting Course for the Institute of Applied Science, and other books and articles. He was Identification Director for relocation camps, and was perfecter and manufacturer of the Berkeley (Lie Detector) Psychograph. Lee was one of the founders of the International Association for Identification. Lee died June 2, 1976, at the age of ninety-eight in Kentfield, California. (*Howard Lee*)

training. Evans later withdrew, and Cooke's sons, Donald G. and T. Dickerson Cooke, joined the staff, as did many of America's foremost identification specialists, including A. J. Renoe, B. C. Bridges, Fred Sandberg, and Bert Wentworth. In 1938, Clarence D. Lee, coauthor of *Classification and Identification of Handwriting*, joined IAS and wrote the original handwriting and typewriting lessons. Many handwriting examiners got their start through IAS correspondence and the lessons that were written by C. D. Lee.

The Institute of Applied Science also publishes a monthly magazine, *Finger-*

print and Identification Magazine, which is sent to each student and to law enforcement agencies around the world. The correspondence school is still in business today under the name American Institute of Applied Science, P.O. Box 6309, Teall Station, Syracuse, New York 13203.

Modern Period, 1942–69

The modern period began during the war years, due to the growth of military laboratories and resultant need for new examiners. Close relationships between examiners were developed and this period saw a great exchange of ideas and techniques. As a result of this exchange of information, three document examiners' associations were either formed or enlarged.

Questioned Document Associations

The first hint of an association was an informal discussion group that later became the American Society of Questioned Document Examiners. Albert S. Osborn began inviting document examiners to New York in 1916 to exchange information. John J. Lomas of Montreal; Frank "Curtis" Sherman of Wichita, Kansas; Elbridge W. Stein of Pittsburgh and later of New York; John F. Tyrrell of Milwaukee; Herbert J. Walter of Winnipeg, Canada and later Chicago; Jay Fordyce Wood of Portland, Oregon and later Chicago; and others attended these informal meetings. In 1942, the formal association was formed and Albert S. Osborn was elected president. Clark Sellers of Los Angeles took office as vice president, Elbridge W. Stein of New York City was named secretary; and John F. Tyrrell of Milwaukee was elected treasurer. This is the only one of the three associations exclusively for document examiners. A list of the past presidents of this association constitutes, therefore, a "Who's Who" of the Document Examiners' profession:

Albert S. Osborn	1942–46	Linton Godown	1972–74
J. Clark Sellers	1946–50	Philip L. Schmitz	1974–76
Albert D. Osborn	1950–52	Joe Nemecek	1976–78
John L. Harris	1952–56	John C. Shimoda	1978–80
George J. Lacy	1956–60	David A. Crown	1980–82
Ordway Hilton	1960–62	Charles C. Scott	1982–84
David A. Black	1962–64	Maureen C. Owens	1984–86
Donald B. Doud	1964–66	John F. McCarthy	1986–88
John J. Harris	1966–68	James V.P. Conway	1988–90
Lucile P. Lacy	1968–70	Paul Osborn	1990–92
David J. Purtell	1970–72		

In the early years of the association, attendance at the annual conference was by special invitation.[18] In the early 1970s, the conference was opened up to all interested document examiners.

In 1915, Harry H. Caldwell of the Berkeley, California, Police Department, with help from his colleague, Captain Clarence D. Lee, and members of other departments in the San Francisco Bay Area—organized the International Association for Identification (IAI). A year later, the California state division of the IAI was organized, with Lee as the first secretary-treasurer. During the following years, many document examiners were speakers at the annual conferences.

In 1947, the parent body decided to reorganize the Science and Practice Committee into five subcommittees: Fingerprints, Firearms, Photography, Miscellaneous Material, and Questioned Documents. Clark Sellers was appointed chairman and started a "Questioned Documents" column for the monthly newsletter. The newsletter was expanded in 1988 to the *Journal of Forensic Identification*.

The American Society of Document Examiners was formed basically for private examiners, while the IAI was for law enforcement examiners. In 1948, the American Academy of Forensic Science was founded, admitting private examiners, and later law enforcement examiners as well. In 1952, Ordway Hilton was named chairman of the Questioned Document Section, and he developed an active group. In 1953, he organized the first sectional meeting, featuring a program of technical papers. Yearly conferences have continued, with as many as two dozen speakers on questioned documents on the program. The association also publishes a quarterly, the *Journal of Forensic Sciences*. It is now the largest of the three document-examiner associations.

Photographic Evidence Book

Charles C. Scott's tremendous volume, *Photographic Evidence*, was published in 1942. This work resembles Osborn's *Questioned Documents* in two ways: it advanced the profession, first by the quality of its information, and second, by its listing of the relevant court decisions. As Scott states in the book, "Whenever a factual situation is capable of photographic proof the attorney should know how to make the most effective use of photographs. This book should enable the attorney to superintend the preparation of accurate photographs for use as evidence." This work was enlarged in 1969 to comprise three volumes.[19]

Typewriter Examinations

The war years brought changes to the typewriter industry. All manufacturers converted their machines for the military except Woodstock, which produced up to 18,000 typewriters a year. The armed forces required about 650,000 typewriters, with the Army needing the most. A few days after the Normandy invasion, an Allied ship was sunk with a cargo of 20,000 Underwood and Royal machines.[20]

The IBM Corporation made a radical breakthrough in typewriter development in 1944, with the introduction of the IBM Executive typewriter. The

Document Examiner Hall of Fame

Charles C. Scott

Scott was born September 1, 1914, in Kansas City, Missouri. He was educated at the University of Missouri School of Law (J.D.). He was Examiner of Questioned Documents with the Federal Reserve Bank (eleven years) and in private practice, 1935 to the present. His major cases were the Select Committee on Assassination of President John F. Kennedy and *Silkwood vs. Kerr–McGee*. He is the author of *Photographic Evidence* (1942) and a three-volume revised edition in 1969. He founded the University of Missouri at Kansas City *Law Review* and was its first editor-in-chief. As Professor of Law he has conducted seminars on scientific document examination. He has served as president of the American Society of Questioned Document Examiners. Scott is currently in private practice in Kansas City, Missouri. (*Charles C. Scott*)

Executive was the first machine with proportional spacing. Typebar letters on this machine varied in width to allow letters from two to five units in width, which simulated the appearance of the printed page.

Electric typewriters date as far back as 1871, when George Arrington and Thomas A. Edison obtained patents for an electrically driven typewriter. Prior to World War II, electric typewriters were not very popular, mainly because of their mechanical faults. After the war, additional research led to the development and production of efficient electric typewriters.

Ink Developments

Ink examinations have always been one of the problems confronting examiners. Prior to the war years, chemical reagents, spectrography, and observation under ultraviolet and infrared light were used. The courts in those days did not allow destruction of a small portion of a document, hence other methods were not developed. With the changing attitude of the courts, Albert W. Somerford and Wilmer Souder of Washington, D.C., developed a method of analyzing ink by paper chromatography. They also demonstrated that only a microquantity of ink was needed, so damage to the document would be minimal.[21] In California, James W. Brackett, Jr. and Lowell W. Bradford of the Santa Clara County District Attorney's office also developed a similar method.[22]

The chromatographic technique is dependent upon the existence of water-soluble dyes in the inks. To achieve desired colors, manufacturers frequently combine two or more dyes in a single ink. The dyes and other organic compounds move up the paper when placed in solution. This procedure separates and arranges components into definite patterns.

With the tremendous popularity of the ballpoint pen beginning in 1953, new methods had to be developed. In 1954, Charlotte Brown and Paul L. Kirk of the University of California developed a method using electrophoresis to separate the dyes, with a technique similar to paper chromatography. They stated that "paper electrophoresis and paper chromatography should be considered to be mutually supplementary to each other in the identification of inks."[23]

David A. Crown, James V.P. Conway, and Paul L. Kirk of the San Francisco area developed a method that would distinguish blue ballpoint ink by chemical spot tests. In Memphis, Tennessee, Linton Godown wrote a paper titled "New Nondestructive Document Testing Methods." This paper dealt with infrared luminescence use as (1) a differentiating test for many writing materials, principally papers and inks; (2) detection of some types of alteration; and (3) deciphering erased, obliterated, obscure, or secret writing.[24] In 1960, Joseph Tholl of the Cleveland Police Department applied thin layer chromatography (T.L.C.) and found that this process effectively separated dye, making possible a more critical evaluation of inks. He also felt that the Eastman Chromagram Sheet, which eliminates the need for costly equipment and time-consuming preparations, should open the door for many document examiners to more extensive work and research in this promising field.[25]

The ink-analysis and ink-dating program of the Bureau of Alcohol, Tobacco, and Firearms was started in 1968. This program was developed by Richard L. Brunelle, who recognized the need for an ink identification program. Ink

Document Examiner Hall of Fame

Richard L. Brunelle

Brunelle was born May 9, 1937, in Littleton, Massachusetts. He earned an MS degree at George Washington University, and has been a forensic chemist with the Alcohol, Tobacco and Firearms Laboratory since 1963. His major cases are the Spiro T. Agnew investigation and the Juan Corona case. He is the author of *Forensic Examination of Ink and Paper* and many articles, and has been an instructor at George Washington University and Northwestern University. Brunelle developed a procedure for the identification and dating of inks, and developed and introduced the forensic and regulatory application of the new laboratory techniques of gas chromatography and atomic absorption spectrometry. He was president of the International Association for Identification. Brunelle is currently President of the Brunelle Forensic Laboratory in Fairfax, Virginia. (*Richard L. Brunelle*)

samples are collected from ink manufacturers, and whenever a company changes an ink formula, a new sample is sent to the ATF ink library. Frequent changes in ink help the ATF experts pinpoint the dates of inks. With the ATF system, standard inks are initially categorized by color, infrared luminescence, and ultraviolet fluorescence; next by solubility and chemical spot tests; and finally by thin-layer chromatography.[26] See Richard Brunelle's book, *Forensic Examination of Ink and Paper*, for advances and techniques in forensic examinations in this field.

Classification of Handwriting

Law enforcement agencies across the United States were encountering major problems after the war years. With the rise in crime and the increase in handwriting identification problems, new methods of classifying handwriting were developed. Prior to that, the authoritative text was *Classification and Identification of*

Document Examiner Hall of Fame

Orville B. Livingston

Livingston was born November 6, 1904, in Livingston, Wisconsin, and educated at Wisconsin Commercial Academy. He served as Handwriting Examiner with the Milwaukee Police from 1938 to 1968 (he joined the police department in 1925). His major cases were the Wells Street murder, and the Wick forgery, as well as many cases identified in the Livingston Classification System. He is the author of "Handwriting and Pen-Printing System for Identifying Law Violators" and other articles. A Plaque of Appreciation was presented to Livingston posthumously by the Secret Service. Livingston died October 6, 1968 at the age of sixty-three in Milwaukee, Wisconsin. (*Hildegarde Livingston*)

Handwriting published in 1922 by Lee and Abbey. In 1929, the Milwaukee Police Department adopted the Lee and Abbey system and began collecting 5-by-8-inch exemplars from prisoners. Orville B. Livingston noted that few identifications were made from the Lee and Abbey system and he began to develop a new system. The Nottingham (England) Police System, started in 1832, used punch cards with eighteen holes to assist in sorting. Livingston improved on this system, using Royal-McBee 5-by-8-inch cards with ninety-nine holes. He also got ideas

Document Examiner Hall of Fame

Ralph B. Bradford

Bradford was born December 14, 1904, in Marion, Indiana. He was educated at California State University at Long Beach and UCLA. He was a Questioned Document Examiner and laboratory technician with the Santa Barbara Police and Sheriff and the Long Beach Police (twenty-eight years), and in private practice, 1931–1971. His major cases were *Hughes vs. Maheu* (firing case) and the Obersmith forged deed case. He was the author of *The Bradford System, Introduction to Handwriting Examination and Identification* (coauthor Russell R. Bradford), and articles published in *Security World* magazine. He was an instructor at C.S.U.L.B. and the Long Beach Police Academy, and president of I.A.I.–California Division, California Check Investigators, and Southern California Association of Fingerprint Officers. Bradford died October 26, 1971, at the age of sixty-six in Long Beach, California.

from Ordway Hilton's "Typewriter Classification Method" and his own knowledge of fingerprint classification.

On November 5, 1953, the Livingston Classification System was put into use. Livingston published an article, "A Handwriting and Pen-Printing Classification System for Identifying Law Violators," which described his system in detail.[27] Based on the classification of handwriting exemplars according to writing characteristics, the system is used by many police departments in this country and as far away as Australia and the Philippines.

On the West Coast, Ralph Bradford began the development of a classification system, based on the M.O. method of filling out a check, rather than on handwriting characteristics. Bradford, a handwriting expert for the Long Beach Police Department, published "The Bradford System" in 1954.[28] (The history and "The Bradford System" are found in chapter 3 of this book.) In 1960, Robert A. Shaw, Clarion (Iowa) Police Department, developed a classification system similar to the Bradford system.[29]

During the next seven years, police departments in twenty-one states and three Canadian provinces obtained copies of the Bradford system. Joseph Tholl, document examiner from Ohio stated, "I have studied this system and believe that it is the answer to the problem of effective check classification. By the elimination of the variable factor of handwriting and the use of the less variable factors of arrangement and check writer identification Mr. Bradford has contrived a workable and practical system of classification." In 1980, my wife and I visited the Metropolitan Forensic Laboratory, London, England, and discussed the Bradford System with officials there. In the 1980s, Israel began to develop a national identification system using the Bradford System as a basis.

Weinberger Kidnapping Case

In 1956, the handwriting manhunt of the century took place. It started on July 4, when thirty-three-day-old Peter Weinberger was kidnapped from his home in Westbury, Long Island. A ransom note was left demanding $2,000 and signed "Your Baby Sitter." The FBI entered the case and a second note was received, written on the stationery of a Long Island company. It was agreed that anyone could have picked up the paper for the note, but the writer probably resided on Long Island. To examine every document on Long Island would take more examiners than the FBI had, so their experts examined the ransom notes and pointed out characteristics to a group of helpers. For six weeks, the examiners, experts, and helpers, looked at voting lists, automobile registrations, school records, and 1,300 probation files. From this material no identification was made, but when the examiners examined a few new probation reports they were able to identify the writer as Angelo John LaMarca. The FBI had examined 1,974,544 documents in the six-week search. LaMarca confessed that he had left the baby alive in a dense thicket (the baby was not found alive). He was later found guilty and died in the electric chair.[30]

New Questioned Document Books

During 1956 and 1958, two handwriting books were published to update the Osborn books. *Scientific Examination of Documents* by Ordway Hilton appeared in

Document Examiner Hall of Fame

Ordway Hilton

Hilton was born July 14, 1913, in Chicago, Illinois, and received an MA from Northwestern University. He served as Document Examiner with the Chicago Police Department and in private practice, 1938 to date (associated with Elbridge W. Stein). His major cases were the Saffian estate, Equitable Plan Co., and *State of New Jersey vs. Yormark et al.* He is the author of *Scientific Examination of Questioned Documents* (1st and 2d eds.), and police science editor and writer of a number of professional articles. He has been an instructor at Northwestern and Georgetown universities, and President of the American Academy of Forensic Science and American Society of Questioned Document Examiners. Hilton is currently working in private practice in Landrum, South Carolina. (*Ordway Hilton*)

Document Examiner Hall of Fame

Wilson R. Harrison

Harrison was born May 16, 1903, in Cardiff, Wales, U.K., and educated at the University of Wales (Ph.D.). He was Document Examiner with the Cardiff Police and Director of the Home Office Forensic Science Laboratory, Cardiff, for twenty-nine years. He has also been in private practice, 1934 to date, associated with his wife, Elizabeth Harrison. At the request of the Prime Minister, he reported on the Casement diaries and the Denning enquiry case. He has examined cases from England, Australia, and China. He is the author of *Suspect Documents* (1st and rev. eds.), and other books and articles. He was elected to University Fellowship. Harrison is currently working in private practice in Cardiff. (*Wilson Harrison*)

1956. Mr. Hilton stated that "the purpose of this book is to discuss all aspects of a questioned document problem in such a way as to be of greatest value to attorneys and investigators." Because of Hilton's expertise, his book is worthy of serious study. A revised edition was published in 1982.[31]

Suspect Documents, Their Scientific Examination by Wilson R. Harrison was published in 1958. This authoritative 583-page volume helped fill the void since the Osborn books. It is well written and covers most of the newer scientific procedures, including paper chromatography, visual infrared viewers, and color photography. Harrison, who was Director of the British Home Office Forensic

Science Laboratory, describes cases that are similar to those examined in the United States.[32]

The Kennedy Assassination

On November 22, 1963, the American public was shocked to hear that President John Fitzgerald Kennedy had been shot, and died a short time later at a hospital in Dallas, Texas. Vice President Lyndon B. Johnson was then rushed to the airport and was sworn in as the thirty-sixth President of the United States. Lee Harvey Oswald was arrested for the murder of Officer J.D. Tippit, and on suspicion as the possible assassin of President Kennedy. Two days later Oswald himself was killed by Jack Ruby during a transfer from the police department.

The assassination of President Kennedy, the murder of Patrolman Tippit by Oswald, and then the murder of Oswald by Ruby less than forty-eight hours after his arrest shocked the nation. The people heard facts, suspicions, and rumors, and wanted answers. On November 29, President Johnson created a President's Commission (Warren Commission) to investigate the assassination and evaluate the facts and circumstances surrounding it. Chief Justice Earl Warren was named chairman. With six additional members: Senator Richard B. Russell, Senator John S. Cooper, Representative Hale Boggs, Representative Gerald R. Ford, Allen W., Dulles, and John J. McCloy. The Warren Commission held its first meeting on December 5, 1963, and issued its final report on September 24, 1964.

Document examiners James C. Cadigan (FBI for twenty-three years) and Alwyn Cole (U.S. Treasury for thirty-five years) testified before the commission. The examiner had numerous exemplars for Oswald, including endorsements on payroll checks, applications for employment, passports, and various letters he wrote. The most important of the questioned documents were the mail order and the money order to Klein's Sporting Goods of Chicago for the purchase of a Mannlicher–Carcano 6.5mm rifle, Serial No. C2766. This was the rifle found at the Dallas School Book Depository and was determined to be the weapon that killed President Kennedy. Another important questioned document was a mail order to Seaport Traders in Los Angeles for the purchase of a .38 Smith & Wesson revolver, Serial No. V510210. This gun was seized from Oswald at the time of his arrest. It was determined that this weapon killed Patrolman Tippit. The two mail orders and the money order were all filled out and signed "A.J. Hidell."

Exhibit 785 (figure 1–8) is the money order written to Klein's Sporting Goods to purchase the rifle that killed President Kennedy. Exhibit 784-B is one of three exhibits prepared by Alwyn Cole, showing the standard writing of Lee Harvey Oswald. The following is part of the testimony of April 30, 1964, before the Warren Commission:

> **Alwyn Cole**: In the word "Dallas," the terminal *s*, still referring to 785, is modified from the conventional or copybook method of making that letter by being flattened out, forced far over its side. In other words, it

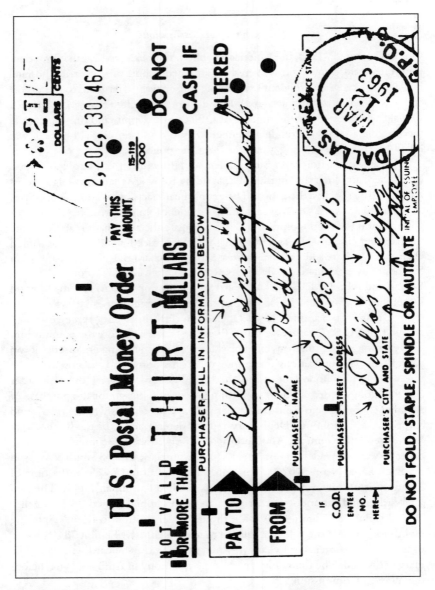

Figure 1–8: Commission exhibit 785 and 784–B. (*National Archives*)

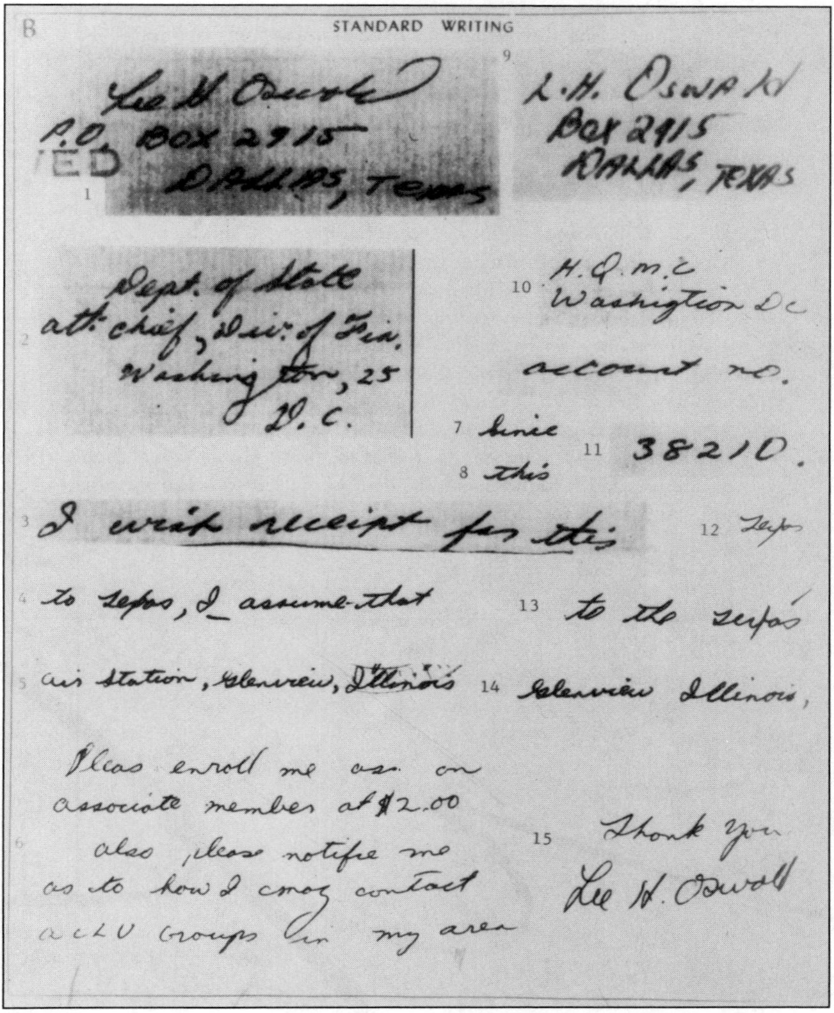
B
STANDARD WRITING
Lee H. Oswald
P.O. Box 2915
Dallas, Texas
L.H. Oswald
Box 2915
Dallas, Texas
Dept. of State
att: chief, Div. of Fin.
Washington, 25
D.C.
H.Q.M.C
Washington DC
account no.
since
this
38210.
I wait receipt for this
to the
Glenview Illinois,
Pleas enroll me as an
associate member at $2.00
also, please notifie me
as to how I may contact
ACLU groups in my area
Thank You
Lee H. Oswald

has an extreme forehand slant rather than standing up in a more vertical position which we would find in a copybook. The same is true of the terminal *s* in the word "Texas" in that area. Now this, too, is a habit found in the standard writings, one good example being chart B (784–B) at the end of item 3, the *s* of the word "this."

In the word "Texas" a very distinctive method of forming the letter *x* is observed. Now, this involves first the production, passing directly from the letter *e*, first the production of a point or cusp, and then an underhand movement similar to that which would be required for the letter *u*, then with the pencil on the paper another point or cusp is produced. The word is finished with the letters *as*, and then the cross bar is made in such a manner that it runs along the side of the second cusp. In other words, the basic part of the *x* form, that is, the part which is connected to the other writings, is somewhat in the shape of a shallow *u*. May I demonstrate that on a pad here?

Melvin Eisenberg: Please, Mr. Cole.

Cole: I have just drawn here an *x* diagramming the form observed on 785 which shows its production of a shallow *u* shape, with the crossbar striking across the second point of that *u*-shaped form. This, I say, is highly distinctive, and is found in the standard writing in several places.

Eisenberg: Pardon me. Mr. Chairman, may I introduce that diagram as 786?

Rep. Gerald Ford: It may be admitted.

Figure 1–9: Commission Exhibit 786.

Document Examiner Hall of Fame

Alwyn Cole

Cole was born on November 8, 1908, in Portsmouth, Virginia, and educated in Shreveport, Louisiana, schools. He was Examiner of Questioned Documents with the U.S. Treasury Department (forty-four years) and in private practice, 1926 to date. His major cases were the Kennedy assassination (Warren Commission), the Lindbergh kidnapping (assisted Bert C. Farrar), and *U.S. vs. Werner Von Klemm.* He is author of many articles and instructor at the Treasury Department Law Enforcement Training School and Royal Canadian Mounted Police seminars. Cole is currently in private practice in Chevy Chase, Maryland. (*Alwyn Cole*)

(Commission Exhibit No. 786 was marked and received in evidence.) [See figure 1–9.]

Cole: This distinctive formation of the *x* is observed on chart B, item 4, in the word "Texas," also in the same chart B, item 13, in the word "Texas," and also item 12 on the same chart.

Eisenberg: Mr. Cole, did you say there was no pen lift after finishing the second cusp, until the letters *as* are added?

Cole: That is correct.

Eisenberg: So that the *x* is not crossed, so to speak, until the entire word is completed?

43

Cole: That is correct.

Eisenberg: How distinctive would you regard this form as being?

Cole: Well, I regard it as highly unusual and carrying a good deal of weight for identification purposes, because it is a wide departure from the copybook method or conventional method of making the letter, and it involves the addition of a part rather than an omission which might come from carelessness.[33]

The post office box application and change-of-address cards were also identified as having been written by Oswald. A fictitious printed Selective Service card and a U.S. Marine Corps certificate of service card (in the name of Alek James Hidell) were compared with retouched negatives and the genuine cards of Oswald. Cole determined that the counterfeits were produced by copying Oswald's cards, a skill Oswald acquired while working for a Dallas photoengraving firm. Several other documents were also examined and identified.

Since the Warren Commission published its report in 1964, many books and articles have been written speculating on other theories and how the assassination happened. One of these theories is that there were two Oswalds. One Oswald went to Russia in October 1959, and a second Oswald returned to the United States in June 1962. It was the second Oswald who assassinated the president.

The House Select Committee on Assassinations was established in 1976 by the 94th Congress to conduct a full and complete investigation into the deaths of President Kennedy and Dr. Martin Luther King, Jr. The committee appointed document examiners Joseph P. McNally, David J. Purtell, and Charles C. Scott to resolve the "two Oswalds" issue. The examiner divided Oswald's handwriting into five periods of time—from 1956–59 (in the Marines); 1959–62 (in Russia); 1962–63 (in Dallas and New Orleans); last week of September 1963 (visiting in Mexico); and October 1, 1963 to the day of the assassination (living in Dallas). The experts examined about fifty documents and determined that "the signatures and handwriting purported to be by Oswald are consistently that of one person."[34]

International Association for Identification, Fiftieth Conference

In 1965, the International Association for Identification held its fiftieth conference in Long Beach, California. President C. Lester Trotter, assistant director of the FBI, presided over this golden anniversary conference. The California Division and its president, Ralph Bradford, hosted this historic conference. James R. Dibowski, director of the Postal Laboratory in Cincinnati, Ohio, presented a Questioned Document program. The program consisted of several outstanding speakers, including: Lon H. Thomas, examiner of questioned documents, Arlington, Virginia; Sidney Goldblatt, Document Examiner, IRS Alcohol and Tax Division, New York; Orville Livingston, chief document examiner, Police Department, Milwaukee, Wisconsin; and Ralph O. Queen, acting superintendent of the Iden-

Figure 1–10: Document examiners at the Fiftieth IAI Conference.

Bottom Row (left to right): Queen, Ralph (Tex.); Rones, Nicanor (Philippines); Sellers, Frances (Calif.); Sellers, J. Clark (Calif.); Somerford, Albert (Washington, D.C.); Trotter, Lester (Washington, D.C.); Bradford, Ralph (Calif.).

Top Row: Wilson, Simeon (Ill.); Mooney, David (Washington, D.C.); Thomas, Lon (Va.); Travis, Robert (Okla.); Dibowski, James (Ohio); Browne, Albert (Sierra Leone); Davenport, Earl (Tenn.); Bunga, John (Tanzania); Livingston, Orville (Wis.); Doulder, Howard (Ill.); Alexander, Floyd (Tex.); Goldblatt, Sidney (New York); unknown; Berry, Samuel (Liberia).

tification Bureau, Police Department, Houston, Texas. The major address, "Questioned Document Examination in the Field of Scientific Identification," was presented by J. Clark Sellers, who forty years earlier had testified in the Lindbergh Kidnapping case. A mock trial session, conducted by Albert W. Somerford, Director of the Postal Service, Washington, D.C., was also an important part of the program at this important conference.

Legal Authority for Handwriting Exemplars

The 1964 *Escobedo v. Illinois* case stated that any statements made by an accused before he or she is informed of the right to an attorney before questioning are inadmissible as evidence. Many attorneys took this to include handwriting exemplars. In June 1964, a Superior Court trial was held in Pasadena, California, in a case in which Jesse James Gilbert was accused of killing a police officer during an armed robbery. Subsequent to the robbery, the suspect was arrested by the FBI in Philadelphia. FBI agents obtained handwriting from the suspect to be compared with a map of the armed robbery. Additional handwriting was needed for the trial, and a Long Beach police exemplar obtained during a 1960 arrest for burglary was used. Since the officer who witnessed the exemplar was no longer available to testify, the exemplar was introduced as an official document of the Long Beach Police Department, and Russell Bradford testified as custodian of the handwriting exemplars. Since the suspect had not been advised of any rights before filling out the handwriting exemplars, the case was appealed to the U.S. Supreme Court. In *Gilbert v. California* 388 US 293 (1967) the conviction was upheld by the Supreme Court. (This and other court decisions are discussed in detail in chapter 6.)

Howard Hughes Period, 1970–78

The 1970s were dominated by the handwriting trials involving millionaire Howard R. Hughes. The four trials were:

1. *Hughes v. Maheu* firing trial (1970)
2. Clifford Irving hoax (1972)
3. *Hughes v. Maheu* defamation trial (1974)
4. Mormon Will trial (1978)

Howard Robard Hughes, Jr., was born on December 24, 1905, in Houston, Texas. When he was eighteen, his father died of a heart attack (his mother had died two years earlier). Hughes inherited $1.3 million and immediately purchased the stock of his relatives and took control of the business.

Hughes wanted to make movies, so he converted one of his subsidiaries, Caddo Rock Drill Bit Company, to a film company and then later purchased R.K.O. Studios.

His next goal was to build and fly airplanes, so he founded Hughes Aircraft Company. The company built several airplanes, including, in 1947, the Hercules HK-1 ("Spruce Goose"), which was then, and still is, the largest airplane every built.[35]

In 1955, Hughes sold R.K.O. Studios, and in 1966, he sold T.W.A. for a record profit of $500 million. He began to have problems with the IRS because of his profits, and on November 27, 1966, he moved his operations to Las Vegas, Nevada. In 1961, Hughes hired Robert A. Maheu, who had moved up to chief executive of Hughes' Nevada operations by 1966. Hughes moved into maximum security on the ninth-floor penthouse of the Desert Inn. He was welcomed in Las Vegas with open arms because it was felt that his money power would give Las Vegas the seal of approval.

Hughes' next role was gambling entrepreneur, which he embarked on in 1967. Within three-and-a-half years, he bought the Castaways, Desert Inn, Frontier, Landmark, Sands, and Silver Slipper casinos in Las Vegas and Harold's Club in Reno. In 1969, he obtained sole ownership of Air West Airlines and then purchased Krupp Ranch, Paradise Valley Country Club, North Las Vegas Airport (Thunderbird Field), KLAS–TV, real estate, and 503 mining claims.

Hughes v. Maheu *Firing Trial (1970)*

In 1970, Hughes' worth was estimated at between $1.5 and $2 billion, and the Nevada operation that Maheu administered was worth about $300 million. In September 1970, Hughes' health took a drastic turn for the worse, and at the same time, he learned that Maheu was skimming profits at the casinos. In Nevada, the normal return on invested capital was 15–20 percent; Hughes' properties returned only 6.15 percent in 1968 and 1.63 percent in 1969. Simultaneously, Hughes learned of other unauthorized Maheu negotiations.[36]

On November 14, Hughes signed a proxy designating "Chester C. Davis, Raymond M. Holliday and Frank W. Gay, or a majority of them, my true and lawful attorneys." They were authorized to carry out "any and all actions with respect to management." (This amounted to an order for the termination of Maheu's employment.) On Thanksgiving eve Hughes flew to the Bahamas. On December 4, Davis informed a friend of Maheu's that he had the proxy and that "Maheu resigns by sundown or he's fired."

Maheu contacted a "handwriting expert" and asked him to examine the proxy. The expert declared it an "imitation." Nevada Governor Laxalt tried to intervene after talking on the phone with Hughes, but the case went to court. Hughes Tool Company hired Ralph Bradford of Long Beach, California, to examine the proxy. Despite the fact that the proxy had been declared a forgery by Maheu's "expert," Bradford was unable to make a positive opinion, due to the lack of exemplars. A search went out for Hughes exemplars. A national defense fingerprint exemplar, autographed photograph, power of attorney dated

April 23, 1968, and three loan notes were located, along with additional exemplars of Hughes' writing.

Hughes was upset with the delay and wrote a memorandum: "Dear Chester and Bill." Ralph Bradford examined it on December 10 and declared the "Dear Chester" document, the proxy, and the exemplars to be written and signed by

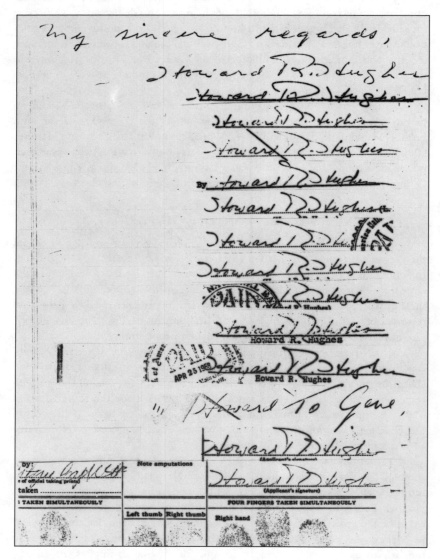

Figure 1–11: Howard R. Hughes, Jr. handwriting exhibit.

Howard R. Hughes Jr. He also identified a fingerprint on the proxy to be the right thumb print of Mr. Hughes. After making the positive identification, he prepared a court exhibit showing fourteen of Hughes' signatures. The exhibit (figure 1–11) starts at the bottom with (1) the 1953 national defense fingerprint exemplar, (3) autograph signature on a photograph, (8) signature on a note to Bank of America, dated March 31, 1954 for $4 million, (12) power-of-attorney document dated April 23, 1968, (13) questioned proxy dated November 14, 1970, (14) the 1970 "Chester and Bill" letter.

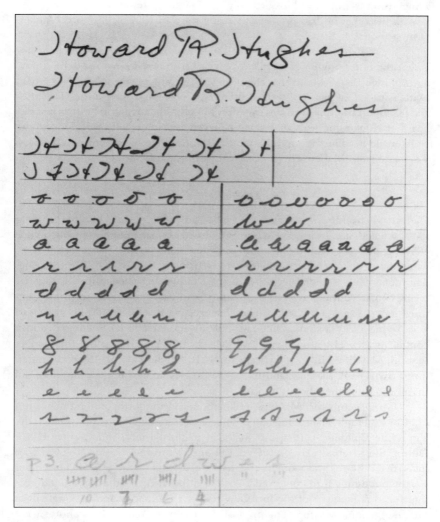

Figure 1–12: Bradford's court work sheet.

On December 8, 1970, trial was held in Las Vegas District Court before Judge Howard Babcock. Maheu's handwriting expert said the proxy "does not have the same general design" as other signatures by Hughes, but added that there are "subtle differences." "It indicates extreme skill, but is nonetheless different," he said. When asked if it was a forgery, he said, "It is a forgery."

Ralph Bradford testified on December 14 that the "Dear Chester" letter and the proxy were written by the same person. He then testified that those two documents were by the same person who signed an autographed photograph and a fingerprint exemplar of Howard Hughes. Bradford's testimony was assisted by a worksheet that he had prepared charting the variations in Howard Hughes' writing (figure 1–12).

Judge Babcock ruled that Maheu was fired legally. He said he could not accept the testimony of "Maheu's expert," that his testimony was "not consistent." Judge Babcock said that Bradford's testimony, plus that of LeVar Myler (witness to proxy signing), proved the proxy "valid and subsisting." The press and television had followed this case very closely. The media and others had not heard of Hughes for years, and many believed he had died. The decision of the court made headlines around the world. The headline in the Long Beach *Press Telegram* read: "Maheu Throws Snake Eyes: House Wins Hughes Stakes."

Clifford Irving Hoax (1972)

Clifford Michael Irving was an author who had written several books, including the best seller *Fake*. Irving saw in Howard Hughes, a man not photographed since 1957, the perfect person about whom to write a bogus book. The "Dear Chester" letter of the Maheu trial was published in the January 1971 issue of *Life* magazine. This document provided Irving with the handwriting needed for his forgery. Irving contacted McGraw-Hill Publishing Company executives, showing them three letters from "Howard Hughes," suggesting that he would be willing to help Irving write a book. McGraw-Hill, Irving, and Hughes entered into a contract which Hughes "signed" on March 5, 1971. During the intervening months, McGraw-Hill issued checks to "H.R. Hughes," which were deposited into a Swiss bank account, and Irving and his researcher, Richard Suskind, did the research for their bogus book.

On December 7, McGraw-Hill announced the forthcoming publication of Howard Hughes' autobiography. Four days later, a meeting took place in the Time/Life Building; participants included Clifford Irving and Chester Davis. During the meeting Davis received a phone call from Howard Hughes, who stated that the book was a forgery and that he had never met Irving. On December 17, the publishing firm contacted a "handwriting firm" to examine the Hughes signatures. A member of the firm flew to Las Vegas and examined originals of Hughes' genuine writing. The originals could not be removed so photos were taken. The McGraw-Hill office would not release the originals of the contract and checks, so again photos were taken. Despite these problems of examination and the fact that some of the signatures were done with felt-tip pen, an identifying oral report was given on December 23 and was followed by a written report.

The Hughes people, unable to convince McGraw-Hill that the autobiography was a forgery, made a dramatic move. Hughes agreed to talk on the phone to a group of newsmen. On January 7, 1972, a conference room in Los Angeles was hooked up through Hughes Tool Company in Miami with the ninth floor of the Britannia Beach Hotel in Nassau. Seven journalists sat around a table talking to a voice coming out of an electronic box, while television cameras recorded it all.

> **Question**: Did you personally sign a letter to Nevada authorities directing that Chester Davis be designated as your representative in gambling licenses issued to Hughes Tool or Hughes Nevada Operation?
> **Hughes**: I don't know if it was in that precise language. It was to that effect. That is the substance of it.
> **Question**: And you personally signed that application?
> **Hughes**: Absolutely!

Hughes was also asked about the firing of Maheu.

> **Question**: Was Maheu fired on your orders?
> **Hughes**: Specifically!
> **Question**: Why?
> **Hughes**: Because he's a no-good dishonest son-of-a-bitch who stole me blind.

Howard Hughes was also asked questions regarding the Irving book.

> **Question**: Did you cooperate or did you know a man named Irving who claims to have taped this biography with you?
> **Hughes**: This must go down in history. I only wish I was still in the movie business, because I don't remember any script as wild . . . I don't know him [Irving]. I never saw him. I had never even heard of him a matter of days ago when this thing first came to my attention.

At the end of the two-and-a-half hour session, all seven interviewers agreed that they had been talking to Howard Hughes.[37]

Clifford Irving agreed to appear on *60 Minutes* with Mike Wallace on January 13, but the day before, Chester Davis appeared before the New York Supreme Court and swore an affidavit preventing the publishing of the book. On January 18, McGraw-Hill filed their affidavits with the court, stating they had learned a "terrible fact." The deposit and withdrawal tellers of the Swiss bank were interviewed regarding the activity of "Mr. H.R. Hughes." "But there was no Mr. Hughes, the customer was a lady." The Swiss account was opened on May 13, 1971, by Helga R. Hughes.[38] On January 24, the U.S. Postal Inspection

Service entered the case, and John Tarpey, postal inspector, brought in the department's document examiner, Robert A. Cabanne, on February 4. On February 7, Clifford Irving and his wife, Edith, appeared before the grand jury. The Irvings pleaded the Fifth Amendment to all questions and also to a request for handwriting exemplars. The judge informed the Irvings that Fifth Amendment rights did not extend to handwriting exemplars and threatened them with contempt of court. The next day, the Irvings wrote the text of the letters, along with endorsements and signatures.

On February 10, the New York handwriting firm that had identified Hughes' writing on December 23 changed its opinion. In the meantime, Cabanne had completed his own examination, begun on February 4. On February 16, Cabanne testified before the Federal Grand Jury, Southern District of New York.

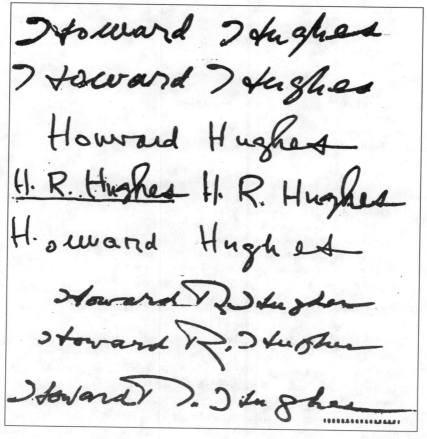

Figure 1–13: Exhibit of Irving's and Hughes' handwriting. (*Robert Cabanne*)

He stated that Hughes was not the writer of the questioned documents or the endorser of the checks. He further testified that Clifford Irving was the forger of several of the checks and that Edith Irving had endorsed at least one of the checks (H.R. Hughes) in the Swiss bank. Cabanne demonstrated his opinion with several illustrative charts.

The top two signatures shown in figure 1–13 are questioned signatures in the Irving case, while the middle three are exemplars of Clifford Irving. The bottom three are exemplars of Howard R. Hughes. Cabanne in his testimony pointed out several characteristics, including the letter *o* in the second questioned signature.

Document Examiner Hall of Fame

Robert A. Cabanne

Cabanne was born February 6, 1919, in St. Louis, Missouri, and educated at St. Louis University. He was Examiner of Questioned Documents with the Postal Inspection Service and State of Illinois Crime Laboratory (twenty-seven years) and has also been in private practice, 1951 to date. His major cases have been the Howard Hughes–Clifford Irving fraud, H. L. Hunt fraud, and the Tylenol case. He has written many articles, and served as instructor at the U.S. Secret Service Document School and the Postal Inspection Service Training Institute. He also organized a new laboratory for the Postal Inspection Service. Cabanne is currently in private practice in Naperville, Illinois. (*Robert A. Cabanne*)

"Compare that with the *o* in the fifth signature by Irving," he said. "The letter has a tendency to be higher on the right side in the questioned writing, whereas in the known specimens of Mr. Hughes, the highest portion is on the left shoulder of the letter *o*. Observe the formation of the *w* in the first two lines as compared with lines 3 and 5 of Irving. Notice the proportion of the letter *w* and the manner in which the bridge of the *w* drops in line 1 and also in line #5."[39]

On March 3, the Irvings confessed to the collection of $750,000 from McGraw-Hill. On March 13, they pleaded guilty in the case of *United States v. Clifford and Edith Irving*.

Hughes v. Maheu *Defamation Trial (1974)*

Robert A. Maheu, fired by Hughes in 1970 (*Hughes v. Maheu* firing trial), sued Hughes for $55 million for wrongful dismissal. After this suit was filed, Hughes employees spent a great deal of time seeking information regarding Maheu's alleged fraud.

On January 7, 1972, during the telephone conference with newsmen, Howard Hughes announced that he had fired Maheu because "he's a no-good, dishonest, son-of-a-bitch, and he stole me blind." A month later, Maheu filed a $17.5 million libel and slander lawsuit in the U.S. District Court in Los Angeles. Hughes commissioned an Intertel private investigating agency to document his charges. Intertel conducted 525 separate investigations. During the five-month trial, Maheu called on John J. (Jack) Harris, a Los Angeles document examiner, to examine many documents. Although only copies were available for court, Harris identified Hughes' writing on several memos from Hughes to Maheu as support for the claim that Maheu was acting under Hughes' instructions. On July 1, 1974, the jury ruled unanimously in favor of Maheu and awarded him $2.8 million in damages. The case was appealed, and in 1977, the United States Court of Appeals for the Ninth Circuit overturned it and sent it back for retrial. The case was ultimately settled between Maheu and the Hughes heirs.

Mormon Will Trial

Hughes left Las Vegas in 1970, and for the next five years his health continued to worsen. Hughes, once 6 feet 4 inches in height had now shrunk 3 inches and he weighed a mere 93 pounds. His starved and dehydrated body was reduced to a pitiful skeleton. His kidneys, damaged in his several airplane crashes, failed, and uremic poisoning racked his body.[40]

It was decided to fly him home from the Acapulco Princess Hotel in Mexico to the Houston Methodist Hospital, where he could be placed on a kidney dialysis machine. A half hour out of Houston, at 1:27 P.M. on April 5, 1976, Hughes died. The official autopsy attributed the death of the seventy-year-old Hughes to renal (kidney) failure.

A massive search was undertaken to locate Hughes' will. More than three dozen "wills" were submitted to various probate courts. Twenty-two days after Hughes' death, Melvin Earl Dummar, a thirty-one-year-old Utah service station owner, brought an envelope to the World Headquarters Building of the Church of Jesus Christ of Latter-Day Saints in Salt Lake City, and quickly left the premises. Two days after finding this envelope with a will inside, Mormon officials flew to Las Vegas and turned over the document (now known as the "Mormon Will") to the district court.

Noah Dietrich, former Hughes executive, was named executor of the Mormon Will. "Experts" from Utah, New York, and two "experts" retained by ABC News all claimed the will was genuine. Dietrich retained Attorney Harold Rhoden, who acquired a silent partner named Seymour Lazar. Lazar went across the United States and then spent weeks in Europe looking for "experts" to support the will. One of the experts was Lon H. Thomas, retired document examiner for the Secret Service, who gave him the bad news—it was a forgery. Many of the "experts" thought that a three-page document like this will would be impossible to forge. That is basically true, except with a handwriting like that of Hughes. Hughes wrote in a disconnected style; for example, note the words *Long Beach* in figure 1–14. Every letter in these words is written individually in the will. A forger need only copy one letter at a time, and this can be done quite successfully.

Jury selection for the "Mormon Will trial" began on November 7, 1977 in Las Vegas. Three foreign experts and one from the United States testified that the handwriting was that of Howard Hughes.

The attorneys for Hughes' relatives and the Summa Corporation, which Hughes founded, attempted to prove to the jury that the will was a forgery. The contestants' attorneys, Jim Dilworth, Clayton Lilienstein, and Paul Freese, called to the stand three leading handwriting examiners, John J. Harris, Lyndel Shaneyfelt, and Donald Doud. Harris, a private examiner from Los Angeles, claimed that he worked two years on the case. He examined three pages of questioned handwriting, comparing them with over 800 pages of known writing. Shaneyfelt, a retired FBI examiner, and Doud of Milwaukee also testified. Doud stated that the name "Howard" on one of the pages was traced, but ultimately, masterful testimony regarding the evolution of Hughes' writing by the three experts decided the case. They explained to the jury how Hughes' writing had deteriorated over the years. In March 1968 (date of the Mormon Will), Hughes' writing still had some quality and had not deteriorated as much as the writing on the questioned will. Four additional experts also had their depositions read into court record.

The jury heard testimony from sixty-nine witnesses, including eleven handwriting examiners, and saw more than 700 exhibits and 480 copies of Hughes' handwriting.

On June 8, 1978, the jury, which had listened to more than seven months of testimony and argument, deliberated eleven hours and gave the following verdict: "We, the Jury, duly empaneled and sworn, find that a certain three-page document written on lined legal paper, dated March 19, 1968, was not written, dated, and signed by the hand of the decedent, Howard Robard Hughes." This marked the end of the Hughes litigation and possibly the longest and richest probate jury trial in the country's history.

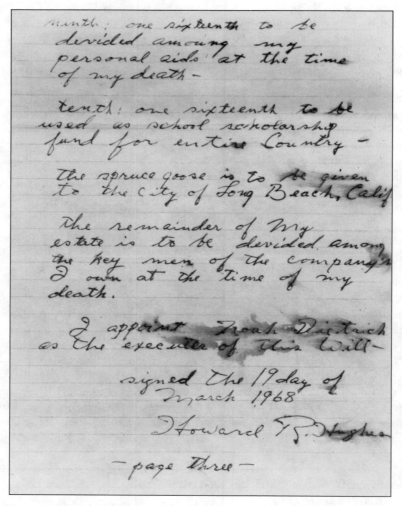

Figure 1–14: Mormon Will, page 3. (*Buddy Hardy*)

Corona Murder Trial

The Hughes trials dominated the 1970s, but two other important events made an impact in the field of document examination. During the early months of 1971, the bodies of twenty-five farm laborers were found in Sutter County, California. On May 21, 1971, Juan Vallejo Corona was arrested and charged with murder. The prosecution requested additional handwriting exemplars, but Corona refused on advice of his attorney, Richard E. Hawk. Judge Richard Patten

Document Examiner Hall of Fame

John J. Harris

Harris was born July 7, 1923, in Seattle, Washington, and educated at the University of California, Los Angeles. He has been a Questioned Document Examiner in private practice since 1948 (associated with his father, John L. Harris, and his wife, Patricia Harris). His major cases have been *Hughes v. Maheu* (defamation case), Howard Hughes, the Mormon Will, and the Corona murders. He has written many articles, and has been an instructor at the University of Southern California and California State University at Los Angeles. He has served as President of the American Society of Questioned Document Examiners and American Board of Forensic Document Examiners. Currently, Harris is in private practice in Los Angeles. (*John J. Harris*)

sentenced Hawk to jail and told Corona he was guilty of contempt, citing a case in which it was found that "persistent refusal to provide handwriting exemplars could be construed as evidence of guilt." Handwriting was obtained.

The trial was held on September 11, 1972, and handwriting experts John J. Harris of Los Angeles, Sidney Goldblatt of the U.S. Treasury Department, and Terry Pasco testified regarding the identification of Corona's handwriting on the "death list." Richard L. Brunelle, Alcohol, Tobacco, and Firearms Laboratory, testified regarding a comparison of ink on the list, with ink from a multicolored ink pen. Corona was found guilty on January 18, 1973. The case was appealed, retried, and again the suspect was found guilty.

Certification Program

In 1977 reputable document examiners decided to attempt to remove the unqualified from the profession. The Forensic Sciences Foundation, Inc. obtained a federal Law Enforcement Assistance Administration (LEAA) grant. With this grant, the American Board of Forensic Document Examiners was organized under the chairmanship of John J. Harris. A program of certification of forensic document examiners was developed, and put in place on July 1, 1978. This certification program was sponsored by the American Society of Questioned Document Examiners and the American Academy of Forensic Sciences.

The objective of the Board is to establish, enhance, and maintain standards of qualification for those who practice forensic document examination, and to certify as qualified specialists those voluntary applicants who comply with the requirements of the Board. Certification is based upon a candidate's personal and professional record of education and training, experience, and achievement, as well as on the results of a formal examination. As an assistance to the examination, Maureen Casey of the Chicago Police Department prepared a "Syllabus/Biography" which was published by the Board in 1979.

It is hoped that the certification program will keep the unqualified and the incompetent out of the courtroom. Certification is the way of the future.

The 1980s, 1990s, and Beyond

Document examiners in the future will be better equipped than examiners of the past. New books, articles, computers, and even lasers will assist tomorrow's examiner. Intensive training and the certification programs will produce true professionals for this new profession.

Hoffman Forgeries

Two professionals worked the major document case of the 1980s, which involved documents relating to the history of the Church of Jesus Christ of Latter-Day

Saints. Mormon history alleges that Joseph Smith received gold plates from the angel Moroni. Smith then wrote the *Book of Mormon* by translating Egyptian type characters from the plates. He copied some of the Egyptian characters on a piece of paper for examination by an Egyptian expert, Charles Anthon of Columbia University. The fate of the document examined by Anthon is unknown, however.

On April 17, 1980, Mark Hoffman confronted officials of the Mormon church with a yellowed sheet of paper that was signed "Joseph Smith." The document was examined by experts to determine its authenticity. On April 28, Hoffman was congratulated for finding the lost Anthon document. In the next five years, Hoffmann "located" forty-eight historical documents which were given or sold to the church. These included a controversial "white salamander" letter.

Salt Lake City was shaken on October 15, 1985, when a bomb exploded, killing Steve Christensen. Three hours later a second bomb killed Kathy Sheets. The following day Hoffman was injured when a bomb exploded in his car. Salt Lake City police detectives Ken Farnsworth and Jim Bell investigated the bombings and interviewed Hoffman. His story did not check out, and the detectives speculated that he was the bomber and was injured when one of his bombs accidentally exploded.

George Throckmorton, Utah Attorney General's office document examiner, contacted the Salt Lake County Attorney's office, and discussed a possible motive for the bombings. When he was told that the Hoffman documents had been examined, he noted that "testing can prove forgery, but it cannot prove authenticity." He agreed to examine the documents, and called on William Flynn, document examiner for the State of Arizona, for assistance.

Throckmorton and Flynn examined the writing with a microscope. They noted that the ink line on some documents was cracked in an unusual alligator pattern. It was later learned that all documents with a cracked line came from Hoffman. The examiners believed that the cracking was a sign of forgery, but wondered how they could prove it.

Flynn returned to Arizona and attempted to duplicate the cracking, which he believed was caused by a chemical reaction between the ink and the chemicals used on the documents to artificially age them. After a period of testing failures, it was recalled that Hoffman had in his library the book *Great Forgers and Famous Fakes*.[41] On page 267, Flynn found a 1770 black-ink formula. He mixed gum arabic with a new batch of iron gallatannic ink in a glass bottle, dipped a steel pen into the bottle, and scratched a sentence across a sheet of century-old paper. He aged the sentence for a half hour with the highest quality sodium hydroxide. Finally he slipped the sheet under his microscope and focused. The letters were smooth at first, but soon began to change to an odd, alligator pattern.[42]

Throckmorton and Flynn hoped this one type examination would prove the forgery of all Hoffman documents, but because the documents dated from

1792 to 1929 this was not possible. Therefore, a series of tests were performed, which included:

1. Ultraviolet examination
   a. *Blue-Haze.* The documents were treated with chemicals to artificially age them. This showed up with a blue-haze when viewed under ultraviolet light.
   b. *Uni-directional Running.* When applied to paper ink bleeds out in all directions from the point of contact. When the Hoffman documents were aged and hung to dry, gravity caused the ink to run in one direction rather than radiate out from the center.

2. Microscopic examination
   a. *Alligatoring.* Examination of the ink at 60× magnification, showed alligatoring of the ink line. Flynn's experiments proved this happened when the 1770 black ink formula was artificially aged with sodium hydroxide.
   b. *Solubility.* Ink, on paper, hardens progressively as time passes. It was discovered that a 15 percent solution of ammonium hydroxide in distilled water would eventually cause the iron-gall formula to become soluble. Application of the formula to 100-year-old documents takes at least three minutes, while the Hoffman documents became soluble in less than 15 seconds.
   c. *Stain.* When iron-gall ink is placed on a document, it slowly begins to oxidize or rust. This iron rust is absorbed into the paper with time. A sharply pointed stylus can pry away the surface and expose the underlying paper. On many of the Hoffman documents, that paper was not stained brown.
   d. *Printing flaws.* Genuine documents were photographed and the negatives were used to make plates. The plates were inked and a forged print was made. Microscopic flaws on the negative would then be reproduced on each plate. Each plate would, therefore, contain the same flaws.

3. Scanning Auger Microscopic Dating (SAMD).
   Roderick J. McNeil, a research scientist and head of Environmental Technologies in Palmer, Montana, developed the new SAMD test which tracked the movement of ions in ink to show how long ink had been in contact with paper. McNeil's test proved the Hoffman documents had not been written before 1920.[43]

Charles Hamilton, nationally known autograph dealer, stated, "Mr. Hoffman perpetrated by far the largest monetary fraud through forgery that this country has ever had," adding, "He fooled me—he fooled everybody." Two persons he did not fool, Throckmorton and Flynn, testified at the preliminary hearing that the "Anthon" document, and the "white salamander" letter were forgeries. (They determined that a total of 107 Hoffman documents were forged.) On January 23, 1987, Hoffman pleaded guilty to two counts of second-degree murder and two counts of theft by deception.

Books

Suspect Documents by Wilson R. Harrison (1958) and *Scientific Examination of Questioned Documents* by Ordway Hilton (1982) update and supplement the landmark volumes of Albert S. Osborn. Numerous articles have been published, and most facets of the subject are well covered.

A recent work on photography is *Modern Photography for Police and Firemen* by Sam J. Sansone (1971). A beginner's book, it complements and updates *Photographic Evidence* by Charles C. Scott (1969). The latter is very good, but was published in 1969. Eastman Kodak has a number of publications, but a new book on the subject of advanced document photography would be welcome.

Reexamination of Old Cases

It is human nature to second-guess a jury's verdict in an important trial. Many articles and books have been written about the verdicts in classic handwriting cases such as the Molineux murder, Rice will, Lindbergh kidnapping, Kennedy assassination, and Howard Hughes cases. In researching the history of handwriting we reexamined all of these cases and confirmed the handwriting opinion in all of them.

In recent times, the appearance of two new books on the subject generated new interest in the Lindbergh kidnapping case. The books are *Scapegoat*,[44] published in 1976, and *In Search of the Lindbergh Baby*,[45] published in 1981. These books reexamine many aspects of the case, including the role of document examiners. Wright's book devotes only four pages to handwriting; its thesis is that the defense expert possessed credentials as a handwriting expert similar to Osborn's. Wright concludes that the prosecution experts were contradicted by several other experts, one of them a professional penman. It is beyond comprehension that anyone could compare the prosecution experts (Osborn, Stein, etc.) with those of the defense.

Scapegoat attacks the testimony regarding the nursery note, on the ground that only the word "is" from the note was used in the exhibits prepared by the prosecution experts, and that numbers were ignored. The experts did, however, identify it as having been written by Hauptman. J. Vreeland Haring and his son, J. Howard Haring, prepared an exhibit based only on the nursery note, and were ready as rebuttal witnesses, if needed, and Clark Sellers made an exhibit identifying the numbers.[46]

Scapegoat alleges that the police had notebooks, ledgers, and other items showing Hauptman's normal writing, but did not use them. However, the only

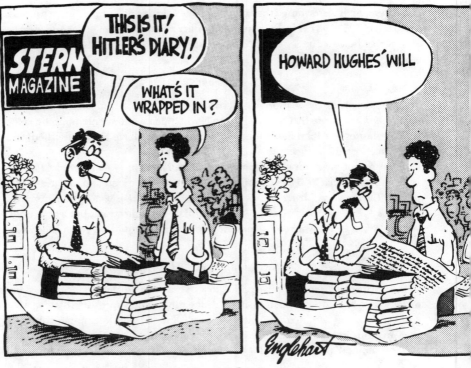

Figure 1–15: Cartoon by Englehart. (*Copyright* © *Robert Englehart*)

usable prearrest writing was signatures; the police could not introduce the note-books, since no witnesses saw Hauptman actually writing in them. A promissory note *was* used, since it had been filled out and signed by Hauptman.

The argument in these two books on the handwriting in the Lindbergh case is totally refutable, and this reduces the credibility of their attacks on other areas.

The Alger Hiss case is the only case I question. The two trials and lengthy typewriter examinations all took place before the question of forgery by type-writer was brought up. (This case is discussed in chapter 10.)

Electronics and Computers

A study by the Insurance and Protective Division of the American Bankers Association revealed that check frauds in the banking industry alone totaled $115 million in 1979 (the latest figure available). This is more than triple the $36 million lost in robberies.

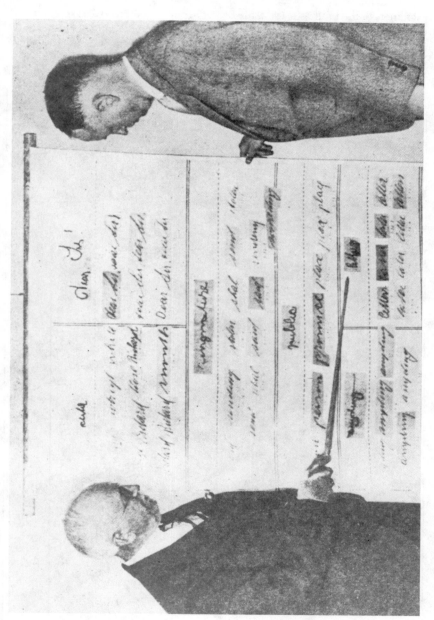

Figure 1-16: J.V. Haring (left) and J.H. Haring examine the "nursery note" exhibit. (*J. Vreeland Haring*)

To combat this problem advanced technology must be used by document examiners of the future. In 1962, the Secret Service attempted to use computers to assist in the identification of forged endorsements on government checks, and in 1971 I attempted to use the Eastman Kodak Miracode Video Computer with

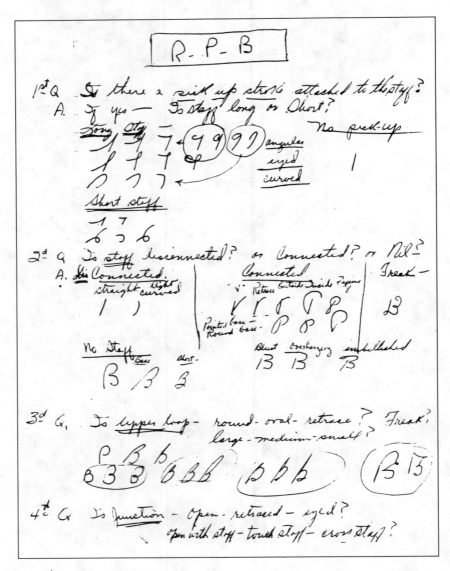

Figure 1–17: Bradford's classification experiment work sheet.

the Bradford System. Neither attempt achieved the desired results. Much of the hardware is here, but the experts must now find a way to utilize it.

One way would be to develop a classification system for handwriting. Lee and Abbey in 1922 and Orville Livingston in 1953 made the attempt. Document examiners may one day develop a system utilizing their work as a starting point. Ralph Bradford believed that a system based on coding key parts of letters and strokes could be developed and had started work on it. He called it "Coded Handwriting and the Identification of Writers," and was conducting experiments shortly before his death.

One day someone will develop a method of classification for handwriting that will assist law enforcement agencies around the world.

A new typewriter was developed in the late 1970s for the electronics and computer fields. The manufacturers and salespeople feel that these new electronic typewriters, with the capability of attachment to and compatibility with computers, are the machines of today and tomorrow.

One of the radical changes in the typewriter is the "daisy wheel." This wheel contains 100 characters and replaces the outdated "golf-ball" element. A ball-element typewriter can type at a speed of 150 to 180 words per minute; the new electronic machines with daisy wheels type at 16-plus words per second (960-plus words per minute). Like the ball, the wheel is interchangeable and is available in various popular styles of type. Another item of interest to examiners is that the machines permit instant switching to 10, 12, and 15 pitch, or proportional spacing.

The Adler-Royal Business Machines brochure promises "Long-life interchangeable print wheels for precise impressions and quiet operation. Typing alignment is always perfect." Some companies advertise a steel daisy wheel, but most use a less-expensive plastic wheel. These can be damaged and produce defects.

Old typewriters produced defects which were very obvious, but defects in the new electronic typewriters are hard to detect. Research will be needed to determine the degree of damage to characters on the daisy wheel. It will also be necessary to determine if alignment is always perfect or whether there might be misalignment problems. Research and practical experience are needed, as problems in this field are on the way for the document examiner.

Lasers

In 1974, the Series 550 Laser system was introduced to provide a reliable, high-performance argon laser at significant cost savings. In 1976, Dr. E. Roland Menzel of the Department of Physics at Texas Tech University, developed a technique for detecting latent fingerprints by using lasers.[47] In 1981, at the IAI conference, Menzel displayed the laser-induced luminescence on fingerprints and items of handwriting. Much work is still to be done with this new forensic technique.

Certification

The Questioned Document program was started in 1978 and is growing steadily. The International Association for Identification sponsored a certification program for fingerprint examiners in 1977. Both programs are growing in recognition every year. There are a few problems in the two programs that must be addressed in the future.

1. Professional titles that would be uniform around the world. At present, examiners with one agency may have one title, and those in another agency a different one. (The legal and medical professions have made their titles uniform, proving that it is possible.)
2. Both certification programs contained a "Grandfather Clause." This allowed members to be certified who did not meet some of the present qualifications (including college degree and testing). This procedure may have been necessary in the beginning to get the program started, but to free the program of any questions it is felt that each person who has not been tested, should be.
3. The qualifications for certification for both programs are very high, as they should be. Law enforcement examiners are a very important part of the program, and for them the requirement of a college degree may be too high, since they enter the training program after their schooling has been completed. This may place certification beyond the reach of too many otherwise qualified examiners. Consideration should be given to the possibility of substituting an Associate of Arts degree for the Bachelor degree requirement.

Up-Date on Handwriting Systems

Recognizing the handwriting systems taught in the United States, and their styles of letters, is important to examiners. In chapter 5, twenty of the most popular systems are listed, including Spencerian, Zaner-Blosser, Bowmar/Noble, and Palmer. In the 1980s, Italic Writing became popular. Calligraphers (writers of beautiful writing) said they did not want to force elegant writing on children. "We want to teach children an efficient hand, one that is legible, fast, and easy to write."

Time magazine (March 21, 1983) reported that Barbara M. Getty and Inga S. Dubay have now taken italic writing one step further. They wrote a handwriting manual for use in the elementary school system. The eight-book series was accepted by the state of Oregon, and schools throughout Oregon now have discretionary permission to use the Dubay-Getty (1980) books.[48]

Figure 1–18: Dubay–Getty writing system. *(Inga Dubay)*

Figure 1–19: Document Examiner Hall of Fame. Front row: (left to right): Osborn, Albert S.; Ames, Daniel T. Row 2: Haring, J. Vreeland; Tyrrell, John F.; Wigmore, John H. Row 3: Lee, Clarence D.; Stein, Elbridge Row 4: Harrison, Wilson R.; Sellers, J. Clark; Livingston, Orville B. Row 5: Bradford, Ralph B.; Hilton, Ordway Row 6: Scott, Charles C.; Cole, Alwyn; Cabanne, Robert A. Row 7: Brunelle, Richard L.; Harris, Jack J.

Document Examiner Hall of Fame

While researching the history of handwriting, I identified certain persons who have made substantial contributions to the field of document examination. At least one of these men, John H. Wigmore, was not a document examiner, but his contributions and those of the others deserve special recognition. I therefore named these men to the "Document Examiner Hall of Fame." The choice was entirely mine, and my opinion is not necessarily shared by other examiners.

—2—

Introduction to Document Examination

An important point to consider before beginning a study of this book, is: Which field in the study of handwriting examination is of prime interest to you? The study of handwriting is basic to two distinctly different professions—document examiner and graphologist—which are not compatible with each other. This book deals with only one of the two professions—Document Examiner, popularly known as Handwriting Examiner.

The examination of questioned documents is the study of handwriting comparison and other sciences relating to documents. It is the comparison of known and unknown documents. The American Academy of Forensic Sciences describes it as "proof of genuineness and detection of forgery in disputed signatures; the identification of extended writing, hand printing and numbers; the identification of makes and models of typewriters and the work they produce; and the detection of eradications, erasures, alterations and substitutions." The examiner's work does not end with the identification of details in the document. He must present these facts in a typed report and be prepared to demonstrate the basis and reasons for his or her opinion to a judge or jury.

Albert S. Osborn stated,

> It has been known in a general way for more than two generations that a new profession of document specialists, usually referred to as "handwriting experts," was being developed. While the identification and proof of hand-writing is the most frequent problem regarding documents, this special work now covers a much wider field than handwriting alone. It now includes typewriting, a growing subject, as well as age and identity of ink and paper, also erasures, additions, alterations, substitutions, forgeries over genuine signatures, anonymous letters, significance of crossed lines, cross marks, kidnapper demands, and other important questions.[1]

The term "handwriting examiner" does not describe the total work of an examiner. Of the titles used today, "Examiner of Questioned Documents" (title used by Albert S. Osborn) is the most popular.

The titles "Questioned Document Examiner" and "Document Examiner" are also widely used. Charles Scott stated that

> the term "document examiner" is preferable to "examiner of questioned documents," which is one-sided and unjust because it places a stigma upon a document submitted for examination and therefore is too favorable to the contestant of a document and too detrimental to the proponent. It is unfortunate that the term "examiner of questioned documents" ever came into wide use. "Document examiner" is not only shorter, it is also more neutral. In my opinion an attorney representing the proponent of a document in a trial should object strenuously to the use of the terms "examiner of questioned documents" or "questioned document," both of which suggest to the average layman that the document involved in the case is questionable. Whether or not it is questionable is a matter to be proved rather than a fact to be assumed.[2]

"Handwriting examiner" is still used by some examiners in law enforcement, since the title makes their profession very clear to the private citizens with whom they deal. This is also the term used by all examiners when listing themselves in the classified pages of the telephone book. Ralph Bradford used the title

AUTHOR OF
QUESTIONED DOCUMENTS 1910-1929
THE PROBLEM OF PROOF 1922
THE MIND OF THE JUROR 1937

ALBERT S. OSBORN

EXAMINER OF QUESTIONED DOCUMENTS
WOOLWORTH BUILDING
233 BROADWAY, NEW YORK
TELEPHONES: OFFICE, BARCLAY 7-3987
RES. 2-1843 MONTCLAIR, N. J.

Figure 2–1: Albert S. Osborn's business card.

"Handwriting Examiner" while in law enforcement, but when he retired, he listed himself as "Questioned Document Examiner."

The basis on which a handwriting examination is made is best illustrated by the testimony of Alwyn Cole, given before the President's Commission on the Assassination of President John F. Kennedy (Warren Commission):

> **Question:** Mr. Cole, could you explain the basis on which you were able to make an identification of a questioned writing as being authored by the person who wrote a standard writing?
>
> **Cole:** This is based upon the principle that every handwriting is distinctive, that since the mental and physical equipment for producing handwriting is different in every individual, each person produces his own distinctive writing habits. Of course, everyone learns to write in the beginning by an endeavor to repeat ideal letter forms, but practically no one is able to reproduce these forms exactly. Even though a person might have some initial success during the active period of instruction, he soon departs from these and develops his own habits. It may be said that habit in handwriting is that which makes handwriting possible. Habit is that which makes handwriting efficient. If it were not for the development of habit, one would be obliged to draw or sketch.
>
> Some habit would be included even in these efforts. But the production of handwriting rapidly and fluently always involves a recording of personal writing habit. This has been confirmed by observation of a very large number of specimens over a long period of time, and it has been further demonstrated by, on my part, having a formal responsibility for rendering decisions about the identification of handwriting based upon an agreement of handwriting habit in situations where there would be a rigorous testing of the correctness of these decisions by field investigators, for example, of the law enforcement agencies, and a demonstration that these results were confirmed by other evidence. This is the basis for identification of handwriting.[3]

The principle, therefore, is that every handwriting is distinctive, because nature never offers her handiwork to us in facsimile. Animal, vegetable, or mineral organisms are never reproduced exactly the same. The statement "As alike as two peas in a pod" is okay as long as you remember no two peas are exactly alike. Study a large tree with its thousands of leaves, and you'll discover that no two leaves are exactly alike. But a botanist can immediately tell you the type of tree they came from.

In many people's handwriting, the difference is even greater. "In the act of writing, the muscular system, the nervous system, and the directive functions of the brain are called simultaneously into play. As a physical act, the expenditure of energy is infinitesimal. But the coordination of the muscles of fingers, wrist, and forearm must be delicately and sensitively balanced to ensure that, within a few hundredths of a second and within a few hundredths of an inch, the direction

Figure 2–2: Carl Bark's Donald Duck cartoon.

of travel of the pen is changed and changed again throughout a bewildering series of motions, and changed, moreover, in a manner at once gradual, even and harmonious."[4]

Given nature's laws, and man's muscular system, brain function, and nervous reaction, no two humans are precisely the same and no two persons write exactly the same. The question always arises regarding twins and students educated in the same school. In fact, heredity and schooling have been the subject of several research projects. We have also examined writing by twins and schoolmates on several occasions, and while, in a few cases the writing was similar, their basic differences were easily determined. (Chapter 8 discusses this subject in greater detail.)

We also conducted considerable research with cartoonists' printing. Cartoonists are trained to print in an exact style. Despite this and the fact that they print in capital letters, the printing of each cartoonist is individual and can be identified. Chapter 9 discusses the statement: "No two persons write exactly alike," and also examines artist Carl Bark's famous Donald Duck cartoons.

In that each person's writing is distinctive, the examination of handwriting is therefore the comparison of known and unknown documents to determine how a document was prepared, and by whom and/or by what instruments.

Graphologists

Graphology is the study of handwriting on documents of a known or unknown person. The examination of the handwriting on a document is the basis for the graphologist's evaluation of a person's character, disposition, and/or aptitudes.

Bonafide graphology doesn't claim to be able to foretell the future or determine if a document was written by someone in a boat who was wearing a hat. It also cannot determine the sex, race, or physical description of a person. Some graphologists have given the profession of graphology a bad name and have downgraded it to a fortune-telling practice.

In recent years, true graphology has gained status in America. The subject is taught in colleges and universities, and through reputable correspondence schools. Some businesses are now using graphology as a screening instrument for new employees.

The International Graphoanalysis Society in Chicago now claims over 10,000 members worldwide. Students are required to complete an intensive correspondence course to earn the title of Certified Graphoanalyst. Mike Winerip, of Knight-Ridder News Service, reported in 1980 that persons in many fields do a better job with a graphology background, citing as examples a United States customs agent who uses graphology when examining declaration cards, and a drug counselor who uses handwriting analysis as an aid to understanding the problems of young people.

Do not, however, confuse graphology and document examination. The two are as different as baseball and basketball (both use a ball but do different things with it). Both handwriting professions examine handwriting, but from completely different perspectives, and there is no connection between the two. It is important to understand that a document examiner is not a graphologist, and a graphologist is not a document examiner. Each profession takes the full-time effort of the practitioner, and if one tries to perform in both fields, he or she will not be proficient in either.

Qualifications for Prospective Document Examiners

Just as a square peg will not fit in a round hole, a person who does not possess the proper amount of personality, education, and physical ability will not make a document examiner. Neither can a person read this book or any other book, or take a handwriting course, and thereby qualify as an "expert." A beginner must invest at least two to five years of dedicated internship to become a qualified examiner. Age, therefore, is important in the decision to begin the study of handwriting. A law enforcement agency preparing to hire a trainee will also consider the applicant's age. No agency wishes to invest in a trainee for several years, only to have him retire. The ideal trainee is usually a mature individual twenty-five to thirty years of age.

Successful document examiners, for the most part, possess many similar personality traits. John Wooden (former head basketball coach at UCLA, and winner of ten national championships in twelve years) believes that the traits of a personality are bound together like blocks of a pyramid. He called it his "Pyramid of Success." For a document examiner these blocks include:

1. *Concentration.* An examiner must be able to focus his energies along a single line of thought. The ability to concentrate, coupled with enthusiasm, will assist in the study of handwriting as well as in preparing a document case. Concentration and hard work will assure that goals are attained.

2. *Analytic approach.* It is believed that any complex problem can be understood if it is broken down into its individual components. Logical analysis therefore gives one the capacity to sort things out by shifting items around and analyzing them. This approach is also called *elementarism,* the opposite of *synthesizing,* in which one sees things as a whole. This book attempts to separate handwriting into its various elements so they can be individually examined and compared. Chapters 2 to 7 inclusive will gradually train you to do that, so that when you reach chapter 8, you can put it all together and arrive at a handwriting opinion.

3. *Organization.* This is the ability to create order from disorder. There are two types of order. The first type is logical organization by dates, categories,

etc., while the second is visual organization by patterns, or a "sixth sense." This type of organized thinking is a slow process by which a final conclusion is gradually attained. Use of this building block results in more thorough and accurate assessments.

4. *Imagination*. This is a "new" form of organization. It involves looking at mental images from past experience in a new way, and reshaping them into a new pattern. Clark Sellers, Elbridge Stein, and John Tyrrell used their photographic skills with imagination to pioneer the application of ultraviolent light in the examination of documents, particularly in the deciphering of erased ink-writing. Sellers wrote of imagination, "It is more unlikely that any document examiner can reach his highest potential unless he acquires a vivid imagination and effectively utilizes it. The higher the degree of intelligence, the keener the imagination. Imagination, as used here, has no reference to fancy, fantasy, or day dreaming. Rather, it is used in the sense of creativeness: the faculty to conceive, to think, to conjecture, to form a mental picture, to invent. The active use of a trained imagination stimulates man's inherent creative force and lifts him above the commonplace. Thomas A. Edison, undoubtedly one of America's greatest exponents of the value of creative imagination, stated that the man with the most keenly developed imagination is the man who is in the position to accomplish the greatest results. Preparation to testify effectively entails the use of a developed imagination."[5]

5. *Reasoning ability*. Examiner Ray Kiser, a training officer for the Los Angeles Police Department Document Section, observed that trainees who failed the training course generally lacked one key element. These trainees had a college education and law enforcement experience, but lacked the ability to reason. He stated that "the three words—reason, reasonable, and reasoning—are the most neglected words in the selection process of trainees."[6]

An examiner must be able to reason and to think logically, and to arrive at the proper conclusion. As Albert S. Osborn pointed out: "Most of the errors in handwriting identification are due not to the failure to see the evidence, but to the inability to interpret correctly what is seen. This failure is, of course, the source of many kinds of error in many fields. Lack of reasoning power, which is the child of ignorance, is the main hindrance and bar to progress."

6. *Integrity and dedication*. These two words say it all. A person must give his all and perform to the best of his ability. In sports, they call it "giving 110 percent." It is a "moral consistency of honesty and truthfulness."[7]

7. *Poise and confidence*. This is the ability to face emergencies calmly and coolly, and to be oneself, and at ease in difficult situations. Confidence—the knowledge that you are prepared for every contingency—comes from within. These two qualities are the keystone of the John Wooden Pyramid

of Success. He defines success as "peace of mind which is a direct result of the self-satisfaction of knowing you did your best to become the best that you are capable of becoming."[8]

Physical Requirements

Healthy eyes and the ability to see accurately are two of the most important assets of an examiner. The eyes of every prospective trainee should be examined by an ophthalmologist to detect any visual problems and/or eye disease, and all trainees and professionals should have a thorough examination every few years or as often as the doctor recommends. A standard eye test should be given for hyperopia (farsightedness), a condition characterized by blurred images in near vision, which requires corrective lenses. A glaucoma test also should be given. Glaucoma is a condition in which eye fluid does not drain off properly, causing increased pressure within the eye. If uncontrolled, this pressure can cause damage to the optic nerve, resulting in loss of sight, or tunnel vision. Eye problems that often occur later in life include cataracts and retinal tears. Neglecting such problems may lead to impaired vision or even loss of eyesight.

Color blindness appears in about 8 percent of males and 2 percent of females, so aspiring examiners should have a color-deficiency test. The commonest form is the inability to distinguish certain reds and greens from each other or from gray. This could be important in examining inks.

Form blindness is the inability to identify or distinguish form or size. This defect can be caused by a physical problem called aniseikonia, in which one eye sees an object as one size and shape, and the other eye sees it as a different size and shape. Dr. Robert Vandervort of the Southern California College of Optometry says that aniseikonia is moderately common, but relatively few patients have severe symptoms.

Another type of blindness, researched by Professor Joseph Jastro of the University of Wisconsin, poses more of a problem for examiners. Albert S. Osborn reported the work of Professor Jastro in his questioned document books.[9] Jastro's research is about Form Blindness. Form blindness prevents a person from carrying form in his mind for even three to five seconds. Also impaired is the ability to determine parallelism in lines. Some cannot see the difference in a comparison of angles until the angles approach five full degrees in width. Examinations of handwriting, hand printing, typewriting, and the like require detailed comparison. An examiner with form blindness would therefore be unable to interpret characteristics and form correct opinions.

Tests of various types should be given to a trainee, such as a jigsaw puzzle, which requires some form memory. Letter puzzles are another way to test a person. A test was published in Osborn's book *Questioned Document Problems* and is shown in figure 2.3. (Answers to the test can be found at the end of the chapter.)

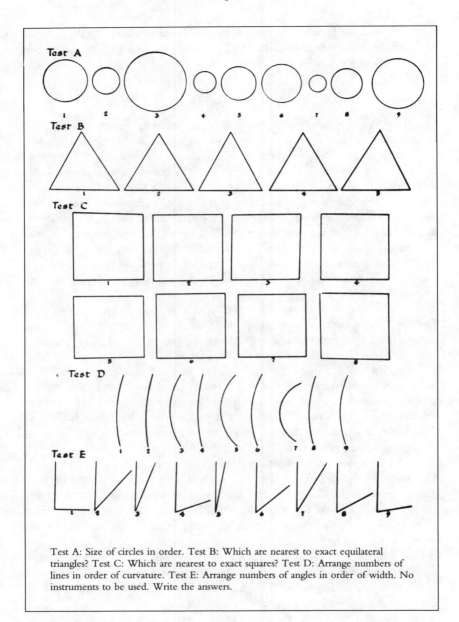

Test A: Size of circles in order. Test B: Which are nearest to exact equilateral triangles? Test C: Which are nearest to exact squares? Test D: Arrange numbers of lines in order of curvature. Test E: Arrange numbers of angles in order of width. No instruments to be used. Write the answers.

Figure 2–3: Form blindness test.

Educational Requirements

The final aspect to be considered is formal education. Both the American Academy of Forensic Science and the American Society of Questioned Document Examiners include a college degree among their qualifications for membership. Certification of document examiners began in the late 1970s. To be certified, an applicant must have a college degree. (Will Rogers once stated, "Instead of giving money to found colleges to promote learning, why don't they pass a constitutional amendment prohibiting anybody from learning anything? And if it works as good as the prohibition once did, why, in five years we would have the smartest race of people on earth.")

It is recommended that the major in college be: chemistry, criminology, mathematics, police science, psychology, or other science. Science courses will introduce the trainee to the microscope and its use in the examination of ink and paper. As photography is of great value to the examiner, beginning as well as advanced classes should be taken. Law and public speaking courses are also important to the examiner.

A recent document examiner task study survey asked for opinions regarding the necessary level of knowledge of a document examiner. The consensus was that document examiners should be able to: *Examine and render opinions on handwriting and handprinting; determine genuineness or nongenuineness of signatures; determine sequence of strokes; and date documents. He or she should be capable of examining typewriting for identification purposes:* of differentiating and identifying photocopying methods, and of examining printed matter, *and other mechanical impressions* (for example, *check writers* and rubber stamps). The document examiner must be able to process charred documents, conduct nondestructive and destructive examinations of ink and other writing instruments, and examine physical characteristics of paper. The examiner should be able to use the following photographic techniques: copying, photomicrography, close-up, ultraviolet, infrared, luminescence, and oblique lighting photography. *The final skills required for training are preparation of written reports and charts for court exhibits and court testimony.* The above is the recommended course of study for a document examiner.[10] (Topics in italic are covered in this book.)

Getting Established as a Document Examiner

Office Space and Furnishings

Your office can be as elaborate as your finances permit. However, you can conduct a handwriting examination with as little equipment as a pocket magnifier and a ruler. The majority of your examinations will probably be made with these two instruments.

For best results, you should choose an office in which you will feel comfortable and at home. Most examiners prefer a quiet office, which permits absolute concentration on the work. Your office should be large enough to hold the necessary desk, work table, file cabinet, bookcase, and visitor's chair. It is vital that the office be well lit, preferably with a white light. Chemical eradicators are sometimes a pale yellow, and this makes certain problems difficult to distinguish if other than a white light is used.

Your desk should be at least 30 inches by 60 inches, with a conference-type work table (72 inches long) perpendicular to the desk. The desk and conference table combination gives the ample space needed to spread out the documents. Why waste time looking for lost documents on a crowded desktop, when handling can be kept to a minimum with a large uncluttered work space? The most important reason for a large work area is that it permits you to organize the documents. Moving an identified document from one side of the table to another, or placing documents in chronological order can expedite the examination. An examiner's ability to study all the pertinent documents simultaneously can be of vital importance.

A good example of this is a case investigated by Senior Special Investigator Terry Taylor, of the California Department of Health. This case involved more than three hundred forged narcotic prescriptions. To assist in his investigation, Taylor wanted to know how many writers were involved. A large work table enabled the examiner to lay out the prescriptions and sort them by handwriting into separate stacks.

Handwriting on the prescription area may tie two or more prescriptions together, and so can a handwritten address or other writing. In this case, Bradford determined by studying the handwriting that about thirty-five suspects wrote the three hundred forged prescriptions. Further investigation pinpointed suspects, and on November 17, 1981, reports were submitted identifying one suspect responsible for writing seventy-one prescriptions, and another suspect responsible for fifty-five. On December 1, 1981, fifty-nine additional prescriptions were attributed to a third suspect. A large work area was essential to this case, as the examiner was thus able to spread out the three hundred prescriptions in order to conduct a thorough handwriting examination.

A swivel chair designed for serious work is needed. A chair without arms, and with a soft seat that angles slightly downward from front to back, is best. It should have a posture back that will make you sit up straight. It should also have a wide base and large wheels. A telephone is another important item in the office, and just as important is an accompanying answering machine. It will answer calls when you are in the middle of an examination. You'll also want a bookcase for your reference books and examination equipment.

Examination Equipment

Once the office is selected and furnished, it is time to equip it with instruments for conducting examinations. A swing-arm lamp, with an adjusting swivel base, is an important item. The light must be movable to show up indentations in the paper. By adjusting the lamp so the bulb faces up, you can have transmitted light. Documents can thus be superimposed to assist in the examination of possible traced forgeries.

In the Eunice W. Rowe case, a signature on a special contract and the endorsement on an Equitable Life Insurance check (signatures 1 and 2 of figure 2-4) were questioned. Mrs. Rowe, her husband, and Harriet F. Myers all submitted exemplars. Examination of the two questioned signatures using a drafting lamp disclosed that the two signatures were almost identical. The conclusion that the two signatures were traced from the same master was arrived at with the help of a light that swivels.

The two most important instruments in a document laboratory are a hand magnifier and a microscope. Hand magnifiers are available with magnification from four power (4x) to fifteen power (15x), and are available in many price ranges and styles. Some can be clipped on eye glasses or on a desk light, and some have a built-in illumination system. I recommend the Agfa Lupe 8×, which can be purchased for around $5.00 in most photography stores. The Agfa Lupe is made of plastic and has a clear base which allows light to enter from the side. This high-quality magnifier is used by photographers and graphic artists the world round. It is lightweight and a compact $1^1/_4$ inches high and $1^{15}/_{16}$ inches in diameter.

The magnifying glass is the examiner's most-used instrument. When making an examination, it is important to determine exactly how each letter is formed to determine whether it has straight or curved lines; sharp or curved angles, retraced or open. These and many more comparison points are important and

Figure 2–6: Agfa 8× magnifier. (*Agfa-Gevaert Inc.*)

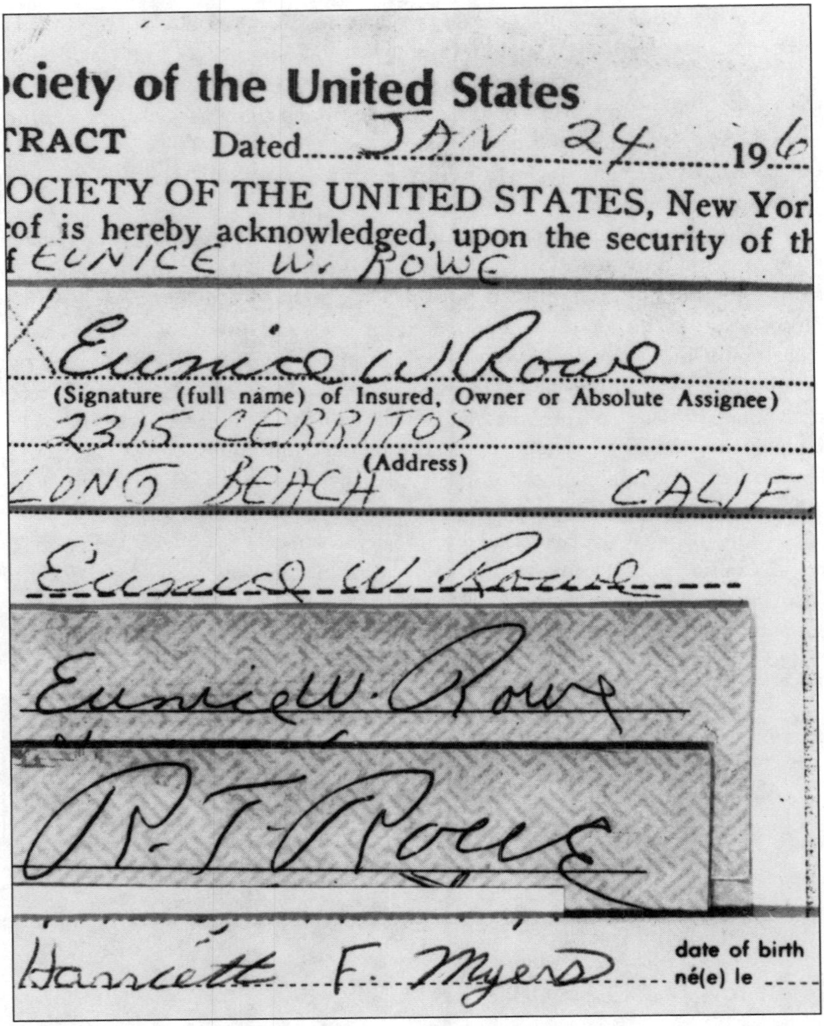
ciety of the United States

TRACT Dated JAN 24 196

OCIETY OF THE UNITED STATES, New Yor
of is hereby acknowledged, upon the security of th
f EUNICE W. ROWE

Eunice W Rowe

(Signature (full name) of Insured, Owner or Absolute Assignee)

2315 CERRITOS

(Address)

LONG BEACH CALIF

Eunice W Rowe

Eunice W. Rowe

P. T. Rowe

Harriett F. Myers date of birth né(e) le

Figure 2–4: Eunice W. Rowe forgery.

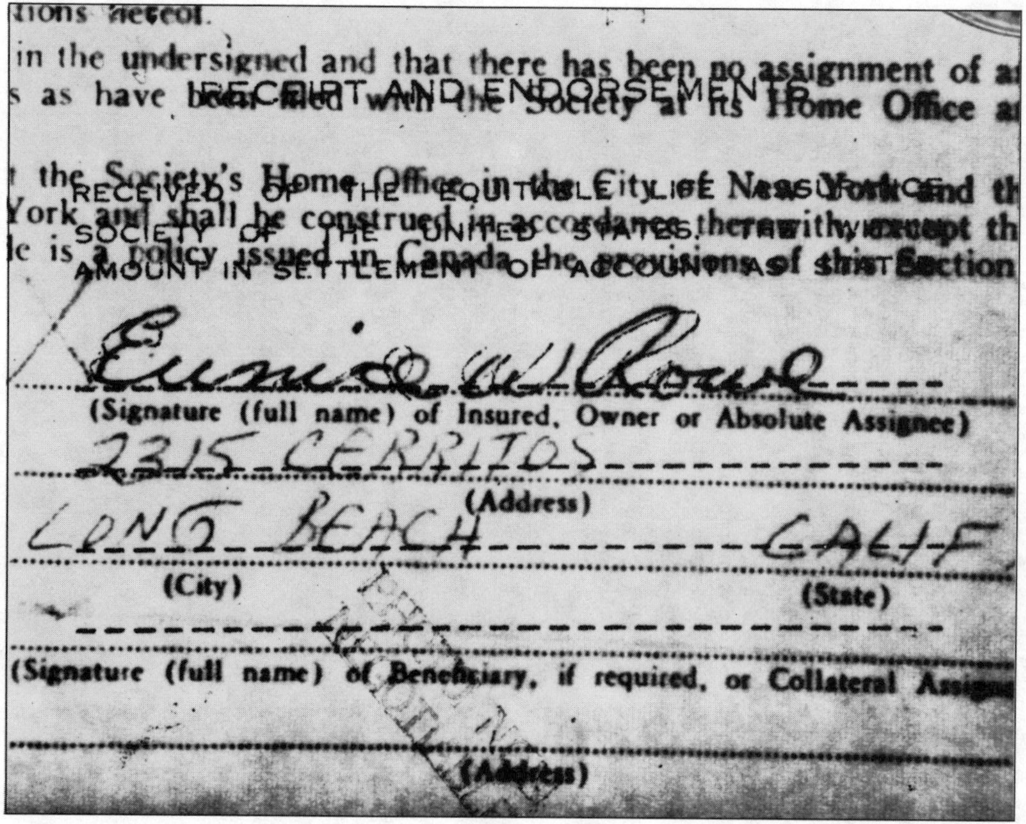

Figure 2–5: Superimposed tracing.

can sometimes be seen only with a glass. Tremor of fraud, and the hiatus in writing, which you'll learn about in chapter 8, can best be seen with a magnifying glass or microscope.

The microscope is the second indispensable tool for the examiner. There are many types of microscopes in use, such as the comparison and the stereoscopic models. The comparison microscope brings two separated images into the same field of view, so they can be compared for color, texture, size, and shape. The quality of written lines can be compared in this manner. A comparison microscope manufactured by the Bausch & Lomb Optical Company was designed to the suggestions of Albert S. Osborn.

The stereoscopic microscope is an important instrument in many handwriting examinations. It can be used in any problem where depth or a third dimension must be considered, such as where an ink line crosses a fold in the paper. Its real value, however, is in the examination of a possible copy, or a forged signature. The keys in determining a copied signature are tremor (which is caused by the slow drawing of a signature), and retouching or patching. This is an attempt to correct any mistakes in the copy, and can be clearly seen under magnification. Carbon paper forgeries and typewritten documents can be examined thoroughly with a stereoscopic microscope. This instrument also has the advantages of stereoscopic vision—revealing depth, wide view area view, ease in movement, and examination of the total document with various powers that range from 6× up to about 150×.[11]

Measuring instruments, such as a finely graduated glass ruler, are also of great value. Glass is preferred by many, since it can be brought into actual contact with the document, while its transparency allows easy measurement. The ruler should be graduated down to a sixty-fourth of an inch. This permits an examiner with average eyesight to measure accurately. You should also purchase a second ruler made of steel, which is graduated to hundredths of an inch on one side and to millimeters on the other. When an extremely delicate measurement is made, you should span the distance with a needle-pointed parallel divider, which then can be transferred to the fine measurements on a steel ruler. Drafting rules approved by the U.S. Bureau of Standards make excellent instruments for document examiners.

Other available types of measuring instruments include a protractor (for measuring angles and slant), and a micrometer caliper actuated by a ratchet (for measuring thickness of paper). A typewriter test plate is a must for examiners. A test plate can assist in measuring for type size, etc., and more importantly, it can assist in the examination of horizontal and vertical misalignment. A large test plate ($8^1/_2$" × 11") can assist in determining whether portions of a document were prepared at different times. "A Test Plate for Proportional Spacing Typewriting Examinations" describes a test plate with vertical rulings every $^1/_{32}$ inch and horizontal rulings every 0.19 inch, which would be useful in a large percentage of the proportional typing problems you are likely to encounter.[12]

One must-buy item, a supply of protective plastic evidence bags, is needed to protect questioned documents. Heavy-duty (4 mm thick) bags in sizes 4" × 9" (for checks), 9" × 12" (for letters), and 13" × 18" (for large documents) are essential in every document office.

The final item of equipment that must be on your desk is a record book. This book should contain a daily record and list of all cases examined. Each entry should contain information as to who brought the case in, results of the examination, and whether a report was submitted. A second section of this book should contain a record of court testimony . Statistics are of great importance to a new examiner, especially when testifying in court.

Accessory Equipment

The equipment listed in this section need not be owned by an examiner, but you should know where you can locate and have access to it. The most valuable of these is a duplicating machine such as the IBM Copier III or a Xerox 1075 Copier. Some duplicating machines slightly reduce the images in a copy, while others enlarge. To determine the type you have, you should copy a ruler. All questioned and known writing should be copied prior to examination. (The reasons will be covered later in this chapter).

Photographic equipment and a dark room are of vital importance to all examiners. Copy equipment is essential. The Long Beach Police Department purchased a special 4 × 5 camera and stand in 1942. It was manufactured by Folmer & Schwing Division, Eastman Kodak Co., and did a tremendous job copying documents.

Polaroid manufactures the MP-4, which is a very sophisticated piece of equipment. They also have introduced the CU-70 evidence recording system that uses a SX-70 Sonar Land Camera. Attachments to this camera allow instant photographs at 1:1, 2:1, and 3:1. Kodak manufactures an Ektographic EF Visualmaker using an Instamatic X-35F camera. The latter two products require no photographic experience or expertise to operate, and both are portable and easy to set up and use.

The veteran examiner will prefer more professional equipment. The trainee should therefore begin to acquire photographic knowledge. Joseph Tholl describes in detail the use of a 35mm camera in document examination. This article discussed the use of an "Exakta single lens reflex camera with a complete set of accessories for copying, photomacrography, photomicrography, ultraviolet, infrared and color photography."[13] Today, most of the camera companies manufacture a full line of equipment. Nikon Inc., a subsidiary of Ehrenreich Photo-Optical Industries, Inc., is a good example. Nikon sells a number of very fine cameras, including the FE and F-3. More important is their Al-Micro-Nikkor 55mm F2.8 lens, one of the sharpest lenses on the market. Coupled with a PK-13 Auto Extension Ring, it will allow 1:1 copy. Nikon's Repro-Copy Outfit PK-3

Figure 2–7: William Corson with LBPD copy equipment.

is a sturdy copy stand with a precision counterbalance system (Canon also manufactures a portable Handy Stand F that attaches to the lens and will copy documents from 10 ½ inches by 15 ½ inches in size to 5 inches by 7 ½ inches). A B12 filter (for color work) and floodlamps complete the total system.

The film used in the copy process is also of great importance. A contrast film is needed so that the writing will stand out from the background. A very fine 4 × 5 film for high contrast and medium grain is the Kodak Contrast Process Panchromatic Film 4155 (Estar Thick Base). A major portion of document photography utilizes this film. The examiner working in 35mm should consider Kodak Technical Pan Film 2415. This film replaces Kodak High Contrast Copy Film 5069, which has been discontinued. The new 2415 pan film will produce negatives with the finest grain and highest resolving power of any black and white film ever offered by Kodak.[14] However, Technical Pan Film requires a specific type development for a given speed. It has no specific ISO speed, but speed can be varied depending upon contrast index, etc. So you have an option for selection of film types and speeds.

The second choice for a copy film would be Kodak T-Max 100. This film equals or comes close to the qualities of Panatomi-X film. This film is a good

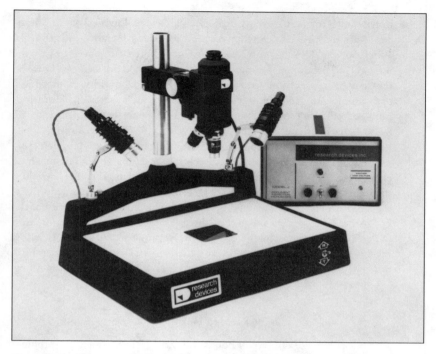

Figure 2–8: Infra-Red Microscope System—Model J. (*Research Devices*).

choice for fine detail, and unlike Technical Pan, it can be processed through standard photofinishers.

There are many other instruments of great value, but they are seldom affordable for the average examiner. These instruments are usually found only in the major laboratories. A check of these labs will provide information as to what is available for possible future use. Four of the sophisticated machines that may be found in the various laboratories are:

1. Projectina. A universal comparison projector for examining questioned documents. This instrument allows side-by-side comparison, superimposition, and a magnification range of 2.5x to 100x. The observed picture can then be photographed. This machine is available through the Fargo Company, 1162 Bryant St., San Francisco, Calif. 94103.

2. Infra-Red Microscope System—Model J. This system allows for the detection of document alterations, obliterations, bleaches, etc. More advanced applications of this system involve the use of filters, observation of IR transmission, and reflection and fluorescence of various materials. The item can then be photographed by Polaroid or 35mm photography. This

instrument is manufactured by the Research Devices Division of the American Optical Corp., 335 Snyder Avenue, Berkeley Heights, N.J. 07922.

3. Video Spectral Comparator, Model VSC-1. This instrument is for viewing infra-red absorption and luminescence in questioned documents. This system has been specifically designed for use in a laboratory to provide a convenient and rapid system of examination in the area of anomalous infra-red effects. This machine is handled by Foster & Freeman Ltd., 35 Swan Lane Evesham, Worcestershire, WR 11, 4 PE, England.

4. Electrostatic Detection Apparatus (ESDA). The ESDA is used for detecting impressions that are too faint to be seen by the human eye. The machine electrostatically charges film (plastic) over documents, and then develops the impression with a black toner. The toner adheres to the plastic, providing a permanent record of the impression. (The extreme sensitivity of the ESDA can be adversely affected by the treatment of paper with ninhydrin to detect latent prints, and the ESDA process can also have an adverse effect on some latents.) This machine is also handled by Foster & Freeman Ltd., in England.[15]

Reference Library

Every office should have a library of books and material to research any problem submitted to it. If the material you need is not in your library, you should contact your local public library or any nearby university. As an examiner, you should have at your fingertips material to research, and answer, any pertinent question.

Listed below is the nucleus for such a library, including references for handwriting, photography, and fingerprinting.

1. *Questioned Documents,* second edition, by Albert S. Osborn. London, England: Boyd Printing Co., 1929. This book is regarded as the "Bible of questioned documents." When it first appeared in 1910, this book revolutionized the science of handwriting examination. The original book, when it can be found, sells for several hundred dollars. Nelson-Hall Publishers has reprinted the second edition (1929), complete and unabridged.

2. *Suspect Documents,* by Wilson R. Harrison. London, England: Sweet and Maxwell Ltd., 1958. This great book contains 583 pages, was reprinted in 1966 with 655 pages, and is in limited supply. It was reprinted again in 1981 by Nelson-Hall Publishers.

3. *Scientific Examination of Questioned Documents,* by Ordway Hilton. New York: Elsevier, North Holland Inc., 1982. This book is a revised edition of Hilton's 1956 book.

4. *The Problem of Proof,* by Albert S. Osborn. Boyd Printing Co., 1926. This book has been reprinted by Nelson-Hall Publishers.

5. *Law of Disputed and Forged Documents,* by J. Newton Baker. Charlottesville, Va.: The Michie Co., 1955.

6. *Evidential Documents,* by James V. P. Conway. Springfield, Ill.: Charles C. Thomas Publishing Co., 1959.

7. *Treatise on Disputed Handwriting,* by William E. Hagan. 1894. This book was reprinted in 1974 by AMS Press, Inc., New York, N.Y.

8. *Forged, Anonymous and Suspect Documents,* by Arthur J. Quirke. London, England: George Routledge & Sons, Ltd., 1930. Quirke is a graphologist, but his Chapter 1, "Individuality of Handwriting," should be read by all.

9. *Century of the Typewriter,* by Wilfred A. Beeching. New York: St. Martin's Press, 1974.

10. *Lockwood's Directory.* New York: Vance Publishing Corp. This is the definitive source of United States and Canadian pulp and paper manufacturing and converting industries, paper and paper products, paper merchants, paper stock, rag buyers and sellers, and mill equipment and supplies sources. Updated each year.

11. *Photographic Evidence,* by Charles C. Scott, St. Paul, Minn.: West Publishing Co., 1969. This very informative three volume work is a revision of Scott's classic 1942 volume.

12. *Modern Photography for Police and Firemen,* by Sam J. Sansone. Cincinnati, Ohio: W. H. Anderson Co., 1977. Photography is very important to the document examiner, and this is a good beginning book.

13. *The Science of Fingerprints,* by the Department of Justice, Federal Bureau of Investigation. Washington, D.C.: U.S. Government Printing Office, 1984. To obtain a copy, write to: Superintendent of Documents, U.S. Government Printing Office, Washington D.C. 20402. Ask for the "Subject Bibliography Index." From that publication, you can order SB-036 (Crime and Criminal Justice), SB-0072 (Photography), and SB-117 (Law Enforcement). From SB-117, you can order "The Science of Fingerprints." Other publications of value can also be obtained through this source.

14. *Single Finger Prints,* by Harry Battley. New Haven, Conn.: Yale University Press, 1931.

15. *Fingerprint Mechanics,* by Walter R. Scott. Springfield, Ill.: Charles C. Thomas Publishing Co., 1951.

16. *How to Develop Self-Confidence and Influence People by Public Speaking,* by Dale Carnegie. New York: Pocket Books, 1975. This book discusses self-confidence, which you will need in your work and in court testimony.

17. *Journal of Criminal Law and Criminology.* This journal was started in 1910, published by Northwestern University. The journal later added *Police Science* to its title. In 1973, the journal split; one part was retitled *Journal of Police Science and Administration.* This journal is now published by the International Chiefs of Police Association. Past and present issues contain some of the most valuable information for examiners.

18. *Journal of Forensic Science.* This is published by the American Academy of Forensic Sciences.
19. *Journal of Forensic Identification* (formally *Identification News*). This is published by the International Association for Identification.
20. *Syllabus/Bibliography of Selected Books and Articles Related to Forensic Document Examination,* prepared by Maureen Casey, Chicago Police Department. Colorado Springs, Colo.: American Board of Forensic Document Examiners, 1979. This syllabus is an index to the leading articles published in books and journals (including the three aforementioned journals). To obtain this syllabus, write to the American Board of Forensic Document Examiners (225 S. Academy Blvd., Suite 201, Colorado Springs, Colo. 80910).
21. *Eastman Kodak Company Publications.* Requests should be addressed to: Professional and Finishing Markets Division, Rochester, N.Y. 14650. Ask for the "Selected Bibliography on Photography for Law Enforcement Agencies," Kodak Publication no. M-46. Among the publications that can be purchased from the list are:

> *Filters and Lens Attachments for Black and White and Color Pictures*
> *Kodak Filters for Scientific and Technical Uses*
> *Ultraviolet and Fluorescence Photography*
> *Applied Infrared Photography*
> *Close-up Photography and Photomacrography*
> *Kodak Infrared Films*
> *Photography Through the Microscope*

Items 17, 18 and 19 in this list are available through membership in a document association. Experts may belong to several associations, but there are only three national associations for document examiners. For information regarding their publications or requirements for membership, write to the following organizations:

a. American Academy of Forensic Sciences, Inc., 225 S. Academy Blvd., Colorado Springs, Colo. 80910.
b. American Society of Questioned Document Examiners, 585 Tarrton Isle, Alameda, Calif. 94501.
c. International Association for Identification, P.O. Box 2429, Alameda, Calif. 94501-2423.

The final reference material an examiner should obtain is one of the utmost importance. This is the examiner's personal reference notebook. The notebook can be divided into twelve sections, corresponding to this book's twelve chapters, but I suggest that you add two additional sections: 13: *Ink*, and 14, *Photography*. In the future, when you find an article on exemplars, make a copy and add it to section 6. If you read about an important handwriting case, make a copy and put it in section 1—*History*. Filing these articles in a notebook will keep things organized, and you will be able to keep abreast of current developments. The sections will grow so large that eventually each section will need its own note-book; some may even need two or more.

Acceptance of a Questioned Document Case

The presenting of a document case to an examiner is the first and one of the most important steps that may eventually lead to testimony in a court of law. This discussion deals with one point, accepting a document case. Later chapters comment on obtaining an exemplar and its examination, and the final chapter is concerned with court testimony.

Albert S. Osborn wrote, "From the moment the genuineness of a document is questioned, it should be handled and cared for in a manner that will not impair in the slightest degree its value as evidence."[16] Questioned documents come in all sizes and shapes, but all must be equally protected. There are three basic types of questioned documents: damaged, unusual, and the flat document.

Damaged Documents

Documents may get wet or, in law enforcement, even get soaked with blood. These documents should be dried at room temperature, and when dry placed in a plastic envelope. Handling should be kept at a minimum. Documents that have been torn into pieces should not be re-assembled with tape. They can be correctly pieced together, then copied and placed in protective envelopes.

Charred documents present special problems. The slightest movement may cause the documents to come apart. If the charred paper is found in a container, it should be taken to the laboratory as is. Documents that can be moved should be placed in a crush-proof container, with a cushion layer of cotton on the bottom. Russell F. Scott of the San Diego Sheriff's Office recommends that a solution one-fourth glycerine, one-fourth alcohol, and one-half water be lightly sprayed on charred documents that cannot be moved. This solution makes the brittle documents more flexible and pliable. The examiner may then take the documents to the photographic laboratory, where the documents should be photographed with various filters and lighting from different angles. Both the use of infrared photography and a technique of placing a charred document in contact with a photographic plate may be used.

Unusual Documents

This term refers to the location of the questioned document. For example, if a home, school building, or public library is graffitied, then the wall is the item to be examined. The statue of Abraham Lincoln, located in the Long Beach Civic

Figure 2–9: Murder scene with lipstick writing on the wall.

Center, was defaced with writing and symbols. An elderly woman was brutally murdered, and the murderer tore up the house and wrote on the walls of the death room. In each of the above cases, detailed photographs were taken of the writing. The examiner then went to the scene and compared each of the original writings with the photographs. At the murder scene, the examination disclosed two writings. The first was done in a light color, and the second, on top of the first, was a darker color. A comparison of the original with the photographs revealed the unusual double lines. Handwriting played an important part in the cases, and in the murder case, handwriting played a supporting role.

The Bradfords made many friends within the ranks of the United States Secret Service and have been called upon to assist Agents Pat Boggs, Darwin Horn, Milton Wilhite, and others on numerous occasions. (In 1966, Ralph received the Award of Merit, and in 1978, Russell received a plaque of appreciation from the Secret Service.)

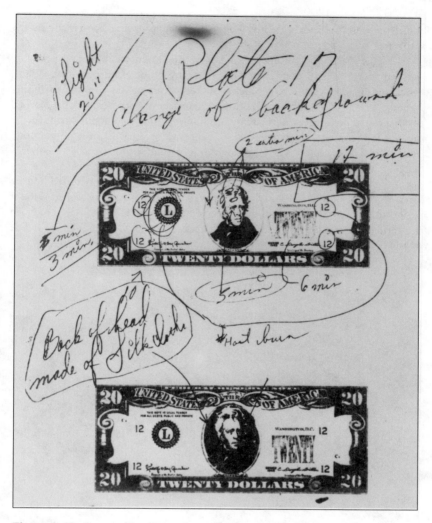

Figure 2–10: Counterfeiter's record.

One of the most unusual cases Ralph Bradford examined was at the request of the Secret Service. A subject had constructed a small room and had numbered each piece of lumber. He then excavated a hole under the cement floor of his garage. The room he had built was taken apart and reassembled (by the numbers) in the hole. A counterfeiting operation was then set up in this underground room. To keep track of the printing operation, the suspect kept a complete diary of different printing runs of counterfeit money. Following his arrest by the Secret Service, photographs were taken of the numbers on the lumber. The numbers and diary were both identified by Ralph Bradford as having been made by the suspect.

J. Clark Sellers, a prominent Los Angeles document examiner, has probably worked more unusual document cases than any other examiner. The Wilson Strickland missing heirs case produced bushels of strange documents, including forged writing on a tombstone, a snuffbox, and an oak tree. Sellers has learned first hand that the forgery of many wills is done on unusual documents. A forger of such a document might contend: "Can't you see that it must be genuine, because nobody would ever forge anything in such a preposterous manner?" Sellers has examined wills on a matchbox, the underside of a stepladder rung, a paper napkin, and a petticoat. One of his most unusual cases concerned lipstick writing on a dead man's back. Sellers proved that the man himself had done it by writing the words in reverse on a piece of cardboard. He then rolled over on the cardboard, transferring the lipstick letters to his back. Thus, the insurance fraud was prevented by an examination of an unusual document.[17]

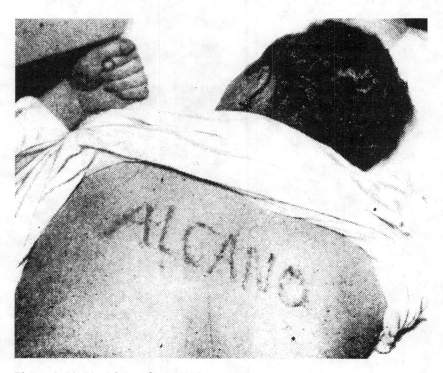

Figure 2–11: Lipstick transfer case. (*Gene Lester*)

Flat Documents

The flat document should be placed in an evidence bag immediately on receipt. The plastic will protect the document, so that, if necessary, it can later be examined for fingerprints. The container will also protect the document against mutilation from other sources, such as accidental writing on the document or additional folding of the paper. Inside the plastic bag, the document will be protected from tearing and erasing. No chemical analysis should be made on the document except under the strictest conditions and then only by an extremely qualified person, with legal permission. There are many caveats, but if the questioned document is placed in a protective bag at once, it will be protected. It should only be removed from the bag to be photographed, and then returned immediately. The immediate placement of the document in a bag is critical.

If the questioned document is an unopened envelope, the examiner should not only protect it, but also be alert to the possibility of a letter bomb. Examination of the envelope with the use of a light should disclose if there is anything suspicious inside. (If the envelope is not transparent, the opinion of bomb experts should be considered.) Once the envelope has been declared safe, it should be opened on the side opposite the flap, and the contents and the envelope placed in separate evidence bags.

The next step is to take the questioned documents and any exemplars to a duplicating machine and make at least three copies of each document. One set will be given to the investigator. After he has answered all your questions, the investigator may leave and continue his investigation. Additional sets of copies may be stapled together and filed, with one set being utilized for your work copy.

At this point, most examiners place a small identifying mark on the document so they can later easily identify it in court. One examiner, for example, places a colored dot in a corner. Documents have been marked with the examiner's full name in the past and this is totally unnecessary. A small identifying mark is acceptable, but as your machine-copy of the document positively identifies that document, no mark is really necessary. We do not place marks on 95 percent and make copies of 100 percent. On 5 percent of the documents, we place an initial "RB-1" on the first, "RB-2" on the second and so on, as small as possible, in a lower corner. These marks are placed on a document so it can be identified in a report. Sometimes there are a number of pieces of paper and the only way they can be identified in a report is by the number placed on the document. Remember, your copies are the best for identifying a document.

With the work copies in hand, you can now go over them with the submitting person, making notes on the work copies. The first thing you should learn from the submitting person is exactly what the problem is, and whether you, the examiner, have all the documents in the case. Make sure you also have all the facts in the case, and thoroughly understand what is to be proved by the examination. In one case, an examiner spent time examining an alteration on a document, when the investigator was interested only in who did the writing on top of the alteration.

Examine the questioned document in detail, determining which parts were written by the complainant. Examine the exemplars, determining which parts were written by the suspect, and who is witness to the document. Make notes of these points on your work copy.

A problem that arises occasionally is the making of a comparison from a photocopy. There are many limitations to using a copy, and no *trainee* should ever express an opinion from one. Trained examiners are extremely careful, and require an original in instances where typing, a possible copy, or a traced forgery has a bearing on the case. Points that determine a copy or traced forgery usually cannot be seen on a machine copy. Tremor, pen lifts, retouching, pen pressure, and color of ink cannot be completely examined from a copy. Also, the document itself may contain indentations, erasures, watermarks, and so on that cannot be seen on a copy. It is permissible for veteran examiners to examine copies because they realize their limitations.

The Preliminary Examination

When the total case is in your possession, it is time to lay out what you have. The background information should be completely written out on the back of your work copy. Any questions concerning this information can usually be resolved by looking over your notes.

Starting with the questioned document, make notes on the face of the copies of whatever you observe on the original document. Remember, anything used in the preparation of a document adds its own characteristics. Each addition, or subsequent handling, adds evidence that you should examine—including, of course, any removal, which also adds information.

The initial examination should be made with a magnifying glass and a light. Examine the entire document, looking for any alteration. Examine the writing, checking for extra lines under the writing. In a traced-writing case, you might find a carbon impression. Use side lighting to detect indentations of this "second writing." Examining the document with an Infra-Red Microscope System Model J will assist in the examination of alterations, obliterations, and other attempts to forge a document.

Many documents contain indentations made by the writing of a cover document. You can obtain all kinds of valuable information from these impressions. *Do not* use a pencil to shade the document and bring out the indentations. Instead, use side lights or photography with oblique lighting to create a shadowing effect, which will permit you to decipher the document. A newer deciphering technique uses a machine called "ESDA," also previously described.

A light positioned opposite the examiner, at the same angle and in the same plane as the angle of the reflection, will produce a glare. This glare is called *specular*

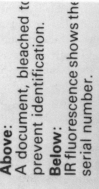

Infrared Microscope

Examination of

and Alterations of

Documents

Above:
Visual appearance of an
obliterated document.

Below:
The obliteration vanishes
in IR reflection.

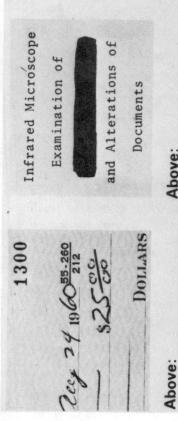

Above:
Visual appearance of an
altered check.

Below:
The same check under the
Model J IR microscope.

DOC.=

Above:
A document, bleached to
prevent identification.

Below:
IR fluorescence shows the
serial number.

Figure 2–12: Applications of the Model J microscope. (*Research Devices*)

reflection. Verle R. Truman, of the U.S. Postal Service, uses specular reflection in document examination.[18] He has found that a variety of document problems can be solved by this method. Impressions made by pencil, pen, typewriter, stamp, or printing process all reflect. Specular reflection is of use in determining sequence of strokes, deciphering obliterations, and identifying spurious entries.

After examining the document with a magnifying glass, use a light at an angle and then try transmitted light (light shining up from below the document). Watermarks can be observed with transmitted light, and the manufacturer should be able to date the paper for you. Alteration can also be seen by this examination. Every examination that you make, and the results, should be noted on your work documents.

One of the most valuable examinations is made by the use of photography. The first photograph you should make is an identifying photograph of the entire document, with a ruler in the photo. Any points you discover in the initial examination should then be photographed with close-up photography. Evidential photography includes:

1. Ultraviolet-reflected photography to make alterations more visible, and faded documents more legible.
2. Ultraviolet-fluorescence for detecting erasures, and for use with fluorescent fingerprint powders.
3. Infrared-reflected for revealing mechanical erasures through carbon or pigment traces.
4. Infrared-luminescence for the differentiation of inks.

Examination and Identification of Handwriting

The actual comparison of handwriting is made from the original document. Make a note of the characteristics of comparison or dissimilarity as your examination proceeds. These notes should be made with a red ball point pen on your work sheets. (All notes prior to this should have been made with a black ball point pen.) Red is preferred since it stands out from other notes, and can easily be referred to during the examination.

When the examination is completed, the back of your work copies will contain a complete history, or background of the case. On the face of the copies will be a record in black ink of the various examinations, defects, and conditions you identified on the questioned document. And all the comparison points that led to these identifications will be noted in red. This system of note-taking will facilitate the planning of an exhibit for a future trial.

The step-by-step methodical examination of the questioned document will lead to a sound identification. There are two principal reasons why examiners make errors. One is the lack of exemplars, and the other is the examiner's failure to make a thorough examination. A self-styled "expert" who systematically stares at a document, hoping it will in some mysterious way proclaim itself as identified, is lost. A step-by-step examination will eliminate any hasty or curbstone opinions. It is desirable to make an examination in two or more settings. As Albert Osborn stated, "It is better to have a reputation for accuracy than for speed."[19]

Form Blindness Test Answers

Problem A (circles) 7-4-2-8-5-6-1-9-3.
Problem B (triangles) 2-4.
Problem C (squares) 2-4.
Problem D (curves) 7-5-3-6-9-8-1-4-2.
Problem E (angles) 5-3-7-2-6-8-4-9-1.

— 3 —

The Bradford System

The Bradford System was developed and first used at the Long Beach, California, Police Department by my father, Ralph Bradford. The system is a simplified method of classifying, filing, searching checks and then identifying check writers. It was published in 1954 and bears copyright A-162181. The Bradford System booklet is included in its entirety in this chapter.

Ralph Bradford discovered, while teaching his handwriting classes, that his system was of great help in teaching handwriting comparison. He stated, "In my opinion, it is the easiest method of beginning the comparison of handwriting on actual cases, in the field of insufficient funds, no account and forged checks. Due to the limited amount of handwriting, there is less confusion in observing all details of the writing and figures. With the Bradford System of Check Classification, all checks are grouped together due to their similarity of construction."

The system is as easily adapted to the needs of a small police agency that handles only a few checks a year as it is to the largest department, where annual check cases number in the thousands. It is a welcome system to the small police department where a handwriting expert is not readily available. One of the most attractive features of the system is the ease with which it may be mastered. It takes only minutes to learn to make proper classifications. The advantages of classifying checks and filing them in a classified check file are evident when several investigators are working check cases in a large department. Once the original check has been filed with the crime report, the classified photograph of the check is just as useful a month or six months later as it was when it was first reported to a law enforcement agency. It is available to all investigators, although some may not have seen the check when it was originally filed. The "memory observation" method is a factor in working check cases, but is not comparable to the system of filing checks by classification. Check writers are notorious repeaters. Thus, when a check has been identified, classified, and filed, it is like a fingerprint card ready to identify the check-writer the next time he issues more checks.

Figure 3–1: (left to right) Jud Drake, Stan White, and Ralph Kortz, Long Beach Forgery Detail.

History of the Bradford System

The Bradford System was developed over a period of fifteen years, starting in about 1940. During this period, Ralph Bradford was a handwriting examiner, first for the Santa Barbara Police Department, and later for the Santa Barbara Sheriff's Department. Working with a limited number of checks at the two departments, Bradford began to observe consistency in the method of filling out the checks. In 1943, he joined the Long Beach Police Department as a laboratory technician. There he designed and was placed in charge of a new scientific and photographic laboratory. The success of this venture led to another new post: Bradford was transferred to the Forgery Detail in 1949 to work full-time as a handwriting examiner.

Working with a greater volume of checks, he found it possible to put his idea of a classification system into practice. Examining thousands of checks, as well as photographing them and spotting their similarities, Bradford was finally able to perfect his system in 1950. Assisted by other members of the Forgery Detail (Inspector Ralph Kortz, Sergeant Stan White, and Detective Jud Drake), Bradford went through the check files to sort out twenty years of checks and more than forty thousand individual documents.

Every check with a different classification written by the same writer (known and unknown) was photographed. Therefore, every bad check passed in the City of Long Beach had a photograph in the system. The "B.S." file was established, and every check reported to the Police Department was searched in the system. During the next four years, the "bugs" were worked out, and in a study of the system, 2,838 different check-writers, or over 90 percent, made no classification change. Less than 3 percent made as many as four changes in the system's five-digit classification. In January 1954, Harold Ely of the Santa Ana Police Department set up the system in his department. This was the system's first use outside the Long Beach Police Department.

The enthusiasm of the Forgery Detail in Long Beach and Santa Ana soon spread throughout Southern California.[1] The Los Angeles Police Department sent two members of their Forgery Detail to Long Beach, where they spent a couple of days learning the system. Within a short time, the volume of requests for information on the system was so overwhelming that it was necessary to publish the information. In 1954, Bradford contacted a retired Long Beach police officer, Inspector Les Dries, to assist in the publication. The two published the "Bradford System" and sold copies for $10. In a short time, the booklet had been sold to police departments in twenty-one states and three Canadian provinces.

The Los Angeles County Sheriff's Department, using the Bradford System as the key, set up a Central Index in 1958. The Bell Police Department was the first to photograph their checks and send them to the Central Index. Half of the first batch were identified with checks already on file. The Whittier Police Department soon followed, and 75 percent of their checks were identified through the index.

The system was so easy to learn and use that many thought anything that simple must have been thought of before, and therefore would not work. The success of the Bradford System is apparent from a letter from Captain Chester A. Welsh, commanding officer of the Forgery Division of the Los Angeles Police Department (see figure 3-2).

The Bradford System brought a great deal of fame to Ralph Bradford in law enforcement circles throughout this country and abroad. In 1952, philanthropist Freeman E. "Free" Fairfield made Ralph a member of the "Bull Shipper Club," which at the time included President Eisenhower, Governor Knight of California, and other notables among its members. In 1956, Bradford was awarded the highly prized Law Enforcement Plaque for Outstanding Service by the Long Beach Elks Lodge 888. On a 1969 trip through Indiana, he found that his reputation had preceded him. During a stop at Ball State University in Muncie, he was interviewed on the local TV station, WLBC-TV.

Ralph Bradford received so many requests for information about his classification system and the field of handwriting examination that he decided to teach a free handwriting class at the Long Beach Police Honor Farm. In March 1957, 104 officers attended the first of his many classes.

THE BRADFORD SYSTEM

A Simplified Method of Classifying and Filing; Searching and Identifying "Check Writers" of

N. S. F. CHECKS
NO ACCOUNT CHECKS
FORGED FICTITIOUS CHECKS

By
Ralph Bradford, Superintendent
Records and Identification Division
Long Beach California Police Department

Including
A System of Classifying, Filing and
Identification of Check Protectors.

PREFACE

Police officials have long recognized the need for a method of classification of spurious checks similar to the method used in fingerprint classification. The Bradford System is the answer to this problem. It is easily adaptable to the needs of the smallest police agency handling only a few checks as well as to the largest police agency where the checks handled number into the thousands.

Because the Bradford System is based on the modus operandi or manner in which the BO check is written rather than the handwriting itself, the need for handwriting experts to establish identification is greatly reduced and in most cases completely eliminated. This is a welcome factor to small police agencies where handwriting experts are not readily available.

The Bradford System has been enthusiastically received by identification men throughout California and may well become the uniform method of check classification throughout the nation.

INSPECTOR L. M. DREIS
Long Beach Police, Rtd.

INTRODUCTION

One of the most attractive features of the Bradford System is the fact that it is so easy to learn. Only minutes are required to learn how to make the proper classification. When the classification has been established it may then be communicated to other police agencies just as fingerprint classifications are exchanged. In such communications the complete classification consisting of five numerals and four alphabetical prefixes should be used. (Example: AAAA 52421)

Smaller police agencies now using this system have found that they did not need to use the complete breakdown afforded due to the small number of checks handled. For them sufficient breakdown was achieved by using only the primary and possibly the secondary classifications. The length to which the classification is extended therefore should be in direct ratio to the volume handled -- except in communications, as stated above.

A recent experience of the Santa Ana Police Department which has been using the Bradford System for only a short time provides a good example of the effectiveness of the system. A victim brought in a "no account" check written by an unknown person. After classifying the check it took only ten seconds to locate another check of the same classification in the file which bore a different maker's name. The handwriting on the two checks was such that it required no expert to know that the same person had written both. It happened, however, that the name used on the check in the files was the true name of the maker who had been arrested and convicted on this earlier check. When shown the true name of the maker the victim stated that he knew the man. The victim later contacted the maker and recovered his money. The victim was greatly impressed by the fact that the investigator was able to go right to the file and pull the correct check in a matter of seconds.

Page 2

This system of classifying checks is based on the method used in writing the check and not on the handwriting characteristics. The classification breaks down the search into small groups of similarly written checks and the final identification is made by handwriting characteristics. A maximum number of variations, which could have been used for a more extended breakdown, have been combined in the classification for two reasons: First to make a search more complete without additional reference searches, and second, to make the system easier to learn and use. A more complicated system with more variations has the proportionate chance for error and misses in the file thereby requiring more reference searches.

CHECKS WRITTEN WITH CHECK PROTECTORS HAVE SPECIAL CLASSIFICATION. The checks with a check protector imprint do not have a five numeral classification as used on all other checks. The imprint on the check eliminates the "written dollar amount", the "conjunction", and the "written cents amount". Only the date and figure cents amount of the check classification are used. That is, in place of the secondary, sub-secondary, and 2nd sub-secondary classification, a special check protector classification is noted. It subdivides that section of the file. The classification is written: "primary classification", "check protector classification", and "final classification". (Example: 5 - CWB - 2) The complete classification of check protectors will be found on page 12.

In all files, except extremely large files, the check protector classification is the only sub-division necessary to break down the collection of checks. All date (primary) classifications are filed together until a section accumulation is too large, then that section is sub-divided by the primary classification. The check protector section of the file is at the beginning of the #5 primary and before the checks without a check protector imprint with a #5 primary. (See photo of file on page 4.)

The identification of an "unknown writer" of a check is made: by the comparison with "known or previously identified check writers" checks filed in the classified check file, or combining checks with the previous checks written by an "unknown and unidentified check writer".

The Bradford System was examined and tested for more than ten years prior to its being put into practice by the Forgery Detail of the Long Beach Police Department six years ago. At that time there were approximately 40,000 checks on file representing over twenty years of "Known Check Writers". Every check by one writer, with a different classification, has been photographed, classified and filed. The names of the writers, if known, with aliases, descriptions, file numbers, etc., were included in the photograph with the check. Finished photographs were enlarged to 5" x 8" to make a standard size file. (See checks on page 4) By actual count covering thousands of checks it is interesting to note that this system has proved to be better than 98% accurate. (See statistics on page 21.)

A CHECK IS PROCESSED THROUGH THE
LONG BEACH CALIFORNIA POLICE DEPARTMENT

The Check is brought to the Forgery Detail.

A Report with all necessary information is filled out.

POLICE DEPARTMENT
CITY OF LONG BEACH
CHECK COMPLAINT REPORT

CR No. 382-234

Name of Victim SEVERIN MOTORS INC.	Where Committed 630 American Ave, Long Beach
Res. Address	Name of Premises Car Dealer - Parts Dept.
Bus. Address 630 American	Reported by Edw. R. Dack
Phone 703-941	Address 760 St. Louis Phone 92-406
(Res.) (Bus.)	Time and Date Reported Oct. 25, 1954 (Mon)
Date Committed Wed, Oct. 13, 1954	Reported to R. G. Kortz Forgery
Time Committed	(Name) (Office)
	Investigating Officers Kortz - Drake - White

S U S P	Name BROOME, Harold E.					Address 239½ Willard (Fict)			Phone
	Race Cauc Sex M Age 27 Ht. 5-8½ Wt. 160					Eyes Haz Hair Blond Comp. Lt			Occ.
						Arrested: Yes No X Bkg. No.			
S U S P	Name -					Address			Phone
	Race Sex Age Ht. Wt.					Eyes Hair Comp.			Occ.
						Arrested: Yes No Bkg. No.			
M O.	Person Male, Auto parts clerk Age Race	Object Auto parts & Cash
	Property Car dealer - Parts Dept	Trademark Penwritten-Personal- No Account
	How Buying and Cashing	Vehicle
	Means No funds - Forged	Type I.D. No.
C H E C K	Color Blue Bank of America	Branch 1st & Pine, Long Beach
	Type (If payroll — Firm name) Personal	No. 26 Date 10-13-54
	Payable to Harold E. Broome	Amt. 31.97
	Maker Mrs. Iva M. Broome	Address Phone
	Endorsed by Harold E. Broome	Address 239½ Willard Phone
	How written (ink, typed, etc.) Ink	Reason rejected No Account
D A T A	Written/endorsed in OK'rs presence Yes X No	Written/endorsed in Acptr's presence Yes X No
	Accepted by C. C. Davidson	Res. Add. 79 Argonne Phone 907-719
	OK'd by B	Res. Add. Phone
	Acpts. can identify ck. Yes X No (S) Yes X No	OK'r can identify ck. Yes X No (S) Yes No
	Victim attempted to locate Yes X No	Agreement to hold Yes No X Pros. Yes No

NARRATIVE: (Other than above) CHECK IDENTIFIED IN CHECK FILE WITH 1950 CASE A-3630

An Index card is made out for the files.

> BROOME, Harold E.   CR-382-234   AAAA 51448
> MWA 27 5-8½ 160 Haz Blond
>
>
> Victim - Severn Motors ($31.97)

The Check and Index Card are Photographed together.
(A 35mm Camera is used to copy all checks)

Page 4

After the 35mm film is developed, 5" x 8" enlargement is made with all information and Face of the check with the endorsement double printed at the bottom. Then - The Check is CLASSIFIED, and the classification marked in the upper right corner of the photographic enlargement.

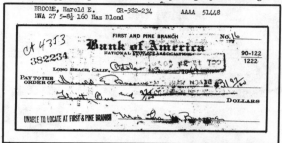

It is now searched by classification, in the section of the file, containing the classification of the check.

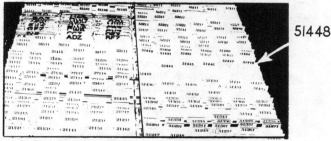

51448

An IDENTIFICATION IS MADE with a check in the file passed in 1950. In that case the defendant was sent to State Prison. His check folder contains a Mug Photo, description, and other information concerning subject.

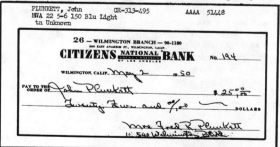

107

THE CHECK AND MUG PHOTO ARE REPRODUCED
ON THE NEXT WEEKLY "Crime Prevention Bulletin"

LONG BEACH POLICE DEPARTMENT
CRIME PREVENTION BULLETIN
This bulletin concerns criminal operations in this area. Should
you have any information concerning any of the operations herein
described, call the Police Department at once.

LONG BEACH POLICE DEPARTMENT	PHONE 6-9811	LONG BEACH, CALIFORNIA
Bulletin No. 133	WILLIAM H. DOVEY, Chief of Police	November 3, 1954

WANTED - FORGERY — HAROLD ELWYN BROOME, MWA, 27 yrs.,
5'8½", 160 lbs., hazel eyes, blonde hair, light complexion. Subject
is currently writing and passing personal type no account checks as
shown, making them payable to himself and forging his purported mother's
name as maker.

ALL POINTS TELETYPES AND OTHER NOTICES
ARE SENT THROUGHOUT THE STATE OF CALIFORNIA.

```
86 LOS    11-3-54    APB  BC 6
WANTED FICT CHECKS
HAROLD E BROOME, TN HAROLD ELWYN BROOME JR., DESC AS WMA, 5'8 1/2"
160 LBS, 27 YRS, BLOND HAIR, HAZEL EYES, LIGHT COMPLEXION. CII NO.
314 537, FBI 4780247.  EX-CON FOR CHECKS FROM LOS ANGELES COUNTY.
PASSES CHECKS DRAWN ON BANK OF AMERICA, FIRST AND PINE BRANCH,
LONG BEACH, PAYABLE TO HAROLD E. BROOME AND SIGNED MRS. IVA M.
BROOME. MAKES SMALL PURCHASE,  BALANCE IN CASH.  SHOWS DRIVER'S
LICENSE AND ARMY DISCHARGE PAPERS AND ID CARD OF FLYING TIGERS.
HAS ARMY SERIAL NUMBER TATTOOED ON RIGHT ARM ABOVE ELBOW
---- ATTN CII SACRAMENTO----
POSITIVELY IDENTIFIED AS YOUR NUMBER 314 537
( KORTZ  FORGERY DETAIL   CR 382 378)
WILLIAM H DOVEY C OF P LONG BEACH LBP CY
```

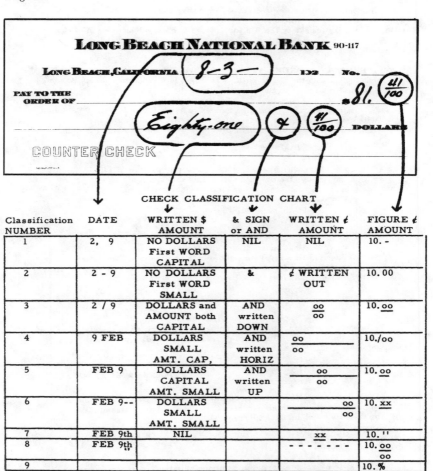

Page 6

CHECK CLASSIFICATION CHART

Classification NUMBER	DATE	WRITTEN $ AMOUNT	& SIGN or AND	WRITTEN ¢ AMOUNT	FIGURE ¢ AMOUNT
1	2, 9	NO DOLLARS First WORD CAPITAL	NIL	NIL	10. –
2	2 - 9	NO DOLLARS First WORD SMALL	&	¢ WRITTEN OUT	10. 00
3	2 / 9	DOLLARS and AMOUNT both CAPITAL	AND written DOWN	oo / oo	10. oo
4	9 FEB	DOLLARS SMALL AMT. CAP,	AND written HORIZ	oo oo	10./oo
5	FEB 9	DOLLARS CAPITAL AMT. SMALL	AND written UP	oo / oo	10. oo
6	FEB 9--	DOLLARS SMALL AMT. SMALL		oo / oo	10. xx
7	FEB 9th	NIL		xx	10. ''
8	FEB 9th			- - - - - -	10. oo / oo
9					10. %

The check classification is divided into 5 divisions, producing a 5 digit number. (Ex. 15286), which is the classification of the check and is used to locate similar checks in the file for comparison and identification of the writer, and finally for filing the check when it has been identified or if not identified, when it has been completely searched.

I - THE PRIMARY CLASSIFICATION is the first division. It is based on the method of writing the DATE on the check. It is divided into 8 subdivisions and is the first figure of the classification.

1 - The date is written, printed, stamped or typewritten in FIGURES only with a space, a period or a comma between the month and the date. And without a dash or diagonal line separating the date and the month.

> 2. 9. 1950   *12, 4, '50*

2 - The date is written, printed, stamped or typewritten in FIGURES only with a horizontal line or dash separating the month and the date. One variation is the combined horizontal line and a diagonal line. Which ever is first, is the only one considered.

> 2 - 9 1950   *12-4-'50*

3 - The date is written, printed, stamped or typewritten in FIGURES only with a diagonal line separating the month and the date. One variation is the combined diagonal line and a horizontal line. Which ever is first, is the only one considered.

> 2 / 9 1950   *12/4 — 50*

4 - The date is written, printed, stamped or typewritten in the style used by the United States Military Services, with the date preceeding the month.

> 9 Feb. 1950   *4 December 1950*

5 - The date is written, printed, stamped or typewritten in the most used style, with the month abbreviated or written out in full, and followed by the date, with no dash or diagonal line.

> Feb. 9 1950   *December 4, 1950*

6 - The date is written, printed, stamped or typewritten similar to #5, except that a DASH or DIAGONAL LINE follows or preceeds the date.

> Feb -- 9, '50   *Dec 4— , '50*

110

Page 8

(Primary Classification continued)

7 - The date is written, printed, stamped or typewritten similar to #5,
except that the contraction of the ORDINAL NUMBER FORM is used
for the date.

Feb. 9th 1950   *Dec. 4ᵗʰ , 1950*

8 - The date is written, printed, stamped or typewritten similar to #7,
except that the contraction of the ordinal number form is used for
the date WITH A TRADEMARK or characteristic mark underneath it.

Feb. 9ᵗʰ 1950   *Dec. 4ᵗʰ , '50*

II - THE SECONDARY CLASSIFICATION is the second division. It is based
on the method of writing the WRITTEN AMOUNT OF DOLLARS on the
check. It is divided into 7 sub-divisions, and is the second figure in the
check classification.

1 - The written dollar amount of the check is CAPITALIZED and the word
DOLLARS is OMITTED.

Ten   *Twenty - five*

2 - The written dollar amount on the check is NOT CAPITALIZED and the
word DOLLARS is OMITTED.

ten   *twenty*

3 - The written dollar amount on the check is CAPITALIZED and the word
DOLLARS is USED BUT IT IS CAPITALIZED.

Ten Dollars   *Twenty Dollars*

4 - The written dollar amount of the check is CAPITALIZED and the word
DOLLARS is USED BUT IT IS NOT CAPITALIZED.

Ten dollars   *Twenty dollars*

5 - The written dollar amount of the check is NOT CAPITALIZED and the
word DOLLARS is USED AND IS CAPITALIZED.

ten Dollars   *twenty Dollars*

6 - The written dollar amount of the check is NOT CAPITALIZED and the

(Secondary Classification continued)

word DOLLARS IS USED but is NOT CAPITALIZED.

ten dollars　　　　　*twenty dollars*

7 - The written dollar amount of the check is BLANK or NIL. No written amount or printed amount is in the normal place for such notation on the check.

- - - - - -

III - THE SUB-SECONDARY CLASSIFICATION is the third division. It is based on the method of writing the CONJUNCTION in the written amount of the check, between the written dollar amount and the written cents amount. It is divided into 5 sub-divisions, and is the third figure in the check classification.

1 - The conjunction AND or & sign is OMITTED, between the written dollar amount and the written cents amount on the check.

　　　Ten dollars twenty cents

2 - The & sign in any form IS USED, between the written dollar amount and the written cents amount on the check.

　　　Ten dollars & twenty cents

3 - The word AND is written DOWNWARDS on the check, between the written dollar amount and the written cents amount on the check.

　　　Ten dollars ^{a}n$_d$ twenty cents

4 - The word AND is written HORIZONTAL on the check, between the written dollar amount and the written cents amount.

　　　Ten dollars and twenty cents

5 - The word AND is written UPWARD on the check, between the written dollar amount and the written cents amount.

　　　Ten dollars $_a$n^d twenty cents

Page 10

(2d Sub-Secondary Classification)

IV - The 2d SUB-SECONDARY CLASSIFICATION is the fourth division. It is based on the method of writing the WRITTEN AMOUNT OF CENTS on the check. It is divided into 8 sub-divisions, and is the fourth figure in the check classification.

1 - NIL. No written amount of cents is indicated on the check.

Ten dollars

2 - The written cents amount on the check is written, printed, stamped or typewritten OUT IN FULL.

Ten dollars & five cents

3 - The written cents amount on the check is written as a FRACTION without a line PRECEEDING or AFTER the fraction.

Ten & $\frac{14}{oo}$

4 - The written cents amount on the check is written as a FRACTION WITH a straight or wavy line FOLLOWING the fraction.

Ten & $\frac{no}{oo}$-----------

5 - The written cents amount on the check is written as a FRACTION WITH a straight or wavy line PRECEEDING AND FOLLOWING the fraction.

Ten & ----$\frac{oo}{1oo}$----

6 - The written cents amount on the check is written as a FRACTION WITH a straight or wavy line PRECEEDING the fraction.

Ten & -----------$\frac{oo}{oo}$

7 - The written cents amount on the check is similar to #3, EXCEPT "xx" is used in the numerator or denominator of the fraction.

Ten & $\frac{xx}{xx}$

8 - The written amount of cents on the check is OMITTED and a STRAIGHT or WAVY LINE is drawn after the written dollar amount on the check.

Ten -------------

113

V - THE FINAL CLASSIFICATION is the fifth division. It is based on the method of writing the figure cents amount of the check. it is divided into 9 sub-divisions, and is the last digit in the 5 figure check classification number.

1 - NIL. No cents or zeros are used.

$ 4 .   4.—

2 - The cents is written WITHOUT a line UNDERNEATH.

$ 4 . 0 0   4.⁰⁰

3 - The cents is written WITH A HORIZONTAL LINE underneath.

$ 4 . ºº   4.ºº

4 - The cents is written with ANY line except a horizontal line. It is usually a diagonal or flourish line.

$ 4 . / o o   4.⌡º

5 - The cents is written with MULTIPLE LINES underneath.

$ 4 . ºº   4.⁰⁰

6 - The cents is written with "xx" in the NUMERATOR OR DENOMIN-ATOR.

$ 4 . ºº⁄ₓₓ   4.ˣˣ⁄ᵇᵒ

7 - The cents is written with a TRADEMARK, other than "xx" in the numerator or the denominator.

$ 4 . ₒ₀   4.⁰⁰⁄₁₁

8 - The cents is written with "oo" or "100" in the DENOMINATOR of the fraction.

$ 4 . ⌐ºº⁄ₒₒ   4.⁰⁰⁄ₒₒ

9 - The cents is written as a percent or In-account sign.

$ 4 . %   4.%

114

CLASSIFICATION AND IDENTIFICATION SYSTEM FOR ALL 'PROTECTOGRAPHED' CHECKS

CODE	CENTS		CODE	DOLLARS		CODE	AND	
A	CTS	VERTICAL	A	DOLS	VERTICAL	A	AND	VERTICAL
B	CTS	LEFT SLANT	B	DOLS	LEFT SLANT	B	AMD	RIGHT SLANT
C	CTS	RIGHT SLANT	C	DOLS	RIGHT SLANT	C	AND	COMPRESSED & UNDERLINED
D	CTS	'C' LARGER THAN 'TS'	D	DOL'S	VERTICAL & APOSTROPHE	D	AND	NOT COMPRESSED & UNDERLINED
E	Cts	LOWER CASE LETTERS	E	DOL'S	LEFT SLANT & APOSTROPHE	E	A.M.D	LEFT SLANT & UNDERLINED
F	CTS	VERTICAL & UNDERLINED	F	DOL'S	RIGHT SLANT & APOSTROPHE	F	AND	RIGHT SLANT & UNDERLINED
G	CTS	LEFT SLANT & UNDERLINED	G	DOLS	VERTICAL & UNDERLINED	G	AND	NEGATIVE
H	CTS	RIGHT SLANT & UNDERLINED	H	DOL'S	VERT' APOST' & UNDERLINED	H	A M D	DIAGONAL DOWN
I	CTS.	RIGHT. UNDERL' WITH A PERIOD	I	DOL'S	LEFT. APOST' & UNDERLINED	I	AND	DIAGONAL UP WITH BLOCKS
J	CTS	'C' LARGER.'TS' UNDERLINED	J	DOL'S	RIGHT. APOST' UNDERLINED	J	and	LOWER CASE LETTERS
K	CTS.	'C' LARGER. UNDER'. PERIOD	K	DOLS	'L' STAFF BENT	K	AND	OVER' AND UNDERLINED
L	CTS.	OVER & UNDER LINED	L	DOLS	'S' SMALL	L	AND	NEGATIVE AND SIGN
M	CTS	'C' ENCIRCLES 'TS'	M	DLRS.	DLRS. PLAIN OR UNDERLINE'	M	&	POSTIVE AND SIGN
N	CTS	DIAGONAL UP SINGLE BLOCKS	N	DOLLARS	'D' LARGER	N	NIL.	NO AND SIGN OR WORD 'AND'
O	CTS	DIAGONAL UP DOUBLE BLOCKS	O	DOL'RS	'DOL' APOST' 'RS' UNDERL'	Z		
P	CTS	NEGATIVE	P	D's	'D' APOSTROPHE 'S'			
Q	CENTS	VERTICAL	Q	DOLLARS	VERTICAL OR SLANTED			
R	CENTS	RIGHT SLANT	R	DOLLARS	UNDERLINED			
S	CENTS	DIAGONAL UP	S	DOLLARS	DIAGONAL UP			
T	CENTS	LEFT SLANT	T	DOLLARS	DIAGONAL UP. BLOCKS			
U	CENTS	DIAGONAL UP WITH BLOCKS	U	DOLLARS	ENLARGING			
V	CENTS	ENLARGING	V	dol's	LOWER CASE LETTERS			
W	CENTS	OVER AND UNDERLINED	W	$	SINGLE STAFF 'OMIT IF ANY OTHER DOL. IS ALSO USED'			
X	¢	CENT SIGN	X	$	DOUBLE STAFF 'OMIT IF ANY OTHER DOL. IS ALSO USED'			
Y	¢	CENT SIGN UNDERLINED	Y					
Z	NIL.	NO WORD OR SIGN FOR CENTS	Z	NIL.	NO WORD OR SIGN FOR DOLLARS			

Examine the imprint of the check protector carefully. First - Look at the CENTS. (CTS) It is slanting to the left. Check down the left hand column, and match the CTS in the chart. The code letter is "B". Second - Look at the DOLLARS. (DOL'S). It is slanting to the left. Check down the middle column, and match the DOL'S in the chart. The code letter is "E". Third - Look at the word AND. There is no AND in the imprint. Check down the right hand column, NIL means "NO WORD or SIGN for AND is present. The code letter is "Z". The classification of the check protector is BEZ. In the upper left hand corner of each check protector imprint is the classification. These are in alphabetical order. Now compare the imprint on the check with the two impressions in the collections with a classification of BEZ It matches with the Paymaster Mod. Y. made in 1937. In the classified check file, look in the section containing all Protectographed-Checks with a classification of BEZ. NEXT, to identify all checks with the same imprint LOOK FOR THE DEFECTS. The vertical lines to the right of the center of the star in the 2nd star from the left are bent forming a pocket. This defect is found in both of the phony print commercial checks, and proves that both checks were imprinted by the same check protector.

CLASSIFICATION OF CHECK PROTECTOR

| AAZ | PAYMASTER Model 400 | |
BEZ	PAYMASTER	

AAZ	PAYMASTER Model 400	*THE SUM* ✱ ✱ I 3 4 DOLS 5 6 CTS
		THE SUM ✱ ✱ ✱ 4 2 DOLS 7 6 CTS
		THE SUM ✱ ✱ ✱ 4 8 DOLS 5 0 CTS
ADZ	TOLEDO Ser R-1000	PAY I 2 3 4 5 DOLS 6 7 CTS
		PAY ◇ ◇ ◇ 9 8 DOLS 6 0 CTS
BEZ	PAYMASTER	DIAMOND TOOL CO ✱ ✱ ✱ 2 9 DOLS 4 0 CTS
BEZ	PAYMASTER Mod. Y 1937	*THE SUM* ✿ ✿ ✿ 9 8 DOLS 6 0 CTS
		THE SUM 1 2 3 4 5 DOLS 6 7 CTS
		INSURED 1◄208062 ✿ ✿ 2 9 9 DOLS 5 8 CTS
BLZ	PAYMASTER Mod. H 1946	*THE SUM* I 2 3 4 5 DOLS 6 7 CTS
		THE SUM 9 8 DOLS □ 7 CTS
CCZ	PAYMASTER Mod. 550 1949	*Bonded* ✱ ✱ ✱ 9 8 DOLS 6 0 CTS
		Bonded 1 2 3 4 5 DOLS 6 7 CTS
		INSURED 1◄2017530 1 2 3 4 5 DOLS 6 7 CTS
CCZ	PAYMASTER Mod. 500	INSURED 1◄1575707 1 2 3 4 5 DOLS 6 7 CTS
CCZ	PAYMASTER	INSURED 1◄5700294 1 2 3 4 5 DOLS 6 7 CTS
CFZ	SAFEGUARD 1940	I 2 3, 4 5 6 *DOLS* 7 8 *CTS*
		R REGISTERED 8771 D ✰ ✰ ✰ ✰ 9 8 *DOLS* 6 0 *CTS*

Page 14

CKZ	HALL–WELTER 88 & 880	*SPEEDRITE* BEST OF ALL 3 65 DOLS 2 1 CTS
		U.S.Silver Co.,Inc. ▷▷▷2 5 6 DOLS 3 1 CTS
CWB	TODD	KERN VALLEY PACKING CO. $1 2 3 4 5 AND 6 7 CTS
CWB	TODD 70, 74, 75, 79	EXACTLY $1 2 3 4 5 6 7 AND 8 9 CTS
		EXACTLY $9 8 AND 6 0 CTS
CXB	TODD	EXACTLY R4572 #$4 3 AND 2 1 CTS
		THE TODD CO., INC. $1 2 3 AND 4 5 CTS
DNZ		EXACTLY 2 4 DOLLARS 3 7 CTS
EVZ	F & E Premier 1953	Pay 2 3 4 5 dolls 6 7 cts
EXJ	F & E KB	The sum of $1 2 3 4 5 6 and 7 8 cts
EXJ	F & E XL3 1949	The sum of $1 2,3 4 5 and 6 7 cts
		The sum of $8 9 and 5 0 cts
EXJ	F & E Ser.1000 1929	The sum of $1 2 3 4 5 6 and 7 8 cts
		The sum of $9 8 and 6 0 cts
		REGISTERED $1 0 and 4 5 cts
FGZ	PAYMASTER Mod. K 1947	SPINA MOTOR LINES 1 3 4 5 6 DOLS 7 8 CTS
		SPINA MOTOR LINES 9 8 DOLS □ 2 CTS
		PAN PACIFIC INDUSTRIES, INC. 4 8 DOLS 5 6 CTS
FGZ	PAYMASTER Keyboard	INSURED 4711236 1 2 3 4 DOLS 5 6 CTS

117

FGZ	HUMPHREY Defender 50 1938	The SUM ≡ 1 2 3 4 5 6 DOLS 7 8 CTS The SUM ≡ ✫ ✫ ✫ ✫ 9 8 DOLS 6 0 CTS
FHZ		✗✗✗✗10 DOLS 00 CTS
FHZ	SPEEDRITE 88, A,S,HW. 1930.	THE SUM OF $1 2 3 4 5 DOLS 6 7 CTS THE SUM OF ✫✫✫$9 8 DOLS 6 0 CTS
FRZ	MONROE "Not Over" H	NOT OVER 1 2 3.4 5 6 DOLLARS 7 8 CTS NOT OVER ✿ ✿ ✿ ✿ ✿ 0 DOLLARS 0 0 CTS
FWC	F & E B	THE SUM OF $2 3 4 AND 6 8 CTS
FWD	F & E. 500 1926	THE SUM OF $1 2 3 4 5 AND 6 7 CTS THE SUM OF $9 8 AND 6 0 CTS THE SUM OF $1 7 AND 2 3 CTS
FWD	F & E 500	THE SUM OF $3 4 6 AND 0 0 CTS REGISTERED NO 3278 $1 2 3 4 AND 5 6 CTS
GIZ	INTERNATIONAL W 1935	THE SUM 1 2 3 4 5 6 DOLS 7 8 CTS THE SUM ✪✪✪✪✪ 9 8 DOLS 6 0 CTS
GWE	CHECKOMETER G	✯ ✯ ✯ 1 2 5 AND 2 5 CTS THE SUM ✯ ✯ $ ✯ 1 0 AND 0 0 CTS
HJZ	SAFEGUARD K 1942	BANK OF 57-GREENWOOD-84 1 2 3 4 5 6 DOL'S 7 8 CTS BANK OF 57-GREENWOOD-84 ✫✫✫ 9 8 DOL'S 6 0 CTS

118

Page 16

Code	Type	Sample
HJZ	SAFEGUARD H	c.g. ATKINS I 2 3 4 6 5 *DOL'S* 7 8 *CTS*
HJZ	SAFEGUARD H 1935	(REGISTERED) I 2 3 4 5 6 *DOLS* 7 8 *CTS*
		(REGISTERED) ★ ✹ ★ ★ 9 8 *DOLS* 6 0 *CTS*
HPZ	SAFEGUARD 6 1953	*THE SUM OF* 7 5 4 2 *D's* 8 6 *CTS*
HWF	TODD 33 1940	*EXACTLY* 🙂 I 2 3 4 5 6 7 *AND* 8 9 *CTS*
		EXACTLY 🙂 9 8 *AND* 6 0 *CTS*
IWD		THE SUM OF $25 AND 00 CTS.
IWF	F & E 700, A, 1928	PAY $ 1 2 3 5 4 AND 6 7 CTS.
		PAY $ 9 8 AND 6 0 CTS.
IWD		THE SUM OF $ 7 0 AND 0 0 CTS.
JWL	TODD 33 1934	EXACTLY 💲 I 2 3 4 5 6 7 & 8 9 CTS
		EXACTLY 💲 9 8 & 6 0 CTS
JWL	TODD Deluxe 33, 55 1937	EXACTLY 💲 I 2 3 4 5 & 6 7 CTS
		EXACTLY 💲 9 8 & 6 0 CTS
KOZ	TODD 25, 29 1925	PAY EXACTLY I 2 3 4 5 DOLRS 6 7 CTS
		PAY EXACTLY XXX 9 8 DOLRS 6 0 CTS
KWL	TODD 30, 1700 1924-29	EXACTLY 💲 I 2 3 4 5 6 & 7 8 CTS.
		EXACTLY 💲 9 8 & 6 0 CTS.
		EXACTLY 💲 I 2 3 4 5 6 & 7 8 CTS.

KXL	TODD 60 1939	EXACTLY $123456 &c 78 CTS.
		EXACTLY $98 &c 60 CTS.
LWK	TODD Personal 500	$23 AND 87 CTS.
MWI	TODD 28, 1928	EXACTLY $123456 &c 7 cts
		EXACTLY $98 &c 60 cts
NWI	TODD Personal 19, H. 1928	PAY $1234567890
		PAY $98 AND 60 cts
OWI		$37 AND 50 CTS
PWG		★★★ $2 AND 7 0 CTS
QQZ		SIXTEEN DOLLARS FIFTY FIVE CENTS
QQZ		EIGHTEEN DOLLARS FIFTY CENTS
QQZ		SEVENTEEN DOLLARS FIFTEEN CENTS
RQZ		TWENTY FOUR DOLLARS THIRTY SIX CENTS
RQZ	TODD Protectograph 1915	EXACTLY ONE TWO THREE FOUR FIVE SIX SEVEN EIGHT NINE TEN
		EXACTLY FIFTY DOLLARS NINETY CENTS
SSZ	SAFEGUARD S. 1925	FIVE HUNDRED THIRTY DOLLARS SEVENTY CENTS
UTZ		EXACTLY TWELVE DOLLARS FIFTY CENTS EXACTLY
		EXACTLY TWENTY FIVE DOLLARS EXACTLY
VUZ		TWENTY SEVEN DOLLARS FIFTY FOUR CENTS

OBSOLETE CHECK WRITERS — ABBOTT, DEFIANCE, DIMINUETTE, NEW ERA, RITEALL, SECURITY, SENTINEL, UNIVERSAL.

Page 18

XWH	🖩$64,82¢
XWC F & E 800, 1929	THE SUM OF $123456 AND 79¢
	THE SUM OF $98 AND 60¢
XWC	THE SUM OF $76 AND 83¢
YJZ SAFEGUARD H, 1929-53	THE SUM OF ★★★269 DOL'S 70¢
	Clauser Chevrolet Kulpmont, Pa. 621742 DOL'S 44¢
ZQZ TODD "Not Over" H.	NOT OVER TWENTY-FOUR DLRS. 24
	NOT OVER FIFTY DOLLARS 50
ZQM MONROE	★★★★ ONE HUNDRED FIFTY-SIX & ★★★ 76/100 DOLLARS
ZWA	EXACTLY $75.00 AND NON
ZWZ TODD Multi Currency 1932	EXACTLY·US$1234567890
ZZZ	EXACTLY·£9■08■14■■■
	EXACTLY·No.345■7■8■5I

ADDRESSOGRAPH
 Addressograph-Multigraph Corp.
 1200 Babbitt Road
 Cleveland 17, Ohio
BLUE STREAK & PROTECTOGRAPH
 Todd Co., Inc.
 1150 University Ave.
 Rochester 7, N.Y.
BURROUGHS
 Burroughs Adding Machine Co.
 6071-2d & Burroughs Aves.
 Detroit 32, Mich.
DEFENDER
 Humphrey, G.W. Corp.
 South Orange, N.J.
ELLIOTT
 Elliott Addressing Machine Co.
 143 Albany St.
 Cambridge 39, Mass.
F & E & SIGN-O-METER
 Hedman Co. The
 1158 W. Armitage Ave.
 Chicago 14, Ill.

INSTANT & SAFEGUARD
 Safeguard Corp.
 Lansdale, Pa.
INTERNATIONAL
 International Register Co.
 Chicago, Ill.
MONROE
 Monroe Calculating Machine Co.
 555 Mitchell St.
 Orange, N.J.
NATIONAL
 National Cash Register Co.
 Maine & K Sts.
 Dayton 9, Ohio.
PAYMASTER
 American Checkwriter Co.
 Chicago, Ill.
SPEEDRITE
 Hall-Welter., Inc.
 46 Mt.Hope Ave.
 Rochester, N.Y.
TOLEDO
 Toledo Checkwriter Inc., Co.
 Toledo, Ohio

PREFIX CLASSIFICATION
    In extremely large files, an additional 4 digit prefix is used to break
down the checks into smaller "Special Files" with 9 x 5 x 7 x 6, or 1890
combinations or files.

1st PREFIX CLASSIFICATION is the TYPE of check. (9 sub-divisions)
    A - Personal checks, without any printing of Company or Names.
    B - Commercial checks, and Personalized personal checks.
    C - Pay Roll checks.
    D - Cashiers checks.
    E - Certified checks.
    F - Travelers checks.
    G - U. S. Government checks.
    H - State and County checks.
    I - U. S. Postal Money Orders.

2nd PREFIX CLASSIFICATION is the HOW MANUFACTURED or "How the
    printed matter got on the check". This classification is sub-divided in-
    to 5 types.
    A - NIL. No printing on the check. All personal checks, except personal-
    ized personal checks.
    B - The standard "Commercial printer" job, with the Business or Company
    name, address, etc., printed on the check. This also includes the Phony
    and Fictitious Company checks.
    C - Blank commercial checks with the company name, etc., RUBBER -
    STAMPED on the check.
    D - Is similar to #C, except that the name, etc., is TYPEWRITTEN on
    the check.
    E - Is similar to #C, except that the name, etc., is written or printed
    LONG HAND with pen or pencil on the check.

3rd PREFIX CLASSIFICATION is HOW THE CHECK WAS FILLED OUT by
    the maker. It is divided into 7 sub-divisions.
    A - Check is made out in pencil or ink.
    B - Check is made out on a typewriter.
    C - Check is made out in pencil or ink and contains the imprint of a Check-
    writer or Check Protector.
    D - Check is made out on a typewriter and contains the imprint of a Check-
    writer or Check Protector.
    E - Check is made out with a Rubber Stamp.
    F - Check is printed on a printing press.
    G - Check is BLANK, where the amount is normally written.

4th PREFIX CLASSIFICATION is based on the sex and race of the passer of
    the check. It is divided into 6 sub-divisions.
    A - White males.   (note) Any part or all of the Prefix Classification
    B - Black males.   may be used to reduce a large collection of
    C - All other males.   checks. However, in a small file, a single
    D - White females.   file is preferred, so that a complete search
    E - Black females.   is made in the one file and with fewer
    F - All other females.   reference searches.

PREFIX CLASSIFICATION CHART

Classification LETTER	TYPE CHECK	HOW Manufacturered	HOW MADE OUT	PASSER
A	Personal	No Printing	Ink or Pencil	Male - White
B	Commercial	Printed	Typewritten	Male - Negro
C	Pay Roll	Rubber Stamp	Ink and Check Protector	Male - Other
D	Cashiers	Typewritten	Typed and Check Protector	Female White
E	Certified	Long Hand Company	Rubber Stamp	Female Negro
F	Travelers		Printed	Female Other
G	U. S. GOV'T		NIL	
H	CALIF. State			
I	Post Office M. O.			

In the Long Beach Police Forgery Detail's Classified Check File, only part of the PREFIX CLASSIFICATION is used. That is, ALL CHECKS with an imprint of a "Check protector", both commercial and personal are in a separate section of the file. They are first classified by the "Classification of the Check Protector", which is the make and model or type of the check protector and further sub-divided by the Primary Classification and the Final Classification.

The Classification of Check Protectors facilitates identifying the make and the model. A 3 letter CODE is used to classify all check protectors.
1 - CENTS or the abbreviation is the first letter. (See chart for details)
2 - DOLLARS or the abbreviation is the second letter.
3 - AND or the & sign is the last letter of the code.

The prefix on check protectors may be changed from "Bonded" to "The Sum" etc., or may be left out of the machine. Also, the stars and various other characteristic marks, may be left out of the imprinting, so these parts of the check protectors were not considered in coding. Considering the small number of different makes and models of machines, the 3 letter code breaks down the imprints so that identification is readily made.

CHECK CLASSIFICATION STATISTICS

2838 different check writer's files were examined to determine the variations in their method of writing checks that would affect or change the classification with each individual. Also, what the changes are and where the changes occur in the classification so that they would be caught in the reference searches.

2838 Different check writers　　-　　2354 Males and 484 Females
2561 Writers made NO CHANGE in classification in all their checks.
- - - of this number　2130 Males and 431 Females.

1 Change in classification was made by	-	180 Males and 45 Females.
2　"　　"　　"	-	32 Males and 6 Females.
3　"　　"　　"	-	9 Males and 1 Female
4　"　　"　　"	-	3 Males and 1 Female

- - - NO MALE OR FEMALE MADE MORE THAN 4 VARIATIONS.

VARIATIONS AND REFERENCE SEARCHES

	DATE				DOLLARS						AND		CENTS						¢				
	3	5	6	7	2	3	4	5	6	7	2	3	3	4	5	6	7	8	3	4	5	6	8
1	1				16	9	7			1	16	15	2	1				4	1	1			
2	3	30	2	1					1		13		6	11	2			2	19	3	3	4	5
3	10	1	3			1	3							21		9	3	2		12	7	11	9
4	5		4			1									1	9	1	11			2	3	2
5		9	13			1										1	1	3				3	2
6		1															1	9					8

79 changes　　40 changes　44 changes　110 changes　　95 changes

Reference searches should be made for a more complete search of the files. In the above chart, the numbers in the left hand vertical column, represents the check classification used in making a check; the numbers above the chart in the horizontal lines, represents the variation in check classification also used; and the numbers in the chart at the intersection of any two numbers, represents the number of persons that used both of those classifications in making out their checks. Example, In the DATE chart, Line 2 and under 5, is 30, the number of persons that used both a #2 date and also a #5 date. From the chart, all variations of the 225 Males and Female check writers that used one variation in their method in writing a check may be observed at a glance.

Variations are uncommon: 79 changes in date were made out of 2786 different check writers; 40 changes in the written dollar amount; 44 changes in the "and" or "and sign"; 110 changes in the written cents amount, and 95 changes in the printed cents amount.

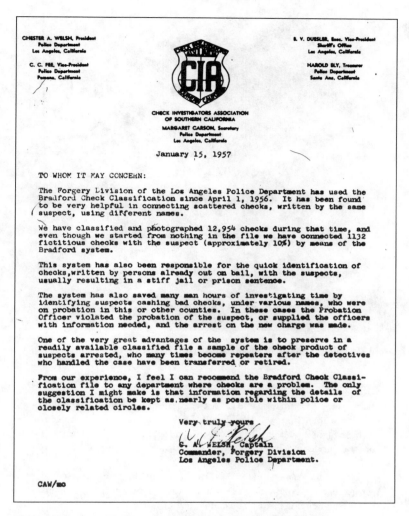

CHESTER A. WELSH, President
Police Department
Los Angeles, California

C. C. FEE, Vice-President
Police Department
Pomona, California

B. V. DUESLER, Exec. Vice-President
Sheriff's Office
Los Angeles, California

HAROLD BLY, Treasurer
Police Department
Santa Ana, California

**CHECK INVESTIGATORS ASSOCIATION
OF SOUTHERN CALIFORNIA**
MARGARET CARSON, Secretary
Police Department
Los Angeles, California

January 15, 1957

TO WHOM IT MAY CONCERN:

The Forgery Division of the Los Angeles Police Department has used the Bradford Check Classification since April 1, 1956. It has been found to be very helpful in connecting scattered checks, written by the same suspect, using different names.

We have classified and photographed 12,954 checks during that time, and even though we started from nothing in the file we have connected 1132 fictitious checks with the suspect (approximately 10%) by means of the Bradford system.

This system has also been responsible for the quick identification of checks, written by persons already out on bail, with the suspects, usually resulting in a stiff jail or prison sentence.

The system has also saved many man hours of investigating time by identifying suspects cashing bad checks, under various names, who were on probation in this or other counties. In these cases the Probation Officer violated the probation of the suspect, or supplied the officers with information needed, and the arrest on the new charge was made.

One of the very great advantages of the system is to preserve in a readily available classified file a sample of the check product of suspects arrested, who many times become repeaters after the detectives who handled the case have been transferred or retired.

From our experience, I feel I can recommend the Bradford Check Classification file to any department where checks are a problem. The only suggestion I might make is that information regarding the details of the classification be kept as nearly as possible within police or closely related circles.

Very truly yours

C. A. WELSH, Captain
Commander, Forgery Division
Los Angeles Police Department.

CAW/mo

Figure 3–2: Captain Chester A. Welsh's letter of January 15, 1957.

These courses were highly regarded in law enforcement circles, as is expressed by a letter written to Long Beach Chief of Police William H. Dovey by Robert K. Lund, Chief of the Intelligence Division, U.S. Internal Revenue Service.

I wish to express my personal appreciation and the gratitude of the Intelligence Division for the splendid contribution your department is making in the field of law enforcement, as evidenced by Mr. Ralph Bradford's

Figure 3–3: Ralph Bradford being interviewed on WLBC-TV.

Handwriting Examination and Check Classification course just completed. The seven men from the Intelligence Division who attended the course offer the highest praise for Mr. Bradford, and speak in glowing terms of his comprehensive understanding of the subject and the quality of his instruction.

May I again thank you and Mr. Bradford and the Long Beach Police Department for conducting the school, and for permitting our men to receive the benefits of this valuable course of instruction.

Updating the System

The twenty-one-page booklet entitled *The Bradford System* was published in 1954.[2] In the years that have passed since the system was published, a few changes have been made, such as specifying a more contemporary camera.

The Bradford System classification was modified slightly by discontinuing a few of the following subclassifications and adding one new classification.

1. Prefix Classification. This part of the system was never put into use. It was described on pages 19 and 20 of the booklet.

[H]ANDWRITING EXPERTS

Ralph Bradford, Long Beach Police Department superintendent of records, seated left, gives tips on handwriting analysis to Chief William Dovey, seated right, and two "graduates" of Bradford's new handwriting and check classification school for police. Bradford taught 104 Southern California officers and special agents in the Monday night nine-week course. Classes were held at Rancho Esperanza, Long Beach Honor Farm. At rear are Joe W. Rice, sheriff of Riverside County, left, and Capt. C. A. Walsh, Los Angeles Police Department.—(Staff Photo).

Figure 3–4: Handwriting Experts. (*Press-Telegram*)

2. Date Classification—Number one, six, and eight were eliminated. (Listed on page 7.)

3. Written Cents Amount. Number seven was removed. (Page 10.)

4. Figure Cents Amount. Number seven and ten are no longer used.

The added classification is Cents Fraction. This is a new sixth division to the five number classification in sections where the file had become unwieldy. This new classification has a three–point breakdown:

1. Nil—no fraction to classify.
2. The numerator and the denominator are separated by a diagonal line.
3. The numerator and denominator are separated by a horizontal line.

In 1970, officials of the Long Beach Police Department decided to computerize the fingerprint identification system. They also believed the Bradford System manual operation would become cumbersome. The Police Department received a federal grant to cover the $60,000 cost of a computer system and the labor to put it into use.

An Eastman Kodak Miracode Video Computer[3] was purchased in 1971, and the fingerprint system was computerized according to the method used by

Figure 3–5: Ralph Bradford using a Bradford System camera.

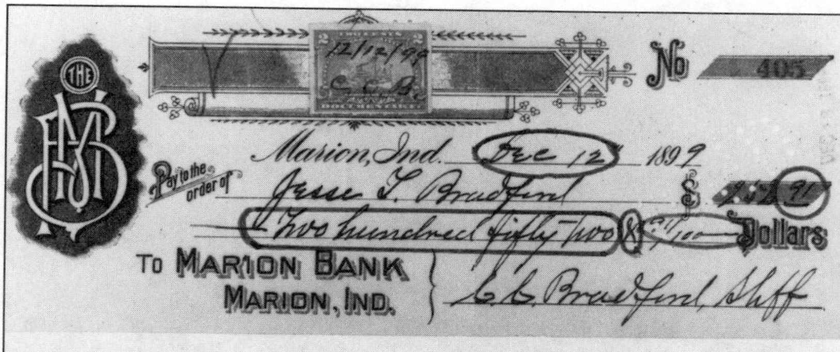

Classification NUMBER	DATE	WRITTEN $ AMOUNT	& SIGN or AND	WRITTEN ¢ AMOUNT	FIGURE ¢ AMOUNT	CENTS FRACTION
1		NO DOLLARS First WORD CAPITAL	NIL	NIL	10.-	NIL
2	11-4	NO DOLLARS First WORD SMALL	&	¢ WRITTEN OUT	10.00	00/00
3	11/4	DOLLARS and AMOUNT both CAPITAL	AND written DOWN	$\frac{00}{00}$	10.00	$\frac{00}{00}$
4	4 NOV	DOLLARS SMALL AMT. CAP	AND written HORIZ	$\frac{00}{00}$	10./00	
5	NOV 4	DOLLARS CAPITAL AMT. SMALL	AND written UP	$\frac{00}{00}$	10.00	
6		DOLLARS SMALL AMT. SMALL		$\frac{00}{00}$	10.XX (any X)	
7	NOV 4th	NIL				
8					$\frac{10.00}{00}$	

Figure 3–6: Bradford System Classification, updated.

the Atlanta Police Department in 1968.[4] Ralph Bradford assisted in computerizing the Bradford System. Ten years of checks (27,877 in all) were placed in twenty-nine cassettes, about 1,000 checks per cassette. This left room for an additional 1,000 checks to be added to each cassette. The conversion was completed and put into use in August 1972.

To convert the system to a computer, it was necessary to make the following modifications:

1. *Personal Checks*
    a. *Cents Fraction*. This classification—already used in the manual system when a section became too cumbersome and needed a further breakdown—was now extended to the entire system.

Figure 3–7: Fingerprint expert Wally Dillon utilizing Miracode.

    b. Checks by male writers and checks by female writers were placed in different cassettes.

2. *Commercial Checks*

    a. Letters could not be used by the Miracode computer, so numbers were substituted. For example, a Paymaster Check Protector Classification of CCZ, is now classified as 030314

    b. A final number classification was added regarding the M.O. of filling out a check, in addition to the money portion of the check protector.

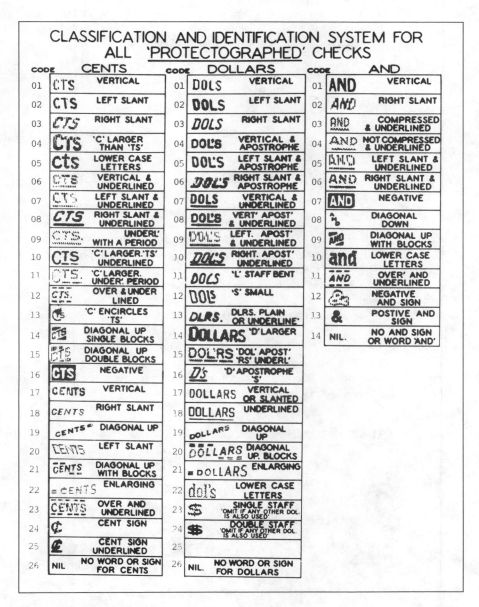

Figure 3–8: Classification changes for the computer.

Final Number Classification

Number	Prefix of protector	Filling in date and payee
1	Blank	Typed
2	Blank	Inked
3	Company	Typed
4	Company	Inked
5	The Sum	Typed
6	The Sum	Inked
7	The Sum (script)	Typed
8	The Sum	Inked
9	Registered, Bonded, Exactly, Pay & The Sum of	

The Coca Cola commercial check shown in figure 3-9 would be classified in the Bradford System as "1023124." The "102312" comes from the old "JWL." The "4" is the Final Number Classification; the prefix of the check protector is a company name (Coca Cola), and the date and payee are in ink, therefore the check is now classified as a "4." Both personal and commercial checks now have a six-digit classification.

In retrospect, changing the manual Bradford System to the computer had both good and bad results. The computer system is staffed by personnel that prepare the computer cards and coordinate them with the camera. The computer, however, is a machine which occasionally breaks down. If any step fails to function the system breaks down. The way of the future may be computers, but I believe the Bradford System works best as a manual system.

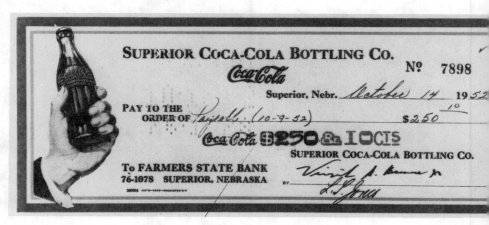

Figure 3–9: Coca-Cola commercial check.

Bradford System Check Comparison

Ralph Bradford contended that the Bradford System comparison of checks is the easiest method of beginning handwriting examination and identification. The document examiner trainee soon learns that most suspects write insufficient-fund checks, account-closed checks, and so on, in their normal handwriting. Even a suspect who signs a different name on every check will still use his normal handwriting. Classification and searching can easily be done by a trainee. In fact the Los Angeles Police Department for many years authorized a secretary to search the system. Working with a large department, she made more identifications than Ralph Bradford did with the smaller Long Beach Police Department.

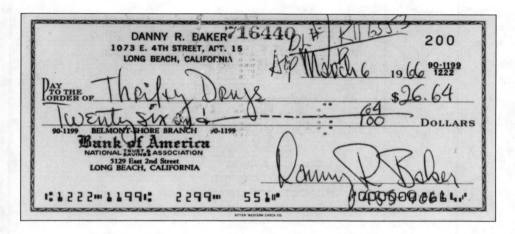

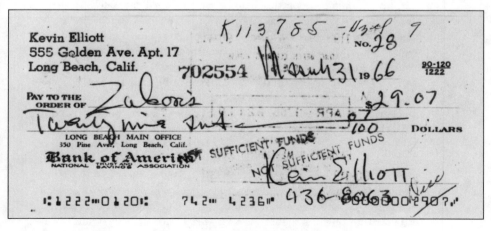

Figure 3–10: Baker-Elliott identification.

A prime point when searching the system is not to place too much importance on the maker's signature of a check. Conduct the examination using the characteristics in the written amount.

Examination of the checks in the Baker-Elliott case (figure 3-10) showed the checks all classified 51462. A comparison of the maker's signature could not be made, due to the fact that one signature is printed while the other is written. But more important, the two names contain different letters. Instead, compare the writing indicating the amount of the checks. You should immediately recognize the unusual characteristics of the *a* in the word *and*. The same letter *a* can be seen in the word *March*. The word *twenty* would be the next comparison, with the letter *y* seen as an individual entity. The signature on a check gives little to examine, but the amount portion of a check affords a wealth of characteristics to examine.

The ease of handwriting comparison the Bradford System affords is illustrated by five cases from the files of the Long Beach Police Department. The suspects in these cases wrote hundreds of checks, and the system was the instrument responsible for connecting and identifying the checks and bringing four of the five cases to a successful conclusion. Harold Edwyn Broome, Jr., and Linda Mae Oliver were notorious for writing bad checks in Southern California. John Waitkunas became nationally known and was the subject of articles in various magazines. Eugene Francis Joyce has been wanted nationwide since 1961. The Chirrick gang consisted of twenty-two forgers and narcotics users.

1. *Harold Edwyn Broome, Jr.* Broome was used as an example when Ralph Bradford wrote the Bradford System in 1954. Broome was arrested in 1955 when his checks were identified in the system, released in 1959, and rearrested in 1962. He was again released in 1966. In November of that year, he returned to Long Beach and passed a forged check to buy a pair of shoes. When the check was reported, I checked the system and quickly identified the check as bearing handwriting that had been placed into the system twelve years before. The suspect was arrested in February 1967.

2. *Linda Mae Oliver.* Oliver is a famous check-writer from Southern California. In 1964, this twenty-four-year-old female obtained a driver's license under the name of "Tanya Lee Parkerson." A bank account was then opened using the driver's license as identification. Every time she ran out of checks, she obtained a new driver's license under another fictitious name and opened another bank account. At the time of her arrest, she had obtained driver's licenses and opened bank accounts using at least fourteen different names. She wrote checks for $50 to $150 in most of the cities in Southern California. Checks bearing all fourteen different names were tied together by using the Bradford System, and the description was broadcast via teletype throughout the area. On May 6, 1965, Sergeant James A. Boyer

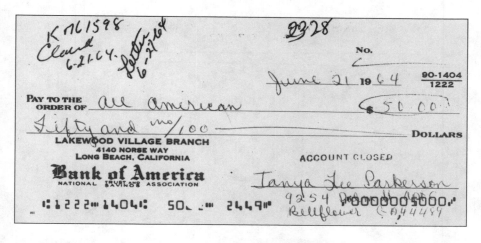

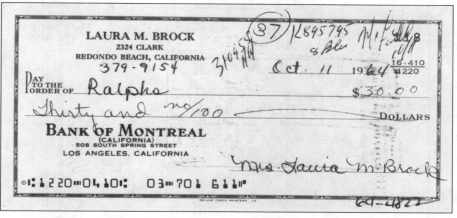

Figure 3–11: Oliver checks, Classification 51442

of the Los Angeles Sheriff's Department reported that the suspect was in custody and had been identified as having passed more than $25,000 in bad checks.

In figure 3-11, the first obvious characteristic is the "and no/100" that appears on all checks of this classification. The hook pick-up on the letter *n* is also individual. The letter *d* in the word *and* also contains a hook characteristic, but this hook is in the body of the letter. The vertical slant is also the same in the two documents. Although the suspect used at least fourteen different names, the handwriting was still easily identifiable.

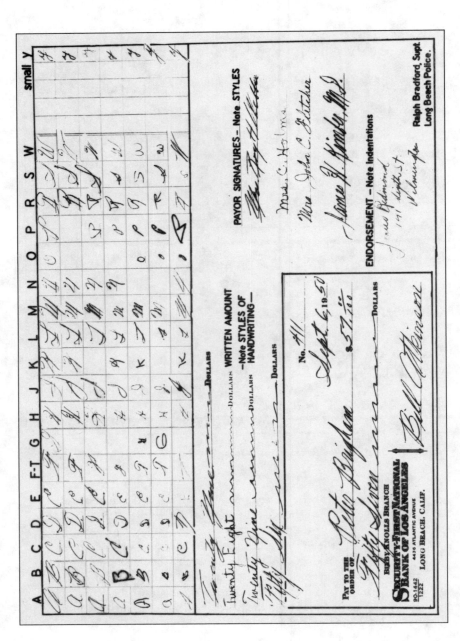

Figure 3–12: Waitkunas check and Bradford's chart, Classification 5118.

3. *John Waitkunas.* Waitkunas was the most famous of the group. On June 18, 1947, the thirty-nine-year-old Waitkunas entered a store in Pasadena and passed a check he claimed he had received for doing odd jobs. The amount of the check was $29. During the rest of the year, he passed sixty checks in Southern California, including seven in Long Beach. Every check bore a different signature, and in many cases a different style of writing, but they were tied together by the new Bradford system.

Bradford advised others on what to look for and soon officers from many cities were finding checks written by the "$29 man," or "Saw Tooth" (so named because of the way he wrote his checks). In 1948, he increased his area of operations, passing checks in Northern California as well as Southern California. In 1949, he was traced by his checks to Connecticut and Massachusetts. The State of California issued warning notices, as did several cities and counties, "on a man now known as Walter Demeter." He was the subject of articles in several national magazines, and was arrested in 1954 in Concord, California, after eight years of passing checks totaling more than $150,000.

In 1947, the chart prepared by Ralph Bradford on Waitkunas's writing was sent to law enforcement agencies throughout Southern California. The outstanding individual characteristic was the line drawn after the dollar amount. It resembled a "saw tooth," hence his nickname. Waitkunas was one of the few persons to disguise his handwriting on checks, but every check classified in the Bradford System had the "saw tooth." Waitkunas was also quite consistent with the pick-up stroke of small letters, which on many occasions started below the base line. The final classification of the "00" over "100" was unusual and much the same on all the checks.

4. *Eugene Francis Joyce.* Joyce had a criminal record with arrests in Massachusetts, Connecticut, and Maryland in the 1950s. In 1961, he was arrested by the Los Angeles police for Nonsufficient Fund Checks—a felony—but a few days later the case was dismissed. From the day he was released until today, he has been passing checks throughout the United States. He passed through Long Beach four times in the 1960s and 70s, and left a few bad checks each time. In 1964 and 1974, he made the Burns Wanted Bulletin. He has been the subject of wanted notices from several agencies, including the FBI. Joyce is still wanted and is passing bad checks using many different names. Since he uses numerous names, many law enforcement agencies do not even know they have a Joyce check.

The two checks shown in figure 3-13 were written over a two-year period and were easily tied together by the Bradford System. Handwriting characteristics are many and individual. The base line pick-up on the capital *T* is unique, as is the initial stroke of the capital *M*. Normally, capital letters are not main points of an examination. In submitting exemplars to law

Figure 3–13: Joyce checks, Classification 51168.

enforcement officers, arrested persons often disguise their handwriting. The two main points of disguise are the slant and the capital letters. When using the Bradford System, you will usually be looking at checks written with a normal hand. John Waitkunas was one of the few who used several disguises when writing checks. Joyce, in all his checks, uses the same style of writing, and all are classified as 51168.

5. *The Chirrick Gang.* This gang was comprised of about twenty-two members from Southern California. Most of them were narcotics users, who used check monies to supply their habit. The group committed burglaries to obtain commercial checks and then went to Tijuana, Mexico, to obtain

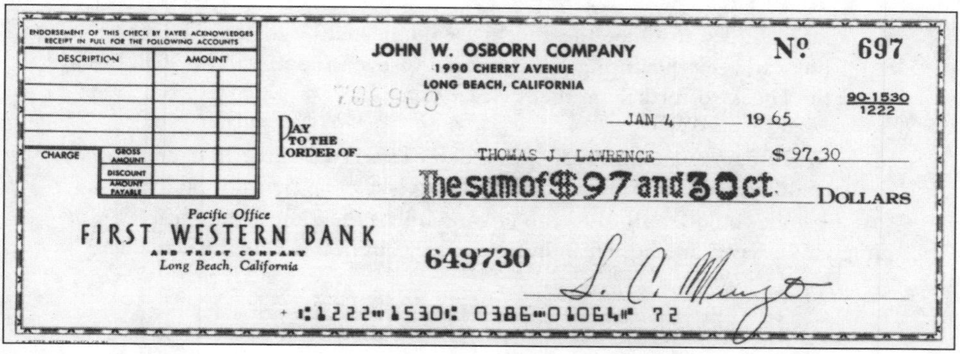
ENDORSEMENT OF THIS CHECK BY PAYEE ACKNOWLEDGES RECEIPT IN FULL FOR THE FOLLOWING ACCOUNTS
DESCRIPTION AMOUNT
CHARGE GROSS AMOUNT DISCOUNT AMOUNT PAYABLE
JOHN W. OSBORN COMPANY
1990 CHERRY AVENUE
LONG BEACH, CALIFORNIA
Nº 697
90-1530
1222
JAN 4 19 65
PAY TO THE ORDER OF THOMAS J. LAWRENCE $ 97.30
The sum of $ 97 and 30 ct. DOLLARS
Pacific Office
FIRST WESTERN BANK
AND TRUST COMPANY
Long Beach, California
649730

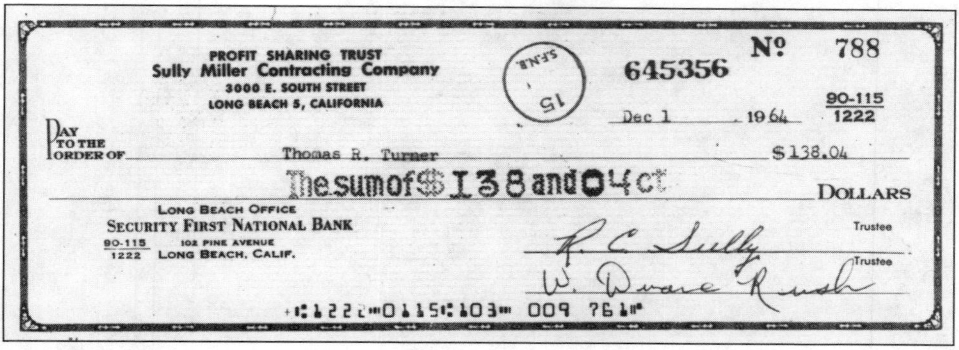
PROFIT SHARING TRUST
Sully Miller Contracting Company
3000 E. SOUTH STREET
LONG BEACH 5, CALIFORNIA
Nº 788
645356
90-115
1222
Dec 1 19 64
PAY TO THE ORDER OF Thomas R. Turner $ 138.04
The sum of $ 138 and 04 ct DOLLARS
LONG BEACH OFFICE
SECURITY FIRST NATIONAL BANK
90-115
1222
102 PINE AVENUE
LONG BEACH, CALIF.
Trustee
Trustee

Figure 3–14: Chirrick checks, classification EXJ.

fictitious driver's licenses. Returning to Southern California, they passed the stolen checks, about $100 each, throughout the area. The checks were tied together by the check-protector of the Bradford System.

Several members of the group were identified and arrested. The gang dissolved when a few members went to Mexico in search of phony driver's licenses, checks, and narcotics. On the return trip, they encountered a border-patrol immigration stop. They panicked, and during an exchange of gunfire, one suspect was killed. The others were arrested.

The EXJ classification check-protector, used by the Chirrick gang, is an F & E check-protector, model L. A large number of these check-protectors were manufactured, so it is important to look for a defect in the check-protector to tie the checks together. The Chirrick check-protector contained a defect that was very easy to see: the "C" in "CTS" was damaged and therefore the "C" was missing. Defects will usually show up on the serif of a letter. Once the checks are connected by the check-protector, one can use typewriting, handwriting, or even the method of filling out the check to further tie them closer together.

Will Rogers stated in 1932, "We don't seem to be able to check crime, so why not legalize it and put a heavy tax on it? Make the tax for robbery so high that a bandit couldn't afford to rob anyone unless they knew they had a lot of dough. We have taxed other industries out of business—it might work here."

— 4 —

Vocabulary

I t is very important in the study of any subject that one knows and understands the terminology. Each science or profession employs words and terms peculiar to that discipline. When you enter the field of document examination, it is vitally important that you master the professional vocabulary. It will be necessary to explain and use correct terminology when you describe handwriting in court. When you're reading study material, confusion will result if you don't recognize and understand the terminology.

The vocabulary that follows contains the basic words and terms you'll encounter most frequently in your studies and professional work. . . . In this chapter there are two vocabulary sections. Part 1 contains general terms that are used in all phases of document examinations. Part 2 deals with terminology used in the descriptions of handwriting terms. This terminology is put into use in chapter 5.

Part 1: General Terms

The following terms may be found throughout the book. Some may not appear, but should be understood.

- *ABA Numbers* (American Bankers Association). President Woodrow Wilson signed the Federal Reserve Act in 1913. The act provides that each Federal Reserve Bank serve as a check-clearing and collecting center for the banks in their district. There are now twelve Federal Reserve Districts:

1.	Boston	7.	Chicago
2.	New York	8.	St. Louis
3.	Philadelphia	9.	Minnesota
4.	Cleveland	10.	Kansas City
5.	Richmond	11.	Dallas
6.	Atlanta	12.	San Francisco

State prefix's are numbered 50 to 99:

Eastern	Southeastern	Central	Southwestern	Western
50. NY	60. PA	70. IL	80. MO	90. CA
51. CT	61. AL	71. IN	81. AR	91. AZ
52. ME	62. DE	72. IA	82. CO	92. ID
53. MA	63. FL	73. KY	83. KS	93. MT
54. NH	64. GA	74. MI	84. LA	94. NV
55. NJ	65. MD	75. MN	85. MS	95. NM
56. OH	66. NC	76. NE	86. OK	96. OR
57. RI	67. SC	77. ND	87. TN	97. UT
58. VT	68. VA	78. SD	88. TX	98. WA
59. AK, HI, Puerto Rico	69. WV	79. WI	89. —	99. WY

City prefixes are numbered 1 to 49:

1. New York, NY	26. Memphis, TN
2. Chicago, IL	27. Omaha, NB
3. Philadelphia, PA	28. Spokane, WA
4. St. Louis, MO	29. Albany, NY
5. Boston, MA	30. San Antonio, TX
6. Cleveland, OH	31. Salt Lake City, UT
7. Baltimore, MD	32. Dallas, TX
8. Pittsburgh, PA	33. Des Moines, IA
9. Detroit, MI	34. Tacoma, WA
10. Buffalo, NY	35. Houston, TX
11. San Francisco, CA	36. St. Joseph, MO
12. Milwaukee, WI	37. Ft. Worth, TX
13. Cincinnati, OH	38. Savannah, GA
14. New Orleans, LA	39. Oklahoma City, OK
15. Washington, DC	40. Wichita, KS
16. Los Angeles, CA	41. Sioux City, IA
17. Minneapolis, MN	42. Pueblo, CO
18. Kansas City, MO	43. Lincoln, NE
19. Seattle, WA	44. Topeka, KS
20. Indianapolis, IN	45. Dubuque, IA
21. Louisville, KY	46. Galveston, TX
22. St. Paul, MN	47. Cedar Rapids, IA
23. Denver, CO	48. Waco, TX
24. Portland, OR	49. Muskogee, OK
25. Columbus, OH	

Many forgers print fictitious checks using the names of well-known commercial companies, but they do not understand the ABA coding that appears on all checks. They use an ABA number that cannot be correct. Knowledge and awareness of this code, established by the American Bank-

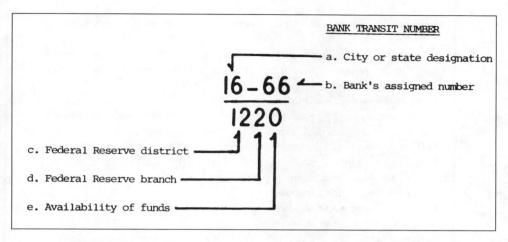

Figure 4–1: ABA fraction.

ers Association and uniform throughout the country, will help you discern many fictitiously printed checks.

Every ABA number has both a numerator and a denominator, as if it were a fraction. The numerator is the bank's assigned transit number, and is always a hyphenated number. The numbers to the left of the hyphen indicate either the city or the state in which the bank is located, and will never be more than two digits. The number to the right of the hyphen is the bank's own number.

In the denominator, the first digit (or the first two digits in the case of a four-digit denominator), indicates the federal reserve district. Naturally, an ABA number which begins "90" in the numerator must begin with "12" in the denominator, since California is in the twelfth (San Francisco) Federal Reserve District. The next digit of the denominator is the branch, and the last digit the availability of funds, with 0 designating immediate availability.

As you can see, checking the city or state code and the Federal Reserve District number against the bank address on the check will readily reveal nonexistent numbers. These ABA numbers in the upper right corner of a check can then be double-checked with the magnetic numbers (ERMA) at the bottom of the check.

- *Abrasion*. Roughness or irregularity of a surface as a result of erasing, rubbing, or scratching.
- *Anonymous Document*. A paper bearing no name or signature, or an "unknown name," with the intent to conceal the identity of the author. Examples include blackmail, ransom, extortion, poison pen, and other letters or documents that are unsigned. Information leading to the suspect

143

may also be found in the paper envelope, typewriter, or even the grammar, spelling, and so on.

- *Arraignment*. A criminal court proceeding in which the defendant is advised of the charges against him or her, at which time he or she may plead guilty and have bail set.
- *Bank—Central or Federal Reserve*. A bank that is usually a government agency and operates in the broad public interest. Deals chiefly with other banks and holds the banking reserves of its county or district.
- *Bank—Commercial*. A financial institution that accepts deposits that are transferable by the depositor's check. Banks make loans, invest in government securities and municipal and corporate bonds. They also provide various services for their customers.
- *Bank—Correspondent*. A bank that serves as a depository, and performs banking services for other banks.
- *Bank—Member*. A commercial bank that is a member of the Federal Reserve Bank System. All national banks are automatically members, while state banks may be admitted. By law, member banks must hold reserves (consisting of their own vault, cash, and deposits with their Federal Reserve Bank) equal to a percentage of their customers' deposits.
- *Bearer*. A person in possession of a check or draft, or the person presenting an instrument for payment.
- *Calligraphy*. The fine art of beautiful writing or writing as a decorative art.
- *Charred Paper*. Document that is burnt or damaged by fire. Such a document is brittle, but restoration is possible if it is properly handled and preserved.
- *Checks—Account closed*. Usually in true names, these are accounts closed by the customer for any of several reasons; or closed by the bank as a bad account.
- *Check—Cashier's*. A bank check drawn by a bank on itself.
- *Check—Certified*. A check drawn against a depositor's account for which the bank sets aside funds from the depositor and guarantees its encashment.
- *Check—Counterfeit*. An exact copy of a genuine check of a legitimate company (usually an offset print of the original). It will have correct bank routing numbers and may even have similar paper.
- *Checks—Fictitious Printed*. Payroll or business checks that are completely fictitious, including paper stock. May use legitimate business name, but no attempt is made to copy the actual company check. Usually contains the wrong bank and ABA or transit numbers, and other errors.
- *Checks—Fictitious Imprints*. Regularly issued or printed blank checks bearing the bank name and transit numbers. Company names, real or fictitious, are imprinted on the checks by printing press, a rubber stamp, or typewriter.
- *Checks—Insufficient Funds (NSF)*. Lack of enough funds in account to cover the check. Often returned by the bank stamped "refer to maker."
- *Checks—No Account*. "Unable to locate" (U.T.L.) an account in the name

on the check. Many times these are old checks that were closed out years before and the bank no longer has records for them.

- *Checks—Obsolete.* Both payroll and business checks originally printed legitimately, but later discarded because of mistakes in the printing, a change of company name and/or address, or closing the company.
- *Checks—Stolen.* Payroll, business, personalized, and travelers' checks, money orders, and so on that are stolen, usually in a burglary. The maker's name may be fictitious, or even a copied forgery, obtained from a bank statement. If checks are already signed, the endorsement is then forged.
- *Check—Stop Payment.* Usually these are civil checks. Payment may be stopped by the writer, usually because of unsatisfactory service. Banks may also place "stops" on checks that are reported lost.
- *Checks Protector.* Machine that imprints an amount of money on a check, used for clarity and to discourage alteration of amount.
- *Comparison of Hands.* This older term and the term "similitude of hands" was used when a person would testify that he had seen a person write several times in the past, and this looked like his handwriting.
- *Complainant.* One who files charges.
- *Copy Book.* Writing systems published in penmanship texts. Students are taught to write by copying the letters in the texts.
- *Cross Mark.* An "X" or similar mark made by a person who cannot write in place of a signature. This mark must be properly witnessed to be legal.
- *Defendant.* The accused—one against whom criminal or civil charges are brought and who must stand trial.
- *Deposition.* A sworn, written statement by a witness for use in court. A deposition may be an examination and cross-examination by attorneys, recorded, typed out, and signed. Such a deposition can be used in court in another state or country.
- *Document.* Anything of substance that bears writing in ink or pencil. It may be typed, printed, or even a copy of another document.
- *ERMA (Electronic Recording Method of Accounting).* The magnetic number at the bottom of a check which assists in its routing through the banking system. A fictitious check will not have numbers printed in magnetic ink.
- *Encashment.* To cash a check.
- *Endorsement.* A signature on the back of a check which makes the item negotiable.
- *Erasure.* The removal of writing, printing, or typewriting by an abrasive (i.e., eraser or sharp instrument) or by chemicals.
- *Examination.* The close and critical study of a document and everything on it. This examination may be made with a simple magnifying glass, microscope, special instrument, or photography.
- *Exemplar—Nonrequest.* Known writings of a subject, written in the day to day business. Checks are a good example of the normal unconscious writing

of a person. Deeds, contracts, and other known writing are examples of consciously written writing.

- *Exemplar—Request*. Dictated writing, or the filling out a form that is then witnessed. This type of handwriting is consciously written writing.
- *Expert Witness*. A legal term used to describe a person who has training and experience in a special field. He or she is permitted to express an opinion regarding his expertise and interpret technical information in court. For example, a handwriting examiner can testify as an expert witness after being qualified.
- *Facsimile*. An exact copy or likeness. The copied document must be the same size as the original.
- *Fluorescence*. Visible light which can be seen when ultraviolet light is focused on fluorescent material.
- *Forged Writing*. An imitation or copy of a signature or writing. Usually it is only a copy of the general form without any of the microscopic or fine detail of the genuine writing, or it is a forged writing by freehand simulation. A more professional forgery may be made by tracing on the original signature, leaving an indentation that can then be written over. A simple copy can also be made using a window glass or shadow box.
- *Guided Signature*. A signature by a writer whose arm is steadied and/or assisted by another person. Guided signatures are common with seriously ill or dying persons.
- *Graphology*. The art of interpreting the character or personality of an individual from a written document.
- *Hand Printing*. Writing of disconnected letters, as taught to children in the first years of school. Also known as "manuscript writing."
- *Handwriting—Conscious*. Writing made when a person is thinking about the writing process. Genuine conscious writing may be found on a marriage license, birth certificate, or other important documents where the appearance of the handwriting is important. Conscious writing can also be an attempt to disguise writing.
- *Handwriting—Unconscious*. This type of genuine handwriting would be normal where penmanship is not important. A note, memo, and check are all unconsciously written.
- *Holographic Document*. A document that is completely written, dated, and signed by one person. A holographic will is accepted in many jurisdictions and will be probated.
- *Infra-Red*. A radiation of a wave-length too long to be seen by the human eye. The rays can only be seen by photography or a special instrument. Used in the examination of cancellation marks, chemical erasures, pencil marks, secret writing, and forged documents.
- *Instruments*. Anything with which one writes—ball-point pens, fountain pens, steel pens, pencils, liquid lead pencils, or brushes. A spray paint can is one of the newest instruments with which to write, and a quill pen is

one of the oldest.

- *Kiting.* The "floating" of checks and deposits between two or more accounts, which gives a false representation of funds.
- *Maker.* The drawer or person who makes and signs a check.
- *Modus Operandi.* The manner or mode of operating or working. Usually applied to the unconscious routine of doing anything from habit. Law enforcement agencies use the M.O. system to solve many crimes, and the Bradford System is based on M.O.
- *Nontestimonial Evidence.* Laws and rules of the United States and local governments. The court acceptance of English words and phrases, and legal expressions. It also includes facts and generalized knowledge that are so universally known that they cannot reasonably be the subject of dissent. This is also known as "Judicial Notice."
- *Norms—Standards.* The writing and printing regarded as "penmanship norms" and found in penmanship copy books.
- *Notary Public.* An officer licensed by a secretary of state (1) to attest to or certify documents and (2) to perform other acts in an official capacity for the convenience and security of the business transacting public.
- *Oblique or Sidelight Examination.* In this type of examination, the light is controlled so it strikes the document at one side and at a very low angle, bringing into prominence any physical fault in the paper, such as a raised portion or an indentation.
- *Opinion.* A qualified and experienced handwriting examiner's conclusion in a given case. This conclusion is based on thoughtful study of the specific material involved, and on the many years of study and experience of the examiner. In court an examiner not only states his or her conclusion, but also demonstrates the reasoning behind it.
- *Payor.* The maker or drawer who orders the payment of a check or draft.
- *Payee.* The person to whom payment of a check or draft is to be made.
- *Pen Nibs.* Pen points, or the two divisions of the points of steel pens and fountain pens. Pen position can be determined by the nibs.
- *Photostat.* A photographic copy, usually direct without the acetate negative. Paper negatives are used in reflex copy photostats. A contrast paper process is used for making line copy, maps, and records.
- *Plaintiff.* The complainant, or one who brings charges against the defendant in a civil case.
- *Printing.* Placing individual letters on a document with the use of a machine (printing press) or by hand lettering.
- *Qualifications.* Education, training, and experience combine to make up one's qualifications. These must be testified to before an examiner is allowed to express his opinion.
- *Questioned Document.* Any document or item in which an issue has been raised. (Synonymous with *Disputed document.*)

- *Reference Material.* Books, articles, or request information that is compiled and organized by a document examiner to assist in answering special questions. This material should contain samples of typewriters, obtained from the manufacturers, plus new or unique information that may be referred to at a later time.
- *Restoration.* Any process through which writing, typewriting, or information in any form that has been removed can be restored to a condition that can be examined.
- *Simulated Writing.* Writing done in an attempt to copy or imitate the writing of another. The dictionary definition is "to have the mere appearance of another's writing."
- *Spurious Signature.* A forged signature in which no attempt has been made to simulate or copy the true signature. When commercial checks are stolen, the thief usually has no idea what the true maker's signature looks like, so he or she will write it in a disguised writing.
- *Specular Reflection.* The observation of a reflection of light on a document, caused by having a light source opposite the viewer. A basic principle of physics regarding specular reflection is: "The angle of incidence is equal to the angle of reflection."[1]
- *Standards.* The methods of handwriting and handprinting published in copybooks. In typewriting, the standards are derived from samples furnished by the manufacturer. Many confuse the words *exemplar* and *standards*.
- *Subpoena.* A legal order issued to a person to appear in court and provide testimony or requested evidence.
- *Thin Layer Chromatography (TLC).* A technique for separating chemical compounds of ink, so that the patterns can be identified.
- *Transmitted Light Examination.* An examination made when a light source is placed beneath the document and the light passes through the paper revealing watermarks and other points of importance.
- *Ultra-Violet Light.* A light of short wavelength, invisible to the naked eye, that can be seen by photography or special instrument. Used in the examination of adhesives, charred documents, erasures, ink, pencil writing, paper, sealing wax, secret writing, and forged documents.
- *Watermark.* The translucent design with which papers are marked during manufacture. It can be seen when a light is held under paper.
- *Writ.* Any type of court order.

Part 2: Handwriting Terms

This section of the vocabulary includes the terms used in describing the characteristics of handwriting. These descriptions are used in this book and in other books on the subject as well. The terminology will also be used to some degree when testifying in court.

The Ball and Frank Sporting Goods murder was a major case in Long Beach, California, because of the popularity of the victims. One of the questioned documents that was found contained information for making explosives. The documents were identified, and during the trial the examiner had to describe its characteristics to a jury. An examiner cannot tell a jury the line goes up here and down there. Instead, standard terminology is used. For example, the small letter *b* on a document was described as follows: "After the body of the small letter *b* is made, the final stroke retraces to the base line in the connecting stroke to the next letter. The norm is for the final stroke of the *b* to go in a straight line to the next letter. The proportion of the body of the letter to the loop is one third." This description can be read in a transcript and understood; the proper way to use terminology is very important to handwriting trainees.

- *Ability-Skill.* The capability or competence of a writer to control strokes. The ability may vary due to internal (mental or medical) or external (poor writing surface) conditions.
- *Alignment—Base Line.* The evenness of letters along the base line, the ruled or imaginary line upon which the letters rest.
- *Alignment—Head Line.* The imaginary line to which the average tops of the small letters reach. Certain letters are smaller and others are larger or taller.
- *Alignment—Top Line.* The imaginary line to which the average tops of the loop or longest letters reach.
- *Alteration.* Any change or modification of the original. Includes additional writing (such as adding numbers to raise amounts) or obliteration by mechanical or chemical erasures.
- *Ampersand.* The character "&" and its variations, meaning *and*.
- *Angle or Angularity.* The change of direction at a point. Right angle refers to one that is 90 degrees; acute angle is one less than 90 degrees. An obtuse angle is more than 90 degrees, and a reflex angle is more than 180 degrees.
- *Angular Meeting.* The meeting of two lines or strokes at an angle.
- *Arch.* An arcade form in the body of a letter.
- *Arrangement.* (1) Placement of the name, address, and city on an envelope. (2) The M.O. or method of writing a check. (3) The relationship of parts to the whole.
- *Ascending.* Rising obliquely upward, from either a straight or a curved point.
- *Asymmetrical.* A lack of bilateral symmetry that results when identical halves are alternately placed.
- *Average.* To reduce to a mean or find the typical. To find the usual or ordinary in form, size, height, etc.
- *Base Line.* The ruled or imaginary line upon which letters rest.
- *Beard.* The rudimentary curved initial stroke, or the slight up-and-down introductory stroke or double hitch.

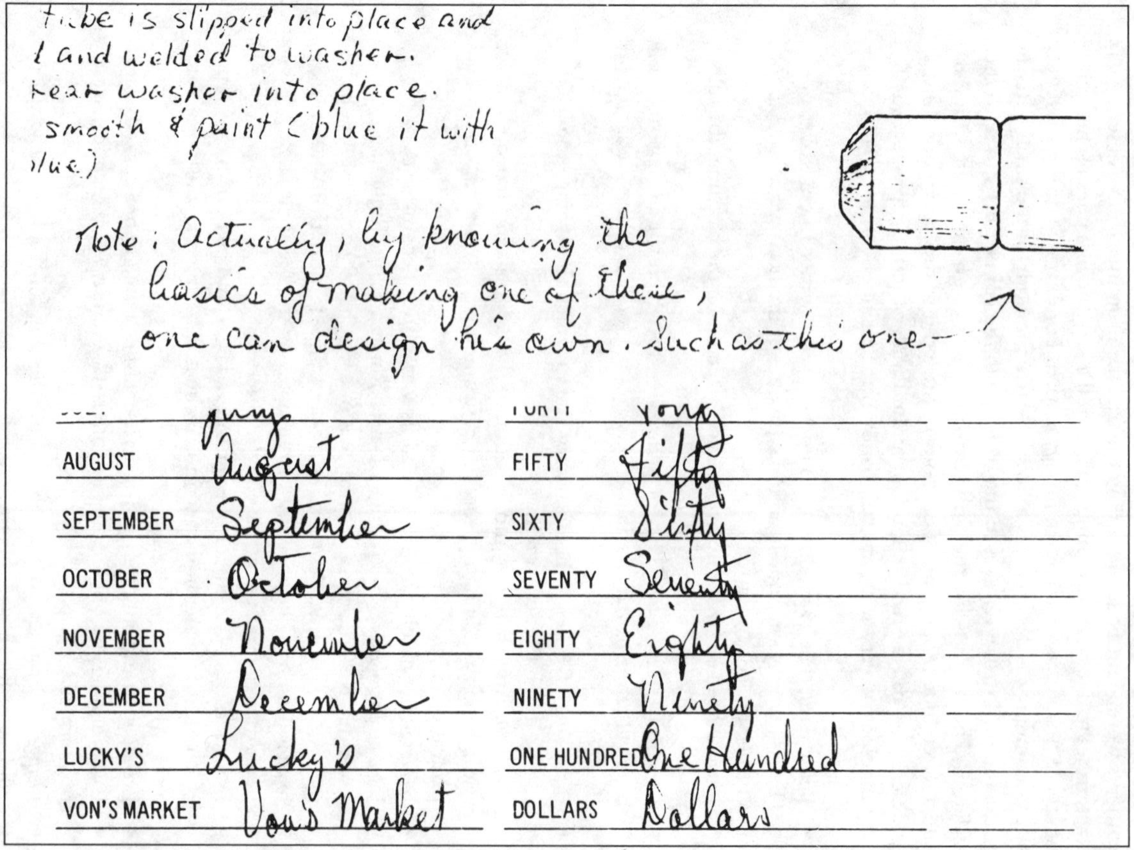

Figure 4–2: Ball and Frank murder case.

- *Block Letters.* Printed letters in the most simple form.
- *Blunt.* The untapered beginning or ending stroke of a letter or character. Usually made when the pen rests on the paper before movement is made, or when the pen stops movement while it is still resting on the paper. Often seen in a copied writing.
- *Body.* The part of the letter that remains, if upper and lower projections, initial strokes, terminal strokes, and diacritics are omitted.
- *Buckle.* Horizontal and looped strokes used to complete a letter. The connection stroke between the two down strokes of a letter. (*A* and *H* are examples of a buckle.)
- *Bulb-Knob.* A pear-shaped, rounded, or swelled part in a line caused by a change in direction of a ballpoint pen.
- *Cap-Crown.* The crossing of the *T.*
- *Capital Loop. See* Spencerian Element #7.
- *Capital O. See* Spencerian Element #5.
- *Capital Stem. See* Spencerian Element #8.
- *Characteristic.* In handwriting terminology, every part of every written line is a characteristic.
- *Choice of Words.* The wording used in anonymous letters, etc., that helps in evaluating the education, experience, and background of the writer.
- *Class Characteristic.* Any characteristic that is common, or letters that are made the same as in a copy book, and lack individuality.
- *Compound Curve.* A line bends in opposite directions. Arcs of two or more circles.
- *Concluding Stroke.* The final stroke of a letter. It may be written upward, horizontal, downward or hooked, straight, curved or compound. (*See also* Terminal Stroke or Toe.)
- *Connecting Stroke-Link.* The stroke between letters. It can be angular, straight, or curved; short or wide spaced; heavy or thin and threadlike; shaded writing or plain.
- *Consciously Written.* A person's requested writing, usually under pressure of arrest. The subject is thinking about handwriting as he or she writes, and therefore some of the normal characteristics may not appear. The person, if guilty, will consciously try to alter the handwriting. Conscious writing is also the attempt to write well on important documents.
- *Contracted Capital O. See* Spencerian Element #6.
- *Crown-Cap.* The horizontal straight or curved stroke at the top of the staff in capital letters *F* and *T.*
- *Cursive Writing.* Letters that are connected, or words written continuously without lifting the pen. (Usually flows without sharp angles.)
- *Curve.* A bent line without angles, or a part of a circle.
- *Curves—Similar.* Curves that follow the same general direction, though not necessarily parallel.

- *Deviations or Variations.* In genuine writing, these are the changes in the form of letters due to the position of the letter in a word, and the normal variations in the form of letters dependent upon the speed, type of material, and importance of the writing.
- *Diacritic Marks.* Elements added to complete certain letters. Examples are the dot of an *i*, the cross of a *t*, or the accent marks in foreign writing.
- *Disconnected Writing or Hiatus.* Pen-lifts which occur between letters in a word that are without a connecting stroke.
- *Direct Pointed Oval.* Occurs when a right curve and a left curve are united in a lower turn. In the Spencerian system it is at an angle of 34 degrees. The inverted pointed oval is a right curve and a left curve united in an upper turn at a 34 degree angle.
- *Disguised Writing.* Used to conceal the writer's identity. Characterized by grotesque capital letter forms, changes of slant, different letter forms, and changes in the size of writing. Disguised writing is usually carefully drawn. Characteristics that are found include tremor, angles, hesitation, stops, patching, and overwriting.
- *Divergence.* The difference of a writing from copybook standards, or dis-agreement between two samples of handwriting.
- *Dot or Period.* A characteristic with its many variations at the end of a sentence, or may be a diacritic mark for the letter "i." The many variations are: a circle, or a vertical, angular, or horizontal line.
- *Elements.* The constituent parts of letters and figures.
- *Embellishment.* Ornamentation not necessary to the legibility of the writing.
- *Equidistant.* In handwriting, refers to lines that are parallel. The lines may be straight or curved.
- *Eradication.* To eliminate, erase, or remove.
- *Eyelet.* A small loop or circle made vertically, angularly, or horizontally. Usually found in: *a,b,o,r,s,v,w,f.*
- *Feathered Stroke.* A line without smooth edges. May be serrated on one side while sharp and smooth on the other side. Sometimes caused by one nib of a pen not touching with the same pressure as the other.
- *Filiform Script.* Cursive writing that tails off into a single line without any distinguishable letters, resembling a thread or filament.
- *Flourish—Embellishment.* The ornamentation of letters by decorative strokes, usually pick-up or ending strokes. Also the extension of lines above and below the signature.
- *Flowback.* Ink writing that has a tendency to flow back on an ink line that is crossed or touched. The sequence of writing may be determined by the flowback of ink on the line crossed.
- *Fold.* The lower part of the small letter *f* or *q*.
- *Foot.* The part of a downstroke that rests on the base line of a letter.

- *Foot Loop.* The horizontal loop on the base line in the figure *2* and capital *O.*
- *Form, Arc-Curve.* A part of a circle. In handwriting it can refer to a connecting stroke between letters, an ending or pick-up stroke, or a part of the body of a letter or upper and lower loop.
- *Form, Arcade.* The inner side of upper loops or the humps of *m, n,* or *h.*
- *Form, Garland.* The inner side of lower loops or the curve of the *u, v,* or *w* and connecting strokes.
- *Formal Writing.* The methodical, ceremonial, or due form of consciously written writing.
- *Free Hand.* Writing done without guidance or aids. Free handwriting is usually considered as memo writing or unconsciously written handwriting. A freehand forgery is a copy by visual means without the aid of tracing, as in a traced forgery.
- *Handwriting Types.* Classification of writing, according to M.O., into five categories:
  1. Normal Unconsciously Written
  2. Normal Consciously Written
  3. Consciously Written Disguised
  4. Freehand Copied
  5. Traced Writing
- *Head Line.* The imaginary line to which the top of the short letters reach.
- *Hiatus.* A disconnected, noncontinuous, broken, or unjoined stroke between letters made by lifting the pen.
- *Hook.* An involuntary formation made at the beginning of a stroke or at the end of a terminal stroke, or on diacritic marks or periods.
- *Horizontal Alignment.* The base line of a word in which letters vary from below the base line to on or above the line. It is also a complete line of writing which may be slanting continuously upward, downward, or at a curve.
- *Horizontal Bar.* A stroke parallel to the base line made in the letters *t* and *f.*
- *Individual Characteristic.* A characteristic that deviates from the norm or standard. It is peculiar to the handwriting of one or a few persons.
- *Initial Stroke or Pickup Stroke.* This is the first stroke. It can be connected to the staff of letters. For example, the capital letter *M* could have a 6 o'clock, 9 o'clock, 12 o'clock, or 3 o'clock pickup.
- *Intersection.* The point where two lines that cross each other meet.
- *Inverted Pointed Oval.* A right curve and a left curve that are united in an upper turn at an angle of 34 degrees.
- *Junction.* The meeting of two lines that do not cross. (*See* Intersection)
- *Knob.* A tiny pool of ink that can be found in the initial or ending stroke, or at a change of direction during the writing.
- *Labored.* Writing produced with difficulty or under strain.
- *Left Curve or Convex.* A curve in the left side of a circle.

- *Letter—Extended.* Loop portion of letters, that may be extended above or below the base line, such as: *h,k,l,b,j,y,g,* long *s,z,* and *f.*
- *Letters—Semi-Extended.* Short stem letters that are extended above and below the base line, such as: *t,d,p,* and *q.*
- *Letters—Short.* Small or minimum letters that are one space high, such as: *i, u, w, n, m, x, v, o, a, e, c, r,* and *s.*
- *Lines—Parallel.* Lines that run in the same direction and are equidistant from each other throughout their entire length. May be straight or curved.
- *Line Quality.* The visible record of a line showing the smoothness or irregularity in its straight lines and curves. To be noticed in line quality are abnormal angles, tremor, hesitation, retouching, sequence, breaks, heavy or thick lines, thin or thread-like lines. The line quality may be simple or complicated, as well as uncoordination from illness, old age, drunkenness, or the "Tremor of Fraud." (See chapter 7.)
- *Loop.* Two opposite curves, a right and a left, united at one end in a turn. A loop may be upper, lower, or horizontal (see Foot Loop).
- *Manuscript Writing.* Writing that omits the joining of letters as in cursive-w-riting. Printing is often referred to as manuscript writing. (See Uncial.)
- *Memo Writing.* Notes, notations, or other information written without the usual care or patience of formal correspondence and business writing.
- *Model Signature.* The genuine writing which is used to copy or trace in order to produce a forgery.
- *Movement.* Method in which a writing instrument is moved. Includes finger writing, finger and wrist movement, and full-arm writing.
- *Nib Marks.* Writing made with steel pens and fountain pens usually show the two divisions of the pen point in the ink line, and thus is identifiable from ball point writing. (Drawing pens may have more than two nibs.)
- *One Space High.* Without the dot the lowercase letter *i* is one space in height and is the standard measurement for the height of all lowercase letters.
- *One Space Wide.* The lowercase letter *u* is the same as a double *i* with the dot omitted. It is one space in width, and the standard measurement for the width of lowercase letters.
- *Oval.* The body of the small letters *a, d, g, o* and *q.*
- *Oval—Direct Pointed.* A right curve and a left curve united in a lower turn at an angle of 34 degrees.
- *Oval—Inverted Pointed.* A right curve and a left curve united in an upper turn at an angle of 34 degrees.
- *Parallel Lines.* Lines that run in the same direction and are equidistant from each other throughout their entire length.
- *Patching.* The retouching of defects in a copied signature.
- *Pen Position.* A pen, when held for writing, can be held at a slant or upright position. This position is indicated by the shading in the ink line.

- *Pen Pressure*. The average force with which the pen contacts the paper. In a drawn signature, the pen pressure will be heavy.
- *Perpendicular*. Vertical, or at a right angle, to the base line.
- *Position of Letters in Words*. A letter may be in the beginning or initial position; intermediate letter in the middle of a word; and last letter in a word. This is important, because the letter will contain variations depending on the position of the letter in a word.
- *Proportion*. The relation of one part to the other, as height in relation to width, or one letter in relation to another.
- *Punctuate*. To separate written matter into clauses or sentences by points or stops. These include periods, colons, semicolons, commas, question marks, exclamation points, parentheses, dashes, brackets, hyphens, apostrophes, quotation marks, braces, and ellipses.
- *Quality*. An identifying factor related to the writing movement.
- *Retrace*. That portion of a letter in which a stroke is superimposed upon another.
- *Right Curve*. A curve which appears on the right side of an oval or circle.
- *Rubrica*. Any mark or flourish added to one's signature.
- *Shading*. The distribution of light and shade (thin and heavy) to parts of the writing due to the pressure or type of pen used.
- *Shank-Staff*. The most basic of the long downstrokes applied to letter.
- *Shoulder*. An abrupt projection that forms an abutment on an object. In handwriting, it is the point at which a recurving line changes into a straight line or different curve.
- *Stem or Extended Letters*. Lowercase letters that rise higher than the standard, such as *t* and *d*, or extend below the base line, such as *p* and *q*.
- *Similar Curves*. Curves that follow the same general direction but are not necessarily parallel.
- *Similarities*. Resemblances of one object to another in parts, elements, or form.
- *Slant*. The angle of writing relative to the base line. Writing can have vertical, right, left, changing, or multiple slant.
- *Skill*. Control, dexterity, and coordination of the writer.
- *Speed of Writing*. The actual speed of writing cannot be precisely determined, but it can be termed as slow, average speed, or very fast.
- *Spacing*. Distance between letters, words, or lines of writing.
- *Spencerian Elements*. The eight elements that form all Spencerian letters.
- *Spur*. The short horizontal stroke in the lowercase letters *b, f, v,* and *w*.
- *Staff—Stem—Shank*. The basic long downstroke of all letters.
- *Staple of Loop*. A right curve and left curve united at the top in a turn or a hairpin form, either crossed or uncrossed above the base line.
- *Straight Lines*. Up or down strokes, angular and horizontal.
- *Superimpose*. *See* Retrace.

- *Symmetrical*. Division by a longitudinal plane into similar halves. Symmetrical halves are proportionately balanced.
- *System*. A uniform, or copy book method of writing. Spencerian and Palmer are two handwriting systems taught in the public schools.
- *Teenybopper*. A style of handwriting used mostly by juveniles.[2] This writing maintains the copy-book style of writing, small letters half the size of capital letters. Both the small and capital letters contain similar pen lifts, height ratios, letter and styles. Adolescents also write an angular style and modification of the above rounded style.[3]
- *Terminal Stroke, Toe or Terminate*. The ending or final stroke of a letter. This may be upward, horizontal, downward, hooked, straight, curved, or with a compound curve.
- *Tick*. A short, straight stroke that is usually a pick-up stroke, but never a beard, spur, or hook.
- *Toe or Terminal Stroke*. The ending stroke of a letter.
- *Top Line*. The real or imaginary line to which the tops of the tallest letters reach.
- *Trace*. To copy by following the lines or letters as seen through a transparent sheet superimposed on the original, or to copy using a shadow box with a light underneath.
- *Trademarks*. The original characteristic marks, signs, figures, and forms individual to one person. A M.O. of writing which, through repetition and conscious practice, are ingrained into the writer's subconscious.
- *Tremor*. Shaky line quality caused by feebleness, old age, illiteracy, or poor education. It may also be found in cases of forgery, the result of the slow copying of another writing.
- *Turns*. The short curves at the top or bottom of letters. Turns are the meeting or merging of one line to another without an angle or point.
- *Unconscious Writing*. Writing that shows natural variation as well as carelessness and incompleteness.
- *Uncial (un'shi al)*. Manuscript writing that omits the joining of letters.
- *Variation*. Changes in letter forms made by a writer in his or her genuine writing. Includes changes due to the position of the letter in the word, speed of the writing, importance of the writing, and type of material used.

  To establish that a known and questioned writing have different sources requires that there is at least one basic, significant difference between them— one fundamental identifying characteristic that does not occur in the same way in both sets of specimens.[4] This is discussed in detail in chapter 8.
- *Writing*. In all there are five types of writing: Normal Unconscious Writing, Normal Conscious Writing, Consciously Disguised Writing, and Copied and Traced Writing.

— 5 —

Parts of Letters

The parts of a letter and the different systems of writing taught are of great importance not only to the beginning student, but to the experienced examiner as well. In this chapter, you will begin to develop the fundamental skills that are the basis for handwriting examinations. You will learn:

1. When examining handwriting, the examiner does not look at the words or letters, but at the individual parts of letters. This chapter breaks down a letter into its individual parts, from which an examination can then be made.
2. Once the letter is broken down, the student may use the vocabulary already learned to describe the parts of letters. The act of describing parts of letters is extremely important as it is used in the examiner's court testimony.
3. Also learned are the various copy book letters. This is important as the established individuality of a letter is judged by its deviation from the copy book.

Examine in Detail

To make a comparison, the handwriting examiner must break down a letter into its individual parts. This is a procedure that must be learned. An untrained person will simply compare one word with another word. The student examiner, or a person with little experience, will compare one letter with another. A trained document examiner will examine the whole word, the letters, and their relationship with one another. But of greater importance, the examiner will examine the individual parts of each letter. He or she will note if the first stroke begins with either a blunt or tapered stroke. The examiner knows that drawn or copied writing usually starts with a blunt stroke. Tremor in the pickup stroke is another indication of copied or traced writing. A magnifying glass will aid in seeing the slight hooks at the beginning of a letter, as well as the construction of the letter. The examination of individual strokes is the way to conduct a proper handwriting examination.

The first step in the examination of the individual strokes is to number the letter (in your imagination) at its starting point, at each change in direction, and at its final point. Refer to the terminology in chapter 4 frequently, naming each point.

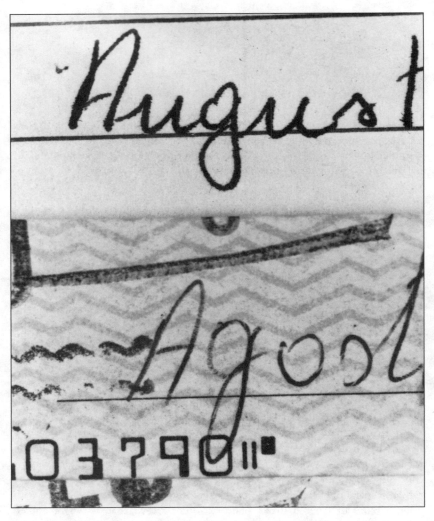

Figure 5–1: Examination of the letter *g*, top signature questioned.

An example of an examination by the numbers is the Pizzo Case (figure 5–1). The letter *g* (questioned signature) starts at the initial stroke (1) at 10 o'clock, curves counterclockwise to the base line (2) and finishes with a final stroke that ends at 1 o'clock (3). The body of the letter (1–2–3) looks like a letter *c*. The second stroke of the letter (4) starts next to the initial stroke and goes up to its head line (5), then dips below the base line to form a lower loop (5–6–7). The examination of the known signature (second signature), the letter *g* starts with

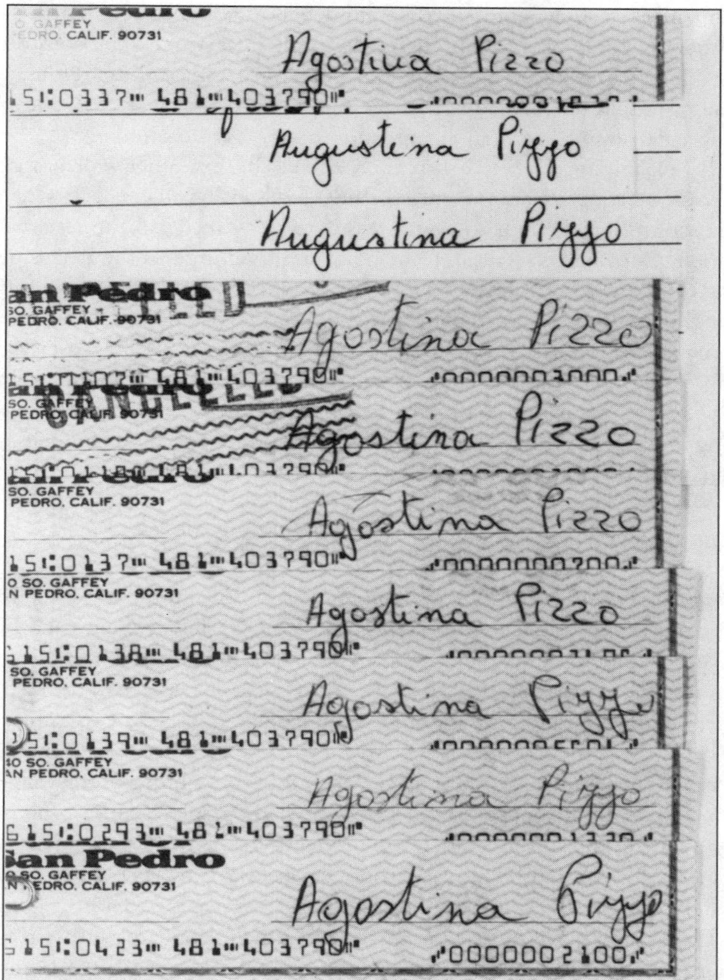

Figure 5–2: Pizzo handwriting exhibit.

159

an initial stroke at 10 o'clock (1). The line then goes counter clockwise in a circle to the base line, continuing around and back to the initial stroke (1–2–3–4). The second stroke starts at the head line (5) and goes below the base line where it forms a loop (5–6–7).

With the detailed information of the exact construction of the letter *g*, by the numbers and with a magnification glass, the differences were noted. An examination of the Pizzo exhibit (figure 5–2) for variations disclosed that all *g*'s were made with a circle. This circle could be seen very clearly in several signatures. The construction of the letter *a* at the end of the first name is also made in the same manner—a circle and then a second stroke to complete the letter. Sometimes there is a drag stroke from the circle to the final stroke. The construction of the *g* in the questioned signature was not a variation, and, therefore, was a characteristic that helped prove the questioned signatures were forgeries. This was all made possible with an examination done "by the numbers."

By examining each letter in such detail, the examiner will not miss a single characteristic. A competent examiner will always make such a detailed examination. One method to assure this is to copy in detail the letters to be examined. Copying the writing to be compared will impress the details of that writing firmly in your mind. It's a good idea not only for the beginner but also for the experienced expert to copy the questioned writing in order to ascertain all its characteristics. (Ralph Bradford used this principle in all of his cases, including *Hughes v. Maheu*, 1970. He also copied the writing again before going to court, memorizing every characteristic for use during testimony. He felt that copying the questioned writing was one of the more important techniques in the examination of handwriting, and you will also find that true.)

Testimony in Court

Handwriting examiners in law enforcement have major problems caused by the volume of cases they must examine. Because of budgeting problems and lack of time, they cannot photograph every case on the possibility that it may go to trial. Experience has shown that they testify in only a small percentage of the cases that are examined. Months after the examination has taken place, the examiner may be called by the office of the district attorney. The examiner may then need to re-examine the handwriting, and testify, all within a few hours of the call. If the examiner has had no opportunity to prepare photographic exhibits, he or she must be able to explain the opinion to a jury with the help of a felt pen or crayon and a piece of paper. With only these tools, the examiner must be able to describe the handwriting, using the proper terminology. Even with a photographic exhibit, the examiner still must describe the writing in detail and testify in such a manner that a court reporter can take down the testimony and, at a later time, it can be read and understood.

The chapter on vocabulary and the description of letters (which will follow in this chapter) are a sample of the words you can use to describe handwriting to a jury.

Unlike many professions, handwriting examination does not have an official or complete vocabulary. The terminology in this book has gained universal acceptance through usage, but is incomplete and should be used only as a guide. As an examiner, you should feel free to use any word that will describe what you see and that will be understood by the jury. Such words usually come from three areas:

1. Familiar objects and shapes. For example, arch, beard, buckle, egg-shaped, foot, hook, and saw toothed.
2. Geometry, which gives us the terms angle, base line, horizontal, oval, parallel, and vertical.
3. Writing movements and qualities, such as cursive, pen lift, proportion, retrace, size, speed, and tremor.

Begin now to use the terminology in chapter 4 and, as you gain experience, other words may be substituted. Testimony, like the original examination, must be detailed.

Copy Book Styles

For the student examiner, the knowledge of the various handwriting systems taught in the United States is essential in order to begin to make comparisons. The copy book styles give you a basis for evaluating writing. Departure from the norm is one of the factors that determines the individuality of handwriting. Albert Osborn wrote, "A handwriting is identified exactly as a person is identified, by a comparison of the general characteristics that, in the case of a person, point to a general class or race, and in addition, the identification must include that which is not general but distinctly individual and personal." Without the benefit of copy book knowledge, most persons think their handwriting is average. But Osborn also wrote: "We look at a peculiar form and are inclined to wonder why anyone for any reason would make a letter like that, and other observers may look at *ours* and think the same thing. As the good old Quaker lady said to her husband, 'Everybody is queer but me and thee and sometimes, dear, thee is a little queer, too.' "[1]

Students in California are taught manuscript writing in grades 1 and 2 and are switched to cursive writing in the second semester of grade 3. Saudek wrote, "There are only three things which concern us to begin with. We have to examine three factors, on whose proper cooperation the success of the first lesson depends:

1. The powers of observation (visual impressionability).

161

2. The attempt to reproduce what is observed (capacity for graphic expression).
3. Technical execution (overcoming the mechanical and physical impediments).

After the first two years of instruction, all doubts as to the form of the individual letters have disappeared. The knowledge of their correct form, that is the form given by the school copies, is already firmly rooted in the consciousness, although the ability to reproduce these ideal forms in pen and ink, without the slightest effort, has not yet been acquired. The child is still writing letters which are put together to form words rather than words which consist of letters.[2]

The key process in learning to write involves both hand and eye coordination. The development of muscular control, especially of the minor hand muscles, is essential for cursive writing. With the development of the minor hand muscles, a person will begin developing his own individual style of writing. The new maturity in writing will contain many variations from the copy book, but the copy book style that was learned will still exert considerable influence on this new writing and later writing as well. This influence is great with regard to the form of the capital letter. The deviation from copy book, *plus the examiner's experience*, determine how individual a character is.

At the beginning of our country in 1776, there were as many different styles of writing as there were nationalities. In the early nineteenth century, the Round Hand System was introduced in the United States. This system retained some of the old English round hand characters. Modern Vertical, another of the early systems, was introduced in 1896.

The Spencerian System was introduced in 1840, and the *Spencerian System of Penmanship* was published in the United States in 1848. This system was still taught in a few New York and Pennsylvania schools as late as 1947, according to a Post Office Department survey. The Spencerian System laid out all kinds of rules, including that a chair should be 16 inches high, and a desk, 27 1/2 inches high.

All Spencerian letters are formed with one or more of eight elements. The first four elements enter into the comparison of small letters; the last four are prominent as the characteristic features of the capitals.[3]

American handwriting instruction reached a turning point in about 1885, when a new type of penmanship was introduced, referred to as "modern American," "commercial," or "business hand." The "new" style has brought forth over fifty systems during the last hundred years. Three of these systems are:

1. The *Zaner-Bloser System*. This system was introduced in 1895 and is currently the most popular system in the United States.[4]
2. The *Palmer System*. Introduced in 1888, this is the second most popular system.[5]

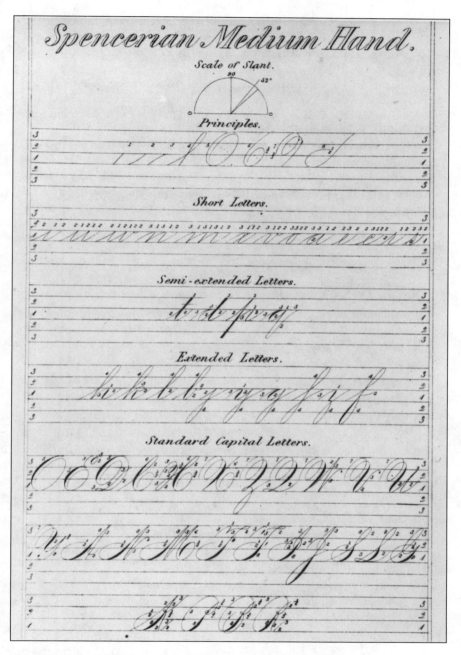

Figure 5–3: Spencerian System of writing. (*Platt R. Spencer*)

3. The *Bowmar/Noble System*. Introduced in 1928 as the New Laurel System, this became very popular. In 1966, its name was changed to Noble and Noble. It is now known as the Bowmar/Noble System.[6]

In the early years of handwriting systems, an examiner could determine which section of the country a person came from by his or her handwriting. But with the increased mobility of people, the systems have spread from area to area, all across the country, so this is no longer possible.

In California, the State Department of Education periodically reviews all handwriting systems published in the United States. In one of their latest reviews they accepted systems published by: W.S. Benson, Bowmar/Noble, McCormick-Mathers, Palmer, Scott-Foresman (D'Nealian), and Zaner-Bloser. Any local school district may incorporate one or more of these accepted books in their curriculum.

Research on the handwriting systems that have been taught in the United States was conducted by the Bureau of Chief Post Office Inspector in 1947.[7] This work was revised by Virgil E. Herrick[8] and Mary S. Beacom,[9] among others. Twenty of the handwriting systems taught in the United States are:

1. American Book
   American Book Co.
   Chicago, Ill. 1937

2. Beckley-Cardy
   Weber Costello
   Chicago, Ill. 1976

3. Bohn/Wool
   Frank E. Richards
   Phoenix, Ariz. 1969

4. Bowmar/Noble
   Bowmar/Noble Co.
   Los Angeles, Calif. 1981

5. D'Nealian Handwriting
   Scott Foresman & Co.
   Glenview, Ill. 1978

6. Kelly & Morriss
   Johnson Publishing Co.
   New York, N.Y. 1921

7. Kittle
   State of Kansas
   Topeka, Kan. 1942

8. Lister Muscular Movement
   Macmillan Co.
   New York, N.Y. 1917

9. Locker
   W.C. Locker
   Richmond, Va. 1943

10. McCormick-Mathers
    Litton Educational Pub.
    New York, N.Y. 1978

11. Palmer System
    A.N. Palmer Co.
    Schaumburg, Ill. 1979

12. Rinehart Functional
    W.L. Rinehart
    Cambridge, Mass. 1940

13. School Zone
    School Zone
    Grand Haven, Mich. 1981

14. Sheldon's Vertical
    Sheldon & Co.
    New York, N.Y. 1896

15. Smilanich Print-Script
    T.S. Denison & Co.
    Minneapolis, Minn. 1969

16. Spencerian
    Ivison, Phinney, Blakeman
    & Co.
    New York, N.Y. 1866

17. Steck-Vaughn
    Steck-Vaughn Co.
    Austin, Tex. 1973

18. W.S. Benson System
    W.S. Benson Co.
    Austin, Tex. 1979

19. Write-Well Handwriting
    Columbia Press
    Bloomington, Ind. 1934

20. Zaner-Bloser
    Zaner-Bloser Inc.
    Columbus, Ohio 1977

Elements of the Capital Letters

All twenty-six capital letters are described in "Norm 1" by the Spencerian System, which is a very exact step-by-step system. Norms 2 and 3 and so on will be used to list the Zaner-Bloser, Palmer System, Bowmar/Noble, and the other sixteen handwriting systems. Each letter will then be broken down and described in its individual parts.

The Spencerian capital letter *A* begins with a capital stem, which joins angularly at the top with a slight left curve, terminating on the base line. A short left curve starts on the last line formed, one space above the ruled line, and descending toward the left one-half space, unites with the short right curve, which crosses the main left curve, and terminates to the right of it, one space above the base line.

Analysis: 8, 3, 3, 2

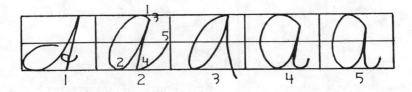

Norm 1—Spencerian makes its letter in this manner.
Norm 2—Zaner-Bloser and Systems 3, 5, 7, 8, 10, 12, 13, 17, and 18 make their letter in this manner.

Line 1–2	Initial Stroke
Line 1–2–3	Forms the oval or body
Point 2	Bottom of oval
Point 3	End of oval
Line 3–4	Second down stroke or staff
Point 4	Foot
Line 4–5	Toe or terminal stroke

Norm 3—Palmer and Systems 6, 9, 15, and 19 make their letter in this manner.
Norm 4—Bowmar/Noble and Systems 1 and 2 make their letter in this manner.
Norm 5—Systems 14 makes its letter in this manner.

The Spencerian capital *B* has the form and proportion of the capital *P* to the point where the right curve touches the capital stem. There a small loop is formed across the stem, at an angle of 52 degrees left of the perpendicular, and the letter is completed with a reversed oval on the regular slant, the base extending a little below the base line, and its last curve terminating opposite the small loop. Measured on a line drawn at right angles with the regular slant, at one-half the height of the oval, the space between the capital stem and the right side of the oval, is one-third the width of the oval and one-fifth the width of the letter.

Analysis: 8, 3, 2, 2, 3

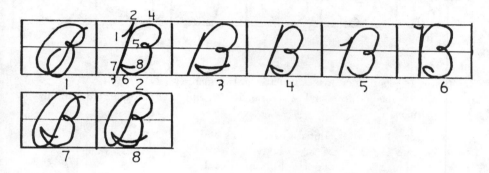

Norm 1—Spencerian and System 9 make their letter in this manner.
Norm 2—Zaner-Bloser and Systems 2, 3, 10, 12, 13, and 19 make their letter in this manner.

Line 1–2	Initial stroke and staff
Line 2–3–4	Second upstroke
Line 2–3	Staff retraced by second upstroke
Line 3–4–5	The upper oval (incomplete oval)
Point 4	Top of upper oval
Point 5	Bottom of upper oval or junction of two ovals. This point may be a retrace or eyelet
Line 5–6–7	Lower oval (incomplete oval)
Point 6	Bottom of lower oval or foot
Point 7–8	Toe or terminal

Norm 3—Palmer and Systems 5, 8, and 18 make their letter in this manner.
Norm 4—Bowmar/Noble and System 6 make their letter in this manner.
Norm 5—Systems 1 and 7 make their letter in this manner.
Norm 6—System 14 makes its letter in this manner.
Norm 7—System 15 makes its letter in this manner.
Norm 8—System 17 makes its letter in this manner.

The Spencerian capital *C* begins at the base line with a right curve, which extends upward three spaces, and then turning to the left, unites with a contacted capital *O*. This crosses the right curve two spaces from the top, forming a loop similar to that in small letter *l*. The space between the two left curves in the oval is equal to one-fourth its width.

Analysis: 2, 6

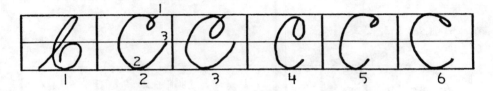

Norm 1—Spencerian makes its letter in this manner.
Norm 2—Zaner-Bloser and Systems 3, 10, 13, and 19 makes their letter in this manner.

Line 1–2	Initial stroke begins with an eyelet
Line 1–2–3	Oval or body
Point 2	Foot or bottom of oval
Line 2–3	Toe or terminal

Norm 3—Palmer and Systems 1, 6, 7, 8, 9, 12, 15, and 18 make their letter in this manner.
Norm 4—Bowmar/Noble makes its letter in this manner.
Norm 5—Systems 2, 5, and 17 make their letter in this manner.
Norm 6—System 14 makes its letter in this manner.

The Spencerian capital *D* begins two spaces above the base line with a compound curve extending downward, and uniting by a short turn at the base with a left curve, which is drawn to the right, crossing the first curve very near the base line. A narrow loop is thus formed, resembling the loop in the small letter *e* made horizontally. After the crossing, the left curve unites at the base line with a right curve, extending upward on the right of the stem and crossing it near its top. The right curve is continued to the top of the letter, where it joins the first curve of a capital *O* which extends downward to within one-half space of the base line, and completes the letter. The space between the two curves on the right of the letter is one-sixth its entire width. The crossing of the loop is midway between the two points where the letter touches the base line.

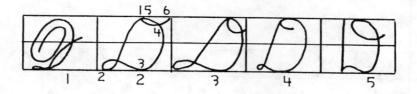

Norm 1—Spencerian makes its letter in this manner.

Norm 2—Zaner-Bloser, Bowmar/Noble, and Systems 1, 3, 5, 8, 13, 15, 18, and 19 make their letter in this manner.

Line 1–2	Initial stroke or staff
Line 1–2–3–4–5	Forms the body or oval
Point 2	Eyelet at bottom staff
Line 2–3–4–5	Forms an essential part of the body or oval and is known specifically as a BOW. In the old round hand and the modern vertical system of penmanship the following capital letters were made with a well defined BOW: B, D, P, R.
Point 3	Bottom of oval or foot
Line 4–5–6	Eyelet
Line 5–6	Terminal stroke

Norm 3—Palmer and Systems 6, 7, 9, and 12 make their letter in this manner.

Norm 4—Systems 2, 10, and 17 make their letter in this manner.

Norm 5—System 14 makes its letter in this manner.

The Spencerian capital *E* begins with a left curve, extending downward one-fourth the length of the letter, then turning to the right, it unites with a right curve extending upward, crossing the first curve near its beginning. At the top of the letter, this right curve joins a second left curve, which is continued downward one-third the length of the letter; then combines with a third left curve by a small loop made at right angles with the regular slant of the letter. The remaining portion of the letter, which is two-thirds its entire length, is the direct capital *O*. The two spaces between the curves at the top of the letter are equal. The space between the two left curves in the lower part of the letter equals one-half the width of the oval. A straight line, drawn on the regular slant through the middle of the letter, will pass through the middle of the first left curve and divide the oval into equal sections.

Analysis: 3, 2, 3, 5

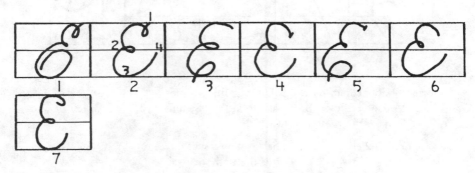

Norm 1—Spencerian makes its letter in this manner.
Norm 2—Zaner-Bloser, Bowmar/Noble and Systems 2, 3, 10, 12, 13, 15 and 19 make their letter in this manner.

Line 1–2	Initial stroke starting with eyelet and forming the upper oval (incomplete)
Point 2	Eyelet, or junction of the two halves or ovals
Line 2–3–4	Forms the lower oval (incomplete)
Point 3	Foot
Line 3–4	Toe

This letter starts and finishes similar to the capital *C*, and is of the same proportions overall—about two thirds as wide as long.

Norm 3—Palmer and System 9 make their letter in this manner.
Norm 4—Systems 5, 8 and 15 make their letter in this manner.
Norm 5—System 6 makes its letter in this manner.
Norm 6—Systems 7 and 18 make their letter in this manner.
Norm 7—System 14 makes its letter in this manner.

The Spencerian capital *F* is the same as capital *T*, with the addition of a left curve one-half space in length, made on the regular slant, on the right side of the stem, opposite the termination of the oval.

Analysis: 3, 1, 3, 2, 8, 3

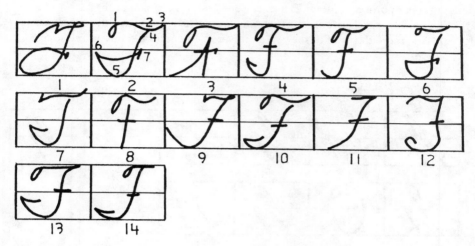

Norm 1—Spencerian and System 18 make their letter in this manner.
Norm 2—Zaner-Bloser and Systems 3, 10, 12, 13, and 19 make their letter in this manner.

Line 1–2–3	It is a curved stroke, starting with an eyelet and terminating to the right of the staff. The crown and staff join.
Line 4–5	Staff
Point 5	Foot
Point 6–7	Crossbar with a final stroke pointing down

Norm 3—Palmer makes its letter in this manner.
Norm 4—Bowmar/Noble makes its letter in this manner.
Norm 5—System 1 makes its letter in this manner.
Norm 6—System 2 makes its letter in this manner.
Norm 7—System 5 makes its letter in this manner.
Norm 8—System 6 makes its letter in this manner.
Norm 9—System 7 makes its letter in this manner.
Norm 10—System 8 makes its letter in this manner.
Norm 11—System 9 makes its letter in this manner.
Norm 12—System 14 makes its letter in this manner.
Norm 13—System 15 makes its letter in this manner.
Norm 14—System 17 makes its letter in this manner.

The Spencerian capital G begins at the base line with a right curve extending upward three spaces, and joining in a turn with a left curve, which descends two-thirds the length of the letter, where it crosses the first curve, forming a loop. The last line is then joined in a broad turn to a right curve, extending upward to half the height of the letter. This curve joins angularly to a capital stem, with its upper portion omitted. The distance from the right side of the loop to the top of the capital stem is equal to one-and-a-half times the width of the loop. A little more than half of the oval in the capital stem is on the right of the first curve.

Analysis: 2, 3, 2, 8

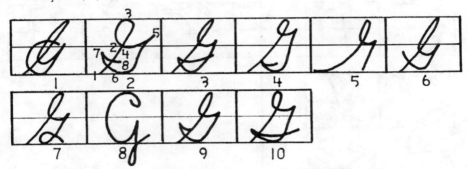

Norm 1—Spencerian and System 1 make their letter in this manner.
Norm 2—Zaner-Bloser, Bowmar/Noble, and Systems 10, 13, 18, and 19 make their letter in this manner.

Line 1–2–3	Initial stroke
Line 2–3–4	Eyelet or loop. (This is a large or a small loop.)
Point 2–4	Bottom of loop or intersection
Point 3	Top of loop
Line 4–5	Shoulder
Point 5	Point or angle of shoulder
Line 5–6	Staff
Point 6	Foot
Line 7–8	Terminal stroke

Norm 3—Palmer and Systems 5, 8, and 12 make their letter in this manner.
Norm 4—Systems 2 and 3 make their letter in this manner.
Norm 5—System 6 makes its letter in this manner.
Norm 6—System 7 makes its letter in this manner.
Norm 7—System 9 makes its letter in this manner.
Norm 8—System 14 makes its letter in this manner.
Norm 9—System 15 makes its letter in this manner.
Norm 10—System 17 makes its letter in this manner.

The Spencerian capital *H* begins one space above the ruled line, with a left curve, which extends upward to four-fifths the height of the letter, then joins a right curve, extending downward to one-half the height of the letter. This line unites with an ascending left curve, which crosses the right curve very near its top, forming a loop. At this point it unites with a descending right curve, which is continued to the base line, where it connects with a compound curve, which is drawn upward and to the right, crossing the descending curve, and extending to the height of the letter. Here it unites with a contracted capital *O*, which crosses the compound curve in descending, and completes the letter. The lower left and the right loop are of equal length and width, and the two sections of the letter are upon the same slant. The spaces on each side of the first loop are equal to the width of the loop, and also equal to the space between the two main portions of the letter. A horizontal line drawn through the letter at one-half its height, touches the lower portion of the first loop and the upper portion of the oval.

Analysis: 3, 2, 3, 2, 3, 2, 6

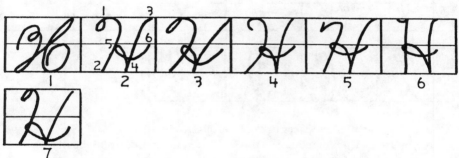

Norm 1—Spencerian makes its letter in this manner.

Norm 2—Zaner-Bloser, Bowmar/Noble, and Systems 1, 3, 10, 13, 15, and 19 make their letter in this manner.

Line 1–2	Initial stroke or first staff, beginning with an eyelet
Point 2	First foot
Line 3–4	Second staff
Point 4	Second foot
Point 5	Connecting eyelet. (When the eyelet is missing, it is called a connecting bar.)
Line 5–6	Terminal stroke

Norm 3—Palmer and Systems 6, 7, 8, 9, and 12 make their letter in this manner.

Norm 4—System 2 makes its letter in this manner.

Norm 5—Systems 5 and 18 make their letters in this manner.

Norm 6—System 14 makes its letter in this manner.

Norm 7—System 17 makes its letter in this manner.

The Spencerian capital *I* commences one space above the base line with a left curve rising one space, then joining a right curve, which descends one space. This curve here unites with a second ascending left curve which divides the oval into two equal sections, and crosses it at its top, rising one space above it. It here unites with a capital stem, which in descending passes through the middle of the loop in oval.

Analysis: 3, 2, 3, 8

Note: In the English alphabet, *I* was noted as a privileged letter. In effect, this means that the custom permits of its being exaggerated out of proportion to the remainder of the capitals. There are several reasons for this. To begin with, English is the only language in which the symbol *I* is used to designate the first person singular of the personal pronoun. English is also the only language in which the personal pronoun of the first person is indicated by a capital letter. There is no one letter in any language which revels in as great diversity of forms as this English *I*.

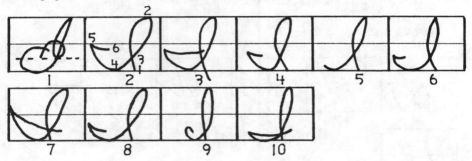

Norm 1—Spencerian makes its letter in this manner.
Norm 2—Zaner-Bloser and Systems 5, 10, 13, 15, and 19 make their letter in this manner.

Line 1–2	Initial stroke
Line 1–2–3	Loop
Point 1–3	Bottom of loop
Point 2	Top of loop
Line 2–3–4	Staff
Point 4	Foot
Line 5–6	Toe

Norm 3—Palmer and Systems 7 and 12 make their letter in this manner.
Norm 4—Bowmar/Noble and System 3 make their letter in this manner.
Norm 5—Systems 1 and 9 make their letter in this manner.
Norm 6—System 2 makes its letter in this manner.
Norm 7—Systems 6 and 18 make their letter in this manner.
Norm 8—System 8 makes its letter in this manner.
Norm 9—System 14 makes its letter in this manner.
Norm 10—System 17 makes its letter in this manner.

The Spencerian capital *J* is five spaces in length, three spaces above the base line, and two below it. The upper portion of the letter is like that of capital *I*. The lower portion of the letter is a modification of the inverted loop, extending two spaces below the base line. Its left curve crosses the main line of the letter one-half space above the ruled line.

Analysis: 3, 2, 3, 3, 4

Note: In capital *J*, the upper loop is slightly larger than the lower loop. A great deal of variation is found between the relative sizes of these two loops among different writers.

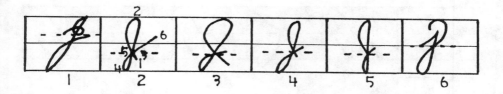

Norm 1—Spencerian makes its letter in this manner.
Norm 2—Zaner-Bloser, Bowmar/Noble, and Systems 3, 10, and 13 make their letter in this manner.

Line 1–2	Initial stroke
Line 1–2–3	Upper loop
Point 1–3	Bottom of upper loop
Point 2	Top of upper loop
Line 2–3–4	Staff
Line 3–4–5	Lower loop
Point 4	Bottom of lower loop
Point 5	Junction of the two loops
Line 5–6	Terminal stroke

Norm 3—Palmer and Systems 1, 2, 5, 6, 7, 8, 12, 13, 17, 18, and 19 make their letter in this manner.
Norm 4—System 9 makes its letter in this manner.
Norm 5—System 14 makes its letter in this manner.
Norm 6—"KINTE J." This letter is not taught in any known system. The letter will be discussed in detail following the section on "Elements of the Small Letters."

The Spencerian capital *K* begins with a right curve, extending upward three spaces, and connecting angularly with a capital stem at its top. The second section begins at the full height of the letter with a compound curve, which is drawn toward the capital stem, touching it at its middle height, and connecting at this point with another compound curve, by a small loop, made across the capital stem on a slant of 52 degrees to the left of perpendicular. This compound curve extends to the base line, uniting at the base with a compound curve, extending upward one space, and completing letter.

Analysis: 2, 8, 3, 2, 2, 3, 2, 3

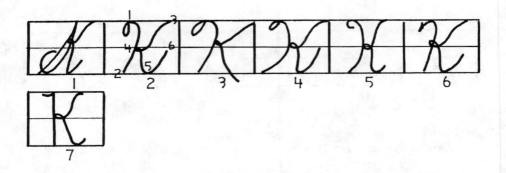

Norm 1—Spencerian makes its letter in this manner.
Norm 2—Zaner-Bloser, Bowmar/Noble, and Systems 3, 10, 13, 17, and 19 make their letter in this manner.

Line 1–2	Initial stroke or staff, beginning with an eyelet
Point 2	First foot
Line 3–4	Initial stroke of second half
Point 4	Connecting eyelet or junction point. (Sometimes this point is a retrace instead of an eyelet.)
Line 5	Second foot
Line 5–6	Terminal stroke

Norm 3—Palmer and Systems 6 and 13 make their letter in this manner.
Norm 4—Systems 1, 7, 8, 9, and 12 make their letter in this manner.
Norm 5—System 2 makes its letter in this manner.
Norm 6—Systems 5 and 18 make their letter in this manner.
Norm 7—System 14 makes its letter in this manner.

The Spencerian capital *L* is like the letter *S* from its beginning to its return to the base line. From this point, a returning compound curve crosses the stem, forming a loop, and again touching the base line, terminates one space above it. The last curve resembles that in the capital letter *Q*. The first curve divides the horizontal loop into two equal sections.

Analysis: 2, 8, 3, 2

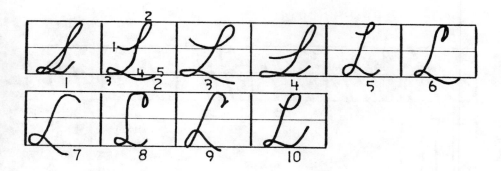

Norm 1—Spencerian makes its letter in this manner.
Norm 2—Zaner-Bloser, Bowmar/Noble, and Systems 3, 5, 13, and 19 make their letter in this manner.

Line 1–2	Initial stroke or staff, beginning with an eyelet
Point 2–3	Bottom of staff is eyelet
Point 4	Foot
Point 4–5	Toe or terminal

Norm 3—Palmer and Systems 6, 8, and 12 make their letter in this manner.
Norm 4—System 1 makes its letter in this manner.
Norm 5—Systems 2 and 10 make their letter in this manner.
Norm 6—System 7 makes its letter in this manner.
Norm 7—System 9 makes its letter in this manner.
Norm 8—System 14 makes its letter in this manner.
Norm 9—System 15 makes its letter in this manner.
Norm 10—Systems 17 and 18 make their letter in this manner.

The Spencerian capital *M* begins like capital *N*. The first two sections are identical with the first two in *N*, the straight line being continued to the base line. This is retraced one-half space by a left curve, rising one-half the height of the letter and uniting by an upper turn with another straight line. This line unites by a lower turn at the base with a right curve, rising one space and completing the letter. The entire width of the letter is equal to ten times the distance between its first two curves.

Analysis: 7, 3, 1, 3, 1, 2

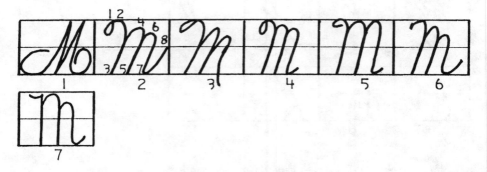

Norm 1—Spencerian makes its letter in this manner.
Norm 2—Zaner-Bloser, and Systems 1, 3, 7, 12, 13, 17, and 19 make their letter in this manner.

Point 1	Eyelet
Line 1–2–3	Initial stroke forming first arc
Point 2	Top of first arc
Point 3	First foot
Line 3–4	Second up stroke
Point 4	Top of second arc
Line 4–5	Second down stroke
Point 5	Second foot
Line 5–6	Third up stroke
Point 6	Top of the third arc
Line 6–7	Third down stroke
Point 7	Third foot or terminal
Line 7–8	Terminal stroke

Norm 3—Palmer and Systems 6, 8, 9, and 15 make their letter in this manner.
Norm 4—Bowmar/Noble and System 10 make their letter in this manner.
Norm 5—System 2 makes its letter in this manner.
Norm 6—System 5 and 18 make their letter in this manner.
Norm 7—System 14 makes its letter in this manner.

The Spencerian capital N begins with a capital loop, the lower half of the last line made straight. A left curve retraces this line, separating from it, one space above the base line, and continuing to two-thirds the height of the letter, where it unites, by an upper turn, with a straight line, which descending on the regular slant, joins by a lower turn at its base with a right curve. This rises one space and completes the letter. The entire width of the letter is equal to eight times the distance between its first two curves.

Analysis: 7, 3, 1, 2

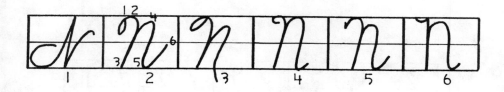

Norm 1—Spencerian makes its letter in this manner.
Norm 2—Zaner-Bloser, Bowmar/Noble, and Systems 1, 3, 7, 10, 12, 13, 17, and 19 make their letter in this manner.

Point 1	Eyelet
Line 1–2–3	Initial stroke forming first arc
Point 2	Top of first arc
Point 3	First foot
Line 3–4	Second up stroke
Point 4	Top of second arc
Line 4–5	Second downstroke
Point 5	Second foot
Line 5–6	Terminal stroke

Norm 3—Palmer and Systems 6, 8, 9, and 15 make their letter in this manner.
Norm 4—System 2 makes its letter in this manner.
Norm 5—Systems 5 and 18 make their letter in this manner.
Norm 6—System 14 makes its letter in this manner.

The Spencerian capital *O* is made on the regular slant, and is composed entirely of curved lines. Care should be taken in its formation to avoid the slightest appearance of angularity. It is three spaces in height. Its width, without shape, is one-half its slanting height. Commencing three spaces above the ruled line, a full left curve is produced, extending to the ruled line, where it unites with a full right curve. This line is drawn upward very nearly to the height of the first curve, joining a second left curve similar to the first, which proceeds downward, and terminates one-half space from the ruled line. The right and inner left curves bend equally. The distance between the outer and inner left curves, measured at one-half the height of the letter, is one-fifth its entire width.

Analysis: 5

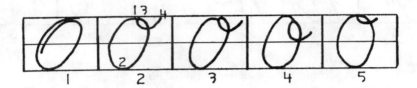

Norm 1—Spencerian makes its letter in this manner.
Norm 2—Zaner-Bloser, and Systems 3, 10 and 13 make their letter in this manner.

Line 1–2	Initial stroke
Point 1	Beginning of oval
Line 1–2–3	Forms the oval
Point 2	Bottom of oval or foot
Point 3	End of oval
Line 3–4	Horizontal bar

Norm 3—Palmer, Bowmar/Noble, and Systems 2, 7, 8, 18, and 19 make their letter in this manner.
Norm 4—Systems 1, 5, 6, 9, 12, 15, and 17 make their letter in this manner.
Norm 5—System 14 makes its letter in this manner.

The Spencerian capital *P* begins two-and-a-half spaces above the base line with a capital stem, which connects at its base with a full left curve continued to the height of the letter, and similar to the left side of the inverted capital *O*. At the top, it unites with a right curve, which crosses the capital stem, and extending downward to one-half the height of the letter, recrosses the capital stem, and unites with a short left curve, which terminates with a dot upon the stem. The distance between the stem and the curve on the right is one-fifth the width of the letter.

Analysis: 8, 3, 2, 3

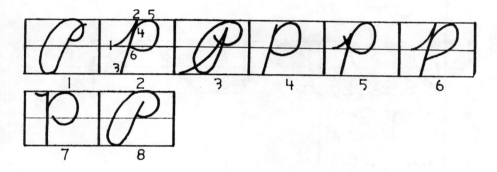

Norm 1—Spencerian and Systems 9 and 15 make their letter in this manner.
Norm 2—Zaner-Bloser, and Systems 2, 10, 13, and 19 make their letter in this manner.

Line 1–2	Initial stroke
Line 2–3	Staff
Point 3	Foot or Bottom of staff
Line 3–4	Staff retraced by second upstroke
Line 3–4–5	Second upstroke
Line 4–5–6	Oval
Point 6	Bottom of oval or junction with staff

Norm 3—Palmer makes its letter in this manner.
Norm 4—Bowmar/Noble and Systems 5, 6, 8, and 18 make their letter in this manner.
Norm 5—Systems 1 and 7 make their letter in this manner.
Norm 6—Systems 3 and 12 make their letter in this manner.
Norm 7—System 14 makes its letter in this manner.
Norm 8—System 17 makes its letter in this manner.

The Spencerian capital Q begins with a capital loop that is slightly modified by drawing its terminating curve toward the left, to a point directly under the oval. The horizontal loop is then formed, similar to the one in the base of capital D, and the letter is finished with a compound curve, rising to the height of one space to the right of the main portion of the letter. This letter touches the base line at the middle of the horizontal loop, and also at a point in the finishing curve. The crossing of the lower loop is midway between these two points. A line drawn on the regular slant through the middle of the capital loop will divide the horizontal loop into two equal parts.

Analysis: 7, 3, 2

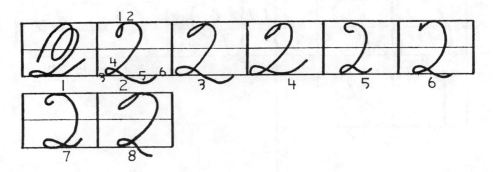

Norm 1—Spencerian makes its letter in this manner.
Norm 2—Zaner-Bloser, Bowmar/Noble, and Systems 10, 12, 13, and 19 make their letter in this manner.

Line 1–2–3	Initial stroke beginning with an eyelet
Point 2	Top of arc
Line 2–3	Staff
Point 4	Eyelet
Line 4–5–6	Terminal stroke
Point 5	Foot
Line 5–6	Toe

Norm 3—Palmer and Systems 3, 6, 7, 8, and 9 make their letter in this manner.
Norm 4—Systems 1 and 17 make their letter in this manner.
Norm 5—System 2 makes its letter in this manner.
Norm 6—Systems 5 and 18 make their letter in this manner.
Norm 7—System 14 makes its letter in this manner.
Norm 8—System 15 makes its letter in this manner.

The Spencerian capital *R* is precisely like the capital letter B as far as the upper end of the loop. The remainder is like the last portion of capital *K*.

Analysis: 8, 3, 2, 2, 3, 2, 3

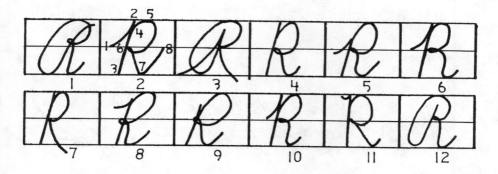

Norm 1—Spencerian and Systems 9 and 15 make their letter in this manner.
Norm 2—Zaner-Bloser, and Systems 3 and 13 make their letter in this manner.

Line 1–2	Initial stroke
Line 2–3	Staff
Point 3	Bottom of staff or foot
Line 3–4	Retrace of staff by second upstroke
Line 4–5–6	Oval
Point 6	Junction eyelet
Line 6–7	Downstroke to foot
Line 7–8	Terminal

Norm 3—Palmer makes its letter in this manner.
Norm 4—Bowmar/Noble and Systems 5 and 18 make their letter in this manner.
Norm 5—System 1 makes its letter in this manner.
Norm 6—System 2 makes its letter in this manner.
Norm 7—System 6 makes its letter in this manner.
Norm 8—System 7 makes its letter in this manner.
Norm 9—System 8 makes its letter in this manner.
Norm 10—Systems 10, 12, and 19 make their letter in this manner.
Norm 11—System 14 makes its letter in this manner.
Norm 12—System 17 makes its letter in this manner.

The Spencerian capital *S* begins on the base line with a right curve, extending upward three spaces. It then unites in a turn with a capital stem, which crosses the right curve midway between the top of the letter and the base line. The upper end and lower sections of the compound curve are very much increased in fullness. This is a distinctive feature of capital *S*. The right and left sides of the oval are equally curved, and the oval is divided into two equal sections by the right curve.

Analysis: 2, 8

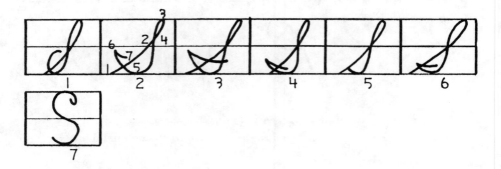

Norm 1—Spencerian makes its letter in this manner.
Norm 2—Zaner-Bloser, and Systems 2, 5, 13, 17, 18, and 19 make their letter in this manner.

Line 1–2–3	Initial stroke starting near base line
Line 2–3–4	Loop
Point 2–4	Bottom of loop or intersection
Point 3	Top of loop
Line 3–4–5	Body
Point 5	Foot
Line 5–6	Toe
Line 6–7	Terminal stroke

Norm 3—Palmer and System 6 make their letter in this manner.
Norm 4—Bowmar/Noble and Systems 3, 10, 12, and 15 make their letter in this manner.
Norm 5—Systems 1, 7, and 9 make their letter in this manner.
Norm 6—System 8 makes its letter in this manner.
Norm 7—System 14 makes its letter in this manner.

The Spencerian capital *T* begins two spaces above the base line with a left curve, rising one space, and uniting by a turn with a slanting straight line, which descends one-fourth the distance to the base line, then joins angularly to a compound curve, made horizontally. This curve unites with a capital stem with the upper curve slightly increased. It crosses the compound curve, forming a small loop, then descending to the base line, completes the letter. The straight line, if continued to the base line, would pass through the middle of the oval in the capital stem.

Analysis: 3, 1, 3, 2, 8

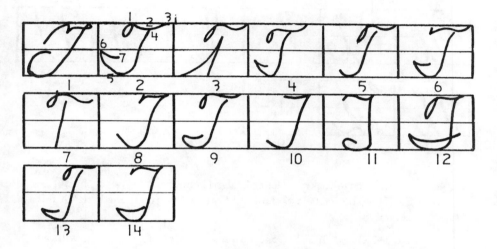

Norm 1—Spencerian makes its letter in this manner.
Norm 2—Zaner-Bloser, and Systems 2, 10, 12, 13, and 19 make their letter in this manner.
Norm 3—Palmer makes its letter in this manner.
Norm 4—Bowmar/Noble and System 3 make their letter in this manner.
Norm 5—System 1 makes its letter in this manner.
Norm 6—System 5 makes its letter in this manner.
Norm 7—System 6 makes its letter in this manner.
Norm 8—System 7 makes its letter in this manner.
Norm 9—System 8 makes its letter in this manner.
Norm 10—System 9 makes its letter in this manner.
Norm 11—System 14 makes its letter in this manner.
Norm 12—System 15 makes its letter in this manner.
Norm 13—System 17 makes its letter in this manner.
Norm 14—System 18 makes its letter in this manner.

The Spencerian capital *U* begins with a modified capital loop. It unites in a turn at the base with a right curve, extending upward two-thirds the height of the letter. A slanting straight line retraces the right curve one-half the length of the letter, and continuing to the base line, unites by a lower turn with a right curve, drawn upward one space. The last two right curves are similar. The width of the letter may be divided into six equal spaces.

Analysis: 7, 2, 1, 2

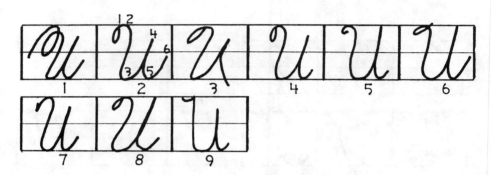

Norm 1—Spencerian makes its letter in this manner.
Norm 2—Zaner-Bloser, and Systems 1, 12, and 13 make their letter in this manner.

Line 1–2–3	Initial stroke forming the arc, and beginning with an eyelet
Point 2	Top of arc
Point 3	Foot
Line 3–4	Second up stroke
Point 4	Point, or top of second arc, is rounded
Line 4–5	Second downstroke or terminal
Point 5	Second foot
Line 5–6	Terminal stroke

Norm 3—Palmer and Systems 6, 8, 9, and 15 make their letter in this manner.
Norm 4—Bowmar/Noble makes its letter in this manner.
Norm 5—System 2 makes its letter in this manner.
Norm 6—Systems 3, 10, 17, and 19 make their letter in this manner.
Norm 7—Systems 5 and 18 make their letter in this manner.
Norm 8—System 7 makes its letter in this manner.
Norm 9—System 14 makes its letter in this manner.

The Spencerian capital *V* begins with a capital loop, which is slightly modified at the base by a turn to the right, connecting it with a compound curve extending upward two spaces, and terminating with a dot as in *W*. Measured on a straight line, drawn at right angles with the regular slant through the middle of the loop, the letter may be divided into five equal spaces.

Analysis: 7, 2, 3

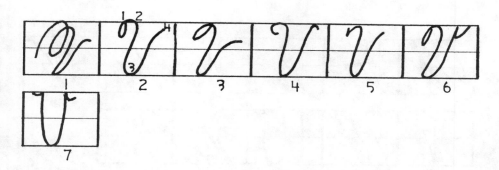

Norm 1—Spencerian makes its letter in this manner.
Norm 2—Zaner-Bloser, Bowmar/Noble, and Systems 3, 10, 12, 13, 17, and 19 make their letter in this manner.

Line 1–2–3	Initial stroke forming an arc and beginning with an eyelet
Point 2	Top of arc
Point 3	Foot
Line 3–4	Second upstroke

Norm 3—Palmer and Systems 1, 6, 8, 9, and 15 make their letter in this manner.
Norm 4—System 2 makes its letter in this manner.
Norm 5—Systems 5 and 18 make their letter in this manner.
Norm 6—System 7 makes its letter in this manner.
Norm 7—System 14 makes its letter in this manner.

The Spencerian capital *W* begins with a capital loop. A right curve is joined angularly to its base and is continued upward three spaces, then joins angularly with a straight left curve, descending to the base line on a slant of 60 degrees. At its base, it is united to a left curve which rises two spaces, and turning a little to the right, terminates in a dot, made on the regular slant. Measured at one-half the height of the letter, the three spaces on the right of the capital loop are equal.

Analysis: 7, 2, 3, 3

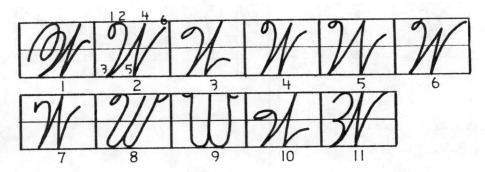

Norm 1—Spencerian makes its letter in this manner.
Norm 2—Zaner-Bloser, and Systems 13 and 17 make their letter in this manner.

Line 1–2–3	Initial stroke forming an arc and beginning with an eyelet
Point 2	Top of arc
Point 3	Foot
Line 3–4	Second upstroke
Point 4	Point, or top of second stroke (arc when rounded)
Line 4–5	Second downstroke
Point 5	Second foot
Line 5–6	Third upstroke

Norm 3—Palmer and Systems 6 and 8 make their letter in this manner.
Norm 4—Bowmar/Noble and Systems 1, 12, and 19 make their letter in this manner.
Norm 5—Systems 2 and 10 make their letter in this manner.
Norm 6—Systems 3 and 9 make their letter in this manner.
Norm 7—Systems 5 and 18 make their letter in this manner.
Norm 8—System 7 makes its letter in this manner.
Norm 9—System 14 makes its letter in this manner.
Norm 10—System 15 makes its letter in this manner.
Norm 11—"Kinte W." This letter is not taught in any known system. It is discussed in detail at the end of this chapter.

The Spencerian capital *X* is a combination of the capital loop and the contracted capital *O* meeting at one-half their height. Their original slant and proportions are preserved.

Analysis: 7, 6

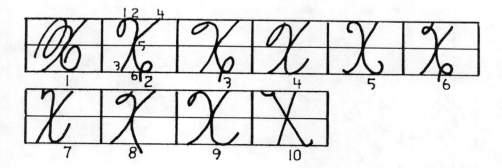

Norm 1—Spencerian makes its letter in this manner.
Norm 2—Zaner-Bloser, Bowmar/Noble, and Systems 10, 13, 17, and 19 make their letter in this manner.

> Line 1–2–3   Initial stroke beginning with an eyelet. This line forms the first half of the letter.
>
> Line 4–5–6   Second downstroke, ending in an eyelet. This forms the second half of the letter.
>
> Point 5   Junction

Norm 3—Palmer and Systems 7, 8, 9, and 15 make their letter in this manner.
Norm 4—System 1 makes its letter in this manner.
Norm 5—System 2 makes its letter in this manner.
Norm 6—System 3 makes its letter in this manner.
Norm 7—Systems 5 and 18 make their letter in this manner.
Norm 8—System 6 makes its letter in this manner.
Norm 9—System 12 makes its letter in this manner.
Norm 10—System 14 makes its letter in this manner.

The Spencerian capital *Y* begins with a capital loop, its last line extending down to a point three-fourths of the length of the letter from its top, where it unites in a turn with a right curve, which is continued upward to two-thirds the height of the letter. Here it joins angularly with a capital stem that extends to the base line and terminates in a dot one-sixth the height of the letter from its base. A straight line drawn on the regular slant through the last line of the capital loop will touch the right side of the dot. The width of the letter may be measured as in capital *U*.

Analysis: 7, 2, 8

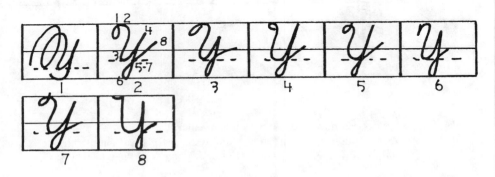

Norm 1—Spencerian makes its letter in this manner.
Norm 2—Zaner-Bloser, Bowmar/Noble, and Systems 13 and 17 make their letter in this manner.

Line 1–2–3	Initial stroke, beginning with an eyelet
Point 2	Top of arc
Point 3	Foot
Line 3–4	Second upstroke
Point 4	Point or angle
Line 4–5–6	Second downstroke or staff
Line 5–7	Loop intersection or top
Line 5–6–7	Loop
Line 7–8	Toe

Norm 3—Palmer and Systems 1, 6, and 12 make their letter in this manner.
Norm 4—System 2 makes its letter in this manner.
Norm 5—Systems 3, 7, and 10 make their letter in this manner.
Norm 6—Systems 5 and 18 make their letter in this manner.
Norm 7—Systems 8, 9, 15, and 19 make their letter in this manner.
Norm 8—System 14 makes its letter in this manner.

The Spencerian capital Z is five spaces in length, three spaces above the base line and two below. It begins with a capital loop that extends to the base line where it is joined to a left curve, rising one-half space and crossing the last curve of the capital loop, forming a small loop. The left curve is then united to a modification of the extended inverted loop, as in the small letter z.

Analysis: 7, 3, 4

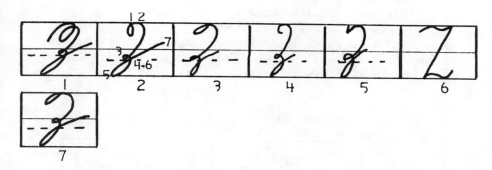

Norm 1—Spencerian makes its letter in this manner.

Norm 2—Zaner-Bloser, Bowmar/Noble, and Systems 3, 7, 10, 12, 13, and 17 make their letter in this manner.

Line 1–2–3	Initial stroke, beginning with an eyelet and ending with an eyelet
Point 2	Top of arc
Point 3	Junction eyelet. This is frequently made as a retrace
Line 4–5–6	Loop
Point 4–6	Loop intersection
Line 6–7	Terminal or toe

Norm 3—Palmer and Systems 1, 6, 8, 9, and 19 make their letter in this manner.

Norm 4—System 2 makes its letter in this manner.

Norm 5—Systems 5 and 18 make their letter in this manner.

Norm 6—System 14 makes its letter in this manner.

Norm 7—System 15 makes its letter in this manner.

Elements of the Small Letters

The Spencerian small letter *a* has generally been considered the most difficult of all letters to construct. It is one space in height and one space in width. A left curve beginning at the base line extends upward on an angle of 27 degrees, and rises to the height of one space, where it unites with a second left curve, which retraces the first half its length. At this point, which is three-fourths of a space from the base line, it separates from the first left curve, and continues to the base line, the entire second left curve beginning on a slant of 34 degrees. It is joined in a lower turn at the base to a right curve, which proceeds upward meeting the left two curves, and joining angularly with a straight line. This straight line descends on the regular slant, uniting in a turn at the base with a right curve, which proceeds upward one space and completes the letter.

Analysis: 3, 3, 2, 1, 2

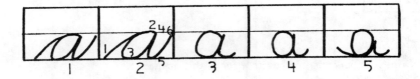

Norm 1—Spencerian and Systems 1 and 6 make their letter in this manner.
Norm 2—Zaner-Bloser, Palmer, Bowmar/Noble, and Systems 3, 5, 7, 8, 9, 10, 12, 13, 17, 18, and 19 make their letter in this manner.

Line 1–2	Initial or beginning stroke
Line 2–3–4	Forms the oval
Point 3	Bottom of the oval
Point 4	End of the oval
Line 4–5	Downstroke
Point 5–6	Foot

Norm 3—Systems 2 and 15 make their letter in this manner.
Norm 4—System 14 makes its letter in this manner.
Norm 5—"French a." This letter is not taught in any American system. The letter is discussed in detail at the end of this chapter.

The Spencerian small letter *b* is three spaces in height and one-half space in width. It is simply the letter *l* with a termination like the small letter *v*. The distance between the crossing of the loop and the dot is equal to the width of the loop.

Analysis: 4, 2, 2

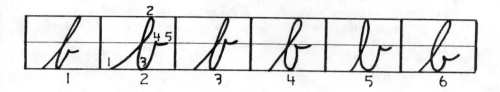

Norm 1—Spencerian and System 6 make their letter in this manner.
Norm 2—Zaner-Bloser, and Systems 7, 13, 15, and 18 make their letter in this manner.

Line 1–2	Initial stroke
Line 1–2–3	Forms the loop
Point 2	Top of loop
Line 2–3	Staff, stem or shank (of the small letters, only those of double space are referred to as having a staff. In these the staff is formed by the first downstroke).
Point 3	Foot
Line 3–4	Second upstroke
Line 4–5	Horizontal bar or terminal (If connected with a following letter, it is called a link.)

Norm 3—Palmer and System 1 make their letter in this manner.
Norm 4—Bowmar/Noble and Systems 2, 3, 5, 8, 9, 10, 12, and 19 make their letter in this manner.
Norm 5—System 14 makes its letter in this manner.
Norm 6—System 17 makes its letter in this manner.

The Spencerian small letter *c* is one space in height, and one–half space in width. It begins at the base line with a right curve, like that of the letter *e*, which extends upward nearly one space, uniting with a short straight line made downward on the regular slant. Turning to the right, a right curve is made, uniting with a left at the top. This left curve descending, crosses the first curve one-third space above the base line. It continues to the base line, where it unites with a right curve similar to the first, which completes the letter. The curves right and left of the short straight line near the top should be equidistant from it, and this portion of the letter should be one-third of its entire length.

Analysis: 2, 1, 2, 3, 2

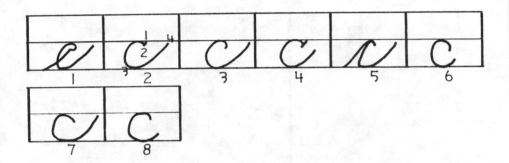

Norm 1—Spencerian makes its letter in this manner.
Norm 2—Zaner-Bloser, and System 13 make their letter in this manner.

      Line 1–2   Initial stroke
      Line 2–3–4   Spiral or downward turn
      Point 3   Foot
      Line 3–4   Toe or terminal

Norm 3—Palmer and Systems 8, 9, 18, and 19 make their letter in this manner.
Norm 4—Bowmar/Noble and Systems 3, 5, and 15 make their letter in this manner.
Norm 5—Systems 1 and 6 make their letter in this manner.
Norm 6—System 2 makes its letter in this manner.
Norm 7—Systems 7, 10, 12, and 17 make their letter in this manner.
Norm 8—System 14 makes its letter in this manner.

The Spencerian small letter *d* is two spaces in height and one space in width. All the lines that compose it are of the same kind, and on the same slant, as in the small letter *a*, the only difference being that the right curve is continued upwards two spaces from the base line, and the descending straight line blends with it one-half the length of the letter, as in small letter *t*.

Analysis: 3, 3, 2, 1, 2

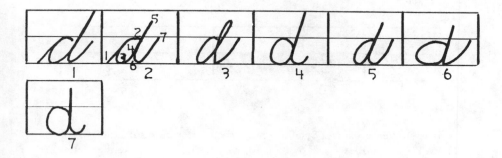

Norm 1—Spencerian makes its letter in this manner.
Norm 2—Zaner-Bloser, Bowmar/Noble, and Systems 1, 5, 8, 10, 12, 13, 15, 17, 18, and 19 make their letter in this manner.

Line 1–2	Initial stroke
Line 2–3–4	Forms the oval
Point 3	Bottom of oval
Line 4–5	Retraced by following downstroke
Line 5–6	Staff
Point 6	Foot
Line 6–7	Toe

Norm 3—Palmer and Systems 6 and 9 make their letter in this manner.
Norm 4—System 2 makes its letter in this manner.
Norm 5—System 3 makes its letter in this manner.
Norm 6—System 7 makes its letter in this manner.
Norm 7—System 14 makes its letter in this manner.

The Spencerian small letter *e* is one space in height, and one-third space in width. A right curve begins at the base line, and continues upward one space, uniting in a short turn to a left curve, which forms the left side of a loop and continues downward, crossing the right curve one-third space from the base line. This left curve joins at the base to a right curve which is continued upward one space, and finishes the letter.

Analysis: 2, 3, 2

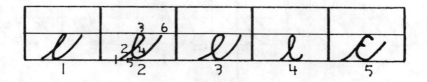

Norm 1—Spencerian and System 6 make their letter in this manner.

Norm 2—Zaner-Bloser, and Systems 10, 12, 13, 17, and 19 make their letter in this manner.

Line 1–2–3	Initial stroke
Line 2–3–4	Forms the eyelet which constitutes the body of this letter
Point 2–4	Intersection of first up- and downstrokes
Point 5	Foot
Line 5–6	Toe

Norm 3—Palmer, Bowmar/Noble, and Systems 1, 3, 7, 8, 9, and 18 make their letter in this manner.

Norm 4—System 14 makes its letter in this manner.

Norm 5—"Greek e." This letter, not taught in any American system, is discussed in detail at the end of this chapter.

The Spencerian small letter *f* is five spaces in length and one-half space in width. Three spaces are above the base line and two spaces below it. It is formed by combining a direct loop with a reversed inverted loop. The direct loop is precisely like the one in the small letter *h*. The curve forming the right side of the lower loop crosses the straight line one-half space above the base line, and joins angularly with a right curve, which also crosses the straight line and terminates one space above the base line, and one space to the right of the straight line.

Analysis: 4, 4, 2

Norm 1—Spencerian and Systems 6 and 9 make their letter in this manner.
Norm 2—Zaner-Bloser, Bowmar/Noble, and Systems 7, 8, 10 and 13 make their letter in this manner.

Line 1–2–3	Initial stroke
Line 2–3–4	Intersection of up- and downstrokes, or bottom or upper loop
Point 3	Top of upper loop
Line 3–4–5–6	Staff
Line 5–6–7	Lower loop
Point 5–7	Closing of lower loop
Point 6	Bottom of lower loop
Line 7–8	Bar or terminal

Norm 3—Palmer and Systems 1, 12, 17, 18, and 19 make their letter in this manner.
Norm 4—Systems 2, 3, 5, and 15 make their letter in this manner.
Norm 5—System 14 makes its letter in this manner.

The Spencerian small letter *g* is three spaces in length and one space in width. It begins with a pointed oval, as in the small letters *a, d* and *q*. To this is added an inverted loop, joined to it angularly one space above the base line.

Analysis: 3, 3, 2, 4

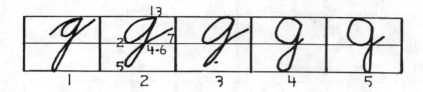

Norm 1—Spencerian makes its letter in this manner.
Norm 2—Zaner-Bloser, Bowmar/Noble, and Systems 3, 7, 8, 10, 13, 17, and 18 make their letter in this manner.

Line 1–2–3	Forms the oval
Point 2	Bottom of oval
Line 3–4–5	Staff
Line 4–5–6	Forms a lower loop
Point 4–6	Top of loop or point of intersection of staff and loop
Point 5	Bottom of loop
Line 6–7	Toe

Norm 3—Palmer, and Systems 1, 5, 6, 9, 12, 15, and 19 make their letter in this manner.
Norm 4—System 2 makes its letter in this manner.
Norm 5—System 14 makes its letter in this manner.

The Spencerian small letter *h* is three spaces in height and one space in width. Beginning at the base line, a loop, or right curve, left curve, and straight line, form the first part of the letter. The second part is precisely like that of small letter *n*, consisting of a left curve, straight line, and right curve, each of which is one space in height. It is united angularly to the base of the first straight line. The two straight lines should be parallel, and the two right curves similar.

Analysis: 4, 3, 1, 2

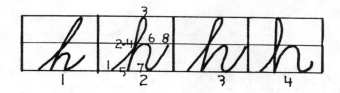

Norm 1—Spencerian and System 17 make their letter in this manner.

Norm 2—Zaner-Bloser, and Systems 3, 7, 9, 10, 12, 13, 15, and 18 make their letter in this manner.

Line 1–2–3	Initial stroke
Line 2–3–4	Forms the loop
Point 2–4	Loop intersection or bottom of loop
Point 3	Top of loop
Line 3–4–5	Staff
Line 5–6–7	The arc or up-curve
Point 6	Top of arc
Point 7	Foot
Line 7–8	Toe

Norm 3—Palmer, Bowmar/Noble, and Systems 1, 2, 5, 6, 8, and 19 make their letter in this manner.

Norm 4—System 14 makes its letter in this manner.

The Spencerian small letter *i* is one space in height without the dot, and is the standard measurement for the height of all letters. It begins on the base line with a right curve extending upward one space, where it is joined angularly to a slanting straight line, which descends to the base line, uniting in a turn with a second right curve. This curve is similar to the first and, ascending one space above the base line, completes the letter. The dot is placed one space above the straight part of the letter and on a line with it.

Analysis: 2, 1, 2

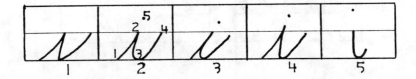

Norm 1—Spencerian and Systems 1 and 6 make their letter in this manner.
Norm 2—Zaner-Bloser, Palmer, and Systems 7, 8, 9, 10, 12, 13, 15, and 17 make their letter in this manner.

Line 1–2	Initial stroke
Point 2	Top or point
Line 2–3	Downstroke
Point 3	Foot
Line 3–4	Toe
Point 5	Dot

Norm 3—Bowmar/Noble, and Systems 2, 3, 18, and 19 make their letter in this manner.
Norm 4—System 5 makes its letter in this manner.
Norm 5—System 14 makes its letter in this manner.

The Spencerian small letter *j* is three spaces long and one-half space wide. One space is above the space line and two below it. It begins on the base line with a right curve, extending upward one space. This connects angularly at the top with the main part of the letter, which is an inverted extended loop. When in this position, the crossing of the loop is on the base line. The finish is a small dot, one space above the straight line, as in the small letter *i*.

Analysis: 2, 4

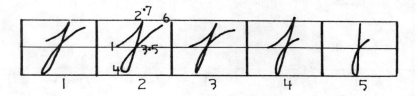

Norm 1—Spencerian makes its letter in this manner.

Norm 2—Zaner-Bloser, Bowmar/Noble, and Systems 2, 10, 13, and 18 make their letter in this manner.

Line 1–2	Initial stroke
Line 2–3–4	Staff
Line 3–4–5	Forms the loop
Point 3–5	Loop intersection or upper end of loop
Point 4	Bottom of loop
Line 5–6	Toe
Point 7	Dot

Norm 3—Palmer and Systems 1, 3, 6, 7, 8, 9, 12, and 19 make their letter in this manner.

Norm 4—Systems 5, 15, and 17 make their letter in this manner.

Norm 5—System 14 makes its letter in this manner.

The Spencerian small letter *k* is three spaces high and one space wide. Beginning with a loop of the same dimensions as in the small letter *h*, the straight line is retraced one-half space, and a left curve is carried upward and to the right to a point one space from the crossing of the loop, and one-and-one-fourth space from the base line. This line is united to a descending right curve one-half space in length, including toward the straight line. This short right curve is united angularly with a slanting straight line, which joins at the base line by a lower turn to a right curve, continuing upward one space and completing the letter. The two straight lines should be parallel and one-half space apart.

Analysis: 4, 3, 2, 1, 2

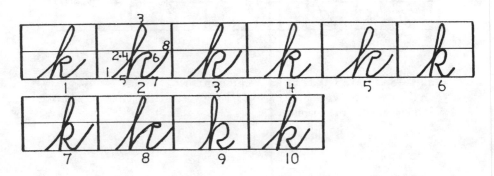

Norm 1—Spencerian and System 10 make their letter in this manner.
Norm 2—Zaner-Bloser, and Systems 13 and 15 make their letter in this manner.

Line 1–2–3	Initial stroke
Line 2–3–4	Loop
Point 2–4	Loop intersection or bottom of loop
Point 3	Top of loop
Line 3–4–5	Staff
Line 5–6–7	Buckle
Point 7	Foot
Line 7–8	Toe

Norm 3—Palmer and System 5 make their letter in this manner.
Norm 4—Bowmar/Noble makes its letter in this manner.
Norm 5—Systems 1, 8, and 18 make their letter in this manner.
Norm 6—System 2 makes its letter in this manner.
Norm 7—System 3 makes its letter in this manner.
Norm 8—Systems 6, 7, 9, 12, and 19 make their letter in this manner.
Norm 9—System 14 makes its letter in this manner.
Norm 10—System 17 makes its letter in this manner.

The Spencerian small letter *l* is three spaces in height and one-half space in width. It is formed by joining to the loop, or fourth element, by a lower turn, a right curve, as in the termination of the small letter *i*. By cutting off the loop, we have remaining all of the *i* except the dot.

Analysis: 4, 2

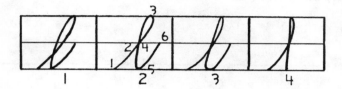

Norm 1—Spencerian and System 17 make their letter in this manner.
Norm 2—Zaner-Bloser, Bowmar/Noble, and Systems 1, 2, 3, 8, 9, 10, 13, 15, and 18 make their letter in this manner.

Line 1–2–3	Initial stroke
Line 2–3–4	Loop
Point 2–4	Loop intersection
Point 3	Top of loop
Line 3–4–5	Staff
Point 5	Foot
Line 5–6	Toe

Norm 3—Palmer, and Systems 5, 6, 12 and 19 make their letter in this manner.
Norm 4—System 14 makes its letter in this manner.

The Spencerian small letter *m* is one space in height and two in width. The left curve begins at the base line, rises one space, and is joined to a descending slanting straight line by an upper turn. The straight line is joined angularly at the base line to a second left curve, which is also joined angularly at the base to a third left curve, which is joined by an upper turn to a third straight line. The latter is joined by a lower turn to a right curve, which rises one space and completes the letter. The three left curves are similar and equidistant and the four turns are uniform.

Analysis: 3, 1, 3, 1, 3, 1, 2

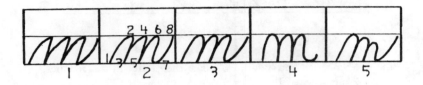

Norm 1—Spencerian makes its letter in this manner.
Norm 2—Zaner-Bloser, Palmer, Bowmar/Noble, and Systems 1, 3, 5, 6, 7, 8, 9, 12, 13, and 17 make their letter in this manner.

Line 1–2	Initial stroke
Line 1–2–3	Forms the first arc
Point 2	Top of first arc
Point 3	First foot
Line 3–4–5	Forms the second arc
Point 4	Top of second arc
Point 5	Second foot
Line 5–6–7	Forms third arc
Point 6	Top of second arc
Point 7	Third foot
Line 7–8	Toe

Norm 3—Systems 2, 10, 18, and 19 make their letter in this manner.
Norm 4—System 14 makes its letter in this manner.
Norm 5—System 15 makes its letter in this manner.

The Spencerian small letter *n* is one space in height and one in width. It is composed of five lines, combined as follows: beginning at the base line with a left curve, it is joined to a slanting straight line by an upper turn. The straight line is united angularly at the base with a second left curve, which is also joined to a slanting straight line by an upper turn. This line is joined to a right curve by a lower turn at its base. The two left curves are similar, the two straight lines parallel, and the three turns are uniform.

Analysis: 3, 1, 3, 1, 2

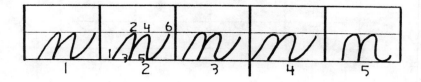

Norm 1—Spencerian makes its letter in this manner.

Norm 2—Zaner-Bloser, Palmer, Bowmar/Noble, and Systems 1, 3, 5, 6, 8, 9, and 13 make their letter in this manner.

Line 1–2	Initial stroke
Line 1–2–3	Forms the first arc
Point 2	Top of the first arc
Point 3	First foot
Line 3–4–5	Forms the second arc
Point 4	Top of the second arc
Point 5	Second foot
Line 5–6	Toe

Norm 3—Systems 2, 10, 15, 17, 18, and 19 make their letter in this manner.

Norm 4—Systems 7 and 12 make their letter in this manner.

Norm 5—System 14 makes its letter in this manner.

The Spencerian small letter *o* is one space high and one-half space wide. A left curve, beginning at the base line, proceeds upward one space on an angle of 34 degrees, joins angularly at the top with a second left curve, which returns to the base line on the regular slant, where it is joined to a right curve. This curve proceeds upward, uniting at the top with the two left curves. The letter is finished with a right curve made horizontally.

Analysis: 3, 3, 2, 2

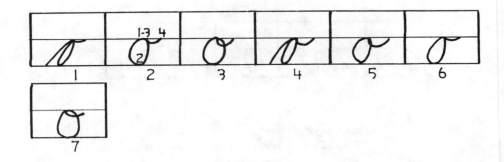

Norm 1—Spencerian and System 6 make their letter in this manner.
Norm 2—Zaner-Bloser, Palmer, and Systems 2, 3, and 13 make their letter in this manner.

Line 1–2	Initial stroke
Point 1	Beginning of oval
Line 1–2–3	Forms the oval
Point 2	Bottom or foot of oval
Point 3	End of loop
Line 3–4	Horizontal bar

Norm 3—Bowmar/Noble makes its letter in this manner.
Norm 4—System 1 makes its letter in this manner.
Norm 5—Systems 5, 7, and 8 make their letter in this manner.
Norm 6—Systems 9, 10, 12, 15, 17, 18, and 19 make their letter in this manner.
Norm 7—System 14 makes its letter in this manner.

The Spencerian small letter *p* is three-and-one-half spaces high and one space wide. A right curve begins at the base line, extends upward two spaces, and joins angularly at the top with a slanting straight line, which descends three-and-one-half spaces, crossing the base line. The line is retraced to the base line, and a left curve, slanting straight line, and a right curve are added of the same form and dimensions as those which compose the second portion of the small letter *n*. The two straight lines are parallel, and on the regular slant. The turns are short and uniform.

Analysis: 2, 1, 3, 1, 2

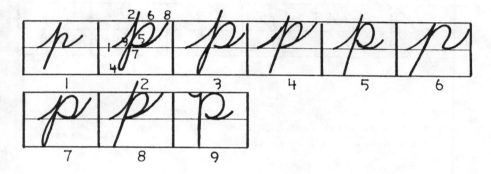

Norm 1—Spencerian makes its letter in this manner.

Norm 2—Zaner-Bloser, Bowmar/Noble, and Systems 3, 13, 15, and 18 make their letter in this manner.

Line 1–2	Initial stroke
Point 2	Top or point of staff
Line 2–3–4	Staff
Point 4	Bottom of staff
Line 5–6–7	Body
Point 7	Foot
Line 7–8	Toe

Norm 3—Palmer and Systems 5, 6, 8, 9, 17, and 19 make their letter in this manner.

Norm 4—System 1 makes its letter in this manner.

Norm 5—System 2 makes its letter in this manner.

Norm 6—System 7 makes its letter in this manner.

Norm 7—System 10 makes its letter in this manner.

Norm 8—System 12 makes its letter in this manner.

Norm 9—System 14 makes its letter in this manner.

The Spencerian small letter *q* is two-and-one-half spaces long and one space wide. The pointed oval that forms the first part of this letter is like the oval in the small letter *a*. Beginning at the top of this oval, a straight line is drawn on the regular slant, extending one-and-one-half spaces below the base line. A turn is then made to the right, and the letter is finished with a compound curve, rising to its full height. The distance from the top of the oval to the termination of the curved line is one space.

Analysis: 3, 3, 2, 1, 2, 3

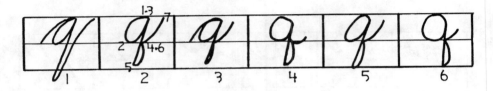

Norm 1—Spencerian makes its letter in this manner.
Norm 2—Zaner-Bloser, Palmer, Bowmar/Noble, and Systems 3, 8, 10, 13, 15, and 18 make their letter in this manner.

Line 1–2–3	Forms the oval
Point 2	Foot or bottom of oval
Line 3–4–5	Staff
Line 5–5–6	Forms the loop
Point 4–6	Forms the loop
Point 6–7	Terminal stroke

Norm 3—System 1 makes its letter in this manner.
Norm 4—Systems 2 and 7 make their letter in this manner.
Norm 5—Systems 5, 6, 9, 12, 17, and 19 make their letter in this manner.
Norm 6—System 14 makes its letter in this manner.

The Spencerian small letter *r* is one-and-one-fourth spaces high and one-half space wide. It begins at the base line with a right curve, extending upward one-and-one-fourth spaces on an angle of 39 degrees. A dot is made at the top of this line, followed by a compound curve one-fourth of a space in length, made on an angle of 85 degrees to the left of perpendicular. This is joined by a short turn, to a slanting straight line, which continues to the base line, where it is joined by a lower turn to a right curve. This curve extends upward one space and completes the letter. The width of the base is one-half space.

Analysis: 2, compound of 3 and 2, 1, 2

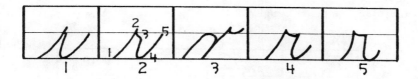

Norm 1—Spencerian makes its letter in this manner.
Norm 2—Zaner-Bloser, Bowmar/Noble, and Systems 1, 3, 5, 7, 8, 10, 12, 13, 15, 17, 18, and 19 make their letter in this manner.

Line 1–2	Initial stroke
Point 2	Tick or top
Line 2–3	Shoulder
Point 3	Angle or shoulder
Line 3–4	Downstroke
Point 4	Foot
Line 4–5	Toe

Norm 3—The "Palmer *r*." Palmer and Systems 6 and 9 make their letter in this manner. This letter is discussed at the end of this chapter.
Norm 4—System 2 makes its letter in this manner.
Norm 5—System 14 makes its letter in this manner.

The Spencerian small letter *s* is one-and-one-fourth spaces in height, and one-half space in width. The first curve, like that in the letter *r*, begins on the base line, and rises on an angle of 39 degrees to the height of the letter. At this point a compound curve unites with it angularly, the first portion being a left, and the second being a right curve. This compound curve, which resembles the capital stem, diverges gradually from the first right curve, for a distance of two-thirds the length of the letter, then turns toward it, and still descending, touches the base line, and rises from this point one-fourth of a space, terminating with a dot on the first curve. From the dot a right curve retraces the last curve to the turn at the base of the letter, and is carried up one space, on a slant of 34 degrees, completing the letter.

Analysis: 2, compound 3 and 2, 2

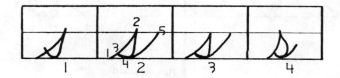

Norm 1—Spencerian makes its letter in this manner.
Norm 2—Zaner-Bloser, Palmer, Bowmar/Noble, and Systems 1, 2, 5, 6, 7, 8, 9, 10, 12, 13, 15, 18, and 19 make their letter in this manner.

Line 1–2	Initial stroke
Point 2	Top of point
Line 2–3	Downstroke
Point 3	Junction of downstroke with initial stroke
Point 4	Foot
Line 4–5	Toe

Norm 3—Systems 3 and 17 make their letter in this manner.
Norm 4—System 14 makes its letter in this manner.

The Spencerian small letter *t* is two spaces high. It begins on the base line with a right curve and rises two spaces. A slanting line retraces the first curve for one space, then separates from it, and continues downward on the regular slant, uniting at the base line by a lower turn to a right curve that extends upward one space. The letter is finished with a right horizontal line, one space in length, drawn across the slanting straight line, one-third of the length of the letter from its top. One-third of this line should be on the left of the slanting straight line and two-thirds on the right.

Analysis: 2, 1, 2, 1

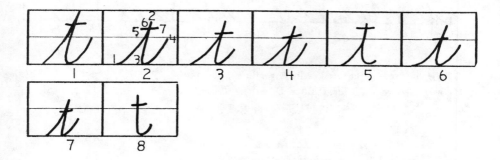

Norm 1—Spencerian makes its letter in this manner.
Norm 2—Zaner-Bloser, Bowmar/Noble, and Systems 3, 12, 13, and 15 make their letter in this manner.

Line 1–2	Initial stroke
Point 2	Top or point
Line 2–3	Staff retraces about one-third of its length
Point 3	Foot
Line 3–4	Toe
Line 5–6	Crossbar
Point 7	Intersection of bar and staff

Norm 3—Palmer and Systems 5, 6, 8, 9, and 17 make their letter in this manner.
Norm 4—Systems 1 and 19 make their letter in this manner.
Norm 5—System 2 makes its letter in this manner.
Norm 6—System 7 makes its letter in this manner.
Norm 7—System 10 and 18 make their letter in this manner.
Norm 8—System 14 makes its letter in this manner.

The Spencerian small letter *u* is the same as a double *i* with the dot omitted. It is one space wide and is the standard of measurement for the width of small letters. The same rules for connecting lines at top, and making turns at base, are to be observed as in the letter *i*. The curves are similar, and equidistant. Straight lines are parallel.

Analysis: 2, 1, 2, 1, 2

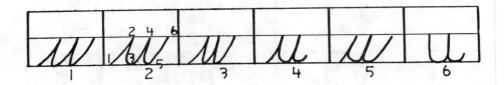

Norm 1—Spencerian makes its letter in this manner.
Norm 2—Zaner-Bloser, Palmer, Bowmar/Noble, and Systems 8, 10, 12, 13, 15, 18, and 19 make their letter in this manner.

Line 1–2	Initial stroke
Point 2	First point or top
Line 2–3	First downstroke
Point 3	First foot
Line 3–4	Second upstroke
Point 4	Second point or top
Line 4–5	Second downstroke
Point 5	Second foot
Line 5–6	Toe

Norm 3—Systems 1 and 5 make their letter in this manner.
Norm 4—System 2 makes its letter in this manner.
Norm 5—Systems 3, 6, 7, 9, and 17 make their letter in this manner.
Norm 6—System 14 makes its letter in this manner.

The Spencerian small letter *v* is one space high and one-half space wide from upper turn to dot. The left curve, upper turn, slanting straight line, lower turn and right curve on an angle of 45 degrees finishing with a dot on a level with the upper turn, and a right curve in a horizontal position, as in the letter *w*, form this letter.

Analysis: 3, 1, 2, 2

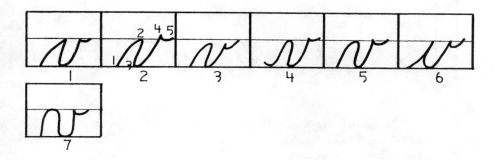

Norm 1—Spencerian makes its letter in this manner.
Norm 2—Zaner-Bloser, Palmer, Bowmar/Noble, and Systems 3, 8, 9, 13, 18, and 19 make their letter in this manner.

Line 1–2	Initial stroke
Line 1–2–3	Forms the arc
Point 2	Top of arc
Line 2–3	First downstroke
Point 3	Foot
Line 3–4	Second upstroke
Line 4–5	Bar

Norm 3—Systems 1, 6, and 12 make their letter in this manner.
Norm 4—Systems 2, 10, 15, and 17 make their letter in this manner.
Norm 5—System 5 makes its letter in this manner.
Norm 6—System 7 makes its letter in this manner.
Norm 7—System 14 makes its letter in this manner.

The Spencerian small letter *w* is one space in height. The first four lines are formed and combined the same as in *u*. A third right curve is then drawn a half-space nearer the straight line than in *u*; then making a slight downward pressure to form a dot, the letter ends with a right curve in a horizontal position, one-half space long.

Analysis: 2, 1, 2, 1, 2, 2

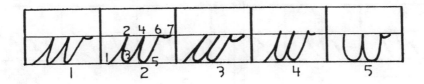

Norm 1—Spencerian and System 6 make their letter in this manner.
Norm 2—Zaner-Bloser, Palmer, and Systems 1, 7, 8, 9, 10, 13, 17, 18, and 19 make their letter in this manner.

Line 1–2	Initial stroke
Point 2	First point or top
Line 2–3	First downstroke
Point 3	First foot
Line 3–4	Second upstroke
Point 4	Second top or point
Line 4–5	Second downstroke
Point 5	Second foot
Line 5–6	Third upstroke
Line 6–7	Bar or terminal

Norm 3—Bowmar/Noble, Systems 3, 5, and 12 make their letter in this manner.
Norm 4—Systems 2 and 15 make their letter in this manner.
Norm 5—System 14 makes its letter in this manner.

The Spencerian small letter *x* is one space in height and one-half space in width. The last three lines in the letter *n* or *m*, the left curve, slanting straight line and right curve, combined by the upper and lower turns, form the main portions of this letter. It is finished with a straight line, beginning on the base line, half way between the left curve and the lower turn, extending upward, crossing the first straight line midway between the upper and lower turns, and extending midway between the upper turn and right curve. This is the only instance in which a straight line is made upward.

Analysis: 3, 1, 2, 1

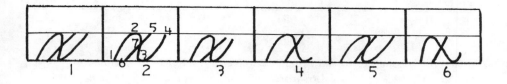

Norm 1—Spencerian makes its letter in this manner.
Norm 2—Zaner-Bloser, Palmer, Bowmar/Noble, and Systems 3, 5, 8, 9, 10, 13, and 18 make their letter in this manner.

Line 1–2	Initial stroke
Line 1–2–3	Arc
Point 2	Top of arc
Line 2–3	First downstroke
Point 3	Foot
Line 3–4	Toe
Line 5–6	Crossbar
Point 7	Intersection of crossbar and downstroke

Norm 3—System 1 makes its letter in this manner.
Norm 4—Systems 2 and 17 make their letter in this manner.
Norm 5—Systems 6, 7, 12, 15, and 19 make their letter in this manner.
Norm 6—System 14 makes its letter in this manner.

The Spencerian small letter *y* is three spaces long and one space wide. It is simply the small letter *h* inverted. The first part is just like the second part of the small letter *n*, and is joined to the downward line of the loop angularly, at the top, which is one space above the base line. The two turns are uniform, and the two straight lines are parallel.

Analysis: 3, 1, 2, 4

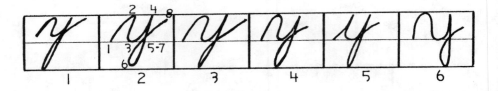

Norm 1—Spencerian and System 12 make their letter in this manner.
Norm 2—Zaner-Bloser, Bowmar/Noble, and Systems 2, 3, 10, 13, and 15 make their letter in this manner.

Line 1–2	Initial stroke
Line 1–2–3	Arc
Point 2	Top of arc
Line 2–3	First downstroke
Point 3	Foot
Line 3–4	Second upstroke
Point 4	Second top or point
Line 4–5–6	Staff
Line 5–6–7	Lower loop
Point 5–7	Loop intersection or top of loop
Point 6	Bottom of loop
Line 7–8	Toe

Norm 3—Palmer and Systems 1, 6, 8, 9, and 19 make their letter in this manner.
Norm 4—Systems 5 and 17 make their letter in this manner.
Norm 5—Systems 7 and 18 make their letter in this manner.
Norm 6—System 14 makes its letter in this manner.

The Spencerian small letter *z* is three spaces long and a half-space wide. The first curve and straight line are like those in the first part of the small letter *n*, and one space in height. A short upper turn is joined angularly to the base of the straight line, and is connected at the base line with a modification of the inverted loop. This modification gives a little more than the ordinary curve to the line that forms the right side of the upper section of the loop.

Analysis: 3, 1, 4

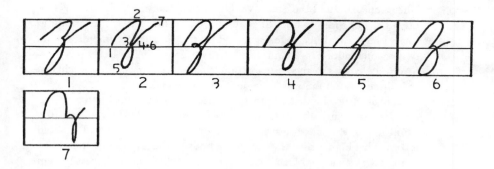

Norm 1—Spencerian and System 12 make their letter in this manner.
Norm 2—Zaner-Bloser, and Systems 2, 3, 13, 15, 18, and 19 make their letter in this manner.

Line 1–2	Initial stroke
Line 1–2–3	Oval (Sometimes more in the form of an arc)
Point 2	Top of oval
Line 2–3	First downstroke
Point 3	Foot. There is a short retrace at this point formed by the first and second downstrokes. Often an eyelet replaces the retrace.
Line 4–5–6	Loop
Point 4–6	Loop intersection or top of loop
Point 5	Bottom of loop
Line 6–7	Toe

Norm 3—Palmer and Systems 9 and 10 make their letter in this manner.
Norm 4—Bowmar/Noble makes its letter in this manner.
Norm 5—Systems 1, 6, 7, and 17 make their letter in this manner.
Norm 6—Systems 5 and 8 make their letter in this manner.
Norm 7—System 14 makes its letter in this manner.

Examination of the Elements

A careful examination of the preceding elements of the capital and small letters discloses several interesting facts:

1. The School Zone System which constructs all its letters exactly like Zaner-Bloser is a subsidiary of Zaner-Bloser. (In 1984, Western Publishing Company published "A Golden Book" of cursive writing. These letters are also the same construction as "Zaner-Bloser.")

2. The Spencerian and the Steck/Vaughn systems are the only systems that use a ratio of three to one: the size of the staff of a letter in relationship to its body. All other systems, including the three most popular, use a two-to-one ratio. The examination of juvenile writing discloses this two-to-one ratio. As the teenager matures, this two-to-one ratio will change to a three-to-one ratio or an even larger difference.

3. The small letter *p* is one letter that does not follow the rules listed earlier in this chapter—particularly the rule "establish individuality by the deviation from the copybook." Most of the systems teach that the top of the staff is somewhat higher than the top of the body of the letter. The true norm written for a small *p* is Norm 7, taught by the McCormick-Mathers System (no. 10). This system teaches that the top of the staff and the top of the body reach the same head line. This is the norm, and the letter which has a higher staff is individual.

4. The small *r* that looks a little like the letter *v* has been for years called the "Palmer r." It was interesting to note that the Kelly & Morris and Locker systems also teach the "Palmer r."

5. The "French a" (small letter *a*, Norm 5) was the subject of a paper by F. Harley Norwitch in 1981.[10] Mr. Norwitch (Metro Dade Police Department, Miami, Florida) examined a routine document case and observed a peculiar lower-case cursive *a*. The letter is constructed with the initial stroke as a right curve in place of the normal left curve. The right curve continues to the top of the body, then curves to the base line with a left curve (the first loop appears like an open *e*). After the loop is formed, the stroke continues as a retrace of the initial stroke to the top of the letter. At the top, the letter is finished with a normal terminal stroke to the base line. The seemingly unique construction of this letter *a* would have normally indicated that it was an individual characteristic. However, within the next few days, the same type of letter *a* by another writer was observed. In both instances, the persons who made the letter were French-speaking Haitians, so it then was referred to as the "Haitian a." I received a copy of Norwitch's paper and while conducting an examination in a credit card case, I saw the same letter *a* in the writing of the victim. The victim was contacted, and it was learned that he was a forty-one-year-old Egyptian

who had been educated for three years in a French college in Cairo, Egypt. He stated that throughout the Middle East, the French influence is found in Arabic writing. The French use a rounded letter form, such as that found in the letter *a*. The "French a" is, therefore, considered a class characteristic.

6. The "Greek e" (small letter *e*, Norm 5) is another letter of interest. This letter, which looks like a capital *E*, is not taught in the twenty systems of the United States. It is estimated that 12 percent of the English vocabulary is of Greek origin. The "Greek e" is one of these letters of Greek origin.

7. There are also two letters that are phenomenons, in that they are not taught in any known penmanship system. These are the capital letters *J* (capital letter *J*, Norm 6) and *W* (capital letter *W*, Norm 11). Both letters are found frequently, mostly in writing by male blacks from the South.

The capital *J* has an unusual construction in that its lower loop is made before its upper loop. The *J* can possibly be explained by the fact that a person may write a small *j*, and then add the extra loop to make it a capital. However, it is still not known why it is prevalently used by southern Blacks.

The deviation in the capital *W* lies in its initial downstroke resembling the number "3." Handwriting examiners have observed this unusual construction also in the writing of southern Blacks. Examiners have investigated schools in the South, including the old black schools, and found that the letters were never taught in any of the southern schools nor are they taught in any known system in the United States. Over the years there have been several theories on why the letters are written primarily by southern Blacks. A few theories are as follows:

a. A resemblance to the introductory stroke of the *W* can be seen in the Spencerian initial stroke, suggesting that the *W* is perhaps a derivative of the Spencerian *W*. This is a possibility, but does not explain why this *W* initial stroke is not seen in the capital letters *U, V,* and *Y*, which all share this same initial stroke in the Spencerian system.

b. One youth stated he learned to write a capital *H* by copying the signature "John Hancock" on the Declaration of Independence. Important documents were therefore examined, such as the Declaration of Independence and the Emancipation Proclamation, and the *W* was not there.

c. The possibility was suggested that the letter was perhaps copied from the handwriting of a prominent black. The handwriting of George Washington Carver, Martin Luther King, Jr., Booker T. Washington, and others were examined, but the unusual *W* was not found.

d. Symbols, signs, and signets of all types were also examined, including cattle brands, heraldry signets, signs of astronomers and symbols of gods. Nothing examined has turned up an answer to this problem.

e. Another theory suggests that if the letter is not learned in the school system, it must be learned at home, being passed down from father, grandfather, or another relative to a son. This is the way that Alex Haley (author of *Roots*) learned of his family history and of his ancestor, Kunta Kinte. Haley was educated in Henning, Tennessee, and his parents were both teachers. Asked if he knew anything about the origin of the peculiar *W*, Haley wrote, "I wish I could shed some light on an origin of that *W* with the '3' beginning, but I'm afraid I can't. It intrigues me, and I've shared your letter with a couple of very well known Black historians, who don't have anything helpful either. So, as you say, it must be simply historical." We have named the unusual *J* the "Kinte J" and the *W* the "Kinte W," after Kunta Kinte, the ancestor so graphically portrayed by Alex Haley in his book *Roots*.

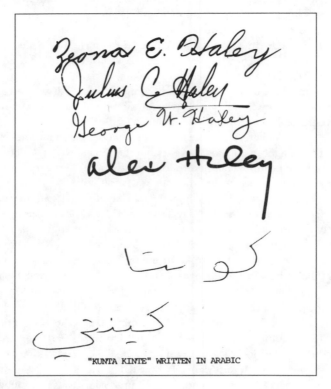

"KUNTA KINTE" WRITTEN IN ARABIC

Figure 5-4. Alex Haley family roots.

—6—

Exemplars

T his is the most important chapter in this book. Students and examiners alike should study and restudy it. The exemplar chapter in every handwriting book should be thoroughly read and digested. Without exemplars, the examiner cannot form an opinion. But most important is the *type* of exemplar that should be obtained. This is the key to the solution of any questioned handwriting problem.

Handwriting exemplars are the "known" writing of an individual. They may be letters written to a person, requested writing obtained by a law enforcement department, or anything in between. Prior to 1913, request exemplars, or even writing not related to the court case, could not be introduced into court. Handwriting examiners were allowed to use only the documents that were part of the case on trial to form their opinion. This changed when Congress enacted the Statute of 1913, Chapter 19, which states:

> Be it enacted by the Senate and House of Representatives of the United States of America in Congress assembled, that in any proceedings before a court or judicial officer of the United States where the genuineness of the handwriting of any person may be involved, any admitted or proved handwriting of such person shall be competent evidence as a basis for comparison by witnesses, or by the jury, court or officer conducting such proceeding, to prove or disprove such genuineness.

In approving this statute, Congress gave the green light to handwriting comparison with the obtaining of a proper exemplar.

Thus, the exemplar is the one most important link in the chain of identifying and solving any handwriting problem, whether it is an anonymous letter, extortion note, bookmaking betting marker, narcotics prescription, altered accounting record, forged will and deed, or forged and anonymous check.

Chapter 6

The Importance of Handwriting Exemplars

The important key to the solution of all questioned handwriting is *sufficient, suitable handwriting exemplars*. Handwriting exemplars are the *known* handwriting of a person, and *must be so proved, conclusively,* in court, or they will not be admitted into evidence. Without exemplars there is no case, from a handwriting standpoint. There are exceptions, but as a rule, a witness *must* be present in court to testify to the authorship of the exemplar *before* it may be admitted into evidence and used in comparison with the questioned handwriting to identify the writer of an unknown document. Comparing unknown handwriting with known handwriting can determine if sufficient elements and characteristics are present in both writings to base an opinion on.

Handwriting exemplars should re-create, as exactly as possible, the questioned document with which they are to be compared. The object of handwriting exemplars is to illustrate fairly and completely the writer's characteristics and elements of handwriting in creating the type of document in question. Only complete, accurate exemplars will give you the basis for a reliable and sound conclusion. Incomplete exemplars not only preclude conclusion, but also may result in an inconclusive opinion that may lead to errors. The procurement of handwriting exemplars may be a hit-or-miss procedure if performed by someone unaware of this evidence's grave importance. Many exemplars are obtained as routine investigation, rather than as an afterthought after examining the questioned writing in which compiled representative exemplars are then compared with it.

If one were to seek a suspect, one would not initiate a manhunt without a description of the person sought including probable attire, any probable disguise, known peculiarities, or everything else of identifying significance. All of the identifying elements and characteristics of the individual would be studied *before the search commenced*. It would be considered inefficient and downright foolish for one to seek a suspect without some idea of what the person looked like. Handwriting exemplars present an analogous problem and one which has even greater tangibility.

The first rule when procuring proper handwriting exemplars is: *Study the questioned document*. The handwriting exemplars must be obtained in light of the handwriting in question. In every case, make an examination of the questioned handwriting, listing its identifying elements and characteristics. Keep these elements constantly in mind in your search for exemplars. You are not seeking just *any* handwriting. Your object is to develop exemplars which fairly and completely illustrate the subject's handwriting in the creation of the same type of document that you have under investigation. Only such writing will reveal the truth of the matter and perhaps the innocence of the subject.

There are two general classes of handwriting exemplars. The first includes writings prepared in the course of daily personal affairs or business. These are "Informal Exemplars" or "Unconsciously Written Handwriting." The second consists of those writings which are prepared in the course of the investigative interview, in the presence of the investigator and on request, referred to as "Request Exemplars," "Normal Consciously Written Handwriting," or "Consciously Written Disguised Writing." The relative value of informal exemplars and request exemplars should be recognized, and it should be understood by everyone how each of these general classes of exemplars can be utilized most effectively.

Personal writing habits are the basis upon which handwriting identifications are made. These habits are the result of penmanship schooling, handwriting usage, and handwriting experience. In most adults, habits are developed through constant repetition until they become automatic. They are essentially automatic, or unconscious, and are more manual than mental. They are produced outside the conscious concentration of the individual. Ordinarily, one does not have to concentrate on handwriting—one just writes. When one writes informally in the normal course of business and in personal affairs, one has no motive to disturb usual writing habits. One has no reason to distort or disguise this ordinary and routine expression of one's personality, so one writes in a habitual manner. One is not self-conscious or under any mental strain, nor is one trying to deceive anybody. One is neither nervous nor afraid, and thus does not resent normal writing.

It should be apparent that informal, course of business exemplars are inherently more personal and more natural, and thus are apt to embody the writer's true unvarnished and unembellished habits and characteristics. This is important, and if we proceed with this understanding that normal, free, day-to-day writing is more apt to be a true expression of the writer's habits, we are on solid ground.

Request exemplars, on the other hand, are prepared within the law enforcement atmosphere. The writer is usually under some suspicion, or at least thinks so regardless of what he or she has been told at the time the specimens are prepared. Whether the writer is guilty or innocent, deceptive or just plain scared, cooperative or antagonistic, clever or stupid, first offender or an old customer, his or her attention is directed to the act of writing. Therefore, self-consciousness, nervousness, intentional disguise, mental stress, fear, and other like factors must be carefully considered and recognized when interpreting the habits and characteristics of request exemplars. Request exemplars are not free, easy, day-to-day writings: rather, they are writings done consciously for a particular purpose. The purpose, many times, is to "hook the guy" that is doing the writing, so of course the person is thinking about what he or she is doing. The mental attitudes and mental ability of some writers enable them to disturb or even alter their normal and true habits when they're preparing request exemplars. Do not underestimate these writers—particularly the more skilled forgers. They are good and may be able to write for some time without showing their normal habits. This makes it difficult to identify their writing from a request sample. Don't take this to mean that request exemplars are not valuable, for they are. There is always a place, an important place, for this second team. However, you may well find that you have been ignoring the "first team"—those informal, normal course-of-business writings—and have been attempting to rely exclusively on the request exemplars. They are good substitutes, but they are only substitutes.

Many handwriting cases fall short of solution due to exemplars. Still more cases necessitate torturous and protracted examinations in the laboratory that still produce borderline conclusions because of the unavailability of the informal, normal, course-of-business exemplars. It is these cases that give document examiners grey hair, as request exemplars may produce inconclusive, and even conflictive, handwriting opinions.

When reading handwriting books on exemplars, I have observed page after page devoted to how exemplars should be obtained during the investigative interview. Little or nothing is said, however, about the greater intrinsic value of normal course-of-business writings. (This one point is especially noticeable in check cases.) So much attention has been devoted to the mechanics of request examplars that the fundamentals of handwriting exemplars as a whole have at times been submerged and neglected. Any investigator who has gotten into the request writing routine for too long may easily come to an improper understanding. To pin-point the principle involved, and one that is analogous, reference to verbal statements may be made. Let us not think of them as handwriting exemplars, but rather as "oral exemplars." Certainly, statements made by the accused to sympathetic family, friends, girlfriend, boyfriend, or mother, completely removed from the law enforcement atmosphere, would be liable to elicit truthful data. A subject reacts characteristically when talking to friends, family, and mother. They know the suspect well and could not readily be deceived in any event. The suspect's statements made prior to accusation, would, of course, be augmentative to prosecution or release. Handwriting exemplars present similar considerations. When writing in the normal flow of daily affairs, under no possible aura of deception or unreliability, they are clearly of great value in isolating the author's true, normal writing habits. I have referred to two general classes of exemplars, but there are also subclassifications. But the *first rule* remains, *Study the questioned handwriting,* and investigate its identifying elements and characteristics thoroughly.

In searching the exemplars, it is important to get the proper type of writing. For example, many writers have an informal, free, intimate sort of writing in letters. Then there is another type of writing—the more formal business hand—used in signing special documents or big checks. Finally, there is a careless type of handwriting often used on delivery receipts or for hasty writing, such as scratching out a telegram—quick writing. Some writers have a very formal signature, used on contracts, deeds, or other really important documents. One of the reasons there is so much consternation in some important will cases is that a will is such an important document to many signers that they wind up using special signatures that they have never used before. They may be formal, flowery, and overall quite different in general form from the writing they use everyday. Numbers and accounting entries may also deviate from ordinary writing. Accountants are accustomed to writing in small places on the job, but they may write differently when addressing an envelope. Engineers also sometimes have different styles when making notes on blueprints or plans. Many people handprint upper- and lowercase letters interchangeably. This is because youngsters who are first taught manuscript writing and later learn cursive writing may carry over a combination of styles, using one for one purpose and another for another purpose, and sometimes mixing the styles.

Some people have special signatures for special occasions, for example, movie stars when signing autographs. They may concoct a scrawl that will differ from the signature they place on a check. Therefore, you must consider the class of writing that confronts you on the questioned document. *That is the key,* and it can't be avoided. When you search for handwriting exemplars, remember you are not looking for just any writing, but for the same as that in question. If printed letters only are found on the questioned documents, don't obtain script writing exemplars. Here no comparison is possible. Study the questioned writing, then obtain the same type or class of writing in the exemplars. Request the same type of script as well as the same slant. If initials are printed and the rest of the writing is script, obtain printed capitals or initials and script writing. Continue requesting exemplars until you obtain satisfactory and sufficient exemplars. This is not to say that there is no relationship between a subject's various styles of writing—of course there is. He or she has only one brain, and it directs the hand even when the eyes are closed, or even when the person is drunk. Many subjects say, "I've forgotten how to make a letter Q," but after a short period of recall they are able to form one.

To get back to the rule: first study the questioned writing. In a check case, isolate identifying elements before running around the country looking for exemplars. Don't look for just any exemplars, but exemplars that relate to checks. Note the identifying elements: first, you are dealing with a check, not a telegram, letter, or delivery receipt. Concentrate on checks to fix your thoughts on *How the suspect writes a check.* A look at a check will show you that it is written, not printed. Hence, this case is concerned with script writing, not printing. Think about the characteristics of the check. Note the date and how the dollar amount of the check is made. Notice also the actual placement of the words on the check. The Bradford System of check classification has grouped all the factors of check writing. Each method of making the date is separated from the others. Further subdividing places similar methods of writing the dollar amount together, and separates them from all other methods. Handwriting on previously written checks is photographed and then classified in a file which falls into the category of the informal exemplar of unconsciously written or consciously disguised checks. The previousl written checks in the file are good standards of the method used by the check writer. Notice how easy it is to compare two checks written by the same

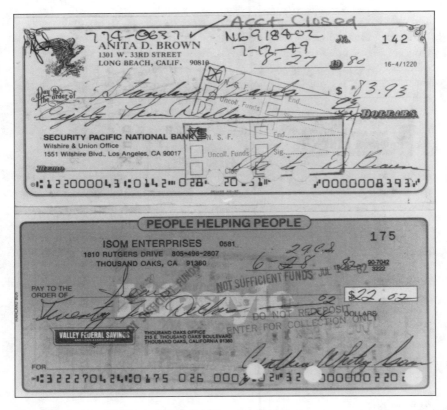

Figure 6–1: Identification of a check with a check exemplar.

person. One should have no difficulty in concluding that the same person wrote both checks.

When you compare a check with handwriting exemplars, however, they do not compare so easily. So, it is necessary to know how the suspect writes checks. Everyone has a set of letter forms, with one or more variations of these forms for each letter, depending on the position of the letter in a word. Forms of the same letter may vary, depending on whether the letter is at the beginning, in the middle, or at the end of a word.

Exemplar checks drawn on the suspect's own bank account about the same time or shortly before the checks in question are good exemplars. These should be checks written in the normal course of business with no motive to disguise and no knowledge at the time the checks written might be used as exemplars. Checks of this sort re-create that which we are investigating. Checks written during a previous check-writing spree, and which are filed away in a classified check file, are as near a re-creation of the questioned material at hand as can be found.

How many exemplars are needed? There is no definite answer to that question. An examiner requires sufficient exemplars to form a definite conclusion or opinion. If an examiner concludes an investigation and still cannot conclude whether the suspect did or did not do it, then the exemplars were inadequate. Some experts will testify "on the fence," although *an identification is not made until it is a definite conclusion*. Handwriting, like everything else, varies with individuality. Individuality is the basis of handwriting identification. If there is distinctive handwriting on a check and it is different or outstanding enough, you may find that a single exemplar check is sufficient for comparison. However, most handwriting experts prefer fifteen to twenty exemplars for use in any comparison. (It would be nice to have a witness who saw the check written, but we cannot have everything.) In a forgery case, especially with a copied signature, more exemplars are required. The act of forgery is considerably less automatic than writing one's own name. For a successful forgery, the signature forged should have the general appearance of the genuine one and little, if any, appearance of the suspect's writing. All outstanding parts of the letters, especially the capital letters and the tails of *y* and *g,* should look like the genuine. All embellishments on capital letters, pickup strokes, and ending strokes will look like the genuine and possibly nothing like the suspect's own writing. However, variation in microscopic parts of the writing can still help you determine the true writer of the signature. To supplement the checks, one may have to rely on request exemplars for the precise work combinations. There is a complementary relationship between the informal request exemplars. They should dovetail together. The examiner may find some things in one and other things in the other. One thing you must learn for sure is whether the request exemplar was purposely disguised and in what way it was changed.

There are various procedures for obtaining request exemplars. First, seat the writer comfortably, and ask him or her to write the material you dictate. *Never* let a subject copy from a master card, especially a card filled out in the same manner as the questioned material. You need to obtain a true sample of the subject's normal handwriting habits, not of just any writing. *Never show the suspect the questioned writing before the exemplars have been completed*. Do not let the suspect control the situation; you must maintain control. Schedule the writing at several intervals throughout the interview, and, while the suspect is writing, keep him moving at the speed you desire, either slow or fast. Supply the subject with the same type of writing instrument used on the questioned material, as well as the same size and texture of paper. If the case concerns checks, use blank check forms. Since the writing space is the same for the date, name, and amount, this may have a bearing on how large or how small the suspect will write. (Size of writing is one of the disguises used very often.) The subject may write with a cramped style on the face of the check and endorse in a flowing free hand.

Dictate the material to be written. *Never show the check and never show how to make out a check. Do not spell words for a suspect.* I have seen many exemplars with the words "Print the alphabet" printed across the space on the card for the printed alphabet, and the words "Write the alphabet" written across the space for the written alphabet. This shows poor supervision in obtaining exemplars. Also, when exemplars are not carefully supervised, a *foreign hand* may show up on a suspect's exemplar card. We have seen several persons' exemplar cards filled out by one obliging prisoner, intentionally or otherwise. Suspects asked other prisoners to fill out their exemplar cards for them because, they said, they could not write so good.

Number and date each of the exemplar cards and specimens of writing, and then sign them *as a witness to the writing.* You will need this information if the exemplars are used in court, and it assists the examiner when testifying. If the subject was directed to write with the opposite hand, note that on the card, or, if the subject is cooperative, ask him or her to write, "This is a sample of my left-hand writing." If any unusual writing position is used, note that on the card.

Usually, the best sources of handwriting to compare with endorsements on stolen checks are cancelled payroll checks from a previous employer when available. In addition to the writing, the placement of the name, address, and city have identifying characteristics. Everyone has his or her characteristic way of endorsing a check. Some indent the address, while others write block form. Look for employment applications, fraternal records, government records, union records, and so on. The potential list is long. Don't overlook papers and cards found on the suspect at the time of arrest. Do not say, "Did you write this?" but, "What didn't you write on this sheet?" It takes time to dig up good exemplars, but complete exemplars solve cases.

When you are conducting an interview, do not sit the suspect down and say, "Write John Doe" (the questioned signature). Dictate some other writing first, so you will have a style, and then ask the suspect to write the specific names in the case. With rare exception, there is nothing to be gained by being mysterious. If you are talking to a person and expect to obtain request exemplars, be open. Ask the subject, "Where am I going to get some writing, written before this incident?" Say, "You produce the writing; we want only the truth." Many suspects will come up with some writing they will identify as their own writing, so you will not have an admissibility problem later. It follows that if the subject is willing to voluntarily furnish request exemplars, he may also furnish informal exemplars which he wrote before the interview. In addition, you may save yourself a lot of time and effort by endeavoring to develop informal exemplars at the time you interview the suspect for request exemplars. Timing can be as important at this stage as your method of questioning. The use of a straight, casual manner during the interview usually produces good results. The contrary is true of a blundering antagonistic approach. During the interview, casually ask where the subject has worked and how you can get there. You may be able to procure an application containing the subject's informal handwriting from this source. You can also obtain much information directly from the suspect. Many suspects tend to be uncooperative, but if you handle them properly, they can yield a great deal of information at the time of the initial interview.

Disguised handwriting can sometimes be turned to your advantage by a proper interview when you are obtaining request exemplars. Disguise is no problem—*if you recognize it.* If the suspect says, "This is the way I always write," ask him to write that at the bottom of the page and sign his name; or, ask him to write, "This is my normal handwriting and "written freely and voluntarily," to which his name should be signed. Disguised writing may backfire when informal exemplars become available, because these may prove that a suspect has disguised his writing. *In all cases,* the likelihood of a definite handwriting opinion is proportionate to the quality of the exemplars obtained.

Police departments that require every prisoner to fill out a handwriting exemplar card *regardless of the crime,* find these cards to be invaluable later. They often bridge the gap between the informal exemplars and the request exemplars. Because prisoners accept these forms as part of the booking procedure, they tend to write informally, especially if they are arrested for a crime in which handwriting plays no part, and if they are handled correctly. These initial exemplars may show a different set of characteristics than the exemplar filled out when the suspect is subsequently arrested on a check charge or when handwriting is obtained later. Obtain a card every time a subject is arrested. In a recent case, the suspect said he could not print, but a check of his exemplars in the files revealed a card with printing on it. Another case involved a subject who claimed he could not write small; however, an old card of his showed small writing. All of these examplar cards are part of a suspect's variations. If you have only one card, *you have only one style.* By itself, it could lead to an incorrect interpretation. There is no knowing how much a person can vary his handwriting. In one case, two different interviews on the same day produced two entirely different exemplars of handwriting. The point is, with only one of these styles, an examiner may have only part of the picture. To make the job easier, the exemplar cards should be standardized. If the same information appears at the same place on all cards, you can easily find certain letter combinations without hunting through a mass of writing material.

Make a note of anything unusual about the suspect, such as arthritis or a broken finger. Make sure that the witness to the handwriting signs the card, because an unwitnessed card can spoil the evidence.

The preceding paragraphs stress that without handwriting exemplars, there can be no handwriting examination. Without proper exemplars, the examination will be very difficult, and inconclusive opinions may result. Every time you approach a new case, you must decide what kind of exemplars will be needed for comparison with the questioned material. You must examine the questioned document carefully, and seek exemplars that will match its style. The questioned document and exemplars should also be as close to each other in age as possible.

Types of Handwriting

Normal Unconscious Writing

This type of writing is the spontaneous writing of a person made in the normal course of daily events. This is a very desirable type of writing for an exemplar, since it contains writing in a normal state. When collecting this type of exemplar, be certain to accomplish three things:

1. The exemplars must contain words, letters, and numbers needed to make a comparison.
2. Gather documents dated at approximately the same time as the questioned material.
3. Check that the document is properly witnessed for possible use in court.

Cancelled checks are best for this type of exemplar. Checks written to a market, telephone company, etc., are unconsciously written, and these documents are dated and signed. The face of the check contains a fair amount of written words, letters, and numbers. Other sources of unconscious exemplars are change of address forms and other post office documents; bank information, such as loan applications, deposit slips, etc.; charge invoices; church pledge cards; personal correspondence; diaries; employment writings; insurance applications; library applications; memoranda; motor vehicle registration; notebooks; pawn shop tickets; paychecks (endorsement); personal records (address book); rental application; school records, such as notebook, work pages, or research papers; traffic tickets; union records; and voting registrations.

Normal Conscious Writing, Non-Stress

In this type of writing, a person is making a conscious effort to write to the best of his or her ability, as people do when they sign their marriage certificate, for example. You will need this type of writing for your exemplar, if the questioned writing is on a will or deed.

There are two problems to keep in mind when you are looking for exemplars of this type:

1. Formal writing is usually found on documents that are difficult to obtain, so you may have to work with copies.
2. Some documents may contain only one signature. A major problem in all the "Howard Hughes" cases was sorting out the genuine signatures. Some of these "genuine signatures" turned out to be written by secretaries.

Some of the best exemplars in this area are applications for employment, as a person tries to write his best to impress his employer. Job applications of this

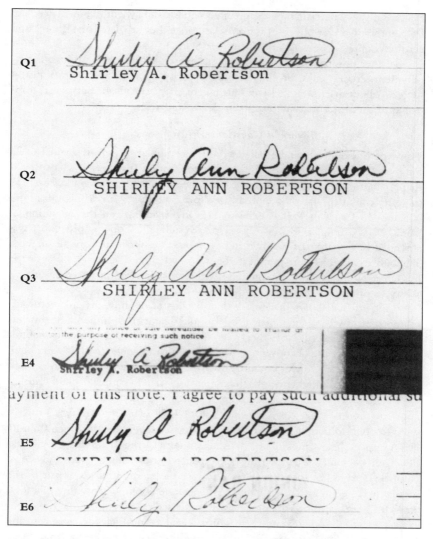

Figure 6–2: Shirley A. Robertson forgery. A case involving signatures on a Quit Claim deed (Q1), Deed of Trust (Q2), and Note Secured by Deed of Trust (Q3) were all questioned. To compare the conscious writing on the documents, a Petition for Amendment (E4), Agreement of Sales (E5), and some personalized checks (E6) were obtained as exemplars. The documents were then placed in order by date and examined. Tremor was found in the word "Shirley," along with missed characteristics that show a retrace at the top of the letter *S* and no loop in the *y*. Obtaining these consciously written exemplars assisted in forming a correct opinion in this case.

type are always dated and signed, and often witnessed. Law enforcement agencies frequently use driver's licenses as exemplars, since they are dated and signed, and certified copies can be obtained from the State.

Other possible sources for conscious exemplars are: applications for employment, credit, loans, or club memberships; autographs; birth certificates of subject's children; contracts; driver's license; marriage certificate; personal records (some of these are unconscious); trust deeds; and wills.

Normal Conscious Writing, Stress

This type of exemplar can be called a request exemplar. A person is asked to fill out an exemplar in order to eliminate or to identify that person as a suspect. Ralph Bradford revised the Long Beach Police handwriting exemplars in 1952 to complement the newly adopted "Bradford System of Check Classification" (chapter 3). Chief of Police William H. Dovey authorized the obtaining of handwriting exemplars from every person arrested. The booking procedure was amended to require that handwriting exemplars be obtained from all subjects. The only exceptions were intoxicated persons, whether due to alcohol or drugs. In such cases, the Jail Division officers use their own discretion as to the subject's ability to submit an exemplar.

Experience shows that fewer than 5 percent of those arrested refuse to submit a handwriting exemplar. Forgery investigators have noted that suspects in custody for forgery, NSF checks, credit card frauds, etc., frequently submit exemplars of disguised handwriting to the investigating detectives. If you obtain the exemplar at the time of booking, however, the suspect may be more relaxed and more likely to submit a normal unconsciously written sample of handwriting.[1]

This type of exemplar played an important part in a case submitted to the Supreme Court—*Gilbert v. California*, 288 U.S. 293 (1967). This was a case in which a police officer was killed during an armed robbery in Alhambra, California. A suspect, Jesse James Gilbert, was subsequently arrested in Philadelphia, and FBI agents obtained a handwriting exemplar without Gilbert having advice of counsel. During the trial, Bradford introduced a handwriting exemplar of the suspect obtained in Long Beach during the routine booking procedure of a 1960 arrest for burglary. Since the officer who witnessed this exemplar was no longer available to testify, the exemplar was introduced as an official document of the Long Beach Police Department, and Mr. Bradford testified as custodian of those records. The case was appealed to the Supreme Court on the grounds that the FBI obtained the exemplar illegally. The conviction, however, was upheld by the Supreme Court on July 12, 1967.

Types of Exemplars

The handwriting exemplar illustrated in figure 6–5, used by the Long Beach (California) Police Department, was designed with two purposes in mind. The first was to make it such a simple exemplar that the suspect can fill it out with

Figure 6–3: Lt. G. W. Workman (left) obtains an exemplar at a special shelf, with a ball point pen on a chain, in the booking area.

Figure 6–4: Detective Barbara Summers searches the Long Beach Police Department files of 112,000 exemplars.

little outside help. Since the intention is that every arrestee submit an exemplar, speed and ease of completion are pertinent factors. The second purpose was to make sure the exemplar meets the needs of the examiner. Since printing is found on a number of suspect documents, the upper half of the Long Beach exemplar is printed. The lower half contains items suitable for comparison with endorsements on checks, forged drug prescriptions, bookmaking cases, and so on. These consist of names, street, city and state address, and numbers. To expedite the examination of handwriting on checks, space for the months of the year, written

LAST NAME FIRST	OFFENSE	BN	RACE	SEX

LONG BEACH POLICE DEPARTMENT

PRINT   DR_____

Name _____ Address _____

City_____ State _____ _____

Date of Birth_____ Place of Birth_____

Occupation_____ Employer _____

Hair_____Eyes _____ Comp._____ Hgt._____Wt._____

Father's Name _____ Address _____

A	B	C	D	E	F	G	H	I	J	K	L	M	N	O	P	Q	R	S	T	U	V	W	X	Y	Z

a	b	c	d	e	f	g	h	i	j	k	l	m	n	o	p	q	r	s	t	u	v	w	x	y	z

WRITE - DO NOT PRINT

Art	Bob	Charles	Don	Edward	Frank	Gus	Henry	Imig
Joe	Kenneth	Lamb	Mary	Nan	Olson	Paul	Quentin	Ray
Sam	Tom	Unthank	Verne	Will	Xavier	Yolanda	Zomora	
Long Beach, Calif.			L. A., California			Anaheim, Calif.		
125½ N. East Ave.			346½ S. West Blvd.			7890 E. North Place		
901 1/3 W. South Pl.			3434 No. 1st. St.			5665 So. 2nd Street		
8796 3rd Ave. West			65½ 4th Blvd. SW			89¼ No. 5th St.		

PD-3134.001 (9/73)

Figure 6–5: Long Beach Police Department handwriting exemplar.

amounts, and even a sample check, appear on the reverse side of the exemplar. One column on the reverse is left blank to permit the accused to submit any special request writing. There is also a place for the right thumbprint of the person submitting the exemplar. Thus, if the witnessing officer is no longer available for testimony, or if there is any doubt as to who submitted the exemplar, the thumbprint can be compared. The document is completed by the witness's signature.

The Long Beach handwriting exemplars are printed on the same $8'' \times 8''$ stock as fingerprint cards and are filed alphabetically in the same type of files. This

---

WRITE the following words: (DO NOT PRINT)

JANUARY	FIVE
FEBRUARY	TEN
MARCH	FIFTEEN
APRIL	TWENTY
MAY	TWENTY-FIVE
JUNE	THIRTY
JULY	FORTY
AUGUST	FIFTY
SEPTEMBER	SIXTY
OCTOBER	SEVENTY
NOVEMBER	EIGHTY
DECEMBER	NINETY
LUCKY'S	ONE HUNDRED
VON'S MARKET	DOLLARS

Fill out the form dated this date, in the amount of $25.46. Payable to yourself and signed by same.

Date _____

_____
Witnessed by   Photo #

SAMPLE ONLY

Bank of America

No. ___

90-1193
1222

Long Beach, Calif. _____ 19 _____

PAY TO THE
ORDER OF _____ $ _____

_____ DOLLARS

RIGHT THUMB

CHICAGO POLICE DEPARTMENT
CRIMINALISTICS DIVISION

LAB NO. _____

NAME _____

R A C S C D N A N S H D R L Y M S L

NAT   S   B   H   W

NAME		DATE
ADDRESS	CITY & STATE	PHONE
MARRIED OR SINGLE	NAME OF SPOUSE	
CITY & STATE OF BIRTH		DATE OF BIRTH
NAME OF PERSON LIVING WITH		RELATIONSHIP
OCCUPATION (IF STUDENT LIST SCHOOL)		SOCIAL SECURITY NUMBER
NAME OF EMPLOYER OR FORMER EMPLOYER		SALARY
ADDRESS OF EMPLOYER		PHONE
NAME OF NEAREST RELATIVE		RELATIONSHIP
ADDRESS OF NEAREST RELATIVE		CITY & STATE

WRITE THE FOLLOWING

ALBERT JOHNSON	DONALD O'CONNOR
EDWARD YOUNGBERG	ROBERT OLSEN
MICHAEL SMITH	PETER FISHER
CHARLES QUINN	JACK KOWALSKI
GEORGE KELLY	U. X. ZIMMERMAN
DAVIES McINTYRE	ELIZABETH VAUGHN
WILLIAM BROWN	FRANKLIN PATRICK
RAYMOND TAYLOR	LAWRENCE HARRISON
THOMAS NOVAK	YOUR SIGNATURE

WRITE THE FOLLOWING

INSTRUCTIONS TO INVESTIGATOR IN OBTAINING REPRESENTATIVE WRITING SPECIMENS: 1. To complete this form, sit the writer at a desk provided with a normal nib fountain pen. Instruct him to answer every question in handwriting or handprinting using no abbreviations. 2. ADDITIONAL STANDARDS should be obtained by duplicating the original paper and writing instrument and dictating, at least 3 times, selected portions of the questioned document without aiding in spelling or punctuation. In check cases use voided checks. 3. Also obtain driver's license, identification cards, applications, personal letters, etc. 4. Officer obtaining standards will see that every line is completed and then sign as witness.

WRITE THE FOLLOWING

NAME

DATE

6739 N. FOURTH AVE.   LAKE PARKER, WASHINGTON

4258 S. INDIANA BLVD.   MANCHESTER CITY, VIRGINIA

6125 W. KILPATRICK RD.   BLACK WOODS, NEW JERSEY

8039 E. 47TH ST.   ANDERSON HILL, GEORGIA

| FIFTY | SEVEN | DOLLARS | AND | THIRTY | TWO | CENTS | $ | 57.32 | JUNE 24, 1967 | 19___ |
| ONE | HUNDRED | EIGHTY | NINE | DOLLARS | & | NO CENTS | $ | 189.00 | DEC. 30, 1958 | 19___ |

HANDPRINT THE FOLLOWING MESSAGE ABOVE THE WORDS SHOWN

THE   MONEY   IN   DOLLARS   WHICH   DICK   ZASS   RECEIVED   FROM   VIRGINIA

MCLONG   WAS   PLACED   IN   HER   AUTO   WITHOUT   ANY   TROUBLE.   IT   WAS   LAYING

COVERED   BY   A   SLICK   CAPE   AND   WITH   LUCK   WOULD   NEVER   BE   FOUND

BUT   A   PUSSY   JUMPED   ON   THE   SEAT   AND   KILLED   THE   OBNOXIOUS   TRICK.

USE THIS SPACE FOR DICTATED MATERIAL

SIGNATURE   WITNESSED BY

CPD-33.351 (5/71)

Figure 6–6: Chicago Police Department handwriting exemplar, Form 1.

exemplar was designed to obtain unconscious handwriting exemplars from every-one arrested, for possible use in future cases, is also the standard for the current case. It is simple enough to be understood by nearly everyone.

Albert Osborn in his book *Questioned Documents* wrote,

> The selection of the matter to be written is of vital importance. The para-graph below about the "London business," containing only about eighty words, contains all the capital and small letters and figures, and is of a nature that will not be likely to arouse suspicion. If it is written three or four times, once rapidly at the last, it will furnish an excellent basis for comparison. It is nearly always advisable to include some additional matter, as suggested above, that contains words, especially misspelled words, or peculiar letters, in the anonymous writing. The copy of the matter to be written from dictation is as follows: "Our London business is good, but Vienna and Berlin are quiet. Mr. D. Lloyd has gone to Switzerland and I hope for good news. He will be there for a week at 1496 Zermott St. and then goes to Turin and Rome and will join Col. Parry and arrive at Athens, Greece, Nov. 27th or Dec. 2d. Letters should be addressed: King James Blvd. 3580. We expect Chas. E. Fuller Tuesday. Dr. L. McQuaid and Robt. Unger, Esq., left on the 'Y.X.' Express tonight."[2]

While the handwriting obtained from the London business letter may be useful to the handwriting examiner, it leaves much to be desired, as the exact words on the questioned material are not present. Without these exact words, it is (1) difficult to prepare exhibits for court, and (2) much more difficult to make a handwriting comparison. Since two of the most important elements in the comparison of handwriting are proportion and alignment (the relationship of letters to each other and to the base line), the ideal exemplar would contain the exact words appearing in the questioned material. This is the reason for the design of the Long Beach Police exemplar. It provides law enforcement with an all-purpose exemplar.

Other law enforcement departments are using different methods to reduce the stress of filling out an exemplar. Some police agencies disguise their exemplars as personal-information questionnaires that list next of kin, places of employment, schooling, etc. The Chicago Police Department used this method in the upper section of Form 1 of their exemplar (figure 6–6). The completeness, simplicity, and familiarity of this form (compared with business applications) are the qualities that produce valuable comparative material. The names and address with the exemplar were piced to reflect the area. The Chicago Department went one step further; they developed two additional forms to make a three-set exemplar. Their Form 2 contains a check to be filled out and Form 3 is used for dictation.

A unique feature of the Chicago exemplar is that it is printed on an $8^{1}/_{2}$ inch by 11 inch piece of paper. The space in which the suspect writes is slightly under 8 inches by 10 inches, which can be photographed for court. It is also

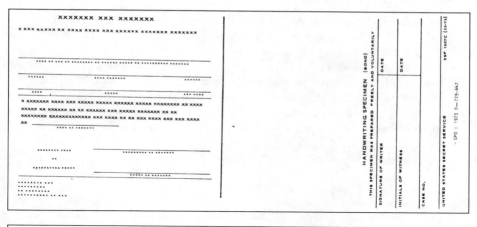

Figure 6–7: United States Secret Service handwriting exemplar.

recommended that the inner lines be printed in a light blue ink so they are deleted when photographed with filters.[3]

The Secret Service handles a large number of cases involving endorsements of forged checks. Therefore, they use, in conjunction with their regular exemplar, one that is the size of a 3½ inch by 8 inch check. They submit several exemplars to the suspect for endorsement that are the same size as the questioned check.

The handwriting examiners from the Dane County Sheriff's Department (Madison, Wisconsin), and the Wisconsin crime laboratory jointly have compiled a handwriting exemplar booklet that they hope will satisfy the requirements of the document examiner for a broad range of cases. The booklet is a self-contained unit, complete with instructions, and has two sections. In the first section, the writer is required to write a specified text. In the second section, the text of the questioned document is dictated to the writer, allowing the investigator to minimize disguise by controlling the rate of dictation.

A handwriting booklet type exemplar is also used by the Bureau of Alcohol, Tobacco, and Firearms (U.S. Treasury Department), the State of California, Bureau of Forensic Services, and other government agencies. The booklet form requires the suspect to write on a page and then turn it over—a good idea in that the suspect must then complete his or her disguised writing, without reference to the writing on the flipped page. The State of California booklet contains nine pages, while the A.T.F. booklet has seventeen pages of writing, and the Wisconsin booklet has twenty-one handwritten pages.

ATF
HANDWRITING
FORM

ATF F 7130.7 (12-77)

HANDWRITING
EXEMPLAR

— WITH INSTRUCTIONS —

Additional copies available from:

Wisconsin Department of Justice
Crime Laboratory Bureau
4706 University Avenue
Madison, Wisconsin 53702
(608) 266-2031

Figure 6–8: Bureau of Alcohol, Tobacco, and Firearms (top) and the Wisconsin Department of Justice handwriting "booklet" exemplar.

Obtaining the Request Exemplar

The proper way to obtain a request exemplar is to first completely examine the questioned document. Ralph Bradford believed that the only way to do this was to *copy* the questioned writing in every detail. He stated, *"before any attempt is made to get exemplars, study the questioned material and be 100 percent familiar with the writing, wording, and contents."* Copy the writing in all details as carefully as possible. If necessary, copy the writing more than once. Look at the microscopic characteristics in the parts of letters. Look at pick-up strokes, embellishments, and the connecting strokes between letters, as well as at ending strokes. Look at the proportion of every small letter in relation to all the other small letters and the capitals. Look for angles in parts of letters. Look for retraced parts of letters. Look for degree of curves in parts of letters. Look for the writer's *ability to control the writing instrument*. Is the writing exceptionally good, average, or poor? Look at the base line of the writing. In short: *know everything possible about the document and writing before beginning the most important part of the entire investigation—obtaining the right kind and sufficient number of exemplars*.

William Shulenberger said, in an article published in the *Identification News*,

> Instructions [to the suspect] should be kept to the minimum necessary to the needed standards. The best way usually is to type out the material to be written. If more specific instructions are later necessary, they should be as nondetailed as feasible, and should proceed to more detailed ones. The actual wording of detailed instructions should be recorded on a separate sheet of paper. . . .[4]

Once you are completely prepared, you should take the subject to a room where you will be assured of privacy. Be sure there is a desk that will allow for comfortable, normal writing. At this point, you should establish some rapport with the subject. Because request exemplars are related to the law-enforcement atmosphere, you should try to neutralize his nervousness and fear. You as investigator must take charge and obtain the exemplars on your terms.

Give the subject a prepared handwriting exemplar form (such as the Long Beach exemplar) to fill out. Supply a writing instrument as similar to that used on the questioned document as possible. If a felt pen was used, get an exemplar with a felt pen. Then get a second with a black ball point. Each exemplar should be filled out with as few instructions as possible. When an exemplar is finished, you in your role of examiner should witness the document with the date, time, place of writing, and your signature.

Next, the exemplar should be removed and you should again establish rapport with your subject. The second document you give the subject should be a lined or unlined piece of paper of the same size as the questioned document. Without ever showing the subject the questioned writing, dictate the complete text of that writing to him or her. During this phase, do not spell any words or give special instructions. Witness this document on the back and then remove it. A third paper, the same as the last, should now be dictated. Instruct the subject to print, write, change slant, write faster, use capital letters, or to duplicate as nearly as possible the questioned document. Again, never spell a word or show the subject how you want the letter written. Watch the subject write. Is he or she following your instructions? It may be necessary to stop the writing several times, in order to get it written according to your instructions. Being in charge of the situation means to control this exemplar and obtain the proper writing. As witness to the exemplar, you should be seated at a comfortable distance, but still be able to see all the writing. After witnessing the document, remove it and take a short break.

The number of exemplars that you obtain depends on how long it takes to re-create the elements that fairly and completely get the "true" writing of the writer. During the break, you can make a quick examination of the documents and determine if you are getting the type of writing you are seeking. If not, new instructions can be given to complete the exemplars. If, in witnessing the exemplars, you indicate the time of writing, it will be easy to determine later in what order you obtained them. Each document should have complete witness information and each must be signed by the suspect.

At the 1977 California Check Investigators Conference it was brought out that a successful technique for obtaining exemplars to be compared with credit card invoices was to use a clip board. The suspect would sit on a chair backward and rest the clip board on the back of the chair when filling out the exemplar. These conditions approximate the true conditions as closely as possible.

Finally, it should be remembered that even request exemplars properly obtained are still only second-best. Unconsciously written exemplars are the best and should be obtained when possible.

Legal Authority

The *Escobedo v. Illinois* 1964 case was the forerunner of many cases regarding the legal authority for obtaining handwriting exemplars. Obtaining of handwriting exemplars without having to advise the subject of any constitutional rights, has been upheld in the Supreme Court (*Gilbert v. California,* 388 U.S. 293 [1967]). In the *Gilbert* case, Justice Brennan delivered the opinion of the Court:

> This case was argued with United States v. Wade, 388 U.S. 218,L ed 2d 1149, 87 S Ct 1926, and presents the same alleged constitutional error in the admission in evidence in court identification there considered. In addition, petitioner alleges constitutional errors in the admission in evidence of testimony of some witnesses that they also identified him at the lineup, in the admission of handwriting exemplars taken from him after his arrest. . . .
>
> We pass the question of waiver since we conclude that the taking of the exemplars violated none of the petitioner's constitutional rights.

(1–3) FIRST. The taking of the exemplars did not violate petitioner's Fifth Amendment privilege against self-incrimination. The privilege reaches only compulsion of "an accused's communications, whatever form they might take, and the compulsion of responses which are also communications, for example, compliance with a subpoena to produce one's papers," and not "compulsion which makes a suspect or accused the source of 'real or physical evidence'. . ." (Schmerber v. California, 384 US 757, 763–764, 16 L ed 2d 908, 916, 86 S Ct 1826). One's voice and handwriting are, of course, means of communication. It by no means follows, however, that every compulsion of an accused to use his voice or write compels a communication within the cover of the privilege. A mere handwriting exemplar, in contrast to the content of what is written, like the voice or body itself, is an identifying physical characteristic outside its protection. (United States v. Wade)

Lewis v. United States 382 F 2nd 817 (1967) was another historic case in which it was stated, "Routine procedures, such as taking photographs, finger-prints, or handwriting exemplars of lawfully arrested suspects, invade no conceivable right that the Mallory Rule was designed to protect."

Two cases of the 1970s further confirmed these decisions:

1. Ringer v. United States, 364 F 2d 1083 (8th Cir 1972). This case established that asking the defendant to write the words that were written on a forged instrument did not require Miranda warnings; it merely provided more reliable physical evidence.
2. State v. Ostrowski, 282 N.E. 2d 359 (Ohio 1972) concluded that a hand-writing exemplar, required for comparison purposes, is outside the scope of the Fifth Amendment privilege against self-incrimination. It is not required that Miranda warnings be given prior to obtaining the exemplars. The standards may contain the same words as those contained in a questioned writing.

In the event the defendant refuses to fill out a handwriting exemplar, the most efficient means to compel the defendant to write is to move for a judicial order at the arraignment. This is usually initiated by an oral motion by the district attorney that the defendant submit to the taking of exemplars at a specific place and time, accompanied by an order that is submitted to the judge for his or her signature. Included in the order is a brief reference to the legal authority on which the order be granted by the judge. This order has been upheld in several cases including:

1. *United States v. Rudy*, 429 F 2d 993 (1970). Rudy was charged with mailing a hand-printed ransom note in a kidnapping case. The government obtained a court order directing Rudy to provide hand-printing exemplars. The court held that hand printing is within the handwriting rule of Gilbert,

and that the suspect could be required to write words printed on a forged document.

2. *United States v. Doe,* 295 F Supp 956 (1968), affirmed 405 F 2d 436 (2d Cir). The witness was held in contempt for his refusal to provide handwriting specimens before the grand jury, and his appeal was denied.

3. *United States v. Mara,* 410 US 19 (1973). The Supreme Court held that "a grand jury subpoena is not a 'seizure' within the meaning of the Fourth Amendment and, further, that the Amendment is not violated by the grand jury directive compelling production of 'physical characteristics' that are constantly exposed to the public."

Finally, if the defendant refuses to comply with the court order, and the trial on the original charge proceeds without the handwriting or hand-printing samples, the prosecutor may comment to the jury on the defendant's refusal to prepare them. Such a comment would be very damaging to the subject's defense. A case in point is *United States v. Izzi,* 427 F 2d 293, cert. denied 90 S Ct 2244 (1970). It is the opinion of Irving R. Kaufman, Circuit Judge, United States Court of Appeals, that:

> Appealing from his conviction of stolen securities, Rudolph Izzi alleges that the introduction of handwriting exemplars executed at the demand of the government, in conjunction with testimony that he had intentionally varied his handwriting, violated his privilege against self-incrimination. . . . The government secured a court order compelling Izzi to provide handwriting exemplars or "standards." It is apparent to the eye that the "R. Randolph" signatures executed by Izzi in compliance with this order in the presence of his counsel are noticeably less fluent than his normal signature . . . he contends that the government improperly emphasized the differences between Izzi's normal signature and the exemplars, intentionally suggesting that he had attempted to disguise his normal handwriting and by so doing had indicated consciousness of guilt. . . .
>
> (1) Under Gilbert, the government may compel the execution of handwriting exemplars and introduce them into evidence in order to determine the authorship of another writing. If Gilbert is not to be rendered meaningless, the government must be allowed to explain differences between the exemplars and the signature sought to be identified, particularly where the defense points to these differences as evidence of noncommon authorship.

Court-Ordered Exemplars

How effective are court-ordered exemplars? First, the exemplars should be obtained in *the same manner as in a normal investigation.* This means that you obtain a couple of exemplars, rest, and then obtain additional exemplars of direct writing. It does not mean the mere obtaining of five signatures on a piece of paper. A complete set of exemplars should be obtained that will show the individual's writing habits and natural variations. The "questioned writing" should be included in the exemplars.

The number one problem with court-ordered exemplars is disguise. Court decisions will place the subject in contempt if he disguises his handwriting. But in such cases, disguise is not easily defined. If the questioned document is written in a very fluent handwriting, and the exemplar was written in his or her "best formal writing," this might tend to exonerate the suspect. Remember, exemplars are conscious writing and are therefore "second choice." As the first paragraph of this chapter stated, handwriting exemplars are the most important link in a handwriting case. But even more important than the exemplar is the *type of exemplar* obtained; this is the key to the solution to the questioned handwriting problem.

— 7 —

Elements of Comparison

This chapter begins the study of the elements of comparison. It is fundamental that we perceive accurately only those things which we are able to describe. For this reason, terminology plays an important role in handwriting comparison, both for identification and for communicating the conclusions reached. Handwriting examination requires careful and systematic examination of all the parts of the sample under study, from the individual characteristics of the paper and pen used, to the smallest characteristic stroke or form.

Identification of handwriting through the study of the elements of comparison is effective because so many handwriting characteristics are unconscious—spacing, beginning strokes, terminal endings, arrangements, and so on. A forger will attempt to copy or disguise obvious characteristics, but fail to change or even to perceive the many individual characteristics of his normal handwriting that he carries over into forgery.

From the step-by-step examination of the twenty basic elements of comparison, a highly individual pattern will emerge revealing the unconscious handwriting characteristics and instinctive choices of the unknown writer. When considered against an exemplar which has been examined in the same detailed way, identical combinations of characteristics become clearly apparent. If not, more exemplar material may help or a reexamination of the elements of comparison for each may be in order. If this still doesn't help, you probably have an exemplar and questioned document that are not written by the same person.

The twenty elements of comparison (not in order of importance) are:

1. Alignment
2. Angles
3. Arrangement
4. Connecting Strokes
5. Curves
6. Form
7. Line Quality
8. Movement
9. Pen Lifts
10. Pick-Up Strokes

246

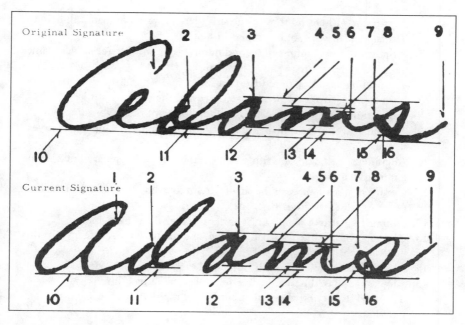

Figure 7–1: Adams identified by elements of comparison.

11. Proportion	16. Spelling
12. Retrace	17. Straight Lines
13. Skill	18. System
14. Slant	19. Terminal Strokes
15. Spacing	20. Trademarks

There are two additional elements that are mentioned in many questioned document books, but because of the use of the ball point pen, the two elements, pen position and instrument, are rarely used.

An example of a handwriting case examined by the elements is the Adams Case. A woman named Adams once wrote and signed a letter to a man stating he was not the father of her child. Twelve years later, she named him as the child's father, denying that she had written or signed the first letter. An examination of the handwriting identified the woman as the writer of the twelve-year-old letter.

Elements of comparison that identified the Adams' writing are:

1. Pick-up stroke. This began on capital *A* with an overhanging curved stroke.
2. Form of small letter *d*. This is open as in a *u* as compared to the closed form of an *o*.
3. Form of small letter *a*. Open as in small letter *u* as compared to closed form of *o*.

4. Alignment. When the tops of the small letters were compared in height, letters *a* and *s* were found similar in height.
5. Proportion. First hump and second hump of the small letter *m* were same height but shorter than the letters *a* and *s*.
6. Connecting stroke. Curved from *m* into *s* and was above the base line.
7. Form. Finish stroke of small letter *s* crossed the pick-up stroke.
8. Proportion. Third hump of *m* was the shorter of first two humps.
9. Terminal stroke. The final stroke of letter *s* ended in a upward curved stroke.
10. Alignment, base line of writing. This is the line or imaginary line that all letters touch.
11. Connecting stroke. From the small letter *d* to *a* did not touch the base line (examine distance from base line).
12. Connecting stroke. Same as 11 except higher from base line.
13. Alignment. Base line for small letter *m,* and the individual base line for the center of the letter.
14. Alignment. Same as 13 with different height.
15. Alignment. Base line of small letter *s* was above base line.
16. Terminal stroke. Final line that cut below the body of the *s* and touches base line.

In addition to comparison characteristics listed above, consideration was given to the ability of the writer and the line quality.

Analysis of Elements

1. Alignment

In determining alignment, imagine that the writing is ruled with a base, head, and top line. The base line is the line on which most of the letters rest. In handwriting, certain letters or strokes are consistently written above or below this line. (The copy book says that all letters shall be written on the base line.) Words that are above the line are sometimes written downhill. Individual letters and connecting strokes are important in your examination of the base line alignment. Look for combinations of letters that show the connecting stroke written above the line. This characteristic is habitual with many writers, and is usually repeated every time this combination of letters occurs. Watch for combinations of letters that have an uneven baseline alignment, where one letter moves to another without the connecting stroke going to the base line. This is also consistent with a writer, especially when in normal memorandum or unconsciously written writing. These same characteristics are found in disguised writing.

In consciously written writing—an attempt to write as well as possible— a writer may try to eliminate this characteristic. There have been many cases in

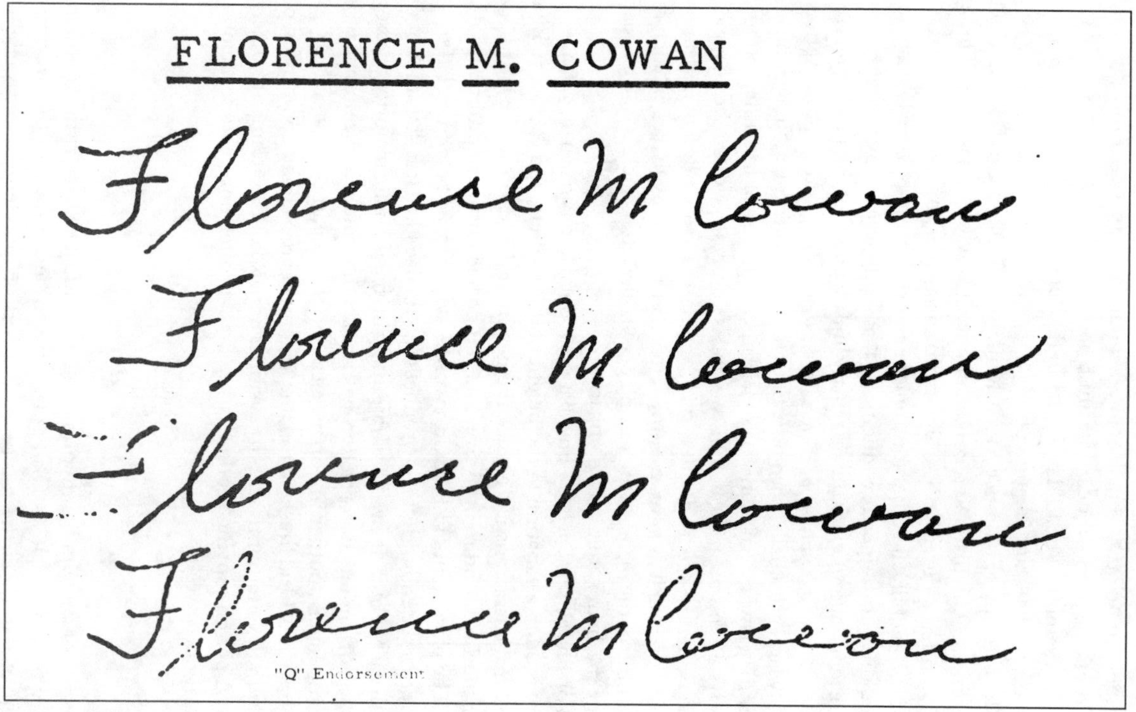

FLORENCE M. COWAN

"Q" Endorsement

Figure 7-2: Cowan base line alignment.

which persons disguised their writing by changing the slant or their capital forms of letters, but still the base line alignment remained the same. You cannot use form of letters when a person disguises or changes his writing. This is because form is seen consciously, but baseline alignment is unconsciously made from habit. Terminal letters on occasion finish above the base line—the body of the small *y*, for example. The fold or eyelet in the center of the small *f* is also a good comparison for base line alignment.

The base line of Florence M. Cowan (figure 7–2) is a good example of base line alignment. The first and second name have a different base line. The letter *w* in Cowan has a different base line from the rest of the name. The base line of the *M* is downhill, and different from the rest of the letters. Base line alignment identified the fourth signature (questioned) as being written by the same person.

Headline alignment is the imaginary line that most of the small letters reach, including *a, c, e, g, i, m, n, o, p, q, r, s, u, v, w, x, y,* and *z*. Some letters are noticeably larger or smaller than other letters. This makes for an uneven headline. A writer may always make his small *r* far larger than any of the other letters, and will always do this even though his writing is consciously disguised. Round-bodied letters, such as *a, b, d, g,* and *o,* will sometimes have a different headline than an angled letter such as *m* or *n*. Some letters get progressively larger, such as the second hump of the *m,* or on the second of two like letters such as *ss*. The headline is one of the better items for comparison.

Top line alignment is the line that the looped letters reach (*b, d, f, h, k, l,* and *t*). There is often a variation in the height of these letters, and each writer has his own habitual characteristics. Notice the height of the letters in the word "will." Usually the *L*s are different in size, and this characteristic is consistent with the writer. The placement of a letter in a word—whether the beginning letter, a median letter, or the ending letter—produces certain size standards that are also consistent with each writer. If a writer is disguising his hand, in the majority of cases, the proportion of combination of letters will remain the same as in the normal writing. So, the top line is another important element of comparison.

The base line, head line, and top line alignment are all good comparison points not only in the attempt to identify writing, but also in the attempt to determine forgery. A person copying another's signature will often not see these unconscious characteristics.

2. Angles

The degree of angle in handwriting is an individual characteristic of writers and will vary from an angle so small as to seem to be a retrace of the previous line (as seen particularly at the top of small letters or loop letters) to a straight line. It is also found between letters in the lower loops, and also in the body of the letters. An angle is formed whenever a line changes direction, whether it is a curved line changing into a straight line, or one straight line going to another

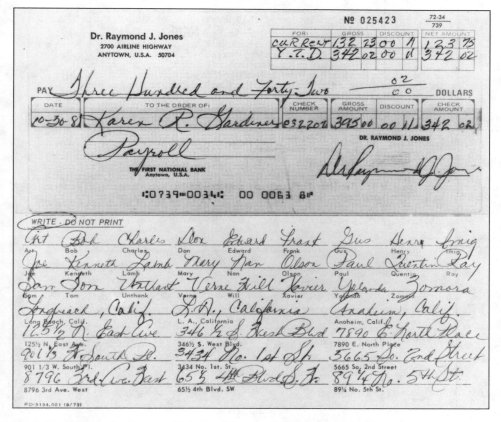

Figure 7–3: Dr. Raymond J. Jones, Anytown U.S.A., sample check.

straight line. Angles may be found after certain letters and not after others; this too is an individual characteristic. Angles may be noted in one or all of the humps of the small letters *m* and *n,* and may be seen in the small letter *h* as well. The Dr. Raymond J. Jones' "sample check" (figure 7–3) that was taken and forged has a sharp angle in the letter *n.* Instead of making a right curve, the letter is made with a left curve. The small *r* has a higher head line alignment and is formed with several angles.

Some persons always make a sharp angle instead of a curve in the connecting stroke after a small *r* or *t.* If a person makes an angled connecting stroke, this characteristic will be consistent with that writer. It should appear every time he or she makes this letter. This characteristic is another element of comparison.

Albert Osborn stated, "The degree of curvature and the slant of connecting strokes is one of the most significant variations in handwriting. Lack of curvature tends to make many angles at tops of small letters, thus making *m* and *n* like *u* and the beginning of *y* and the last of *h* like the small *i*.[1]

3. Arrangement

Another writing habit so deeply ingrained as to be characteristic is arrangement. Writing above or below the line, or indifferently above and below, for example, while not noticeable to the writers themselves, is an unconscious characteristic that persists in disguised handwriting. Margins on the left and right may be wide, normal, or close, but they are consistent.

The spacing between lines can be wide, medium, or narrow and even or uneven. Depth of indentations, and placement of date, signature, names, addresses, city, and state, are also characteristic. Be alert for placement, particularly on the endorsement of checks and on envelopes mailed in anonymous letter cases.

The address on an envelope can be block, staggered, or varied. Watch for instances in which the writer runs out of space, and crowds the last two or three letters or squeezes them together. When writing one's own check signature, the normal writer does not run out of space. Some handwritings, particularly if the writer uses a full arm movement, may run off the paper, but the handwriting will not be crowded.

The arrangement of filling out a check is part of the Bradford System of Check Classification. Arrangement is also an important element in identifying the typist of a typewritten document.

4. Connection

Connecting strokes are characteristically broken before or after certain letters. Some capital letters are always connected to the next letters, while others may never be connected. When they occur, these connections are also characteristically curved, straight, or angular. They may be close, with letters cramped together, average, or widely spaced. The degree of arc or angle will differ with the specific letter being connected, as is seen particularly in small *v* and *w*.

A break between letters, or a "hiatus," is also a handwriting characteristic and frequently occurs between letters such as: *e-g, d-w, w-f, s-t, h-s, n-d*, and the like. Interruptions in the center of long words to cross a *t* or dot an *i* are more frequent. While the *i* is usually dotted and the *t* crossed after the word is written, many writers have a characteristic break for this before completing the word.

Curved or angular connections depend on the construction of the letter. A straight downstroke on a small *l* will produce a sharp angle in the connecting stroke to the next letter. Lee and Abbey's *Classification of Handwriting*[2] lists connections in three classifications: (1) capital connected, (2) capital disconnected, and (3) small letter disconnected.

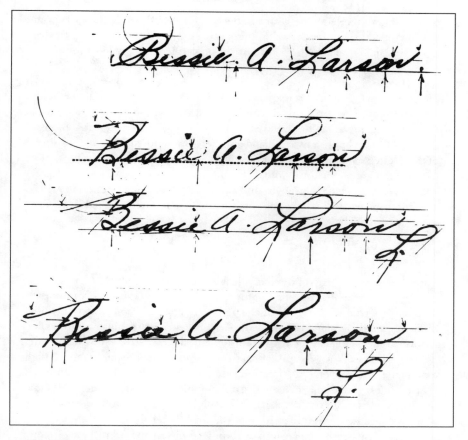

Figure 7–4: Bessie A. Larson forged signature.

5. Curves

Curves are described as "left" curves (the curve found in the left side of a circle), "right" curves (the curve found in the right side of a circle), clockwise curves, inside curves, and outside curves. The degree of arc, or radius of the arc, varies with each letter, and is usually constant in each person's writing. The rule for determining the radius of the arc is to complete the circle which the arc begins.

Curves and arcs are found in the top of small letters, loop letters, connecting strokes, lower loops, bodies of oval letters, parts of capital letters, and pick-up strokes and terminals.

In the case Bessie A. Larson (figure 7–4), curves were important. The upper half of the capital *B* shows different sizes of curves. The curve in the capital *L* is also characteristic. In the top signature (questioned), the *L* is formed with a straight line to the base line with a curve at the base line. A stroke to the right finishes the letter. In the exemplar, the *L* is made with a straight line to the base line, with an angle at the base line. At the angle the stroke then forms a curve to the base line.

The location in a curve where the arc changes is even more important than the curve itself. Examine retrace curves and microscopic parts of letters under magnification. The variations or combinations of curves and angles are crucial identifying factors. Don't overlook the small *e* and *l*, two letters that are looked upon by many as not individual, and are therefore ignored. But, the up-stroke of these letters can be made with a straight line or various degrees of a curve. The letters *e* and *l* are concluded with a straight line down or again various degrees of a curve. At the base line, angles and curves again are made to finish the letter. The curve, angle, and straight line combination is very important in handwriting identification.

6. Form

Form signifies the shape of the individual letters. For example, letter *a* is distinguished from letter *b* by its different form. It is made up of different constituents. The same is true of all letters of the alphabet, small or capital, as well as the numerals, marks of punctuation, and special characteristics. Small *a* is the same in form as small *o* except for a single constituent, the final stroke, in which *a* goes down to the base line whereas *o* final stroke is horizontal. Small *b* is made with exactly the same movements, or writing impulses, as small *f* and could be mistaken for *f* if carelessly written, when the first down stroke is carried considerably below the line. But usually these two letters are easily distinguished from each other by a single constituent, the lower loop in the small letter *f*.

The first step in the analysis of form is to dissect the normal forms (copy book standards) of individual letters into their components, describing and marking each salient feature. The second step is to make an analysis of deviations from the normal forms. This will familiarize you with the terminology and enable you to comprehend and describe the form characteristics which contribute so largely to the individuality of handwriting.

Handwriting may be round, angular, or eyed. Round writing is made with a clockwise overstroke, while eyed writing is made by a counterclockwise understroke. Angular writing is formed by sharp up- and downstrokes. Form is very important, but a letter's form is the easiest copied or changed of all the elements of handwriting. In normal undisguised handwriting, form is quite consistent with most writers. Make a chart of each variation of each letter in order to determine the consistent standard of the individual. This part of the examination should be complete and thorough, so that time will not be wasted in the later examination.

In the examination of any writing, form or other, noting variation is important. The examination of the Robert D. Kelly case (figure 7–5) disclosed individual form and variation. The last two signatures (questioned) show an individual form of the letter *y* in that it has no body. The "no body *y*" can be found in the exemplars with a *y* variation that has a body. Proportion also played an important part in the examination.

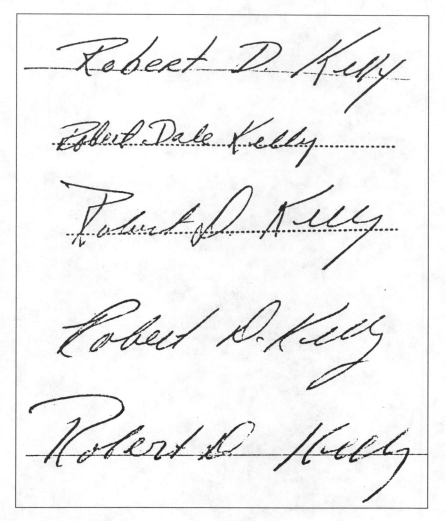

Figure 7–5: Robert D. Kelly form and variations.

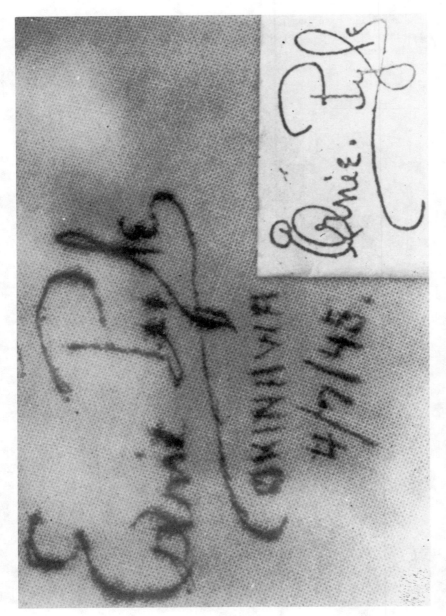

Figure 7–6: Ernie Pyle's signature on a Japanese flag.

7. Line Quality

This element describes the ability of the writer to control the strokes. Line quality is described as: smooth, fast, laborious, slow, weak, rough, jerky, studied, wavy, or even patched writing. Line quality is the quality of the up, down, and forward strokes that constitute letters and figures. Genuine handwriting will be free-flowing writing with some light pressure on the upstroke and heavy pressure on the downstroke (or vice versa). An exception to this may be caused by the document itself. The comparison of Ernie Pyle's signature on a Japanese flag dated eleven days before his death disclosed poor line quality. (Ernie Pyle was a famous World War II correspondent who covered the European and Pacific campaigns and was killed on Okinawa.) In this case, material of the flag may have caused the poor writing quality.

An individual who writes poorly often has a natural tremor in certain strokes, usually the upstrokes, while the downstrokes are smooth. A natural tremor is difficult to simulate or copy. Normally, tremor in writing indicates fraud and identifies the writing as a copy of another's handwriting or signature. Many tests refer to this as the "tremor of fraud."

A low-power microscope or magnifying glass is important in the examination of line quality and patched lines. Old age, and some forms of disease may produce an uncontrollable tremulous line quality. Tremor should be carefully examined as to its location and frequency in horizontal (connecting) strokes, upstrokes, and downstrokes for their intensity.

In genuine tremulous writing, some of the strokes may be free of tremor, while in simulated tremulous writing, the writer often makes the mistake of placing tremor in all lines. It is possible to differentiate between two writers on the basis of tremor alone, but to say that two writings are "identical" because of this characteristic alone would be unjustified.

Another line quality characteristic of some letters is "uncontrolled strokes." These are caused by uncontrollable variation in the writing impulse, which results in sudden changes of direction or spasmodic shading due to irregularity of pressure. This quality has its origin in the nervous, rather than the muscular, system.

8. Movement

There are three distinctly different movements in writing: finger movement, hand movement, and forearm or muscular movement. In finger movement, the thumb, index, and middle fingers are used almost exclusively in the writing of the letters. There is little freedom of movement and frequent shifting of the hand is necessary as the writing goes from left to right across the page. Writing produced by finger movement is characterized by lack of smooth regular lines and usually shows blunt beginnings and endings. It contains numerous broad curves and appears slow and labored.

Hand movement goes a step further and involves the action of the hand as a whole. The fingers play only a minor role, their action being limited mainly to the formation of the small parts of the letters. The wrist serves as the pivot of lateral motion. There is still some restriction, but not as much as in finger movement. Freedom in the long strokes and continuity of motion are not yet possible.

Forearm or muscular movement is produced by movement of both the hand and the arm, and, with some writers, the fingers also. The movement has its origin at the shoulder, and the elbow is the pivot of lateral movement. The arm is supported by resting the forearm on the writing surface. Forearm writing is the ultimate in speed and freedom, as evidenced by this stroke. While it is possible to write by forearm movement alone—without the separate action of the hands and fingers—the most perfect writing is produced by using hands and fingers in the formation of the minute parts of the writing. Muscular or whole-arm writing is distinguished by sharp points at the beginning and ending strokes, as the pen is moving when it touches and leaves the paper.

Lee and Abbey's *Classification of Handwriting*[3] lists movements as Finger, Compound, and Forearm. They also said Finger movement lacks freedom, while Forearm movement shows speed.

9. Pen Lifts

Consistent interruptions of handwriting, or pen lifts, are another unconscious characteristic of handwriting. These can be interruptions to cross a lower *t*, to stop before the small *w* or *v* with their higher pick-up point, or to end a small *y* or *g* with a single downstroke, and so forth. Less evident in copied signatures, although often included, consistent pen lifts are commonly seen in both forged and normal unconscious handwriting. When a person attempts to disguise his or her handwriting, the pen lifts will still remain in the writing, since this is an unconscious characteristic. An example is the forged United States Treasury check bearing the endorsement "Lucy E. Rohwedder." The examined forged endorsement shows pen lifts after the letters *L, h, w, n, w,* and *u.* These same breaks in writing can be seen in the exemplars (2 and 3 signature).

Pen lifts may appear as "breaks" in the writing, or as superimposed strokes, often more clearly seen under magnification. Superimposed strokes following pen lifts commonly are found where the writer "breaks" to cross the small *t,* and the pick-up stroke of the next letter is begun over the terminal stroke of the *t.*

Breaks in long words are common, occurring as the hand is shifted, but are usually not sufficiently frequent in the exemplar to form a basis for comparison. Such breaks are more frequent in finger-controlled handwriting, but they are characterized as that kind of writing rather than as pen lifts.

The "Howard Hughes Mormon Will" was a case in which pen lifts or breaks played an important part. Since Hughes' writing was normally discon-

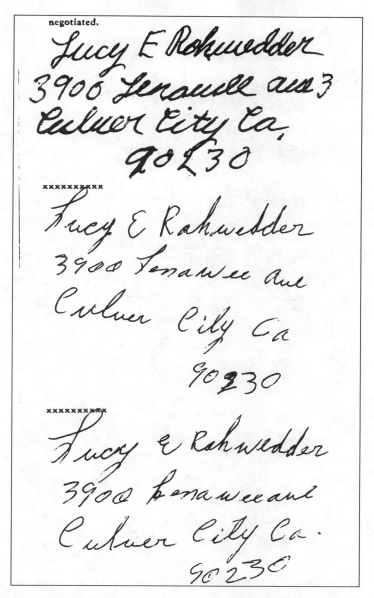

Figure 7–7: Endorsement identified by means of pen lifts.

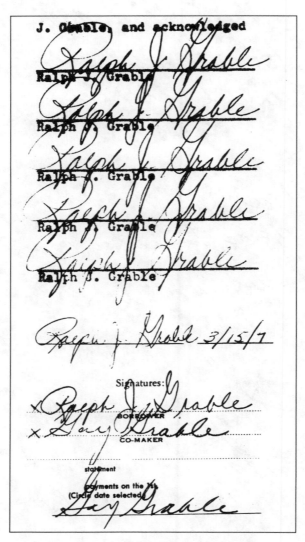

Figure 7–8: Grable identified by pick-up stroke.

nected, the forger in copying the will copied only one or two letters at a time due to the breaks. In fact, one "expert" stated that since it was a three-page will it would be impossible to copy that much writing. Normally, that may be true, but because of Hughes' writing style, the forgers were able to copy a letter at a time and do a job that fooled some experts.

10. Pick-Up Strokes

In normal undisguised handwriting, the pick-up stroke on capital letters and some small letters is so characteristic as to either identify or eliminate a suspect.

Most persons have variations for certain letters that are part of their individuality. Of these, a base line pick-up stroke on capital letters is less common than a 12 o'clock pick-up stroke. The stroke may, however, begin at any position of the clock, and the form of the stroke may be a hook, oval, tick, slight curve, or straight line. Other identifying characteristics are the length of the stroke and the embellishments in the stroke, and whether the beginning of the stroke is blunt or tapered.

Lowercase letters also have varying strokes. For example, a pick-up stroke on the small letter *a*, beginning on the base line, may be a left curve or a right curve. The stroke may be short, or it may begin below the baseline. An absence of pick-up strokes (e.g., on the small letters *i*, *t*, or *y*) is just as important. The unusual pick-up beginning below the base line in the letters *a* and *r* helped identify the two questioned signatures (bottom two are questioned) as being written by the exemplars.

Pick-up stroke characteristics are both habitual and unconscious, making them particularly useful in handwriting comparison. Therefore notes on these stroke characteristics in the questioned writing and comparisons with the same letters in the exemplar writing are very useful.

Also note that the first letter many suspects disguise is the capital letter, which will affect the pick-up. We believe that the pick-up characteristic is consistent and is one of the first characteristics to notice in an attempt to classify handwriting.

11. Proportion

This is one of the more important elements of handwriting comparison. The exact size of basic letters, or parts of letters, is not the important comparison; rather, it is the relative size or proportion of letters to other letters, or parts of letters to other parts, that is of true concern.

An interesting case concerning proportion is the credit-card forgery of the name "Curtis Woods" (figure 7–9). In this case, a variation in the final *s* was characteristic, as it was way out of proportion and very large. Also notable in the writing was the small *i*, which was small in proportion to the other letters.

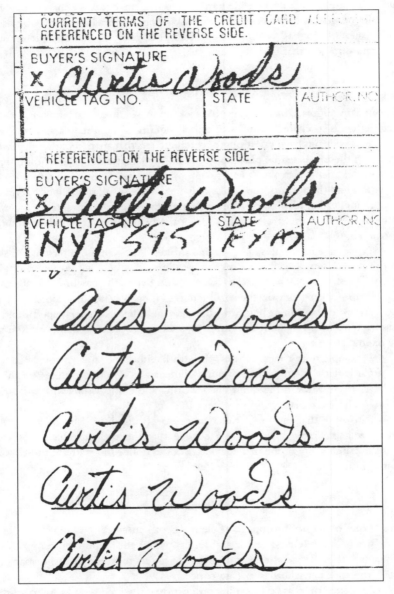

Figure 7–9: Signature forgery identified by proportion.

Proportion is characteristic of a writer even though an attempt is made to disguise the form or slant, or change the size of the writings. Every writer subconsciously and consistently uses a chosen scale of proportion. Proportion may be the width of a letter to the height; the height of small letters relative to capital letters; the body of letters to the upper loops or lower loops (e.g., *h*, *b*, *y*, *g*, *d*, etc.). Examine the small letters to determine average height, then note those letters that are smaller or taller than the average.

Moreover proportion also depends on the location of the letter in a word. In a double *L*, one of the *Ls* is usually shorter than the other; the same often occurs in a double *t*. In a disguised handwriting, many persons change the general size, but the proportion of the letters, being an unconscious habit, is most difficult to change. More specifically, if a person likes long tails on his *y*, a short-tailed *y* will seem not to be a *y* to him.

A letter may be written small or large, narrow or wide, but it is the relationship to the other letters that is most important. In examining a letter, we not only examine the body, but also the loops. Proportion is also important in comparing printing and numbers. Proportion is the most important element in the examination of handwriting and is consistent even in disguised writing. Saudek, in *The Physiology of Writing*,[4] says:

> The standard of large and small writing is, in itself, of very secondary importance. What is very significant is the proportion in size between tall letters and small letters, and what is decisive is not so much the absolute proportion but the degree of variation in this feature of writing, as in all features. The decisive factor is thus the variation which is detected in the same piece of handwriting or in several manuscripts of the same author, in the maintenance of the size between tall letters and middle-sized letters on the one hand, and small letters on the other hand, and between the small letters themselves.

12. Retrace

Retrace is the name given to the superimposed stroke: when an upstroke falls on a downstroke, or when the direction of a stroke is sharply changed. Many letters of the alphabet, both small and capitals, are normally formed with some parts retraced. The failure to retrace, if consistent, becomes an equally significant "retrace" characteristic, and the loops formed are described as "excessive retracing."

Examples of letters in which retrace strokes normally occur are the curve of the small *a* or small *d*, where the top of the oval letter retraces the pick-up stroke. Retraces are also normally seen in the downstroke of the small *h* and the upstroke which begins its hump, as well as in the strokes between the humps of the *m* and *n*. The up-and-down strokes of the small *t* are also more frequently a retrace than are those of the small *l*. This usage is now being recognized in the

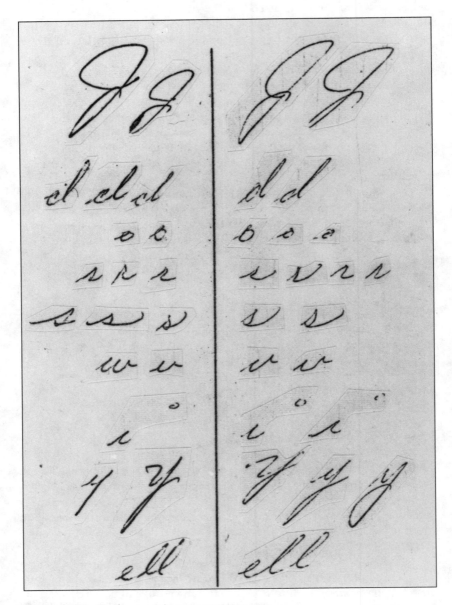

Figure 7–10: Hook retrace in an anonymous note.

teaching of handwriting, and the loop *t* will probably become more infrequent in time, except in instances of excessive retrace.

A retrace stroke may be straight, curved, or partly overlapped, and the amount or length of the retrace is particularly significant. The characteristics of an anonymous note (figure 7–10) point out retrace characteristics. The hook in forming the body of the letter *d* is a retrace. The letter *d* hook retrace is on the top of the body, while an examination of the bottom of the *s* shows a hook retrace from the bottom.

One of the important letters to examine for retrace is the written *y*. The first hump and the second hump of the letter may be open, retraced, or partially retraced, or the two humps may sometimes differ from each other. Also important is the amount of retrace.

The chapter on the Bradford System discussed the case of John "Saw Tooth" Waitkunas. "Saw Tooth" issued more than $150,000 in bad checks and had five distinctive styles of handwriting. However, every *y* he made had a retrace, so the tail came out the bottom of the body of the letter. Although he had written hundreds of checks, all in five different styles, his handwriting exemplars all had that one retrace characteristic.

13. Skill

The legibility and symmetry of handwriting are the indicators of the true ability of the writer. Certain parts of letters signify that the writer is capable of far better writing than the material examined shows.

Although penmanship may range from excellent to just plain terrible, it does not give an accurate account of the writer's ability. Therefore, a person writing illegibly may be capable of excellent penmanship, while a poor writer may write in legible hand. Determine the ability of the writer, not the quality of the writing being examined. All of the elements discussed will help to determine the ability of the writer. Remember, it is possible for a person to write more poorly than he or she is capable of writing, but it is impossible for a person to write better than his or her ability.

Grotesque forms of lettering and poor writing are merely disguises used to hide identity. Microscopic parts of letters show the writer's ability and help to identify writing far better, because these characteristics are subconscious habits, and, therefore, less within the writer's control to change. In disguised writing, the writer may invent new forms, especially in capital letters, never used before and that may never be used again. In these cases it would be impossible to find a duplicate in any amount of the subject's normal exemplar writing. Similarly, if a person were jolted while writing, a characteristic may be created that could never be duplicated. When this problem arises, look for other elements of comparison, ignoring the accidental and foreign characteristics. Consider all of the elements carefully in your examination, and you'll form a quality opinion.

Sufficient exemplar material of the right type is the key to the examination and the eventual solution of the problem. Lee and Abbey's *Classification of Handwriting*[5] lists skill as Poor, Medium, and Good, but also notes that legibility, symmetry, and pictorial aspect of handwriting must be considered.

14. Slant

Lee and Abbey[6] classify slant as: less than 60 degrees, 60 to 80 degrees, or more than 80 degrees above horizontal.

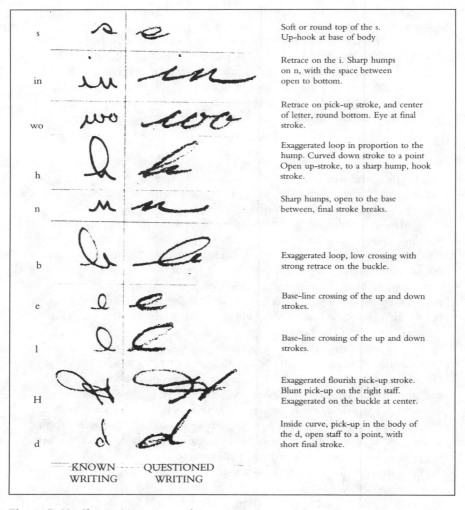

	KNOWN WRITING	QUESTIONED WRITING	
s			Soft or round top of the s. Up-hook at base of body
in			Retrace on the i. Sharp humps on n, with the space between open to bottom.
wo			Retrace on pick-up stroke, and center of letter, round bottom. Eye at final stroke.
h			Exaggerated loop in proportion to the hump. Curved down stroke to a point Open up-stroke, to a sharp hump, hook stroke.
n			Sharp humps, open to the base between, final stroke breaks.
b			Exaggerated loop, low crossing with strong retrace on the buckle.
e			Base-line crossing of the up and down strokes.
l			Base-line crossing of the up and down strokes.
H			Exaggerated flourish pick-up stroke. Blunt pick-up on the right staff. Exaggerated on the buckle at center.
d			Inside curve, pick-up in the body of the d, open staff to a point, with short final stroke.

Figure 7–11: Slant writing compared.

In writing, there are two aspects of slant to be considered: The first is the basic slant of writing in general, which may be a vertical, backhand, or exaggerated right slant. Second, the relationship of the slant of certain letters to other letters in the same word or in different words requires comparison.

Slant varies from 35 degrees above the horizontal on the right, to 80 degrees above the horizontal on the left. (In the Spencerian System, slant was designated at an angle of 52 degrees.) If the slant is noticeably different—for example, between the signature and the endorsement of a forged check—it may have been deliberately changed. If, on the other hand, the examination is of unconsciously written handwriting, slant would be an identifying factor.

Overall, a writing may slant to the right, but certain letters or parts of letters slant backward or to the left. This is characteristic with many writers and is seen in the final *y*, and also in other lower- and upper-loop letters such as *h, l, t,* and *d.*

In disguised handwriting, basic slant is usually the first element to be changed. A disguised request writing survey revealed that: 52 percent of the writers changed the slant of their writing; 8 percent changed the slant of their writing and wrote in a grotesque manner; 18 percent attempted to change the pictorial features and skill of their writing without appreciable change in slant; 15 percent used pen lettering, a third of them writing in the best grotesque blackmail form; 7 percent failed to appreciably disguise their writing.

Inconsistency is the most important indicator of disguised handwriting. Frequent changes in slant, letter forms, spacing, pen pressure, size, and legibility are indicative of the writer's effort to substitute new handwriting characteristics in place of natural writing habits. A suspect, when filling out a disguised handwriting exemplar, will start a line in backhand (left slant writing) and finish the line with right slant writing.

Even when slant is written backhand you can compare it with right slant writing (an attempt should be made to duplicate slant on an exemplar). The comparative slant of the constituent letters will remain constant in respect to each other. The projection of all slanting axis lines to cross other projected lines will form angles which will provide a more accurate comparison than basic slant.

15. *Spacing*

Spacing is another unconscious characteristic element of writing that warrants comparison. Spacing between letter combinations may be noticeably wide or close. The spacing between capital letters and the next letter may be wide or the letters may overlap. Spacing between words, sentences, lines of writing, and wide or narrow margins on the page all have significant value in the comparison, identification, or elimination of suspect writers. Lee and Abbey[7] classify spacing between small letters as small, medium, and great.

16. Spelling

In the examination of handwriting, the misspelling of words may be of great value in identifying a suspect. The most common and consistent variations of misspelling include: "fiftie," "fifity," "fourty," "dollors," and "casheir." In anonymous letters, however, misspelled words are frequently used to ward off suspicion, as are grotesque capital letters. But because these are not habitual to the writer, the misspellings will tend to vary from sample to sample, and even within one sample.

Because spelling is an element of handwriting comparison, it is important to reemphasize that you should *not* spell words for a suspect when you're obtaining a handwriting exemplar. Rather, instruct him to do his best. I find spelling the most difficult element to examine and evaluate. Wilson R. Harrison, in his book *Suspect Documents*,[8] agrees and says, "A great deal of nonsense has been written about spelling mistakes, and they are often made to play far too great a part in court proceedings. They can only be assessed at their true worth as evidence if some thought is given to the matter." Furthermore, names or different words rate less in importance. As Harrison states:

> Spelling mistakes are sometimes found in simple words. These mistakes may be the result of habitual mispronunciation on the part of the writer, or of some personal misapprehension as to how these simple words should be spelled. The significance of such misspelling may be considerable because, unlike the misspelling of difficult words, which is a failing common to the majority of persons, these misspellings of simple words are often personal idiosyncrasies and are likely to be restricted to a very small number of people. For example, if anonymous letters are found to contain consistent misspellings of simple words, this fact should be kept in mind in case other documents of known origin are discovered to contain the same errors. On one occasion, the word "ashamed" was repeatedly spelled "ashaned" throughout a group of anonymous letters, and this curious misspelling was also found in the handwriting of a suspect. This spelling mistake was regarded as being highly significant and an investigation in this direction was suggested. This led to the exposure and conviction of the writer of the anonymous letters.

17. Straight Lines

Because of the difficulty in making straight lines when writing, some writers simply cannot make them. If you are going to cross a *t* you will make a compound curve, deep curve, or tented curve, but rarely a straight line. Straight lines, when located, are good identifying characteristics. They may be identified as pick–up or terminal strokes, the length of and position of, with relationship to the base line, are important and individual.

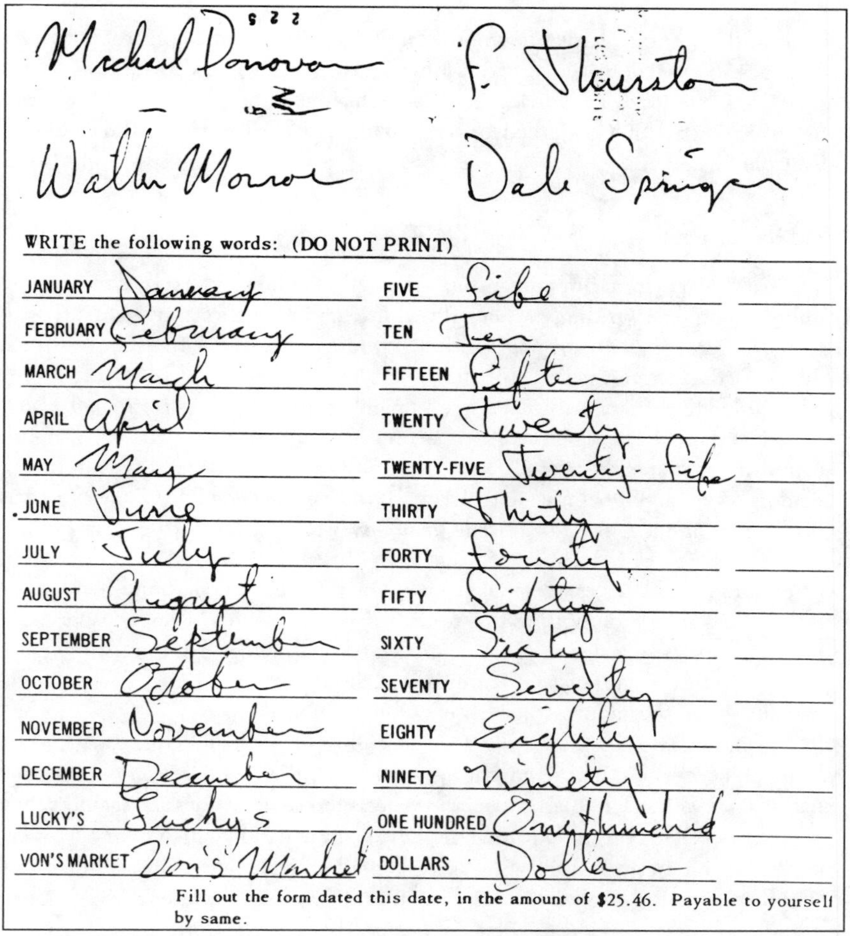

Figure 7–12: Four endorsements identified with straight lines.

Often writers who use a straight pick-up stroke on such letters as *y, d,* or *a,* will cross the letter *x* with a straight line. The staff of the small letter *h* should be examined, as should the tail of the *y,* to determine if they make curved or straight lines. In forged writing, the person unable to make a straight line often shows a curved line, and so offers a characteristic important to the examination.

Many persons believe that straight lines found in loop letters have little value in an examination. However, letters such as *e* and *l* at times do have great individual value. A case in point is the forged endorsements on six commercial checks. (See figure 7–12.) The letter *l* of the forged signature had a curved stroke up as well as a curved stroke down: the letter *t* was of the same construction. The loop of the letter *h* had a curved line up and a straight line down. Also in this same case, the letter *M* is made up of straight lines. Loop letters can therefore be made with either a curved or straight line, with the straight line being a valuable characteristic.

18. System

The particular system of penmanship practiced in childhood exerts considerable influence on later writing, particularly with regard to the form of capital letters. In the different systems of penmanship, a wide variation occurs, and this offers the most distinctive evidence of the system used.

Four distinct systems have been taught in this country: (1) *Round Hand,* introduced in the early nineteenth century, retains some of the old English round-hand characteristics. (2) *Spencerian,* a highly stylized hand with intricate shadings, was taught from 1840 to 1865. (3) *Modern American,* or *Commercial,* was first taught about 1885. (4) *Modern Vertical* was introduced in the year 1900.

A version of Modern Vertical, the A. N. Palmer Method of Penmanship, first published in 1923, is still taught today. The capital letters are quite characteristic in the Palmer method, as are the small letters *r* and *t*. Present systems of penmanship, principally taught in the commercial colleges, are not sufficiently distinctive to offer points of identification, though it may safely be said that all current systems concur in their absence of decoration.

Those who learn to write in a foreign country will often carry over a "foreign accent" in their handwriting. It should be remembered, however, that national (as well as systematic) similarities between two writings are *not* indicative of identity when considered alone; however, these national or systematic differences are significant in indicating *non-identity* between two writings, since few writers possess the versatility to write consistently in two different systems or to assume an aspect foreign to their natural hands. (See chapter 5.)

19. Terminal Strokes

Terminal or ending strokes of letters or words are another writing characteristic. Ending strokes may be upward, downward, or horizontal, as well as convexly curved, spiral, hooked, compoundly curved, straight, or blunt. In addition, they can be a flourished underscoring stroke.

An example of the great variety of terminal strokes is shown in figure 7–13. After the words "for" and "over," the final stroke finishes in an upward position. In the words "be," "me," "Take," and "Tax," the final stroke ends in a horizontal line. And finally, the words "are," "didn't," and "would" all have ending strokes that end downward.

If the final letter is a small *t*, it may end with a bow knot or *t*-crossing without lifting the pen. Another letter subject to variation in the ending stroke is the small letter *y*, where a loop may be replaced by a blunt straight tail ending.

Everyone has his or her own characteristic taste in the use or absence of decorative strokes. As an element of comparison, however, remember that it is apt to be a conscious characteristic and, therefore, the final stroke is subject to change and variation, especially when in disguised, copied, or controlled writing.

Lee and Abbey[9] classify terminal strokes as up, horizontal, and down.

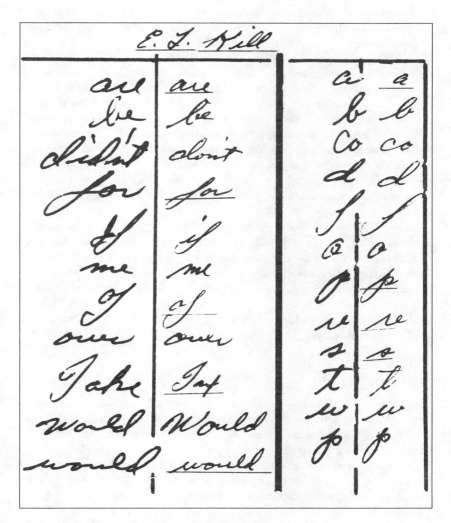

Figure 7–13: Terminal strokes in the anonymous letter.

271

20. Trademarks and Embellishments

A writer's trademarks are the underscoring of a name, a dash after names or words, or marks that are superfluous. These embellishments can be found in the signatures of the famous, such as: Jack Dempsey, former heavyweight champion of the world; and Elvis Presley, legendary performer of rock-and-roll music.

The dot of the *i*, the period, the quotation mark and the manner in which it is used all have identifying characteristics. Similarly, the slash or solidus, dash, or a circle in place of a period are significant in themselves and in the places where the writer uses them, and you should duly note them. Since punctuation shows attention to detail, it is an indication of the writer's education, as is the system of capitalization.

The ampersand, or "and" sign, is one of the most individual and characteristic signs and, in many cases, offers sufficient points of individuality to identify or eliminate a suspect. The flourishes in handwriting may appear on the pick-up strokes, the ending strokes, or in the lower loops (as in the *y* and the *g*), or in the crossing of the *t*. Fancy forms are noticeable and easy to chart, as are their absence.

In disguised handwriting, such as anonymous notes, the educated writer will often attempt to include errors, change of terminal strokes, and embellishments. These changes will be inconsistent within the sample, however, and correct writing will creep back into the exemplars. Because of this regression, when you obtain exemplars, you should take away each one when it is completed and before a new one is submitted.

With the above twenty elements of comparison, any comparison can be made and an opinion given. For the most part the twenty elements focus on small parts of letters, as an opinion is formed from an examination of every small part. In the past, however, two additional elements of comparison were implemented; making twenty-two elements in all. Since the advent of the ball point pen these two elements are seldom used, but most handwriting books, including Osborn's *Questioned Documents,* include information about them. These elements are pen position and instrument.

21. Pen Position

The position in which a pen is held can be determined by examination of writing written by an ink pen. The point of this pen is made of two pieces of metal called nibs. If a line is written straight down, the nibs will separate slightly to create a broad line. If the pen is moved sideways, a narrow line will appear. By examining the thickness or narrowness of a line you can determine the position in which the pen was held at the time of writing. Prior to the ball point pen, this was regarded as a very important element in the examination of handwriting. (See figure 7–14.)

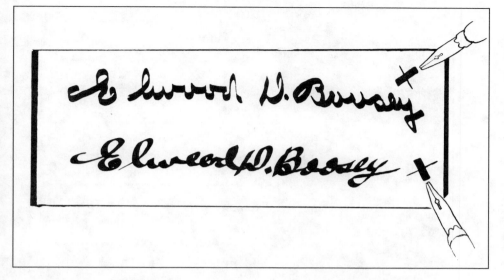

Figure 7–14: Pen position.

22. Instrument

While it may not be too important to the examination, the writing instrument used and its points of identification should be determined. Examples of various writing instruments include: the fountain pen, the old-style steel pen, the ball point pen, the liquid lead pencil, and the ordinary pencil. Important aspects you should note are the color of the ink, the shade of the color (slight differences in shade become noticeable under magnification), and the deposit along the ink line. Also notice the width and striations of the line.

The instrument used once played an important part in the examination. Today it is still a point that you should examine and evaluate. For instance, suppose you work on a case where the suspect alters the amount after the teller writes the deposit in a passbook.

One case where the writing instrument was involved concerned a public official in Long Beach. The official turned in expense claims which, upon examination, showed a great number of alterations. One of the documents concerned the Stock Yard Inn (figure 7–15). The receipt was made out for $9.45 and then initialed by the cashier with a ball point pen. The official then went over the writing with a felt tip pen, raising the amount to $129.45. The altered documents were photographed using filtered lenses and then compared with exemplars of the suspect.

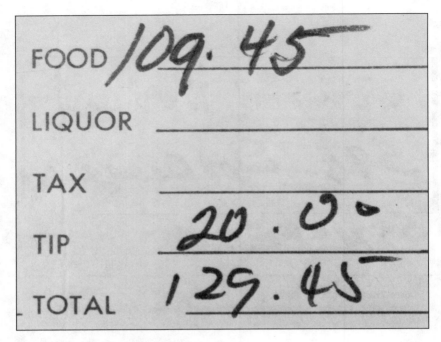

Figure 7–15: Stock Yard Inn receipt.

— 8 —

Five Types of Handwriting

E veryone has examined and compared handwriting. You have probably recognized at first glance the handwriting on a letter delivered by the postman.
Most persons can readily identify the handwriting of a few friends and relatives.
It is difficult to explain just what makes handwriting so distinctive and identifiable
unless your vocabulary includes the proper terminology for describing handwriting.

For comparison, handwriting is divided into five types. The casual memo,
letter, or informal handwriting is the first type, and is called Unconsciously
Written Handwriting. Special documents, important papers, and formal scripts
may contain carefully delineated writing or signatures done with a conscious
effort to achieve the best of the writer's ability. This type is called Consciously
Written Normal Handwriting. It may differ considerably from the first type.

The third type of handwriting is called Consciously Disguised Handwriting,
and is a deliberately disguised and controlled handwriting, designed to hide the
identity of the writer. This type of handwriting may be found on two-party
checks, anonymous letters, and many other types of documents. Exemplars submitted by suspects may be an effort to disguise normal handwriting, and could
fall into this category.

The fourth style of handwriting may be found on many documents. It is
the imitation of another person's signature or handwriting, done freehand. On
certain documents, this is the style referred to as "Copied Handwriting." The
California Penal Code, Section 470, states: "Every person [who] with intent to
defraud, signs the name of another person, or of a fictitious person, knowing that
he has no authority to do so . . . [or] counterfeits or forges the seal or handwriting
of another . . . is guilty of forgery." The copied signature may be on a check,
a will, or any other of hundreds of different documents.

The fifth class of writing in comparison study usually involves only signatures, but may be a complete letter or document. This is Traced Handwriting

of another person. Tracing is often done on a piece of glass, under which a strong light has been placed. Shadow boxes, a photographer's contact printer, and an ordinary window utilizing sunlight have all been used for tracing. With or without these aids, tracings have been made that were sufficiently similar to the original to fool the average person. An example is the traced signature "Jack Firenstein" on three checks (figure 8-1).

The comparison and identification of handwriting falls into different degrees of difficulty, depending on the type of problem; and the quality and quantity of comparison exemplars examined. In order to see and understand handwriting comparison, knowledge and training are necessary in addition to good eyesight.

The problem then remains of, "How do I get started, and what do I do besides just look?" The answer is simple: Do basic study, with progressive advancement through practical problems, so that your ability can develop. In addition, you will need to augment your vocabulary with the proper terminology for clear, concise description of the subject matter and proper evaluation. Proficiency can come only with practice. Examples and problems must be worked, analyzed and then reworked. No one ever learned to play a piano or operate a typewriter without basic practice. Nor does reading a book on the subject make you an expert. Proven, progressive steps and experience in observing and understanding, rather than just looking, is the slow and sure method for developing expertise in the field of handwriting analysis.

Millions of dollars, or often a person's freedom, may depend on a small amount of handwriting. Therefore, the opinions you make must be positive. If a problem is complicated, give it all the time necessary. If there is insufficient exemplar material, get more. Although this may require diligent search, don't give up! Give it all you have until you are sure of the correct and positive conclusion, based on the facts. "No opinion" is *always* the conclusion and rule until the problem has been absolutely completed and a final opinion can be stated.

Whenever there is a dispute about handwriting, only one side can be right; the other side is 100 percent wrong. Every problem must be demonstrated or illustrated to the complete understanding of everyone involved in judging the examination. It is far better to overdemonstrate than to state an opinion without any illustration. In this way the opinion can be proven so clearly that all who observe will feel the extra effort unnecessary, as they can see the facts for themselves.

The problem, generally, is to compare a known writing with an unknown writing to determine who was responsible for the questioned (unknown) writing. In doing so, you may have several exemplars from different persons to compare and examine.

In the study of handwriting examination, we start with the general overall form of the alphabet, including the small and capital letters and their parts, using the descriptions and specific terminology of the examiner's vocabulary. Each part of a letter has a descriptive name. To be able to see the individuality of a word,

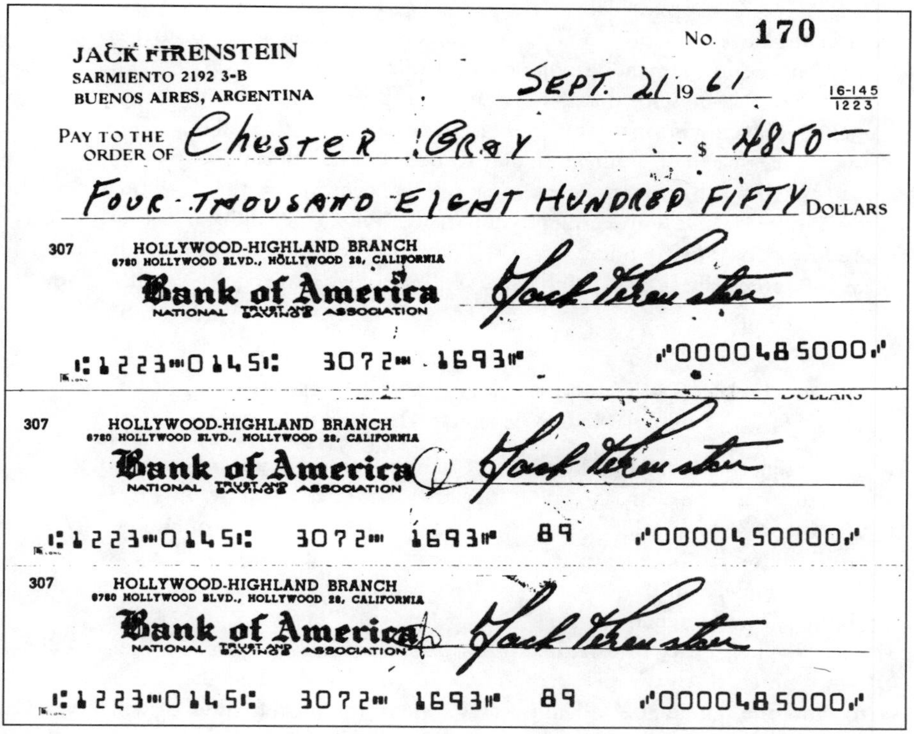
JACK FIRENSTEIN
SARMIENTO 2192 3-B
BUENOS AIRES, ARGENTINA

No. 170

SEPT. 21 19 61

16-145
1223

PAY TO THE ORDER OF Chester Gray $ 4850—

FOUR-THOUSAND EIGHT HUNDRED FIFTY DOLLARS

307 HOLLYWOOD-HIGHLAND BRANCH
6780 HOLLYWOOD BLVD., HOLLYWOOD 28, CALIFORNIA
Bank of America
NATIONAL TRUST AND SAVINGS ASSOCIATION

Jack Firenstein

⑆1223⑈0145⑆ 3072⑈ 1693⑈ ⑈0000485000⑈

307 HOLLYWOOD-HIGHLAND BRANCH
6780 HOLLYWOOD BLVD., HOLLYWOOD 28, CALIFORNIA
Bank of America
NATIONAL TRUST AND SAVINGS ASSOCIATION

Jack Firenstein

⑆1223⑈0145⑆ 3072⑈ 1693⑈ 89 ⑈0000450000⑈

307 HOLLYWOOD-HIGHLAND BRANCH
6780 HOLLYWOOD BLVD., HOLLYWOOD 28, CALIFORNIA
Bank of America
NATIONAL TRUST AND SAVINGS ASSOCIATION

Jack Firenstein

⑆1223⑈0145⑆ 3072⑈ 1693⑈ 89 ⑈0000485000⑈

Figure 8–1: Jack Firenstein traced forgery.

you must examine the component parts of the individual letters. Variations from copybook standards identify each person's handwriting. No two persons have the same combinations of characteristics. In some instances, certain characteristics are so uncommon that you can form an opinion of identity or nonidentity. In other cases, many other characteristics and minute values may be needed before you can reach a definite opinion or conclusion.

Children learn to write by copying or drawing letters from blackboard illustrations or penmanship books. They copy the form of each letter many times until it is memorized and can be formed without referring to the blackboard or copybook standard. After they master printed capital letters, they learn to combine them into words. With practice, the words become expressions of thought on paper. Handwriting becomes an automatic process and habit takes over. The particular style or system of penmanship learned in early childhood influences a person's writing all through life. In later years, other factors have a bearing on handwriting. Education, training, artistic and personal taste, as well as physical and mental health, all contribute to the final development of one's handwriting.

After the development of a facile style of handwriting is attained, there is very little change in the handwriting characteristics.

You can now see that the first seven chapters of this text cover the fundamentals of handwriting examination. In this chapter, we tie it all together, so you can make, first the examination, and second, the identification.

Before you can start the examination, however, you must know and understand three facts. It is interesting to note that in the science of handwriting, there are few axioms (self-evident truths).[1] The axioms of the science of handwriting are therefore called "facts," since they are "partially qualified." Despite this, they are very important.

Fact 1: No Two Persons Write Exactly Alike (and No One Person Writes Exactly the Same Twice)

The absence of absolute repetition is a universal law of nature. No two objects in nature can be exactly the same. It follows that once a handwriting is written, it can never be reproduced in all its detail by the same person, or another. This fact is important, because once a person is identified, it can be correctly assumed that no one else in the world could have written the document, since no one else has the same characteristics.

In the history of examination of handwriting, no expert has ever found two writings that were precisely the same. Many studies have been conducted to show the uniqueness of handwriting, one of the most massive of which was conducted by the U.S. Postal Inspection Service under the direction of Albert B. Somerford. Six qualified document examiners examined five hundred separate sets of fraternal and identical twins. It was reasoned that twins with their physical, psychological, and mental resemblances and similar educational backgrounds, might produce a handwriting similarity or possibly evidence of identical handwriting occurring between two persons. The examiners spent weeks examining and analyzing the handwriting exemplars. Somerford reported that "none could find any greater similarity in the writings than generally found among non-twins. Also, three-quarters wrote in a forward hand." There will, in handwriting, be marked resemblances between two different handwritings. However, differences will occur because of an individual's mechanical, physical, or mental characteristics at the moment of writing. If you find two writings that are exactly the same, one must be a forgery.

Fact 2: Retention of Characteristics

The early school years of a student are the formative years with regard to handwriting, and it is always changing. A teenager's style of writing continues to change until the individual's handwriting matures. From then on, it retains its individual characteristics and remains fairly constant for the remainder of a person's life. Illness, such as arthritis, stroke, alcoholism, or Parkinson's disease, may cause some alteration in the writing. Physical accidents, such as a broken arm or finger or a pulled muscle, can also affect a person's writing.

The fact remains that the characteristics of the mature hand will remain basically the same until death. An occasional problem does arise, however, when a person switches from his or her favored hand to the opposite hand. In some cases, the very lack of skill in the second hand may prevent an identification. But as an individual develops skill in the opposite hand, the writing from each hand can be identified as coming from the same person.

The theory is: *A person has only one mind that learned to write, and that mind will retain the characteristics and attempt to write in the style it has learned.* The theory indicates that the mind, not the hand, does the writing, and this theory is easily proven by examining the writing of a person who is ambidextrous. One can further test this theory by examining the writing of persons who have lost the use of their hands.

One method of writing without hands is by the use of an artificial or prosthetic arm. James H. Kelly, of the state crime lab in Atlanta, Georgia, researched this subject and stated in his summary, "Signatures written with artificial aids and prosthesis are basically similar to normally written signatures. The features found in signatures written with these devices are readily distinguishable from those features associated with forgery. While such signatures can present unusual problems, a thorough examination, complete evaluation, and proper interpretation will render correct conclusions."[2]

Another example of this problem can be seen in the writing of Ealon R. Lamphier. Mr. Lamphier contracted polio many years ago and is almost totally paralyzed. He overcame his disability and learned to write and paint by maneuvering instruments with his mouth. He developed a new method of writing which entails holding the pen in both hands and then moving the body (to move the pen). He now uses this method to write instead of mouth writing. Moving the body to paint would not work, so he still uses his mouth to paint. The two writings by Lamphier were written on the same day and show many identifying characteristics.

Durley B. Davis, document examiner for the Commonwealth of Virginia, also did research on the subject of writing after the loss of the dominant hand. In his conclusion he stated, "It is obvious that the central nervous system and retention powers of the brain combine to produce a new handwriting which contains deep-seated writing habits, which are very strong in most subjects."[3]

Even if a person had the ability to write backwards, the writing would still retain the same characteristics as the normal hand, as it is the mind that really does the writing. Richard L. Clason, document and fingerprint examiner for the Beverly Hills Police Department, was adept at writing backwards. In 1965, Clason took a Bradford handwriting class and left an anonymous note for the teacher (figure 8-3).

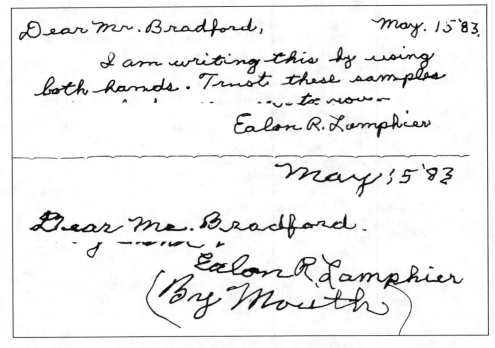

Figure 8–2: Lamphier hand writing (top) and mouth writing.

Copies of the anonymous note were made for each of the students in the handwriting class. They compared the note with the student examplars and were able to identify Clason. The first individual characteristic that stood out was the base line pickup for the capitals *R* and *P* in the questioned writing. The flat top of the *r* and the initial stroke of the capital *Y* also assisted in the identification. Clason then explained that he had used carbon paper to make his backwards writing come out "right" for the anonymous note.

The Lamphier and Clason writings and the Kelly and Davis studies best demonstrated the retention of handwriting characteristics, until the Clarence M. Noonan forgery trial in 1980.

Clarence M. Noonan Forgery

Clarence Noonan and his wife purchased a home in Long Beach, California, in 1927. By 1939, the mortgage was paid off, and the house was free and clear. The Noonan's granddaughter, Mary Margis, moved into the house in 1978 when her grandparents became ill. In 1979 housekeepers were employed to help her take care of Clarence Noonan and in September Noonan died of Parkinson's disease.

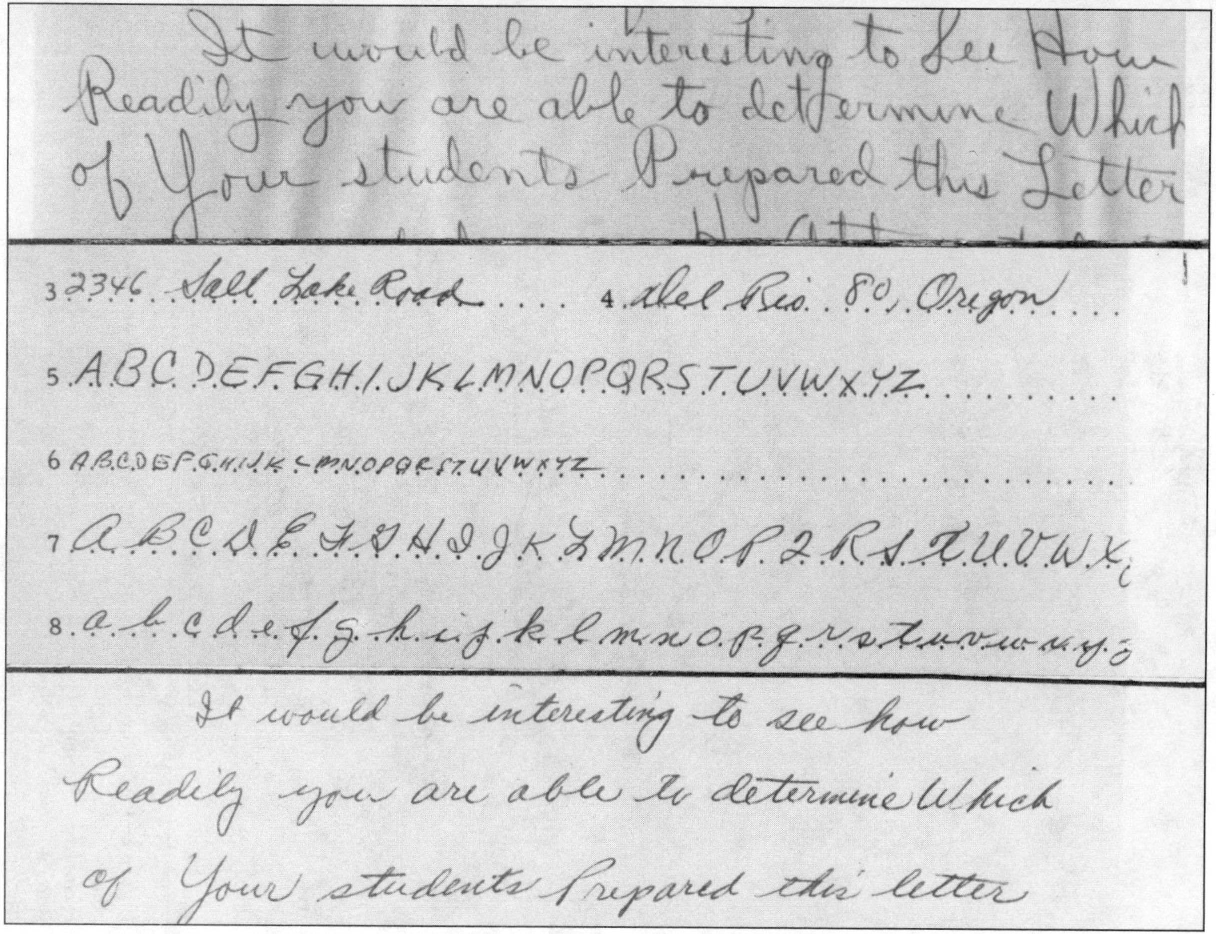

It would be interesting to see how
Readily you are able to determine Which
of Your students prepared this letter

3. 2346. Salt Lake Road . . . . 4. Abel Rio . 80. Organ

5. A.B.C. D.E.F.G.H.I.J.K.L.M.N.O.P.Q.R.S.T.U.V.W.X.Y.Z. . . . .

6. ABCDEFGHIJK-LMNOPQRSTUVWXYZ . . . .

7. A.B.C.D.E.F.G.H.I.J.K.L.M.N.O.P.Q.R.S.T.U.V.W.X.i

8. a.b.c.d.e.f.g.h.i.j.k.l.m.n.o.p.q.r.s.t.u.v.w.x.y.z.3

It would be interesting to see how

Readily you are able to determine Which

of Your students prepared this letter

Figure 8–3: Anonymous note (top), class writings (middle) and request exemplar (bottom).

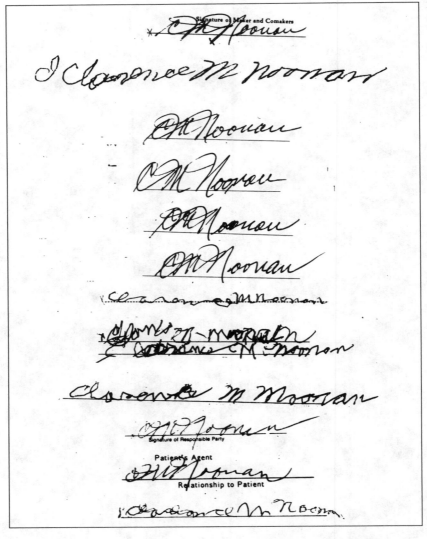

Figure 8–4: Clarence M. Noonan exhibit. Signature 1 is from an August 12, 1958 note; signature 2 is from a 1978 will; signatures 3, 4, 5, and 6 are January 7, 1979, exemplars; 7 is from a 1979 will; 8 and 9 are from January 19, 1979, grant deeds; 10 is from a power of attorney; 11 and 12 are exemplars dated March 3, 1979; and 13 is from a 1979 power of attorney.

After his death, Margis received an eviction notice and hired an attorney, who learned that Noonan had "signed over" the property to a housekeeper for $1 on January 19, 1979. The housekeeper had sold the property to a man who lived in another city for $20,000 in cash, along with a duplex dwelling valued at $100,000.

The case was reported to Detective Jack Starbird of the Forgery/Fraud detail of the Long Beach Police Department. As document examiner, I examined the handwriting and determined that several questioned documents contained signatures not written by Clarence Noonan. On June 18, 1980, the housekeeper was arrested on a 470 PC–Forgery.

On October 17, 1980, a preliminary hearing was held in Long Beach before Judge W. H. Winston. After being called and sworn in, I testified that the signatures on the wills (figure 8-4, 2 and 7), grant deeds (8 and 9), and powers of attorney (10 and 13) were not signed by the person that signed the other documents in the name of Clarence M. Noonan (figure 8-4, signatures 1, 3, 4, 5, 6, 11, 12). I also pointed out that Noonan had retained his characteristics, and that there was very little change in his handwriting over a twenty-year period.

Up to this point, the Noonan case had been a routine fraud by forgery case. The defense attorney then asked me a final question: "If Mr. Noonan was a man of multiple personalities, could a second personality have written the writing you failed to identify?" The answer to this question lies, once again, in the theory that the mind does the writing and in the research done on handwriting of multiple personalities.

Multiple Personalities

This abnormal type of personality goes back in history to the days of the Bible. "What is your name?" Jesus asked, in Mark 5:9. "My name is Legion," he answered, "for there are many of us." The first classic case was written by a prominent Boston physician, Morton Prince. Dr. Prince wrote the story of Claire Brenner in 1905.[4]

Prince's work went unnoticed for many years. The phenomenon of multiple personality was brought to the public with the publication of a work by Corbett Thigpen and Hervey Cleckley in 1957. Their book, *The Three Faces of Eve*, became a best seller, and was later made into a movie for which Joanne Woodward won an Academy Award in 1957. In the book, the character Chris Sizemore (pseudonym Eve) begins having traumatic experiences at the age of two. As a result, by age twenty-five she had developed three personalities. Her parents then brought her to a psychiatrist, Corbett Thigpen. After a few days, Dr. Thigpen received a letter, the second half of which was written in a crude scrawl. Thigpen soon developed the theory that Chris was a person of multiple personalities. He performed several tests on his patient, one of which was to have a handwriting examiner compare the handwriting written by each of the three personalities. After examining the writings, Ward S. Atherton, chief questioned document examiner for the criminal investigation laboratory at Camp Gordon, Georgia, reported:

> As a conclusion of the opinions derived from analysis of the various handwritings of this multiple personality patient, it is believed that the handwriting does not undergo complete subordination to each marked change of personality, even though each group exhibits evidence of emotional instabilities. It readily appears the handwriting of each personality is of a different person. Such apparent or discernible variations may lead the untrained observer to believe that the handwriting of each personality is completely foreign to the other. However, extensive investigation of these handwriting materials establishes beyond any doubt that they have been written by one and the same individual. Nothing was found to indicate a willful and conscious intent to disguise writings executed within a personality or between the first and second personalities.[5]

After publicity from the book and movie drew attention to the case, other psychiatrists realized that Chris's therapy had been incomplete. Chris consulted another psychiatrist, who discovered not three personalities, but thirteen. Chris required twenty years of treatment, after which she wrote her book, *I'm Eve*.

In 1978, David A. Bellomy reported a police case, "A Case of Forgery by an Alleged Multi-Personality Subject."[6] In the forgery investigation, handwriting was obtained from the suspect (personality one). Dr. Somerford, an Orange County psychologist, placed the defendant under hypnosis to obtain exemplars from the second personality, and then the second personality after filling out exemplars, imitated the writing of personality three "from memory" and then filled out a third set of exemplars. Examiner Bellomy found that "each set of writings was consistent unto itself, and that each set was quite separable from the other." Using the three sets of writing, Bellomy identified all the questioned writings.

Research into the multi-personality subject led to other research regarding handwriting and hypnosis. Michael M. Zanoni, a San Jose criminologist, has examined handwriting of both types. He stated that multi-personality handwriting "differed greatly in pictorial effect. . . . But when examined from a scientific basis, the writings shared similar letter and spacing ratios, consistent stroke characteristics, and common microscopic characteristics such as hesitations, pen lifts, etc."

Zanoni's research led to a paper co-authored with Richard W. Chang titled "Handwriting Change and Hypnosis."[7] This paper states that "it is obvious that the experimental series does not approximate an event aimed at fraudulently obtaining signatures. Such situations would require interpersonal variables not easily introduced in experimental work. But at least there is an initial basis to conclude that signatures obtained through the use of post-hypnotic suggestion do not greatly deviate from normally executed signatures."

The retention of characteristics is therefore established as an important fact. A person retains his characteristics over a period of time, even if he uses artificial hands, writes with his mouth or backwards, is a subject of multiple personalities, or is under hypnosis. The mind does the writing, and its characteristics remain fairly constant from early maturity through the remainder of a person's life.

Fact 3: Identification of Handwriting Is Made by Identifying Characteristics

The theory upon which a document examiner proceeds is that every time a person writes, he or she subconsciously places individual characteristics in the writing. An examination of these characteristics will in many cases enable the examiner to determine whether questioned documents and exemplars were written by the same person.

It is therefore important to understand the principles by which the force and significance of characteristics are to be measured. The three basic principles are: first, characteristics that deviate from the norm; second, characteristics that are inconspicuous; and third, class characteristics.

First Principle

Osborn stated, "Those identifying or differentiating characteristics are of the most force which are most divergent from the regular system or national features of a particular handwriting under examination."[8] Ralph Bradford liked to describe an individual characteristic as so individual that it was worth a $20 gold piece. In turn, a class characteristic would be worth 25 cents to him. To be individual is to be different than the norm. But to learn that difference, one must first learn the norm—the systems currently taught in the United States.

In the examination of any characteristics—individual or class—we must evaluate it in relation to other characteristics. It is up to the examiner to determine, in the light of his experience, skill, and training, the value or significance which is to be assigned to each characteristic. It can be said where there is no individuality, there can be no identification. The difference between a trainee and a qualified document examiner is that the examiner has examined thousands of letter *a*'s and can almost immediately put a value to all characteristics in a particular letter *a*. The trainee, with little or no experience lacks the background needed to evaluate the individuality of a letter. As a trainee, one of the most important things you can do is examine as much writing as possible. You should start with the small *a*, examining and noting each variation in its construction. After comparing a hundred *a*'s, you will begin to get an idea of the individuality of the letter. Examiners say that it takes three or four years to develop this ability. It takes so long partly because of the wide experience you need to determine the individuality of a characteristic in a letter. Reading all the top books or taking all the classes will not make you an expert. The only way to achieve expertise is with practice and hard work.

Second Principle

Osborn stated, "Those repeated characteristics which are inconspicuous should first be sought, and should be given the most weight, for these are likely to be so unconscious that they would not intentionally be omitted when the attempt is made to disguise, and would not be successfully copied from the writing of another when simulation is attempted."[9] The importance and description of these characteristics are of such volume that they would be impossible to list. For a starting point, review the twenty elements in chapter 7. The pick-up stroke that starts below the base line is individual because most start on the base line. Proportion is widely considered one of the most important of the elements that formed individual characteristics.

Third Principle

Osborn stated, "Ordinary system or national features and elements are not alone sufficient on which to base a judgment of identity of two writings, although these characteristics necessarily have value as evidence of identity, if present in sufficient numbers and in combination with individual qualities and characteristics."[10] Ordinary system or national features are "Class Characteristics." A suspect described as a male, white, about thirty years of age would be a class-characteristic description, since most of the white males in the United States are between twenty and thirty-nine years old. If a description contained several additional class characteristics as well as the information that the suspect had a deformed left ear, the ear would be an individual characteristic (discussed in more detail as the First Principle).

Class characteristics in handwriting include the handwriting taught in school, since all students attempt to write exactly as they are taught from a penmanship copy book. Class characteristics of one era can become individual characteristics later. An example is the capital *W* of William Bradford and William Brewster. These men were educated in the Scrooby district of central England about twenty years apart. They both were taught to write the letter *W* with a large loop in the center of the letter. This loop gave the letter a two-to-one relationship with the rest of the letters (figure 8-5). This class characteristic of the late 1500s is no longer taught, so when it appears in writing today, it is an individual characteristic.

William Bradford and William Brewster were leaders of the Pilgrims that sailed to Plymouth on the Mayflower in 1620. As William Bradford no doubt taught this letter to his children, this "Class letter *W*" was probably one of the first *W*'s taught in the United States.

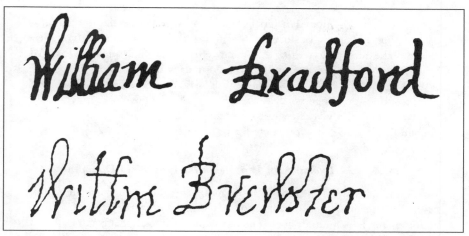

Figure 8–5: The Bradford and Brewster *W*.

The reverse of a class characteristic that becomes individual is an individual characteristic that becomes a class characteristic. An example is the "French A" (chapter 5) which was not taught by any American handwriting system and was therefore thought to be characteristic of one individual. Investigation revealed others who wrote the same *A*, and finally it was learned that this *A* is a French-taught characteristic. Thus, a letter which was thought to be individual has been identified as a class characteristic. A most unusual case is the so-called "Kinte W" (chapter 5). This untypical letter is seen so often that it must be considered a class characteristic.

The Six Examination Procedures

With the knowledge of the three "Facts" as a background, you are now ready to make an examination. To assist you with this, we have broken the examination into six procedures: It is important that these procedures be understood and undertaken in order. Shortcuts should be avoided.

Procedure 1—Gather All Questioned Documents

On many occasions, investigators ask an examiner to compare the endorsement of a check with the exemplar of a suspect. After the examiner has finished the examination, the investigator may give him a second document and ask his opinion of it. Don't allow this to happen. Gather *all* questioned documents in the beginning. In a check case, these may include additional checks, check–cashing applications, signature cards, a suspect's shopping list, and even maps, with writing.

The more questioned material you have available, the easier the examination will be. A volume of documents will furnish you with a more complete record of the questioned writing. Ask the investigator probing questions that may bring forth more questioned writing than originally thought.

The Howard Hughes "Mormon Will" case concerned a three-page will. The examiners examined not only the will, but also the envelopes in which the will was found. Only when you have gathered all documents in the case that contain handwriting, are you ready for procedure 2.

Procedure 2—Examine All Writing on the Questioned Documents

Check the questioned documents front and back to determine which writing could have been written by the suspect. During the examination of a check endorsement, look not only at the endorsement signature, but also at the address. The face of the check may also be of value to you, since many times the endorser of a bad check will also write the payee signature on the face. Credit-card invoices normally contain only a signature written by the suspect. A careful examination of the invoices may reveal that an alert clerk had the suspect write a telephone number or other information on the invoice.

The Bradford System emphasizes that you use all the writing on the check for comparison. Even more important than the date and payee signature is the written amount of money. As an examiner, you should find as much questioned writing as possible.

The object of all document examiners is to identify all handwriting presented to them. If an examiner is shown an initial and then asked to identify it with an exemplar, the investigator may be asking for a miracle. Surprise the investigator and make a difficult case simple by gathering additional questioned documents and then locating additional writing on those documents. Then, instead of having only an initial to examine, you will have all kinds of writing to make the job of identification much easier. Do not try to solve a difficult case, but, rather, make the case easy by utilizing all the questioned writing available.

Procedure 3—Locate Nonrequest Exemplars

The problem most frequently encountered by examiners is that investigators do not understand the problems of an examiner. The investigator who knows little about handwriting may attempt to solve a case in other ways. Such investigators submit for handwriting examination only as a last hope.

It is your job as the examiner to educate the investigator regarding the acquisition of informal exemplars. If, for example, a person says he did not write a certain check in June 1980, an attempt should be made to obtain some cancelled checks from May and July of that year. The will that was signed in a hospital shortly before a person died should be compared with the hospital admission cards, signed a short time before. Any questioned writing should have exemplars written as close to the date of the questioned writing as possible.

Recall the chapter on exemplars; it is important to get known writing of the same type as the questioned writing. Normal unconsciously written writing (such as on a check) should be compared with another exemplar of the same type. Proper informal exemplars will assist you in making an opinion that will aid the investigator in solving his case.

Procedure 4—Examine Request Exemplars

To examine exemplars or questioned documents for disguise, we must first determine what is normal. A simplified definition of normal writing would include:

1. Tapering of initial stroke
2. Difference in pressure on upstrokes and downstrokes
3. Simplification of the forms of letters
4. Hooked or dragged strokes at the end of disconnected letters
5. Consistent slanting.

The first four points in the definition of normal writing listed above change when a person writes slowly or draws the writing. One of the features most characteristic of disguised writing is the lack of consistency throughout the document. The degree of speed or control will determine the possibility for an identification. Suspects who write slowly also write smaller. In the drawn illustration (figure 8-6), the tail of the y has no loop on the final stroke.

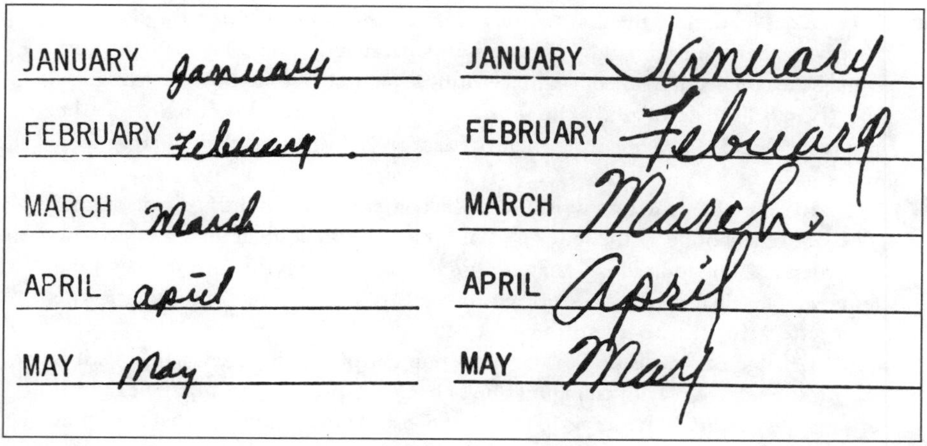

Figure 8–6: Drawn exemplar writing.

The "ch" combination in the word "March" (figure 8-6) is the same in both drawn and normal exemplars. The letter c has a hook, and the body of the letter has a headline that is higher than the body of the h. Reduction in size of writing does not affect the characteristics—this can be seen with a magnification glass. A pure drawn writing cannot be identified since it is not writing, but a drawing.

If an examplar contains a great deal of writing for the suspect to fill out, he will be writing at normal speed by the completion of the exemplar. Handwriting habits are fixed habits, therefore for many practiced writers, writing has become a reflex action over which they have some difficulty exercising control. Exemplars obtained over a period of time will assist in bringing out this normal handwriting.

Several studies have been made of disguised writing. One study was conducted by Jack Harris over a period of seventeen years.[11] Harris asked his students to write a paragraph in normal handwriting on a 5-by-7-inch ruled card. They were then asked to copy the same text, only this time in disguised handwriting. Two of the many observations from this study were:

1. By far, the majority of students failed to disguise their handwriting effectively, even though they were members of a class on questioned documents.
2. Over half (52 percent) of the students changed their slant and wrote backhand in an attempt to disguise their handwriting.

A person who disguises his or her handwriting is doing an unnatural act. Slant best illustrates this, as a suspect may change his or her writing by changing the slant, but as the person continues to write, the slant will gradually revert to normal. The suspect, on noticing the reversion of slant, will again change the slant.

Examination of the handwriting in figure 8-7 discloses that the first four words are written backhand. "Edward" is vertical and "Frank" is slanted to the right. With the second line of normal writing, the suspect remembered to disguise the "Nan, Olson and Paul." The fourth line contains vertical writing, while the rest is backhand. These inconsistencies of slant are a distinct giveaway of disguised writing.

In figure 8-8, the two writings can be compared and identified as the same. The size of the body of the letter h (March) is extremely small in relation to the other letters. The individual characteristic in this writing is the final stroke of the letter a. The final stroke does not go to the base line before continuing to the next letter; this can be seen in many of the a's.

Change of slant is one of the most popular of the disguises. I believe it is the most effective way of changing one's characteristics and making the examiner's job very difficult. Refer again to figure 8-8 and you will notice that the letter a backhand has a hook on the initial stroke, while in the normal writing, the

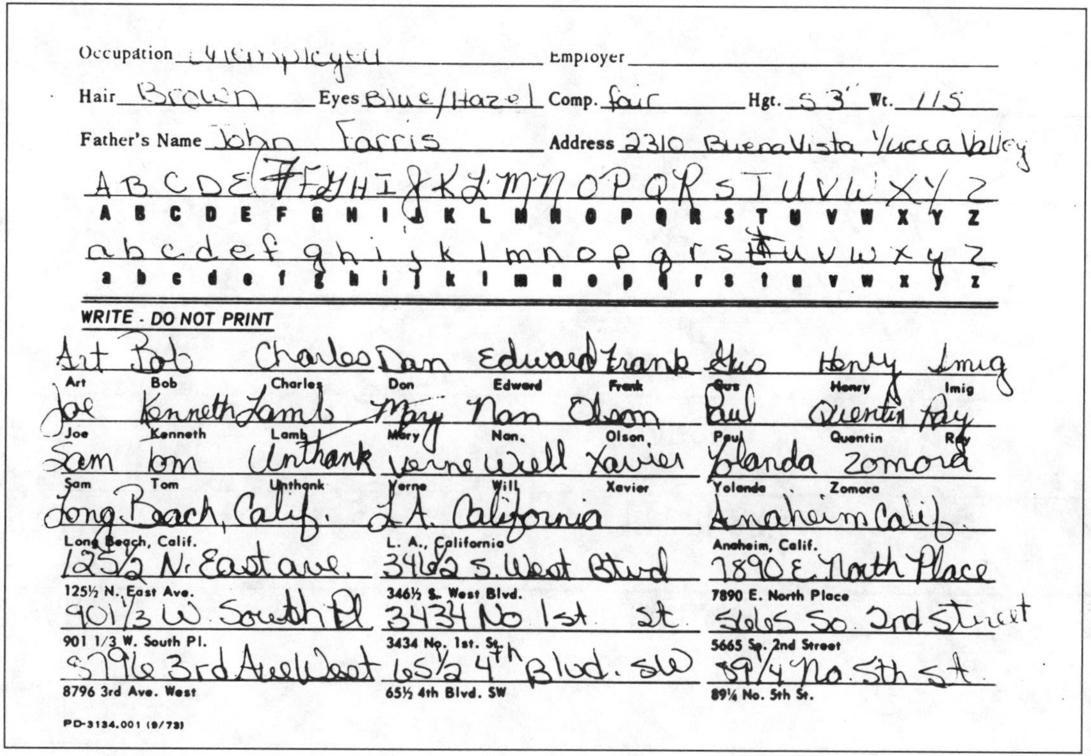

Occupation ___unemployed___ Employer _____

Hair __Brown__ Eyes __Blue/Hazel__ Comp. __fair__ Hgt. __5'3"__ Wt. __115__

Father's Name __John Farris__ Address __2310 Buena Vista, Yucca Valley__

A B C D E F G H I J K L M N O P Q R S T U V W X Y Z
A B C D E F G H I J K L M N O P Q R S T U V W X Y Z
a b c d e f g h i j k l m n o p q r s t u v w x y z

WRITE - DO NOT PRINT

Art	Bob	Charles	Dan	Edward	Frank
Art Bob	Charles	Dan	Edward	Frank	the henry Imig
Joe	Kenneth James	Guy	Don	Olson	Paul Quentin Ray
Joe	Kenneth	Lamb	Nan.	Olson,	Paul Quentin Ray
Sam Tom	Unthank	Verne	Will	Xavier	Yolanda Zamora
Sam Tom	Unthank		young Will Xavier		Yolanda Zamora
Long Beach, Calif.		L.A., California		Anaheim, Calif.
1252 N. East ave.		3466 S. West Blvd.		7890 E. North Place
125½ N. East Ave.		346½ S. West Blvd.		7890 E. North Place
9011/3 W. South Pl.		3434 No. 1st. St.		5665 So. 2nd Street
8796 3rd Ave. West		65½ 4th Blvd. SW		89¼ No. 5th St.

PD-3134.001 (6/73)

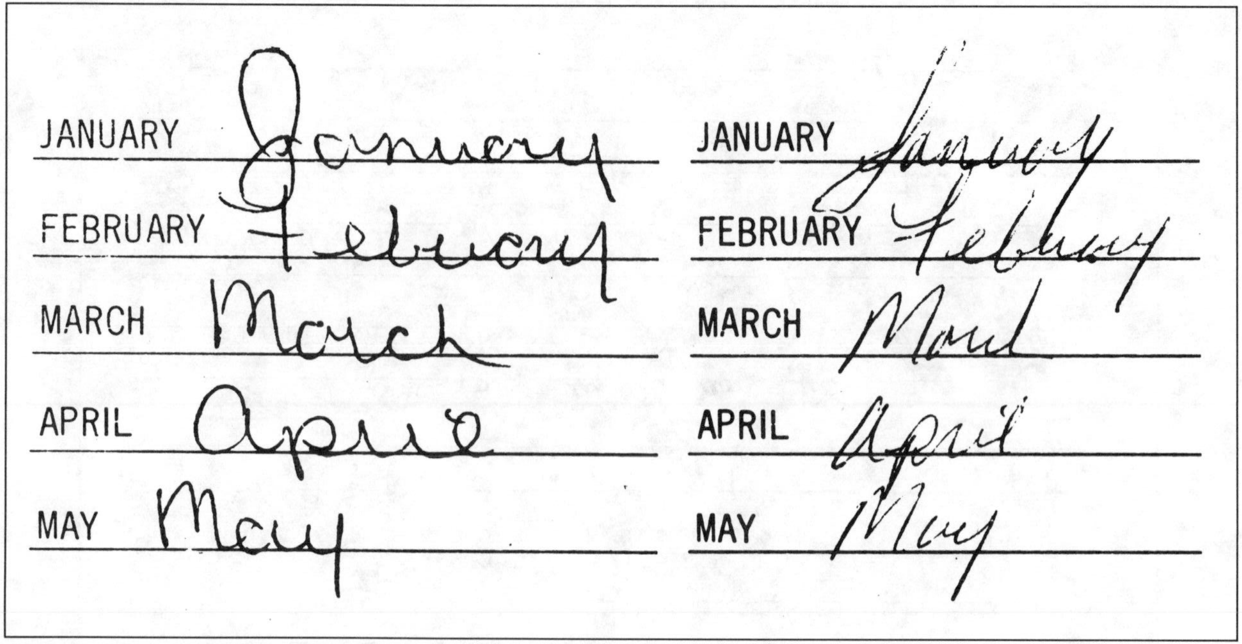

Figure 8–8: Slant exemplar writing.

initial stroke is straight. The capital *J* is all round curves in the backhand writing and angles in the normal writing. Slant can present a very difficult time for examiners and new exemplars should be obtained.

It is important to determine the amount of control in request exemplars. With this in mind, you can choose to request new exemplars or continue to use the old exemplars.

Procedure 5—Copy the Questioned Writing

In chapter 2, entering the date on which the documents were received in a notebook was discussed in detail. You should make copies of all documents, recording the general peculiarities such as creases, tears, spots, or erasures. The documents should be photographed actual size and with a scale, to preserve the original condition of the document. Place the document in a transparent plastic envelope.

Ralph Bradford believed and stated in the strongest terms: "To begin the examination of handwriting, [one must] first *copy* the questioned signature or writing slowly with all microscopic detail. If necessary, copy it two or three times *before* a comparison with known exemplars or any other handwriting is attempted." In copying these details, you will observe more characteristics in the writing than if you merely looked at the document. Over a period of time, you will memorize more and more characteristics. Ralph Bradford could memorize an entire document without knowledge of its content, because he examined characteristics and not words.

On beginning an examination, Albert Osborn stated,

> If it is feasible, it is usually advisable that an investigation of a writing should begin, not with an examination of the questioned writing itself, but by a careful study of the standard writing with which it is finally to be compared, and this study of the genuine writing should, if possible, be made before the questioned writing is seen by the examiner. The genuine writing should be gone over step by step, should be studied and, in some cases, tabulated, classified, averaged and measured, until the examiner actually begins to recognize, as it were, its complexion, features, and characteristic individuality.[12]

The second stage of an examination, according to Osborn, is to study the questioned writing in the same manner as the genuine writing, and, if conditions permit, the careful tabulation and classification of this writing. The third and final operation is an exhaustive comparison of the two writings, with an evaluation and interpretation of all similarities and differences. Too many times the order of an examination is reversed, and time is unprofitably given to the questioned writing with an adequate amount of standard writing for comparison not procured for the examination.[13]

If you are confused regarding Ralph Bradford's statement to "first copy the questioned signature," and Osborn's injunction to compare the standard writing before examining the questioned writing itself, remember that procedure 4, examine request exemplars, precedes copying (procedure 5). I concur with both of these authorities.

Although the above statements are usually correct, they are not always true. If you have a questioned will, the will signature must first be copied and examined. This is true in many cases, but not all. In police work, suspects are frequently arrested for passing stolen personal checks. The suspects, in order to avoid suspicion, write the checks in a fairly normal writing. Like burglars who do not wear gloves, they do not believe they will be caught. When they are apprehended, their only recourse is to disguise their exemplar. In most cases, examiners attempt to locate characteristics in the disguised questioned writing and then compare them with an exemplar. Forged check cases are, in effect, worked backwards, with the examiner first finding characteristics in the disguised exemplars and comparing them with the checks.

No matter which way you choose to do the examination, always copy the writing and mark the characteristics out on your worksheet. This will save you a great deal of looking back and forth between documents, and you will have ensured that you have examined all the characteristics.

Procedure 6—Determine "Type of Handwriting Examination" Needed, Then Proceed with the Comparison

The five previous procedures are followed by all examiners. Procedure 6 is one of the most important of the procedures. Though it hasn't been written about previously, it is the key to any handwriting examination.

First, you must understand that there are two types of handwriting examination: "positive" and "negative." When making a comparison, examiners look for individual characteristics, noting each variation, and then form an opinion. In most cases, this type of positive examination is correct, and will lead to a correct opinion. It is therefore very important to understand when this type of examination is needed and how to perform it.

Positive Type Examination

If two handwritten documents appear to a lay person to have been written by different persons, conduct a "Positive Type Examination." The two writings are different and the examiner must therefore determine if they are written by the same person. If the examiner fails in this attempt, he or she must then go to the original premise that they are different, and therefore written by different persons. An examination of this type is the most common performed by document examiners.

At this point in our handwriting examination, we have followed the five previous procedures; we've photocopied the documents and made notations on the worksheets. The documents have been examined for disguise, and we have copied the questioned documents. We must now compare the questioned and exemplar material with the following comparison elements (chapter 7).

1. Alignment	11. Proportion
2. Angles	12. Retrace
3. Arrangement	13. Skill
4. Connections	14. Slant
5. Curves	15. Size
6. Form	16. Spelling
7. Line quality	17. Straight lines
8. Movement	18. System
9. Pen lifts	19. Terminals
10. Pick-up	20. Trademarks and embellishments

Compare one element at a time, making notes and comparisons. Later, when the examination becomes second nature, you can consider several elements at one time. Albert Osborn said, "It is suggested that in any examination, it is well to make a definite list of all the things to consider and then take them up in order so that nothing will be omitted. One who attempts to see all things at once will not see certain things and others he will not see clearly."[14] In the beginning, it is important to consider one element at a time, as this is the time to be thorough and build a foundation and background on these elements. Just as the purchase of a Stradivarius does not make one a violinist, controlled and extensive practice must be applied in acquiring the expertise of a good examiner. Desire alone cannot replace practice and experience.

Step-by-Step Examination of a Murder Case

Follow the examiner in his solution of a 1979 murder case. Using this step-by-step method, a thorough and complete examination will take place. By following this examination, you will identify the examination procedures that have been discussed.

In this murder case, a motel registration was one of the pieces of evidence. The suspect was arrested and extradited to Long Beach for trial. A request exemplar was obtained by the jailers during the booking process. The investigating officers then submitted the motel registration and exemplar for a handwriting comparison. The officers were asked to obtain, if possible, any nonrequest exemplars that would assist in the examination. Since the suspect had been returned from out of state, no additional exemplars could be located.

The exemplar was examined and found consistent throughout, with no attempt at disguise. The questioned document was then copied in detail and the unusual *a* was examined. A magnification glass was used to determine the exact method of construction of the letter. It was decided to conduct a positive examination, despite the obvious similarities in the form of the writing. If an identification was made, the examiner would then make a negative examination. The purpose was to determine if it was possible for a second person to have copied the suspect's writing onto the questioned document. The twenty elements of handwriting comparison were applied one by one to the questioned documents.

When examining each of the elements of the writing, do not forget to consider *variation*. Since no two words or letters are written by the same person the same way twice, a person's two writings are considered variations of each other. Wilson Harrison stated, "The existence of natural variation means that, as with other handwriting, a reasonable amount of standard material in the form of genuine signatures must be available for comparison, because it is essential that the range of variation in letter design which might be expected in a genuine signature should be determined before any comparisons are attempted with signatures of unknown authorship."[15] To further explain, compare all the variations in the questioned writing. If the questioned writing shows three variations of the letter *a*, for example, and the three variations are found in the exemplar, this can be used in the writer's identification. But if you do not find all the variations in the exemplar, you have found an unexplained characteristic. The variations must be found in the exemplar. Albert Osborn wrote, "If the conclusion of identity is reached, either in a person or a handwriting, there must not remain significant differences that cannot reasonably be explained. This ignoring of the differences, or the failure properly to account for them, is the cause of most of the errors in handwriting identification."[16]

The comparison of the 1979 murder case started with the element of form. *Form* was the first element that determined what type of examination was to be made. Thus, the comparing of the registration to the exemplar should be now made by the additional elements.

The head line *alignment* discloses that the letters *i* and *e* are shorter than the other small letters on the questioned document. In examining the exemplar, you find normal size letters, as well as the variation of a short *i* in "Harris" and a short *e* in "Market." Examination of the base line alignment on the questioned document shows that the first letter rests on the base line while the rest are above it. The exemplar shows great variation with no consistency to use for an identifying characteristic.

Angles are examined, and one immediately sees the connecting stroke of the letters *n* and *m* in "Sam" and "Denver." This connecting stroke is connected to the first downstroke with a sharp angle. Most connections are with a curved stroke. This characteristic can be seen throughout the exemplar.

Arrangement is not as important in this comparison as are *connections*, discussed in the angles element. *Curves* are also not individual in this case, since angles are the individual characteristics.

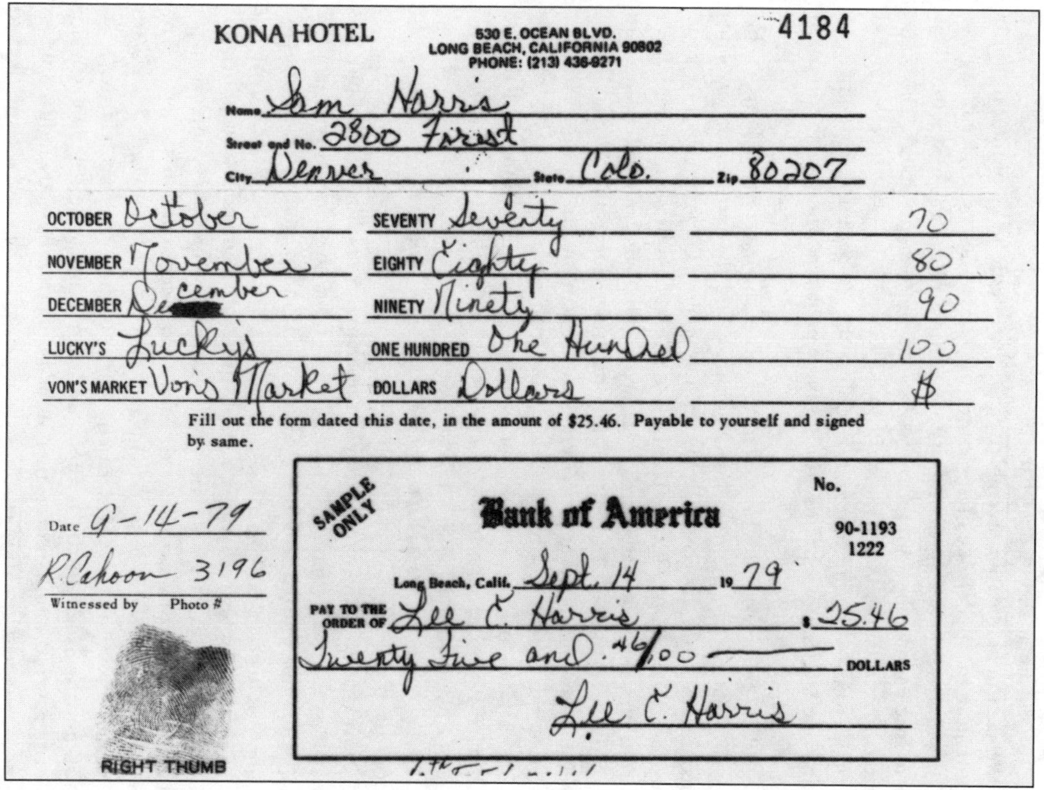

Figure 8–9: Motel registration and exemplar.

Proportion is always an important element. The relationship of the letters *i* and *e* has already been discussed, which also relates to proportion. In the numbers 2800 and 80207, the *0*'s are smaller in proportion to the other numbers. This can be seen to some degree on the limited portion of the exemplar, while the other side of the exemplar shows this characteristic very well.

Retrace can be seen on several letters of the questioned registration slip. It is important in the final stroke of the letter *v* in "Denver." The retrace is halfway down the upstroke before it becomes a connecting stroke to the next letter. This characteristic can also be seen in the words "Seventy" and "Five." This same characteristic can be seen in the letter *w* in "Twenty." (It is not recommended for trainees to use different letters in a comparison. Experienced examiners do examine like letters, but extreme caution must be taken when a *v* is compared with a *w* and so forth.)

A slight retrace can also be seen in the top of the letter *r* in "Harris." This part is also higher than the head line alignment, and the retrace portion slants backhand. The letter also contains curves and angles. These are a lot of good characteristics for a single letter. The lack of retrace can be seen in the letter *t* in "forest," and then compared to the *t* in "Sept." These individual characteristics make retrace, or the lack thereof, an important element in this case.

Slant was considered in procedure 4 of the examination process. The slant of the exemplar was basically vertical, although the writing does vary slightly from backhand to forehand, making the skill inconsistent. This same small degree of slant change can be seen in the questioned writing. In the word "Denver," the "Den" slants to the right, while the "ver" stays vertical.

Spelling, straight lines, system, terminals, and trademarks are not important in this comparison.

Now that you have considered all the elements, use them again and, this time, compare letter by letter. The first letter of the questioned document is a capital *S*. Compare it with a letter *S* from the exemplar, and you find the two *S* letters match almost exactly.

The letter *a* is next to compare. It was first examined under a magnification glass to determine exactly how the letter was made. This is very important, as machine copies many times will not reveal the exact construction of a letter. The letter *a* in "Sam" has the same individuality as it does in the word "Harris" in the questioned writing, and also matches the *a* in the exemplar "Harris."

Comparing element by element and then letter by letter, you will not forget any part of a comparison. The possibility of error is greatly reduced when you use a systematic method of comparison. Alwyn Cole said that he likes to "write descriptions of handwritten forms upon a theory that you cannot be sure you have seen everything until you attempt to describe everything."

There is one more point to be made in a Positive Type Examination. Many document examiners have a rule that when a great number of similarities are found *but* unexplained differences exist, those two writings must be considered as the products of two different authors. This Unexplained Differences Rule is important. Of course, any time you find unexplained differences, you should take extreme caution to fully consider these differences.

Examine the writing of the 1979 murder case (figure 8-9) one more time. Despite the fact that the handwriting examination in this case is a relatively easy positive identification, there still remain two unexplained differences on the questioned document. The capital *F* in "Forest" on the questioned document ends in a straight line to the base line. The written *F* on the exemplar ends with a base line loop as in "Twenty" and "Five." The printed *F* on the exemplar is not seen in the photo, but it is made as a mirror image of the *F* in "Forest." The second characteristic is the connecting stroke with the first downstroke in the letter *v* in "Denver." In the exemplar, there is a short retrace on the left side of the *v* in "Seventy" and "Five." In the questioned "Denver" there is no retrace; it is open. There is a slight hesitation glob, which may explain this characteristic. The capital *F*, however, is an "unexplained difference" that is overruled by the many identifying characteristics in this case. The unexplained differences are not a rule, but caution is.

The Positive Type Examination will yield many individual characteristics. However, since the form of the questioned and known writing is so close, a Negative Type examination should now be conducted. The questioned writing should now be totally examined under a magnification glass for the elements of line quality, movement, and pen lifts.

Negative Type Examination

If two handwritten documents appear to a lay person to have been written by the same person, conduct a Negative Type Examination. The two writings are the same and the examiner must therefore determine if they are written by different persons. If the examiner fails in this attempt, he or she must then go to the original premise that they are the same and therefore written by the same person.

In this type of examination, no attempt is made to identify the writing. Instead, the object is to determine if it is a forgery. The individual characteristics, for the most part, will be the same, whether it is a copy or genuine. As there will have been an attempt to copy the characteristics, do not try to make a Positive Type examination. Writing on wills, grant deeds, personal notes, true name personal checks, suspected forgeries, and so on are items that require negative type examination. It is obvious that in the comparison of a will, you are making a "negative opinion," as you are looking for characteristics that will tell you it is a forgery. In a case of the twenty nonsufficient funds checks that are to be compared with a driver's license application, no information is available that will tell you the type of examination to be made. Therefore, you must go by the rule that, because they look the same, a negative examination is necessary. Examination of the elements, including "line quality," may reveal that the NSF checks are actually forgeries.

Wilson R. Harrison divides "suspect signatures" into seven classes[17].

1. Forged signatures where no attempt has been made to make a copy of the genuine signature of the person purporting to sign the document.
2. Forged signatures of fictitious persons.
3. Genuine signatures which have been obtained by trickery.
4. Genuine signatures which the writers are honestly unwilling to accept as genuine.
5. Genuine signatures which have been deliberately written illegibly or in an unusual manner, to afford the signatories some plausible grounds for disclaiming them should they deem it expedient.
6. A forged signature will resemble the genuine signature, written freehand to produce what is known as a "simulated" forgery.
7. Forged signatures which closely resemble the genuine signature since they have been produced by a tracing process.

Since the signatures in items 1 and 2 are seminormal signatures, and not copies, they will exhibit the characteristics of the forger and can be easily identified.

Items 3 and 4 are no longer the problem of the examiner after it is determined the signatures are genuine. Item 5, like disguised writing, will contain a few characteristics that do not match, but it is the unconscious characteristic that will stand out and announce that the signature is genuine.

Items 6 and 7 are the two most frequently used forgeries today. Copied and traced forgeries have to be examined very carefully with a negative examination.

Free-Hand Forgeries

Usually the forger gives no thought to the elements of a copied handwriting; his or her concern lies totally with the form. Any noticeable flourish strokes, embellishments, or exaggerated characteristics are copied. This makes the copy an unskilled imitation of the original, as the delicate characteristics in the letters are different from those in genuine writing. The line quality and skill of this type of forgery was pointed out in the 1968 Molly C. Putnam case examined by Ralph Bradford, in which he determined the endorsement of a $37,500 will to be a copied forgery. At a glance, the documents looked good, but after examination, sixteen negative characteristics were found.

The two top signatures in figure 8-10 are representative of a large number of exemplars. A comparison between these and the questioned signature below them show the following:

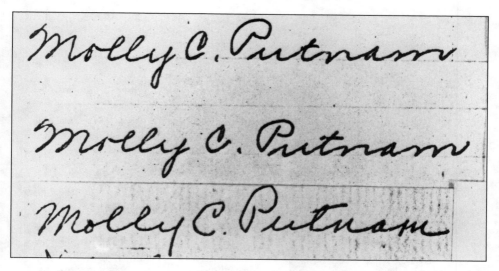

Figure 8–10: Molly C. Putnam $37,500 forgery.

1. The pick-up stroke on the exemplars begins at the top of the letter *M*, while the questioned signature has no pick-up.
2. The downstroke and the upstroke of the *M* is retraced on the top two signatures, while in the questioned signature they form an open angle.
3. The second downstroke of the exemplars is retraced, while on the questioned signature it forms an open angle.
4. Connecting stroke from *M* to *o* (exemplars) is angular, while on the questioned signature, the connecting stroke is more rounded.
5. The form of *o* is narrow or retraced on the exemplars, while the *o* of the questioned signature is rounded.
6. The finishing stroke of *o* is open angle on the exemplars, while the *o* of the questioned signature is eyed.
7. The capital *C* is smooth line quality on the exemplars, while that of the questioned signature has hesitation angles on the left shoulder and side.
8. The capital *P* is smooth line quality on the exemplars, while that of the questioned signature has hesitation angles at the top and left shoulder.
9. In the letter *u*, the retrace between the pickup stroke and body is an open angle, while pickup stroke and body of questioned signature is a retrace.
10. The first stroke of the *u* is short and the second high on the exemplars, while that of the questioned signature is reversed (head line).
11. The second upstroke of the *u* and its downstroke are open angles, while those of the questioned signature are a retrace.

12. The *t* is a retrace on the exemplars, while the questioned *t* has the form of an *l*.
13. The exemplar *t* has a horizontal *t*-crossing, while the questioned *t* has a high angular crossing.
14. The *n* and *m* on the exemplars have curved humps, while the humps of the questioned signature are sharp and angular.
15. The exemplar *m* and the final stroke have angular finishes, while that of the questioned signature is curved.
16. The final stroke on the exemplars slants upward, while the final stroke of the questioned signature is a horizontal curve.

Tremor, when found in handwriting, is usually referred to as the "tremor of fraud." This refers to writing not written fluently when compared with genuine writing. The light and dark shading of normal handwriting will be absent in the copy. Most countersignatures on stolen travelers checks are poorly copied forgeries. Some advanced check gangs use copies of genuine signatures on stolen commercial checks, and cash them at a bank where the company has their account.

Copied forgeries are accomplished in basically one of two ways:

1. Every characteristic is copied slowly and correctly. This slow method of writing causes a tremor or shakiness in the writing. Tremor is an obvious characteristic, and any endorsements written in this manner will be rejected by the skilled teller.
2. Copying the signature at a faster speed. This is the most popular method since it reduces the amount of tremor in the writing. Here, the document examiner will find a wealth of material. Although tremor is still there to some degree, the real giveaway lies in the "patches" a forger makes to mask a missed characteristic. Missed characteristics are one of the main elements that help the examiner determine a copy forgery.

Visible evidence is usually fairly obvious. During the copying of handwriting, the hand no longer glides over the paper, but moves slowly, as the eye moves back and forth from the copy to the pen. This slow movement produces poor quality, stops, and breaks in the writing and angular strokes. This also makes the line quality bad.

Patching is a characteristic found in copied writing. The pen continues to move while the eye looks ahead for the next characteristic to copy. When the eye looks back at the pen, it sees that the pen has moved too far. The pen is removed from the paper so that the line can be retouched to add the missing characteristic. Some retouching is so good that you need a magnifying glass to see the patch. Patchings are found in slower copies and some medium speed ones as well.

Missed characteristics are quite common in copied forgeries. To forge a writing with entire success, one must not only be able to see the significant characteristics of the writing of another person, but also have the muscular skill necessary to reproduce these characteristics, and at the same time eliminate all characteristics of one's own writing. The result usually is failure in both phases of the performance. The forger usually fails to determine the most significant characteristics in the writing which is being imitated, and he is even less aware of the significant characteristics of his own writing and may unconsciously include them in the forgery. Albert S. Osborn wrote, "Simulation, in almost every case, gives attention to the conspicuous features of form only, and the many other elements entering into the task receive no attention whatever."[18]

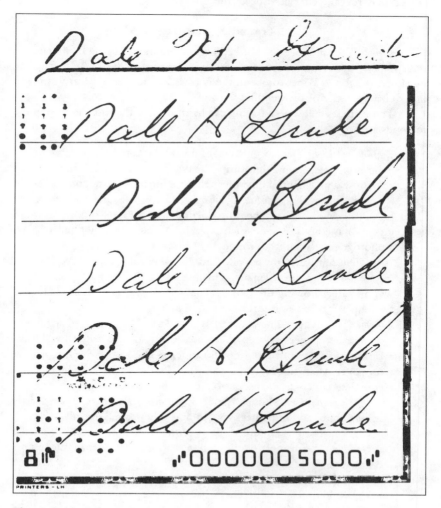

Figure 8–11: Dale H. Grade forgery.

The copied forgery of "Dale H. Grade" is just such a case. While there is some resemblance between the questioned signature and the exemplars, a closer examination of the base line loop shows that the letter G goes clockwise in the questioned signature and counterclockwise in the exemplars. A comparison of the proportion of the small letters also assists in the determination that the signature is a case of missed characteristics.

In a copy, the characteristics of the victim's handwriting as well as the possible forger should be examined. It is rare that the suspect can be identified in a copied handwriting case, but it is possible that characteristics that are not copied may reveal a characteristic of the forger.

Traced Signature

Forgers wishing to produce the perfect forgery and those lacking confidence in their ability, will attempt the traced signature. (See figure 8-12.) By tracing the signature, the forger hopes to obtain the correct spacing, slant, letter form, and other characteristics of the genuine signature.

There are several ways a tracing can be made, but the three most popular methods are:

1. *Transmitted Light Tracings.* A spurious document is placed over the document bearing a genuine signature. The two documents are then placed on a window with a light shining through from the back. If the top document is not too thick, the genuine signature is now visible, and can be copied. It is difficult to copy by holding documents up to a window, so more ingenious methods are used, such as placing a glass over a light bulb or even a photographer's contact printer.

   The signatures on pages 6 and 7 of the will of Dr. Mye Haddox (figure 8-13) were forged in such a manner. To prove the tracing, an exhibit was prepared showing the two signatures with the exemplar and also the two superimposed signatures of pages 6 and 7.

2. *Carbon Tracing.* A genuine signature is placed over the fabricated document with a carbon paper between. A tracing directly on the original will leave a carbon writing on the bottom document. The carbon writing is then traced over. Many suspects use a felt tip pen for the traceover, which assures a complete cover-up of the carbon and eliminates the tremor.

   The signature "Samuel Perrie" on the first (bottom) check (partially missing), third, and fifth checks is genuine. The second, fourth, and sixth checks from the bottom are carbons of the first, third, and fifth checks respectively. The tremor and the carbon writing can be seen, as the suspect did not write over it with a felt tip pen. When the suspect was arrested, the master (first check) and the third check were found in her purse in torn-up condition. The fifth check had been preserved in case she needed it again.

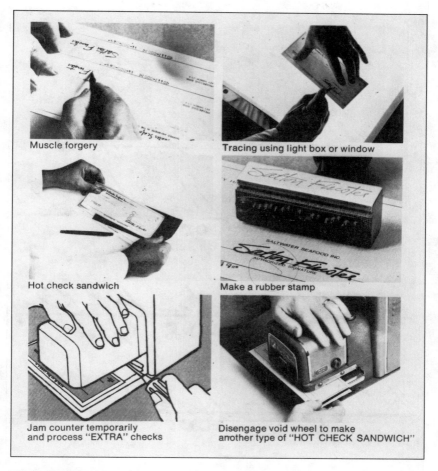

Figure 8–12: 470 PC, forgery. (*Burroughs Corp.*)

3. *Indented Tracing.* This is produced by the same procedures as a carbon tracing, but without the carbon paper. When tracing directly on the original, the writer applies more pressure to make an indentation on the bottom document. The forger then writes the victim's name, using the indentation as a guide.

Tracings by any of these methods requires slow writing, so the forger can be sure to copy it right. Slow writing causes the "tremor of fraud." This slowness also causes the writing to be devoid of shading. Line quality is a very important characteristic to examine in a suspected tracing.

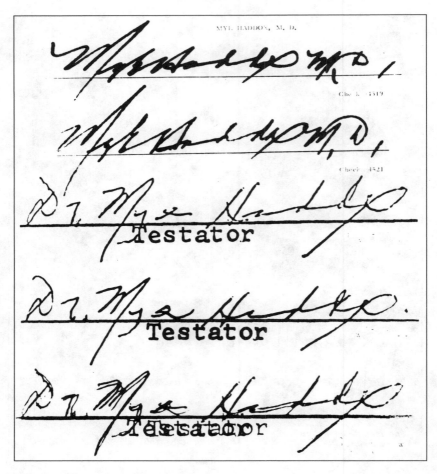

Figure 8–13: Dr. Mye Haddox traced forgery.

On all tracings except direct tracing, a guideline will appear on the document. This guideline will be a carbon line or indented line produced by the type of tracing. This guideline can be seen with a magnifying class or a microscope. The signatures should be photographed with infrared lighting, which will show the carbon guide lines. If there are any alterations, these too will show up in infrared photography. If an indentation forgery is suspected, cross-light photographs should be taken to show the valleys that were used for guidelines.

It is impossible for a person to write two identical signatures. Most tracings show *too many* identical characteristics to be normal. Tremor in the line quality, pressure, shading, and blunt endings and beginnings are indicators of traced

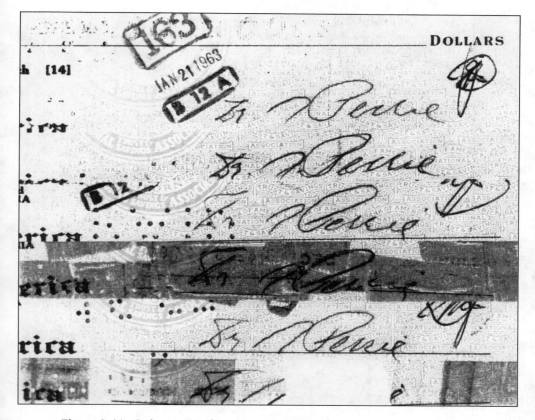

Figure 8–14: Carbon tracing forgery.

forgeries. The only positive proof that a writing is a tracing rather than a simulation is the detection of guidelines or the actual model from which the tracing was made.

Strange as it may seem, in many important cases the model for a traced signature is actually introduced in the case by the forger in order to prove the forged writing is genuine. The reasoning behind this surprising action seems to be the thought that a genuine writing so like the disputed signature will undoubtedly prove the questioned signature to be genuine.

One such "strange as it seems" case was assigned to Ralph Bradford in a 1970 examination of a quit-claim deed. The initial examination disclosed a normal shakiness in the writing of "Myrtle Stewart." Normal shakiness is often difficult to differentiate from the "tremor of fraud." A person who has a normal tremor will nevertheless write part of some letters free of tremor. Thus, a careful examination will usually locate some quality lines in a tremorous writing.

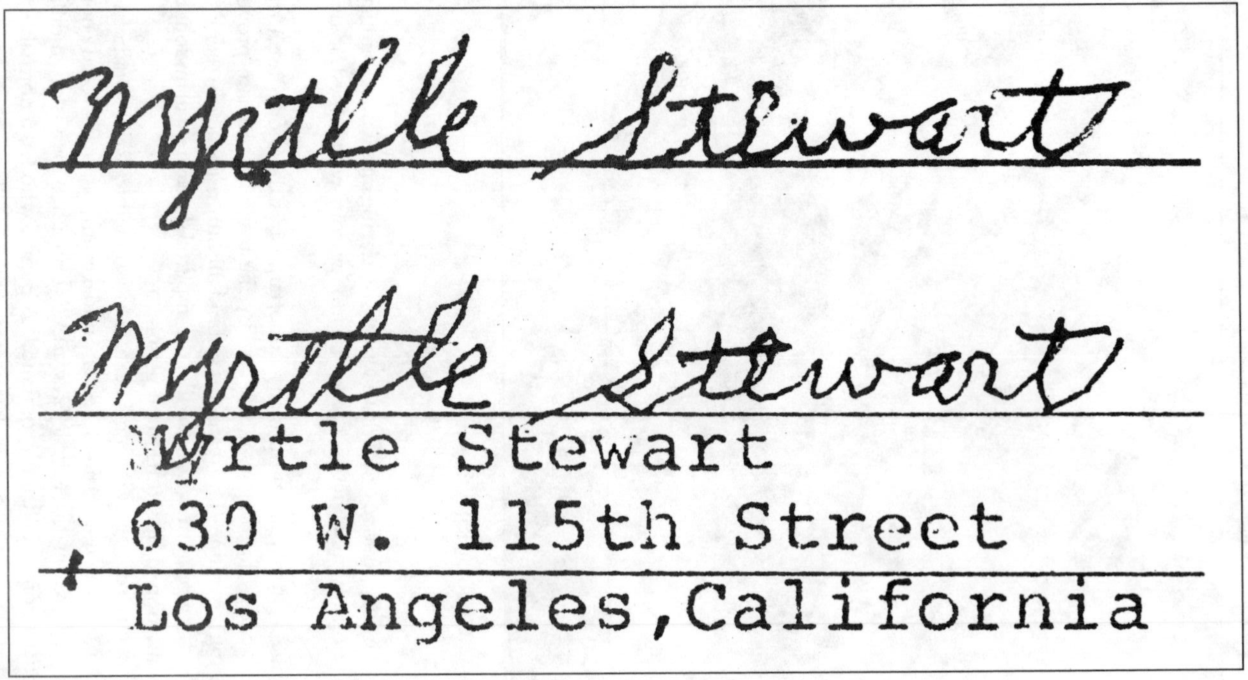

Figure 8-15: Myrtle Stewart tracing.

In the Stewart case, Bradford could not find much consistency in the tremorous writing. At this point, he asked for additional exemplars and also learned of other good signatures on documents already part of the case.

Examination of the additional exemplars revealed that the usual characteristic at the top of the second *L*, which was observed in the questioned writing in the top signature (figure 8-15), was also present on one exemplar. The unusual characteristic on the *L* was not seen in any of the other exemplar writings. It was concluded that it was an accidental characteristic that had been traced onto the questioned document. Additional examination revealed that the measurements of the two *L*'s were very close. It should be noted that when a person traces a signature, the paper will "slip," thus making the traced signatures appear slightly longer than the genuine.

A forger of documents will trace a document with a different line quality than the victim. In the Stewart case, the line quality of the tracing of the accidental characteristic is of better quality than in the genuine signature.

Preparation of a traced forgery for court should include photographic exhibits. Be careful not to use enlargements of extreme size. Paper slippage and the forger's lack of ability will show much differently in extreme enlargements. A tracing forgery should be attacked in court just like a straight forgery. Emphasis should be placed on tremor, patching, and missed characteristics. Albert Osborn wrote, "The discovery of two or more questioned signatures that resemble each other in a suspicious manner and at the same time bear in themselves the inherent evidence of forgery, which writing shows when produced by tracing method, affords the strongest kind of additional proof that the writing is a forgery."[19]

— 9 —

Hand Printing and Numbers

The examination of disconnected letters presents a problem from the start. Authors of books and articles on the subject use a variety of names for this type of writing, including:

- *Hand Printing.* Favored by David J. Purtell and Maureen A. Casey in the article "The Comparison Value of Hand Printing Styles."[1]
- *Handlettering.* Favored by Ordway Hilton in his book *Scientific Examination of Questioned Documents.*[2]
- *Handprinting.* Favored by James Conway in his book *Evidential Documents.*[3]
- *Lettering, Manuscript Writing.* Favored by the school systems and Marjorie Wise in her book *Manuscript Writing.*[4]
- *Pen and Pencil Printing.* Favored by Albert S. Osborn in his book *Questioned Documents.*[5]
- *Print Script, Print Writing, Printing Script.* Favored by Wilson Harrison in his book *Suspect Documents.*[6]
- *Script Writing.* Favored in other books and articles.

The school systems used "manuscript writing" as early as 1924 and still use it. They did not like any name containing the word "print," as it was both misleading and incorrect. Printing is a mechanical procedure, and they felt it was wrong to suggest that children model their handwriting on a uniform and characterless device such as printing. "Script" was rejected on the grounds that it has different means in different countries. "Manuscript Writing," although somewhat redundant and in some ways ridiculous, carries with it a flavor of old books and libraries. So, for its suggestive tendency and for lack of a better designation, it was the name chosen by the school system.[7] *Webster's New Collegiate*

Dictionary defines manuscript writing as: "Writing as opposed to print." For this reason, we object to the name "manuscript writing."

Webster's defines printing as: "To form in characters like those of type, as a letter printed by a child; to write in letters shaped like those of ordinary Roman text type." "Handprinting," as one word, is not found in this dictionary, so we chose "hand printing" as the most descriptive and correct title.

Correct terminology may not seem that important to some, but to others, such as Bill Coleman, it has great value. As a student, Bill heard his history teacher state: "Thomas Jefferson wrote the Declaration of Independence." Bill compared the writing of the Declaration of Independence with the signature of Thomas Jefferson at the bottom; they did not match. Bill took the problem to his father, Dick Coleman, of the Long Beach Police Department, Forgery Detail. Dick had been a student in the Bradford Handwriting Class taught in 1965; he also was unable to identify the writing, so he gave the problem to the Bradfords.

It was learned that Thomas Jefferson did not "write" the Declaration of Independence, as the teacher had said; rather, he "drafted" or "composed" it. When the Declaration was adopted on July 4, 1776, it was turned over to John Dunlap to "print copies." That night, Dunlap set type and, using a hand press, printed hundreds of 15-inch by 18-inch copies to be distributed. It was Timothy Matlack, the contracted engrosser, who actually "wrote" or "printed" the Declaration of Independence. The document was then signed by John Hancock, along with fifty-five other signers, on August 2, 1776. Depending on how you word it, any one of three persons "wrote" or "printed" the Declaration of Independence.

A History of Hand Printing

The history of handwriting and hand printing started with picture writing (hieroglyphics) of the ancient Egyptians in about 3000 B.C. The pictures took shape as letters as they were passed through the Seirite (1850 B.C.), Phoenician (1200 B.C.), Greek (600 B.C.) and Roman cultures (A.D. 114). The Romans used only capital letters, but with careless writing, small letters came into common use. Hand printing faded out with the teaching of cursive writing in the 1500s. John Watson, in 1533, was the first teacher of handwriting.[8]

With the introduction of cursive handwriting, hand printing ceased to be used. Ms. M. M. Bridges in England believed that hand printing could be taught to children, and it would be easier for them to learn. In 1899, Bridges' work was published, but it attracted little attention. Edward Johnston, Grailey Hewitt, Ms. S. A. Golds, and Professor Shelbey have all written on this subject.

In 1922, Marjorie Wise of England came to the United States and offered a course in manuscript writing (hand printing) at Columbia University. Wise's work gave impetus to this new method of writing, and private schools were quick to take advantage of it. At the time, the advantages of hand printing were many:

1. The copy books used letters that were basically the same as the printed letters used in a book. This style was, therefore, easy to learn to write and read, as only one alphabet or style of letter was used.
2. For the same reason, children learned to spell at a faster rate when using hand printing.
3. Hand printing was less stressful on the children, and they therefore enjoyed it more, which resulted in more rapid advancement.
4. Hand printing was more legible than cursive writing.

In those early times, "many predicted that manuscript writing would result in a uniform stereotyped handwriting, and destroy individuality. Were this the case, grave dangers would ensue in banking and business, making forgery an everyday occurrence. No such results seem to have followed. It is asserted that individuality appears in manuscript writing with unfailing certainty, as the same mental and physical peculiarities which produce it in the running hand manifest themselves equally in the manuscript handwriting."[9]

Facts and Procedures

In recent years, hand printing on documents has greatly increased. The words, "Print—Do not write," can be found on documents throughout the business world. Applications for bank or credit institutions routinely request printing for legibility. Individuals also print applications for employment, since the average person can print better than he or she can write. Many businesses require printing, so that no mistake is made when reading the document.

The criminal element uses printing, but as a disguise. Since many do not believe hand printing can be identified, forged documents are often printed. Anonymous letters of all types—kidnap, threatening, and confessional letters sent to the newspapers; robbery notes; betting markers; etc.—are printed in order to disguise. With the increase in printing by individuals, hand printing is an increasing factor in the examination of questioned documents.

Contrary to the belief of many, hand printing is highly individual and, with suitable exemplars, can be identified. "The writer is astonished to learn that so unusual a product of his hand as hand printing is distinctly individual and differs from similar work by others, and astonishment is usually expressed by most observers at the unmistakable identity of an extended disputed document of this kind and a request writing."[10]

In order to be compared and identified hand printing, like handwriting, must contain individual characteristics. Numerous individual characteristics can be seen in the abandoned baby note (figure 9–1), such as the initial stroke of the small letters *a* and *e*. It is also essential that there are a sufficient number of the individual characteristics in the questioned writing. With proper exemplars, a comparison can then be made. With a successful examination, a positive opinion may be expressed regarding a hand printed document.

The examination of hand printing, like writing, requires certain facts and procedures which must be followed. The rules for hand printing are basically the same as the rules for handwriting found in chapter 8, but the emphasis is changed.

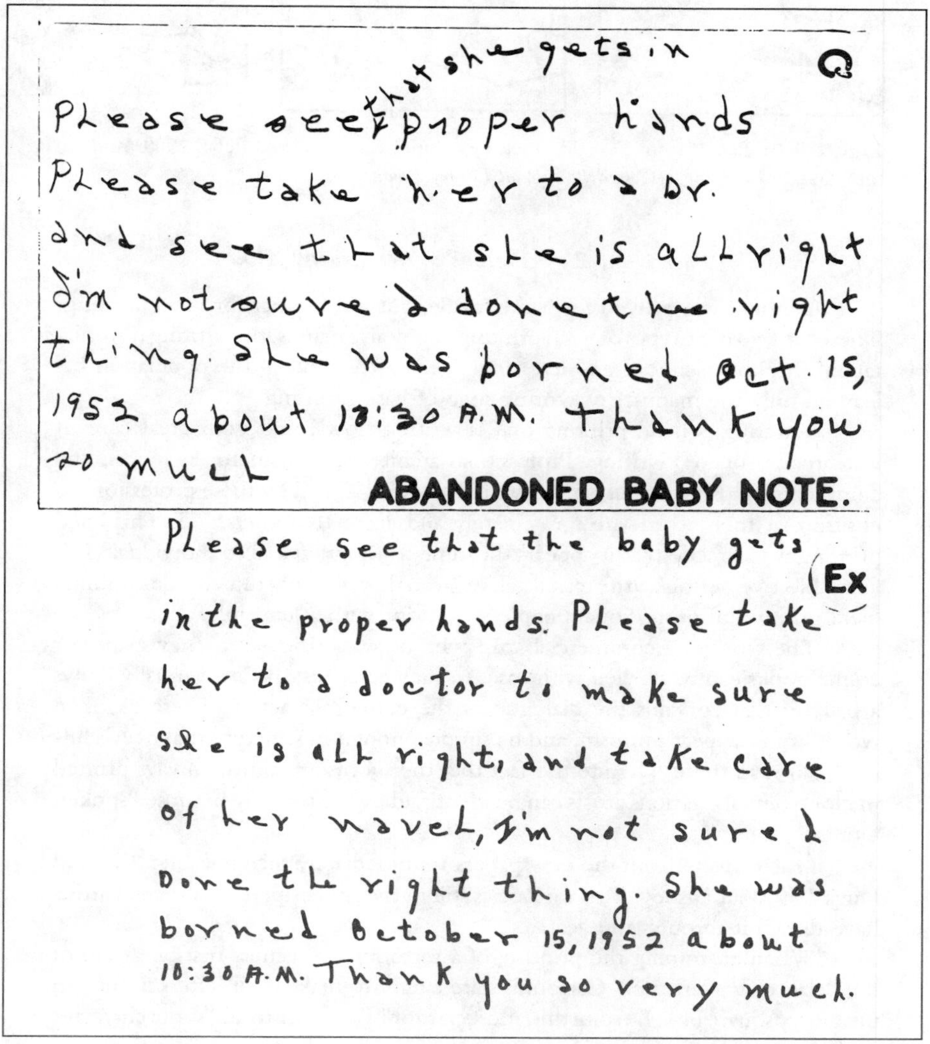
Q

Please see that she gets in proper hands
Please take her to a Dr.
and see that she is allright
I'm not sure I done the right
thing. She was borned Oct. 15,
1952 about 10:30 A.M. Thank you
so much

ABANDONED BABY NOTE.

Ex

Please see that the baby gets
in the proper hands. Please take
her to a doctor to make sure
she is all right, and take care
of her navel, I'm not sure I
Done the right thing. She was
borned October 15, 1952 about
10:30 A.M. Thank you so very much.

Figure 9–1: Abandoned-baby note.

Figure 9–2: Panels from Donald Duck newspaper cartoon–1983 (left), 1980 (middle), and 1975 (right). (*Copyright* © *Walt Disney Productions*)

Fact 1. No Two Persons Write Exactly Alike

This statement was proved for handwriting, but is it correct for hand printing? There are two basic types of hand printing. They are: manuscript writing (printing taught in public schools) and lettering. A major portion of the population has learned only the manuscript writing style of hand printing.

Lettering is hand printing that is written slowly and with great care. It is a precise style of writing. Professional architects, draftsmen, engineers, and commercial artists write using this style. Lettering is used by these professions to ensure that their words are immediately and correctly understood. This hand printing is so precise that it appears the same from individual to individual. The fact, "No two persons write exactly alike," can therefore be studied by examining hand printing of professional people who print with a lettering style.

The work of a commercial artist who draws cartoons for a newspaper or comic books can be studied with ease. In such cartoons, the artist usually draws a balloon that contains the dialogue of the comic characters. These "spoken words" must appear uniform, and be simple enough in structure that even children can read them. Despite the fact that the words are almost always printed in block capitals, various artists can be identified by the printing in those "spoken words."

One cartoon from the newspapers is immediately recognizable: "Donald Duck" by Walt Disney. This cartoon is still in the newspapers, and several artists have drawn it through the years.

When examining the printing of a cartoonist you must first be aware of the "class characteristics." Cartoonists are taught to make their letters fit into an imaginary square box. Despite this, most cartoonists are able to add some character to their printing. This individuality can be seen when examining the printing in a cartoon.

No two persons write (or print) exactly alike. The "Donald Duck" panels (figure 9-2) prove this to be true even of cartoonists. The first individual characteristic that immediately stands out is the initial downstroke of the letter *u*. To get the width for the letter, the artist enlarges the letter with his initial downstroke, making a very characteristic letter. This same artist adds a hook to the letter *c* and slants most of the horizontal lines. It is easy to see, despite the block printing used by these trained artists, that the 1980 and 1983 cartoon panels are by the same person, while the 1975 panel is by another person. This proves that people, even professional cartoonists, do not print exactly alike.

Fact 2. Retention of Characteristics

In chapter 8, it is stated that handwriting remains basically the same from maturity until old age. This is also true for hand printing. Children learn to hand print in the early school years and then change to script for the remainder of their teen years. Because of constant use, handwriting matures into a permanent style. With use hand printing will also develop, mature, and then remain constant until old age.

To determine the retention of characteristics over a period of several years, we shall again examine the comics. One of the most famous of the comic book artists is Carl "Duck Man" Barks. From 1943 to 1953, Barks wrote and illustrated ten pages of the Donald Duck comics every month, along with nearly two dozen Donald Duck one-shots. Barks also created "Uncle Scrooge," and wrote and illustrated that comic from 1952 to 1967.

Carl Barks used to write all the dialogues in his comics, but in 1952 he turned the dialogue printing over to his wife, Gare Barks, who used a special speedball pen to do the lettering. She made use of a bottom-lighted lettering board and a ruled template to determine letter height. Despite the fact she hadn't lettered any "quacks" in seventeen years, she consented to print an exemplar without using any special equipment so it could be compared with her earlier printing.

Gare Barks was asked to print the first two lines of the first panel of the 1956 Uncle Scrooge comic. These particular lines were chosen in the hope that the repetition of letters would bring out the variation of her 1956 printing. Comparison of the two printings (figure 9–4) discloses the letters *A* and *G* are different in the two printings. The spread-out legs of the *M* and the quality of the *P,* on the second line of the exemplar are characteristic and match the 1956 printing. The letter *R* shows great variation throughout the exemplar. The *R* in the first word in the third line of the exemplar displays the same characteristic as in the cartoon. The major characteristic of the 1956 and 1983 exemplars is in the letter *Y.* Comparing the *Y* on the third line of the exemplar with the 1956 printing shows a 2-to-1 relationship. The body of the *Y* is twice as large as its final tail and is very characteristic.

Figure 9–3: First panel of Uncle Scrooge cartoon, no. 13. (*Copyright © Walt Disney Productions*)

A comparison of Gare's hand printing after twenty-seven years showed remarkable similarities. Retention of characteristics is as true in hand printing as it is in writing.

Fact 3. Identifications of Hand Printing Are Made by Identifying Characteristics.

This fact is as correct for handwriting as it is for hand printing. Locating individual characteristics is the major problem in hand printing. An apprentice examiner is more likely to incorrectly identify a common characteristic as an individual one. Therefore, the chance for error is even higher if the document is hand printed.

Variations are also greater in hand printing due to the fact that people print a great deal less than they write. The lack of practice in printing means a lack of consistency. As a person gains practice in printing, the variation is reduced.

When well practiced, this style shows a small degree of variation, and the individual characteristics can be identified.

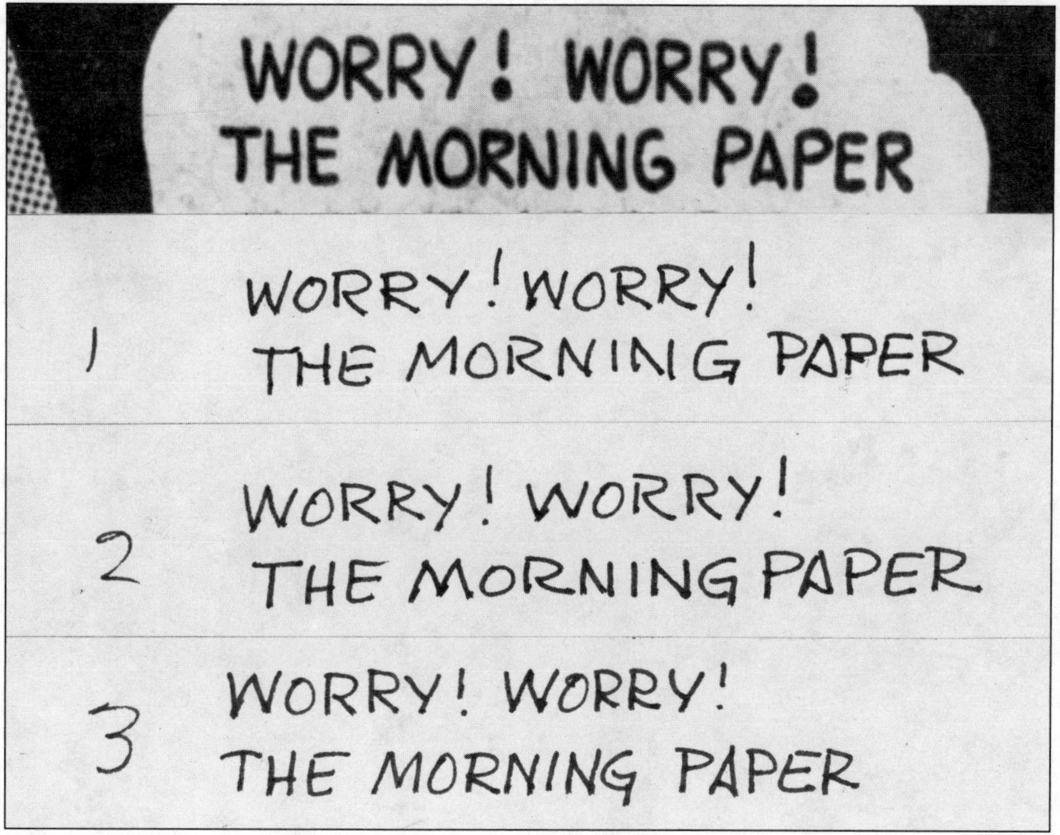

Figure 9–4: Cartoon no. 13 and Gare Barks exemplar.

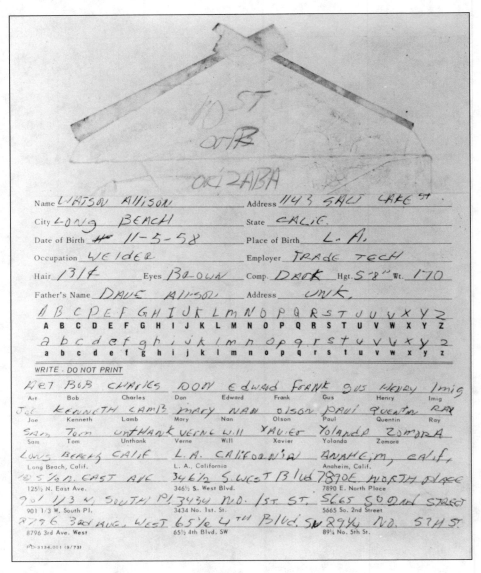

Figure 9–5: Evidence in the Polk murder case.

Identifying characteristics and then determining the individuality, played a part in the Polk murder case (figure 9–5). On the floorboard of a suspect vehicle was an envelope listing the address of the murder. The letter Z was determined to be very characteristic and individual. The capital and small letter R was also identified as characteristic, and assisted in the identification of the envelope printing.

Procedures

The examination of hand printing, like handwriting, hinges on the same three important facts.

- Fact 1. No two persons write exactly alike (and no one person writes exactly the same twice).
- Fact 2. Retention of characteristics.
- Fact 3. Identification of hand printing is made by identifying characteristics.

With these three facts in mind, you are now ready to make an examination. It is important that the following six procedures are fully understood and taken in order.

Procedure 1. Gather all Questioned Documents
Procedure 2. Examine all Printing on the Questioned Documents

These two procedures are as important for printing as they are for writing. The object is to obtain all questioned printed documents available. This will make the examination easier, and increase the likelihood of a positive opinion.

Since printing requires a more difficult examination due to its variations, you, as examiner, should seek all possible help. A large amount of printing will assist you in determining the variations, and help you locate the individual characteristics that are of value.

One case where the gathering of "all" documents made a difference concerned a robbery at the Farmers and Merchants Bank, Long Beach, California. The suspect gave the teller a note printed on a brown paper bag, which read: "I have a gun, give me the money." Both the brown paper bag and the exemplars of the suspect were submitted for examination.

Several characteristics in the robbery note were identified. These included the loop in the final stroke of the G; the four-stroke E; the four-stroke M, with the unusual center; the lowercase h; and the small o, in relation to the rest of the uppercase letters. In the questioned printing the letter U had no final stroke to the base line, and the top of the letter A was disconnected. Because of these final two characteristics, and the lack of a number of individual characteristics, this case

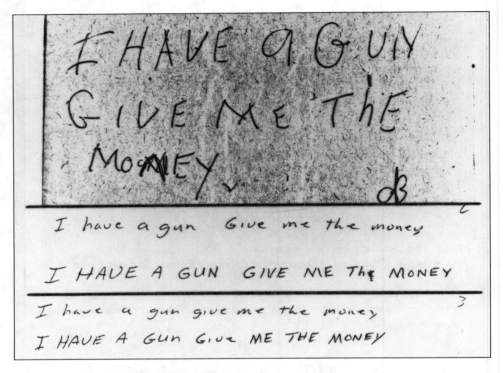

Figure 9–6: Robbery note (top) and exemplars.

was examined at intervals for three days. A "could-be" opinion was verbally given, and since there was so little other evidence in the overall case, the examiner was subpoenaed. The federal prosecutor felt that the could-be opinion would be strengthened if a *second suspect* in the case could be eliminated. An examination of the second suspect's hand printing resulted in a positive opinion.

The examiner's failure to obtain all documents pertinent to the case could have resulted in an incorrect opinion. There were many similar characteristics in the writing of suspect one. If all the documents had been obtained at the beginning, less time would have been spent on examination, and there would have been less chance for error. Once you have gathered all the documents in the case that contain hand printing, and then examined all the questioned writings, you are then ready for Procedure 3.

Procedure 3. Locate Nonrequest Examplars

As previously stated, the criminal element frequently uses hand printing as a disguise. Nonrequest exemplars are, therefore, most important in a hand printing

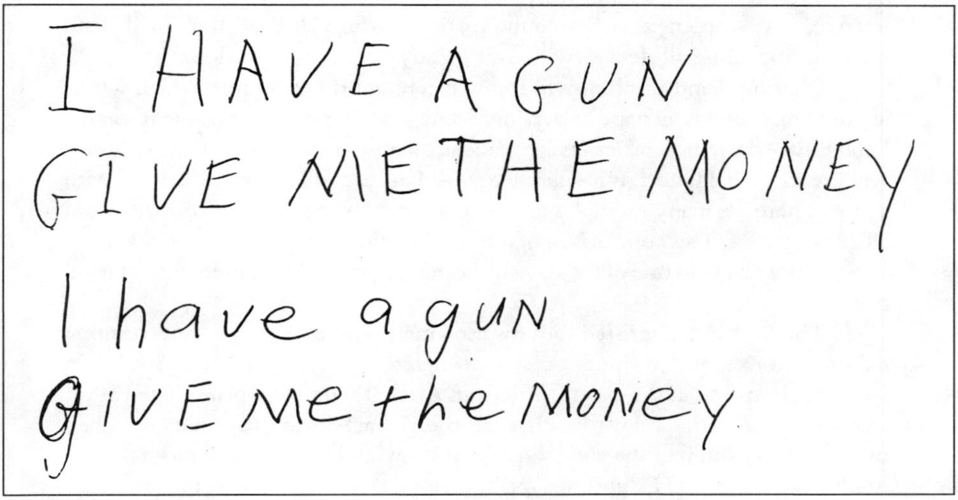

I HAVE A GUN
GIVE ME THE MONEY

I have a gun
GIVE Me the Money

Figure 9–7: Hand printing of second suspect.

case. Because of the changing of a person's printing due to lack of practice, the exemplars should be dated as close to the questioned document as possible. The availability of nonrequest printed exemplars is very good in most cases. Applications for employment or work documents are usually printed and therefore make good exemplars.

Procedure 4. Examine the Request Exemplars

There are two types of request exemplars: Those in normal conscious writing and those in consciously disguised writing. Therefore, *all* request exemplars are considered second class, since they are consciously written. This fact must be remembered and taken into consideration. Request exemplars should be examined with the nonrequest type as they will complement each other.

Disguise in hand printing can be very effective and cause difficulties for the examiner. A suspect writes disconnected letters one letter at a time. When printing in this manner, the suspect has ample time to think disguise. The examiner, however, can readily recognize this nonrhythmic printing. An examination of the total document will also assist the examiner.

Procedure 5. Copy the Questioned Printing

Copying of hand printing should be done on a chart. This method consists of lining a piece of paper with the twenty-six letters written in order down the left side. The questioned word would now be copied letter by letter, placing each letter of the word next to its counterpart. Charting all the questioned hand printing, including all details, will assist greatly in the examination.

Charting hand printing will immediately tell the examiner which letters are uppercase and which are lowercase. Some persons print everything in capital letters, even though some letters are made smaller to simulate small letters. Others will use all capital letters, but will use a small *l* instead of the capital letter *L* with a foot. There are many examples of one small letter being used on a document of all capital letters. This comparison of the combination of uppercase and lowercase letters is the first, and one of the most important, parts of the examination of hand printing.

The same charting listed above is also a method of preparing a hand-printing exhibit. An example of this is a case in which a subject wrote on the wall of a women's restroom at the North American Aircraft Company plant. The janitor was identified as the culprit by charting the characteristics; the chart was then made into an exhibit of the same style. In this way, individual characteristics were found; the *G, N, CTH*, and the spelling characteristic identified the suspect.

Procedure 6. Determine the Type of Hand Printing Examination Needed and Proceed with the Comparison

To determine the type of handwriting examination needed, as discussed in chapter 8, one must decide whether to make a positive or negative examination. In the comparison of hand printing, however, that decision is seldom necessary as all comparisons will be of a positive type and will attempt to identify the writer of the questioned document. Only rarely is printing copied onto another document. Line quality, explained in comparison element 6 in the next section of this chapter, is most useful in keeping you alert to a copied document.

As previously stated, extreme caution must be used during a hand-printing examination. Errors in these examinations can develop for several reasons:

1. Examiners work few hand-printing cases and therefore get rusty in this type examination.
2. Suspects with little printing experience will not have developed a consistent style of printing, which may cause one-time characteristics to be falsely identified.
3. Hand-printed letters are less complicated in form, tempting inexperienced examiners to place unwarranted significance on some letters.

The comparison of hand printing begins with copying the letters in all their detail onto a chart (Procedure 5). Examine each letter with a magnifying glass to determine the number of individual strokes and the direction of each stroke. The direction can be determined by the drag strokes, which will be discussed under element 5, "Form."

The examination of hand printing involves a step-by-step comparison of the elements. While handwriting has twenty elements, hand printing has only seventeen. Connections, pickups and terminals are basically eliminated in a hand-printing comparison. Instead, more emphasis is placed on form. Direction of individual strokes as well as drag strokes are important.

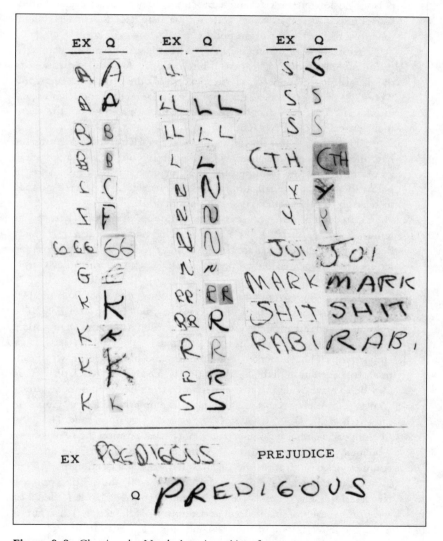

Figure 9–8: Charting the North American Aircraft case.

Elements of Hand Printing Comparison

1. *Alignment*. This element is not only first on the list, but it is also the first element you will see when copying a hand printing chart. The height of the small letters is the first important characteristic. Students are taught to print the small letters half the size of the capital letters. The small letters would rise to an imaginary line that we call the head line, but as many persons no longer print as taught in school, they print all capital letters. Cartoonists also use all capital letters. The height of the small letters is therefore the first comparison point.

   An example of alignment can be seen in the sexual harassment investigation of an employee at Rockwell International. A birthday card sent to the plaintiff had all uppercase letters, except for the *p* and *g*. In the words "You," "Love," and others, the first letter was larger than the other uppercase letters. There are many characteristics in the printing, but the alignment characteristics best identify it.

   The head line (the imaginary line the capital letters rise up to) and the base line (the ruled or imaginary line the letters rest on) are also important in an examination. The printing of a letter (or several letters) on, above, or below the base line is characteristic; it is this characteristic, when examined in relation to other letters, that can be individual.

2. *Angles*. In hand printing, there are a great number of angles in letters. The letters *A, K, M, N, V, W, X, Y,* and *Z* all have angles of less than ninety degrees. Right angle letters are: *E, F, H, I, L,* and *T.* The design of printed letters causes repeated redirection of lines, which in turn causes sharply differing angles.

   If these angles are consistent, they become very characteristic. Determining this consistency in your copy chart will be of great help. The volume of angles that can be used in a comparison makes this an important element in the comparison of hand printing.

3. *Arrangement*. This element is the same in hand printing as in writing. It refers to the position of the hand printing on a page. The M.O. of a person may be to leave wide margins or certain spacing between lines or words.

4. *Curves*. Simple curves and straight lines make up printed letters. Curves in the letters *B, C, D, G, J, O, P, Q, R, S,* and *U* are important. The letter *O* is not just a circle. It is important to note what position the *O* starts in— 9 o'clock, 12 o'clock, and so on. At the point the *O* starts, the line goes counterclockwise to form the *O,* and then stops at an ending point. The location of this ending point, in conjunction with the starting point, is characteristic. The letter *G* has a large curve on the left side (called a *left curve*) and a series of small curves at the bottom of the letter. These curves make the letter *G* one of the most individual letters in hand printing.

   One of the most unusual curve characteristics was found in a ledger

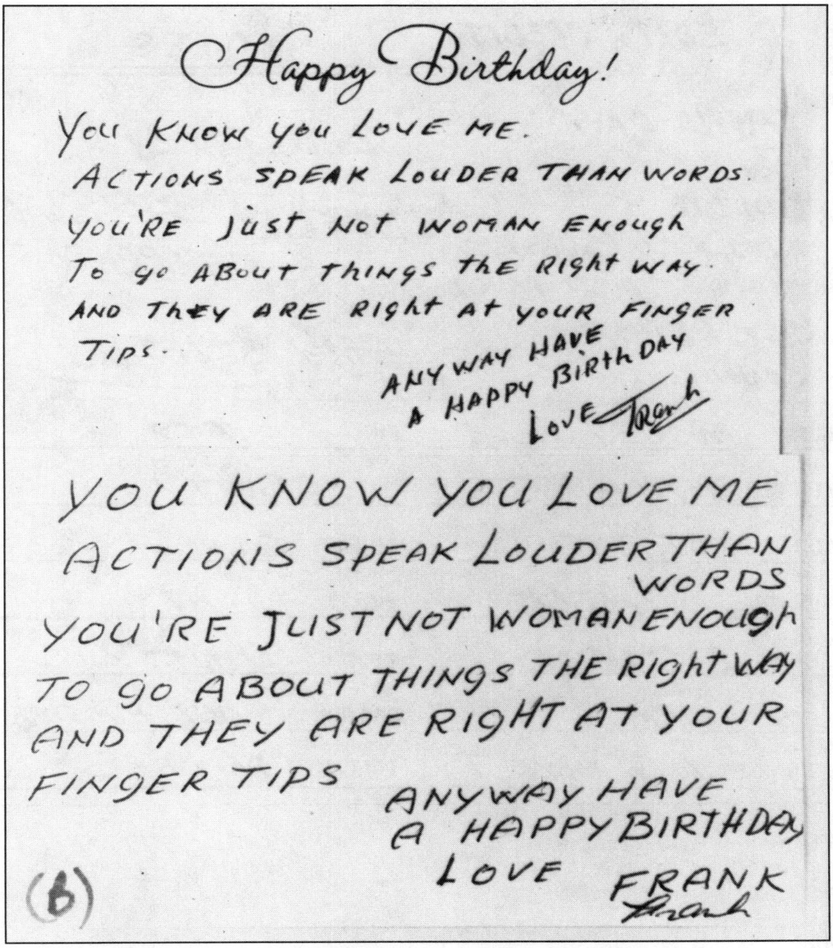

Happy Birthday!

YOU KNOW YOU LOVE ME.
ACTIONS SPEAK LOUDER THAN WORDS.
YOU'RE JUST NOT WOMAN ENOUGH
TO GO ABOUT THINGS THE RIGHT WAY.
AND THEY ARE RIGHT AT YOUR FINGER
TIPS.
ANYWAY HAVE
A HAPPY BIRTHDAY
LOVE Frank

YOU KNOW YOU LOVE ME
ACTIONS SPEAK LOUDER THAN
WORDS
YOU'RE JUST NOT WOMAN ENOUGH
TO GO ABOUT THINGS THE RIGHT WAY
AND THEY ARE RIGHT AT YOUR
FINGER TIPS
ANYWAY HAVE
A HAPPY BIRTHDAY
LOVE
FRANK
Frank

(b)

Figure 9–9: Happy Birthday card.

of a narcotics suspect. The left stroke of the letter *Y* was extremely individual. It was made with such a flair that it could almost be called an embellishment (figure 9–10).

5. *Form*. In handwriting, a letter used at the start of a word may differ from the same letter in the middle or at the ending of that word. This change of form in a letter does not occur in hand printing because the letters are disconnected. Hence form is more important in printing than in handwriting comparison. Hand printed letters, for the most part, will be of a "Gothic form," which has no serifs as in machine printed letters.

The examination of hand printed letters requires the use of a magni-

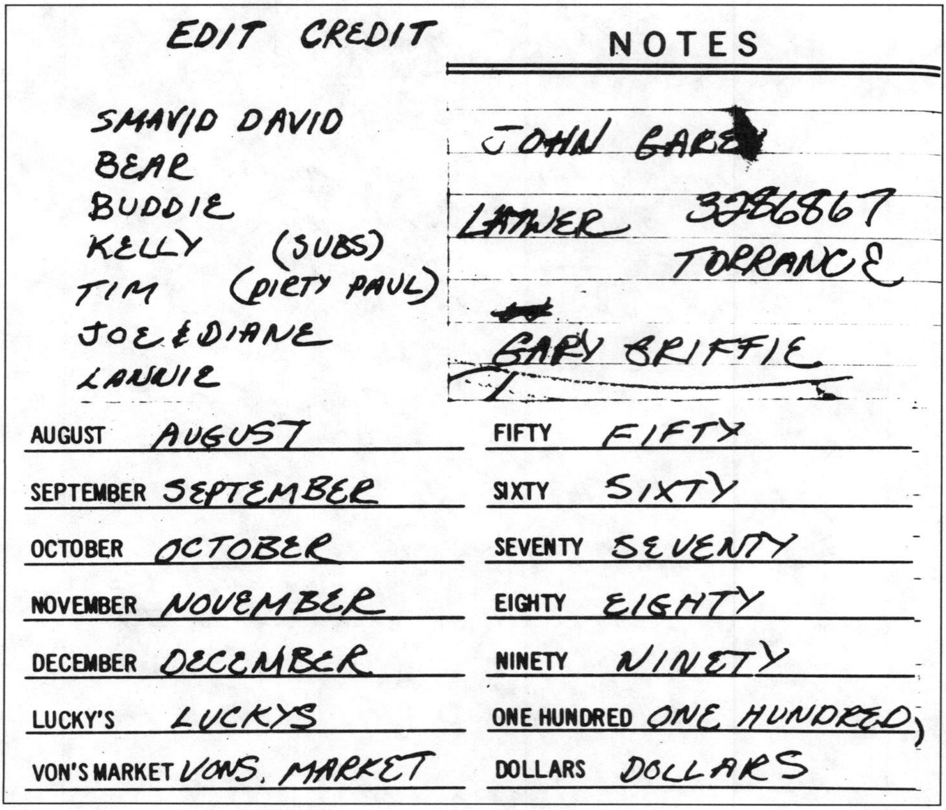
EDIT CREDIT

SMAVID DAVID
BEAR
BUDDIE
KELLY (SUBS)
TIM (DIRTY PAUL)
JOE & DIANE
LANNIE

NOTES

JOHN GARE
LAWER 3786867
TORRANCE
GARY BRIFFIE

AUGUST	AUGUST	FIFTY	FIFTY
SEPTEMBER	SEPTEMBER	SIXTY	SIXTY
OCTOBER	OCTOBER	SEVENTY	SEVENTY
NOVEMBER	NOVEMBER	EIGHTY	EIGHTY
DECEMBER	DECEMBER	NINETY	NINETY
LUCKY'S	LUCKYS	ONE HUNDRED	ONE HUNDRED
VON'S MARKET	VONS. MARKET	DOLLARS	DOLLARS

Figure 9–10: Narcotics ledger.

fying glass. It is important to determine the exact number of individual strokes that make a letter. The letter *E*, for example, can be made with four individual lines. Many persons make an *L*, and then add two additional lines to complete the letter, or, for a more individual letter, some make an upsidedown *L* and then add the additional two lines.

LSD, a hallucinogenic narcotic, was found in a hollowed-out book that was to be mailed by a professor at California State University at Long Beach. A detailed examination of the hand-printed letters on the address label with a magnification glass disclosed an individual letter *K*. The letter was made with two strokes. The first stroke made a *V*, and the second stroke then made the final leg of the letter. A normal examination of this letter might have missed its unusual form.

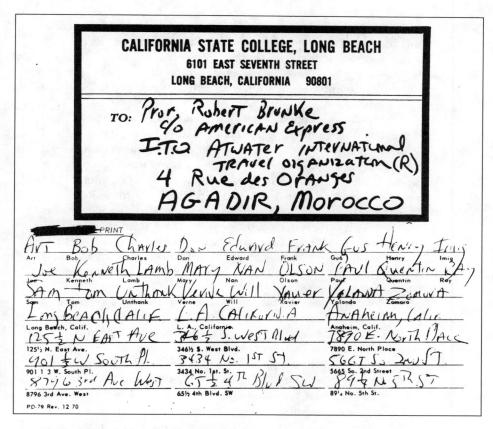

Figure 9–11: Address label in LSD case.

Determining the number of strokes is the first step. The second step is determining the sequence in which they were written. Many times when a person hand prints, he does not totally remove his pen from the paper after completing a stroke. The pen will then make a "drag stroke" to where the pen is used to write the next stroke. These drag strokes will not only tell the sequence of strokes, but will also tell in which direction a line was made. Once you know exactly how a letter was made, you can examine a known hand printing to determine if the two letters are made of the same construction or form.

The letters *E, G, K, M, R, S, W,* and *Y* are all very characteristic letters, especially the letter *K*. What makes the *K* important is its number of strokes, as well as the location of the start of the two downstrokes in

327

relation to each other. Also important is the location where the first stroke joins the second and the angle at which the strokes come together, as well as many additional points which make this letter form.

6. *Line quality (speed)*. This element is important as far as a possible copied forgery is concerned. However, it is an extremely rare case that contains a copy printed forgery.

   Line quality is important when determining the amount of disguise in printing. A lack of fluency in printing is usually due to (1) disguise, and (2) lack of practice. Printing is therefore an act that requires more mental control but less fluency than handwriting. Because of this, the comparison of line quality is important in determining the amount of normal hand printing that must be examined. Line quality is the one element that makes a hand printing comparison more difficult than a handwriting examination.

7. *Movement*. One of the reasons for the movement from cursive to manuscript (hand printing) by the school systems was that hand printing puts less strain on the arms of the children. The printing of individual letters allows for more rest, whereas in writing one cannot stop until an entire word is written.

   Movement does not play an important part in the comparison of printing. The freedom of long strokes and continuity of motion can be found in handwriting. Because of the numerous individual strokes, this complete freedom of movement is rare in hand printing.

8. *Pen lifts*. This element has already been discussed under Form, but it is important to recognize that it is also an element of comparison. The exact construction of a hand-printed letter must be understood by an examiner. A magnification glass will enable you to determine the number of pen lifts in the printing of a letter. Once this is known, you can then compare it to the exact construction of a like letter in the known exemplars. In handwriting, the comparison pen lifts can be found within letters or between letters. In hand printing, pen lifts are strictly within the letter. Pen lifts are for the most part unconscious characteristics, and are therefore important in the examination of hand printing.

9. *Proportion*. This element is basically the same in hand printing as it is in handwriting. The author believes that proportion is one of the most important elements of comparison. The size of a letter in relation to other letters, in height or width, is a comparison of proportion. Proportion may also be a comparison of one part of a letter with another part. The capital letter *B* is normally printed with the upper half smaller in height and width than the lower portion. It is therefore very characteristic if this proportion is reversed, with the upper half the larger part.

   An example of proportion within the letter is seen in a kidnap and assault with deadly weapon case regarding some "religious maniacs." The victim was subjected to beatings and electric shock by a family attempting

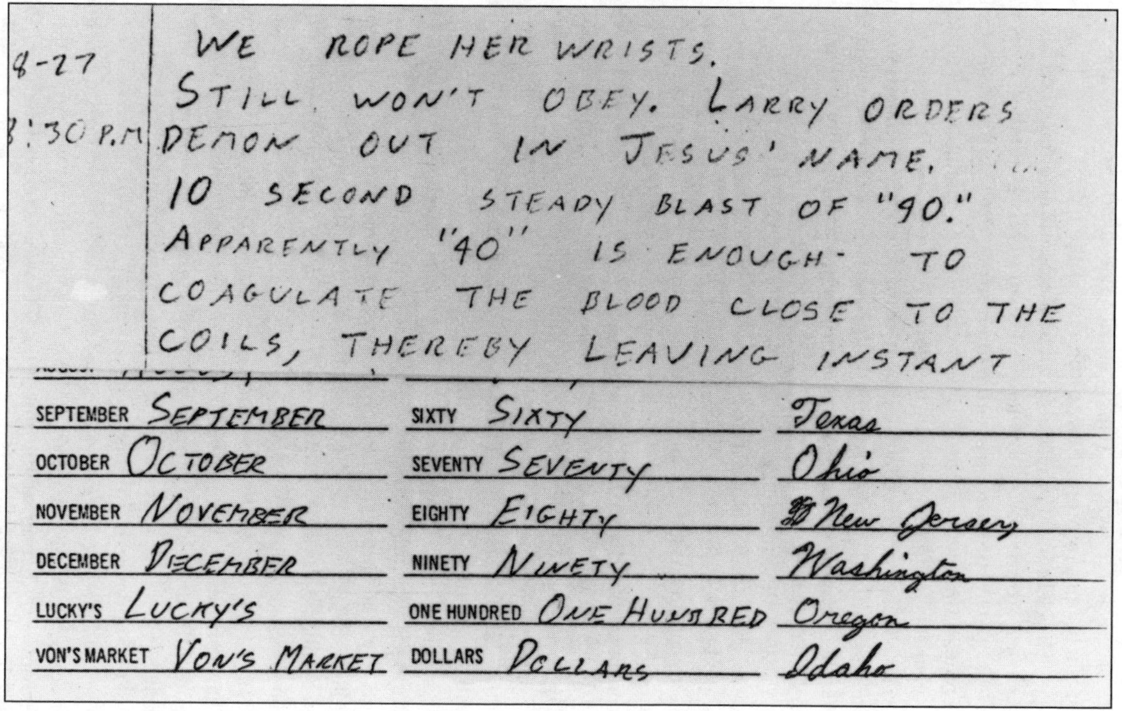

8-27 WE ROPE HER WRISTS.
STILL WON'T OBEY. LARRY ORDERS
8:30 P.M DEMON OUT IN JESUS' NAME. ...
10 SECOND STEADY BLAST OF "90."
APPARENTLY "40" IS ENOUGH- TO
COAGULATE THE BLOOD CLOSE TO THE
COILS, THEREBY LEAVING INSTANT

SEPTEMBER September	SIXTY Sixty	Texas
OCTOBER October	SEVENTY Seventy	Ohio
NOVEMBER November	EIGHTY Eighty	New Jersey
DECEMBER December	NINETY Ninety	Washington
LUCKY'S Lucky's	ONE HUNDRED One Hundred	Oregon
VON'S MARKET Von's Market	DOLLARS Dollars	Idaho

Figure 9–12: Diary of "religious maniacs."

to "get the Devil out of her." The several members of the family were all identified by their hand printing found in a diary. The inner proportion of the letter *M* was individual. The center of the *M,* in proportion to the rest of the letter, was extremely small. The final stroke of the *G* was extremely long in proportion to the rest of the letter.

The element of proportion can be used with all letters of the alphabet when you are comparing one letter in relationship to another. Also, most letters contain proportions within themselves that can be important in a comparison. Every letter is important when making a hand-printing comparison using the element of proportion.

10. *Retrace.* This is an excellent element in handwriting comparison, but is rarely so in hand printing. When it does appear, it is an individual and a fine characteristic. Retrace in hand printing is usually only a retrace in a very small part of the letter.

11. *Skill.* With the words "Print—Do Not Write" appearing on more documents, the population is gaining more practice in hand printing, therefore more skill. The first examination in hand printing will be to examine the exemplar and questioned writing to determine the consistency of characteristics. Lack of consistency within a document may disclose a disguised printing rather than a lack of skill.

Printing is done in most cases for legibility. This legibility or skill can play an important role. A skilled writer will give himself away when he attempts to disguise his printing. He will unconsciously leave characteristics of his skill in the printing. The combination of characteristics and skill may assist in the identification of a hand-printed document.

That a skilled writer will still produce characteristics in disguised writing is exemplified in the case of a burglary of a school. During the burglary, the suspect disguised his writing while writing a note on the bulletin board. Despite the attempt at disguise, the letter *E,* with its bent back and proportionally long center staff, assisted in the identification of the suspect.

12. *Slant.* This is one of the most important items to consider when obtaining a hand printing or handwriting exemplar. Nothing can make a comparison more difficult than the comparison of two documents with greatly different slants. Watch the exemplar as it is being written and make sure you get hand printing with the proper slant.

A slant difference between the known and the questioned documents presents one of two problems: (1) Two hand printings are by two different persons, or (2) one of the documents is in a disguised writing. When examining slant for possible disguise, examine all the printing to determine if the slant is consistent. If the slant varies, you probably have a disguised document.

13. *Size*. Size of letters will be discussed in more detail under element 16 (system). The size of a letter is one method of deciding whether a letter is an uppercase or lowercase letter. The letter O is written the same as a capital and as a small letter, except for the letter size.

Some persons hand print all letters as uppercase letters, but then use size to indicate whether they are capitals or small letters. The M.O., or system, of hand printing used by a suspect is very consistent, and, despite

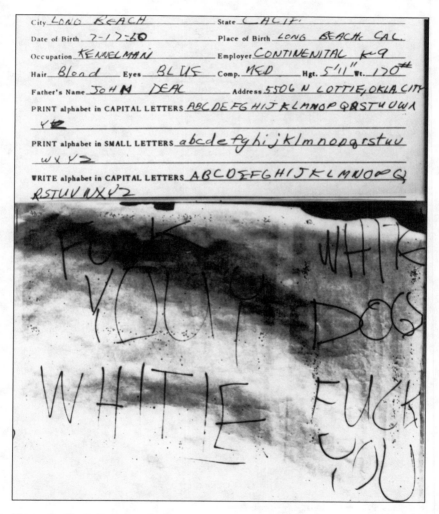

Figure 9–13: Bulletin board printing.

disguise, its size remains the same. The size of a letter, in relationship to other letters, is therefore an important element in the identification of hand printing.

Three checks tied together in the Bradford System are readily identified by examining the hand printing rather than the signature. The printing is all uppercase, with the capital letter larger than the rest. Size was the first

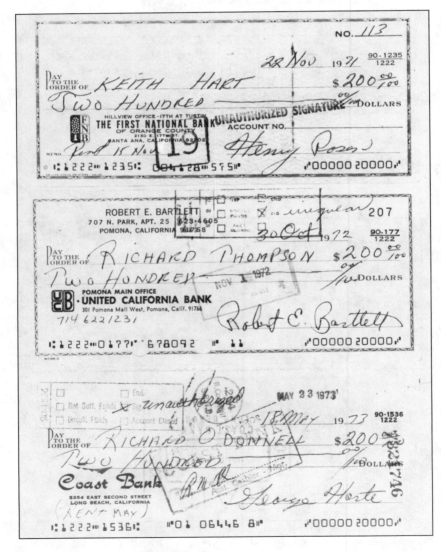

Figure 9–14: Three questioned checks.

element of comparison observed. Once connected, the documents were then compared in a detailed examination.

14. *Spelling.* Misspelled words, poor grammar, lack of punctuation, and incorrect word usage can also be individual characteristics, and can be used as a comparison point in hand printing as well as in handwriting.

15. *Straight lines.* All hand-printed letters contain straight lines and/or simple curves. Straight-line elements can therefore be found in almost every letter. They can be straight or close to it, vertical, horizontal, short, or long. Isolated straight lines are not very individual, but, in conjunction with other straight lines and curves, they can be a very important element.

16. *System.* This refers to the previously discussed system of manuscript writing. Various penmanship publishers now include hand-printing instructions in their books.

Printing is taught with penmanship books in the very early years, but soon supplanted by script writing instruction. Since children do not get years of instruction in printing, the practice copy book is soon forgotten. So most adults use the printed word in the average book or magazine as a model for their own hand printing.

All types of printing can be found on hand printed documents. Some students forget their small letters, so they do all their printing in capital

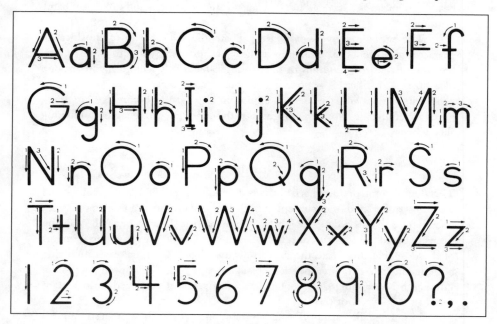

Figure 9–15: Bowmar/Noble Hand Printing System. (By permission from *Better Handwriting for You,* © 1972, Bowmar/Noble Pub., a Division of The Economy Company.)

letters. Most of the time only a few small letters are forgotten, and therefore, the uppercase and lowercase letters are both found in a word. This unusual combination of letters is very consistent and is a good characteristic in the examination of hand printing.

17. *Trademarks and embellishments.* These marks can also be described as unusual additions to a person's writing. Normally, they are unconsciously added to a document. However, many embellishments are consciously added to make it more attractive. These conscious additions will not be found in a questioned printing.

The step-by-step comparison of the six procedures and seventeen elements in a hand-printing comparison should lead you to a successful conclusion of your questioned document case. Your opinion will be positive if:

1. There is sufficient individual hand printing on the questioned document.
2. Exemplars were obtained following the procedures outlined in this book.
3. You have had adequate practice in recognizing individual characteristics.

This chapter attempts to train you in the step-by-step examination of a hand-printed letter. If you follow the rules and develop your skills, you should be able to locate the several "like" characteristics in known and unknown hand printing.

The problem now is how to evaluate the *individuality* of the located characteristic. No book or handwriting class can teach you this point. Only the examination of hundreds of hand-printed letter *A*'s will give you an idea of a normal *A*. For this reason, it is recommended that you work and study handwriting eight hours a day for a minimum of two years before making opinions. Hopefully, the two years will give you the experience to recognize individuality when you see it.

Numbers

The identification of numbers is both possible and important. Numbers are found on almost every kind of document in both civil and criminal cases. Almost every document contains a date, which has numbers in it. In a recent will case, the suspect copied the signature on the will, but since he did not have the numbers of the decedent, he wrote the date in his own hand. Criminal cases involving bookmaking, checks, or embezzlement all use numbers. The ransom note in the Lindbergh Kidnapping Case contained numbers, and they played an important part in the solution of the case.

Numbers, like hand printing, are disconnected, so they can also be positively identified. In a comparison we should consider the dollar sign ($), number sign (#), and the "and" sign (&) as well as numbers. As with handwriting and

Figure 9–16: Clark Sellers with his Lindbergh exhibit. (*Gene Lister*)

hand printing, a positive opinion on numbers is based on quality of the writing and on the individuality of the characteristics. If sufficient characteristic numbers are present, a positive opinion can be made.

The same procedures suggested for handwriting and hand printing apply to number comparison. Procedure 2—examine all writing on the questioned document—was used in a case regarding forged American Express travelers checks. The countersignature was a copied forgery that could not be identified. Following the procedure to examine the entire document, the examiner checked the dates on the travelers checks and was then able to identify these with the

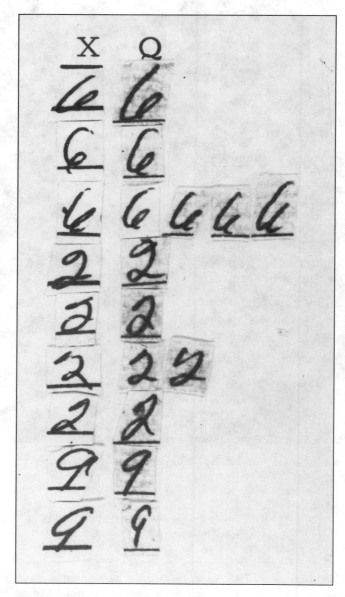

Figure 9–17: Numbers in the dates on travelers checks.

suspect's handwriting. The initial and ending strokes of the numbers were characteristic.

Procedure 3, location of nonrequest exemplars and Procedure 4, examination of request exemplars, are important in the examination of numbers. Printing and writing on an exemplar will not assist in the comparison of numbers. You must have numbers of the proper slant and style. As stated before, the comparison of consciously written numbers with unconsciously written numbers will cause some problems. Disguised exemplars will cause even more. Nonrequest exemplars are the best type. Procedure 6, the copying of the questioned numbers, still applies.

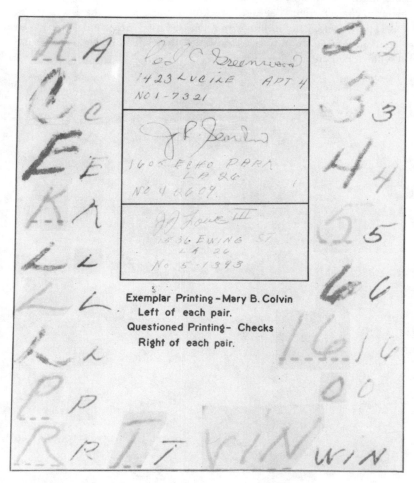

Exemplar Printing–Mary B. Colvin
Left of each pair.
Questioned Printing– Checks
Right of each pair.

Figure 9–18: Savon Drug Store altered record.

Procedure 7, determine the type of number examinations needed and proceed with the comparison. This examination should be a positive examination done by the elements. Numbers usually consist of only one stroke although the numbers 4 and 5 sometimes have two strokes.

Proportion is still one of the most important elements. The 0 (zero) is sometimes smaller than other numbers. The proportion of the numbers 3, 4, 5, and 6 should be relatively equal. The oval in the 6, 8, 9, and 0 can be of different sizes and shapes. The ending stroke of the number 8 can finish at the one o'clock position, as most do, or at nine o'clock. The finish of the number 8 is consistent and makes a very good elimination characteristic. The altered Savon Drug Store record (figure 9-18) shows an ending stroke variation in the 2, 3, and 6, all of which are characteristic. The inside pickup of the 9 is also characteristic.

Handwriting, hand printing, and numbers may each stand alone as a basis for an identification. In most cases, however, they will complement each other and will strengthen any opinions made.

— 10 —

Typewriters and Check Protectors

Q uestioned typewriting cases present a new type of problem to the examiner. This examination is based largely on mechanical defects in the typewriter and only secondarily on the human element. The human element figures
in the "special examination," where one is trying to identify the "typist" of a
document.

Typewriters

This chapter is an all-inclusive one about typewriters. The first section deals with
the invention of the typewriter by Christopher Sholes and its manufacture by
Remington Arms Works. In the legal section, court cases, including the historic
trial of Alger Hiss, are analyzed. A section on vocabulary, exemplars, standards,
and the classification of standards is included. The three types of examination—
preliminary, identifying, and special—are discussed in detail. The final part of
the chapter deals with check protectors. This includes their history, exemplars,
comparison, and identification.

A History of Typewriters

Male clerks, proud of their elegant Spencerian script, were understandably loath
to relinquish their sole mark of distinction. Until the advent of the typewriter,
the job of secretary was a man's role. Though shorthand was used by the ancient
Egyptians, Hebrews, and Persians, it was developed by a Greek slave, Tiro, who
used it to take down the words of the Roman orator Cicero, during debates in
63 B.C. Tiro's system gained widespread popularity in ancient Rome, where the
people who used it were known as "Notarii."

Figure 10–1: Christopher L. Sholes. (*Milwaukee Public Museum*)

No written transaction was faster than that of the man who took shorthand and transcribed it. In the nineteenth century, the progress of the Industrial Revolution was limited by the lack of speedy communications. In 1852 the speed record was thirty words per minute, but the average was only twenty-four words per minute. Writing in beautiful, flowery script with a steel pen and ink was considered first-rate work.

It took more than four-hundred years to progress from Gutenberg's type presses to the typewriter. The first recorded attempt to invent a typewriter was in January 1714, when a patent was granted to Henry Mill by Her Majesty Queen Anne. Today, there is no evidence of a model nor any description of Mill's machine.

In 1829, President Andrew Jackson granted the first typewriter patent to William A. Burt of Detroit, Michigan. Burt's machine was never manufactured, but his ideas were published in the newspaper. However, no commercial use was ever recommended for his "Burt's Family Letter Press."

In 1867, Christopher Latham Sholes, the fifty-second typewriter inventor, developed the first successful typewriter. This Milwaukee inventor developed more than fifty typewriters between 1867 and 1873. Assisted by Samuel Soule and Carlos Glidden, he developed a monstrous wooden cabinet, cut away on one side to accommodate four rows of keys. Sholes contacted James Densmore, a Pennsylvania oilman, who would later become the chief promoter of the typewriter which friends at the time called a "literary piano."

Densmore and G. Yost, a persuasive salesman, went to the Remington Arms Works in Illion, New York, and contacted Philo Remington, the president, and Henry H. Benedict, a director of Remington Arms.

Remington Arms completed the first commercial typewriter in 1874. The Sholes and Glidden machines were mounted on sewing machine stands complete with a foot lever used to rotate the platen. The label on this first typewriter read: Sholes & Glidden Typewriter, manufactured by E. Remington & Sons, Illion, N.Y.[1]

The first commercial typewriter of 1874 was a Sholes typewriter that featured all capital letters. It was difficult to use, as the typist could not see the lines being typed. Sholes' arrangement of letters, "Q W E R T Y U I O P," is still used today. This arrangement of letters, worked out by Sholes, put the most commonly used letters farthest away from each other to keep the type bars from colliding. In 1878, the Remington Company manufactured the "Remington #2"; this was fitted with a shift key that would type both upper- and lowercase letters. The two Remington typewriters were followed by the Caligraph in 1883, the Hammond in 1884, and the Yost in 1887.

In 1894, Underwood distributed the "visible typewriter," which had typebars that struck from the front rather than from below. Christopher Sholes is said to have made his last technical contribution to a similar model developed by his son. Sholes, in one of his last letters, called his typewriter "a blessing to mankind, and especially to womankind" and added that, "I builded wiser than I knew, and the world has the benefit of it." Although Sholes has been forgotten, his typewriter and addressograph are still a vital part of the communications world.

In 1944 IBM marketed their "Executive Typewriter." This was the first machine designed for proportional spacing. The letter I is two units wide, while the letter W is five units wide. Proportional spacing gives typing the printed page look.

Following World War II, manufacturers went back to the drawing boards and produced new machines for the civilian population. Electric typewriters, and then portables in various colors were manufactured. In 1961 IBM introduced their revolutionary "Selectric Typewriter" with the single "ball element." This ball (sometimes referred to as a "golf ball") could be removed and replaced with a ball element of another type style. Each ball contained all the alphabetic

Figure 10–2: The first commercial typewriter was a Sholes. (*Milwaukee Public Museum*)

characters, numerals, and punctuation symbols. The other major feature of the machine was the elimination of the carriage; the ball now moved in place of the carriage.

In the late 1970s, a new typewriter was developed and marketed. This "electronic typewriter" has micro-electronic technology. The printing function is performed with a "Daisy Wheel" (100 characters on a print wheel). The microprocessor technology in these new machines includes very few moving parts, which means they are virtually trouble-free. These typewriters also have the advantages of light weight, memory storage, and the capability of being attached to more sophisticated equipment. They also have the capability to switch instantly to proportional spacing, in addition to 10-, 12-, and space-saving 15-pitch typing. The Daisy Wheel is also interchangeable with other element wheels.

The manufacturers and typewriter salesmen believe the new electronic typewriters have totally outdated all other typewriters. These new typewriters, with their instant changing pitch, and/or interchangeable Daisy Wheel give the document examiner a new set of problems to deal with.

Legal Record

Evidential typewriting cases date back to the early courts. The first case that went to a court for review was *Levy v. Rust*, 49 Atl. 1017 (New Jersey).

The court in *Levy v. Rust* stated

> An expert in typewriting is brought here and that expert sat down by my side at the table here and explained his criticisms on this typewriting, and I went over it with him carefully with the glass . . . it appeared very clearly. . . . I was very much struck by his evidence. . . . If you compare the typewriting work, it contains precisely the same peculiarities which are found in the typewriting in these seven suspected papers.

The judge in ruling on the case did not cite any prior case on typewriter examination. This case was in 1893, just twenty years after Sholes' typewriter was sold to Remington Arms.

An incredible feat occurred two years before the *Levy v. Rust* typewriter trial of 1893. In 1891, Sir Arthur Conan Doyle wrote about typewriter identification in his Sherlock Holmes story "A Case of Identity."[2] "It is a curious thing," remarked Holmes, "that a typewriter has really quite as much individuality as a man's handwriting. Unless they are quite new, no two of them write exactly alike. Some letters get more worn than others, and some wear only on one side. Now, you remark in this note of yours, Mr. Windibank, that in every case there is some little slurring over of the 'e' and a slight defect in the tail of the 'r.' There are fourteen other characteristics, but those are the most obvious." This statement by the character Holmes was made, using sound principles and precise terminology, two years before the first court case.

The Sixty-second Congress enacted the United States Statute of 1913, Chapter 79, which allows for the introduction of admitted or proven handwriting exemplars for comparative purposes. By court decisions, this statute was extended to cover typewriting. In *People v. Werblow*, 209 N.Y.S. 88 (1925), it was stated that "The law is well settled that such specimens of typewriting are properly received in evidence for the purposes of comparison." In the case of *State v. Swank*, 99 Ore. 571, 195 Pac 168 (1921), J.F. Wood, document examiner, testified in clear, analytical and convincing terms the reasons for his brief that the two notes were prepared by the same person on the same typewriter.

Forgery by Typewriter

Chapter 8 discusses various methods of how to commit a forgery. "Forgery by typewriter" is one additional way to commit forgery. A document can be identified as being typed by a particular typewriter, if defects and imperfections can be found on both questioned document and on exemplars. The identification is made by the individuality of the typewriter characteristics.

Forgery by typewriter is committed by obtaining a typewriter of the same make and model as the one used on the questioned document. The forger then alters the keys to create the same defects and imperfections as are on a known document. Theoretically, the two typewriters could type a document containing the exact same characteristics. Forgery by typewriter has been attempted in several cases and is still going on today.

People v. Risley (214 NY 75, 108 NE 200 (1915)) involved the first known attempt at a forgery with the use of a typewriter. Risley, a New York lawyer, altered another lawyer's affidavit by adding the words "the same" with his Underwood typewriter. Examiner William J. Kinsley identified thirteen characteristics that were different from the Remington which had been used to type the affidavit. Kinsley also identified Risley's typewriter as adding the two words.

In the eight months between the charge and the trial, Risley contacted Arthur W. Buckwell of the General Typewriter Company. Risley asked Buckwell to alter an Underwood of the same model as his so that it would contain the same characteristics. Risley hoped at the trial to be able to say, "You say those words 'the same' were written by my machine and no other. But here is another machine which I picked up second hand, and which can also write those words, just like they were written in the affidavit. Now if another machine can write them. . . ." The expert, however, proved that the altered typewriter was different from the Underwood used in the case. The mechanic later testified that he hadn't made as many alterations as he should have.[3]

British Intelligence Uses Forgery by Typewriter

Under the cover of the British Passport Control, British Intelligence established offices in New York. The British Security Coordination (BSC), under the leadership of Sir William Stephenson, had its own agents who developed a full-fledged alliance with J. Edgar Hoover and the FBI.[4] The agents for the BSC trained at "Camp X" in Canada, on the north side of Lake Ontario. This site was chosen because it could be easily reached by FBI agents as well as by the British. At Camp X was a group called "Station M." Station M was an important part of Camp X, as it produced all types of paraphernalia for the spy trade. The production of false documents was one of the important products of Station M. The experts included leading authorities on the manufacture of special inks and paper, and individuals who could reproduce faultlessly the imprint of any typewriter on earth.[5]

In June 1940, the American ambassador in Uruguay cabled to President Roosevelt that unless the United States acted effectively, countries in South America might fall under Nazi domination. The President empowered the FBI to act, and they were greatly helped by Stephenson's agents. Stephenson's men determined that the Italian airline Linee Aeree Transcontinental Italiane (LATI), which flew regularly between Europe and Brazil, carried German and Italian diplomatic bags, couriers, and agents. The Brazilian Government showed no

LINEE AEREE TRANSCONTINENTALI
ITALIANE S.A.

Roma, 30 ottobre 1941 XX

IL PRESIDENTE

Caro Camerata,

ho ricevuto la Vostra relazione che è
giunta cinque giorni dopo essere stata spedita.

La relazione è stata portata subito a
conoscenza degl' interessati i quali la considera-
no di grande importanza. L' abbiamo confrontata con
altra ricevuta dal Fraça Del Frete. Le due relazio-
ni presentano un quadro analogo della situazione
che esiste laggiù ma la Vostra è più dettagliata.
Desidero esprimerVi il mio compiacimento. Il fatto
che, in questa occasione, noi abbiamo ottenuto infor-
mazioni più complete di quelle che abbian S. ed i
suoi, mi ha riempito di soddisfazione.

Non vi è dubbio che il grassoccio sta
cedendo alle lusinghe degli Americani e che soltan-
to un intervento violento da parte dei nostri
amici verdi può salvare il paese. I nostri collaboratori di Berlino, in seguito alle conversazioni
avute con il rappresentante a Lisbona, hanno deciso
che tale intervento deve aver luogo al più presto.
Ma Voi conoscete la situazione. Il giorno in cui si
verificherà il cambiamento, i nostri collaboratori
si preoccuperanno assai poco dei nostri interessi e
la Lufthansa raccoglierà tutti i vantaggi. Per impedire
che questo si verifichi dobbiamo procurarci al più
presto altri amici influenti tra i verdi. Fatelo senza
indugio. Lascio a Voi di decidere quali sarebbero le
persone più adatte: forse Fadilha o E.F. de Andrade

. . . non bisogna dimenticare che sono scaltre di-
sposte a servire chiunque tiene le redini in mano.

Saluti fascisti,

Comandante
Vicenzo CUIGLA
Linee Aeree Transcontinentali Italiane S.A.

Figure 10–3: Forged LATI letter. (*Montgomery Hyde*)

intention of closing down the airline, since powerful Brazilians had an interest in the operation of the airline.

Station M was asked to fabricate a letter from the head of LATI to the airline's general manager in Brazil. Notepaper was produced using the straw pulp normally found only in Europe. The engraved letterhead of Italy's state-owned LATI was copied by counterfeiters, using a genuine letter the agents had succeeded in obtaining. An Olivetti typewriter was rebuilt to conform to the exact mechanical imperfections of the machine upon which the general's secretary had typed the original letter.[6]

The documents were then smuggled into Rio and eventually leaked to President Vargas' friends. Then Brazilian President Getulio Vargas read in the letter that "There can be no doubt the little fat man is falling into the pocket of the Americans, and that only violent action on the part of the green gentlemen can save the country. I understand such action has been arranged for by our respected collaborators in Berlin." President Vargas knew that the "little fat man" referred to him, and that the "green gentlemen" referred to Germans. Vargas cancelled LATI landing rights and ordered the arrest of the LATI general manager in Brazil. A few weeks later, Brazil broke off relations with the Axis and moved under the Allied umbrella. There is no doubt that one of the main factors in persuading Brazil to turn against the Axis was the insulting remarks contained in a letter that was typed by a "forged typewriter."

The Allies were not the only ones to use forged typewriters. Wythe Williams reported in the *Reader's Digest* (July 1940) that the Gestapo had the finest setup for the falsification of documents that has ever existed. This included handwriting wizards, ace chemists, and a typewriter bureau that had every make of typewriter in the world. A Gestapo expert would check a document for the type of typewriter used; lines were then chemically expunged and new ones inserted. There was little that the German experts could not imitate.

United States v. Hiss (107 F. Supp. 128 [1952])

On January 25, 1950, Alger Hiss appeared for sentencing after being found guilty in the second of two trials. Hiss stated to the court, "I am confident that in the future the full facts of how Whittaker Chambers was able to carry out 'forgery by typewriter' will be disclosed."

Alger Hiss was a prominent man and had served in the administration of President Harry S. Truman. The scandal of the Hiss trial could have lost the election for the President if it had been tried earlier. The trial also brought into prominence Richard M. Nixon. Dwight D. Eisenhower stated in his book, *Mandate for Change*, that he picked Nixon for Vice President because: (1) his political philosophy generally coincided with his (Eisenhower's) own; (2) he was young, vigorous, and ready to learn, and (3) "I had read about his record as a congressman in conducting a difficult investigation in the historic Alger Hiss case."

Alger Hiss was born on November 11, 1904, and graduated with a law degree from Harvard in 1929. While there, he attracted the attention of Felix Frankfurter and was recommended for, and received, the post of secretary to Supreme Court Justice Oliver Wendell Holmes. In 1933, he went to work for the government and became director of the Office of Special Political Affairs in 1944. He accompanied President Roosevelt and Secretary of State Stettinius to the Malta and Yalta Conferences. Hiss was the elected Secretary General of the United Nations Conference and was appointed to personally take the United Nations Charter from San Francisco to Washington D.C. for ratification. In December 1946 he was elected president of the Carnegie Endowment for International Peace.

On August 3, 1948, Whittaker Chambers was called before the Committee on Un-American Activities. Chambers was an admitted Communist functionary of the 1930s, and was the then senior editor of *Time* magazine. He shocked the committee when he described Alger Hiss as a member of the Communist Party underground. Hiss asked to testify and did so, stating that he was not a communist sympathizer. The committee was then attacked by President Truman, who dismissed the hearing as a "red herring" that undermined public confidence in the government. The committee was then afraid to continue, but authorized John McDowell, Eddie Hilbert, and Richard M. Nixon to investigate further. In two court sessions, Nixon attacked Hiss with his questions, and "won" the encounter. Chambers appeared on "Meet the Press," where he was asked to repeat his charge. He said that "Alger Hiss was a Communist and may still be one." Three weeks later, Hiss sued Chambers for libel.

Whittaker Chambers stated that Alger Hiss was an aid to Francis B. Sayre, Assistant Secretary of State. Chambers stated that for about two years Hiss copied documents that came across Sayre's desk. The copies were then given to Priscilla (Hiss' wife) for typing. The material was then turned over to Chambers to be photographed and given to Soviet agents. When Chambers left the party in 1938, he kept some of those documents for insurance against assassination. The documents were placed in a package and given to a nephew for safekeeping.

Chambers further stated that ten years later, he went to the hiding place, an unused dumbwaiter, and found the documents. On the day before turning over the documents, Chambers decided to hide the microfilm rolls overnight in a pumpkin. Thus, the Chambers documents became known as the "Pumpkin Papers," although only the film was hidden there, and only for one night. The package contained sixty-five typed pages, microfilm, and other documents. They were introduced into court on November 17, 1948, during pretrial depositions for the libel suit. Hiss' lawyers immediately requested that the typewritten copies (referred to as the Baltimore Documents) be turned over to the Department of Justice.

The Hiss family no longer owned the Woodstock typewriter used in 1938.

The family therefore turned over to the FBI four communications that could be used as exemplars (referred to as the Hiss Standards). They consisted of:

1. A December 6, 1931, letter typed by Daisy Fansler to the Philadelphia Free Library.
2. September 9, 1936, documents sent to the Landon School, among which was an application for admission and a letter listing the description of personal characteristics of Timothy Hobson, Alger's stepson.
3. A 1936–37 report typed by Priscilla Hiss when she was president of the Bryn Mawr Club.
4. A May 25, 1937, application typed by Priscilla Hiss for admission to the University of Maryland, for a summer course in chemistry.

Ramos C. Feehan, of the Document Section, FBI, examined the documents and stated that the questioned "Baltimore Documents" were typed by the same typewriter that had typed the "Hiss Standards," with the exception of one document. Ordway Hilton, then employed by *Time* magazine, arrived at the same opinion. Hiss' lawyers hired a succession of experts, J. Howard Haring, Edwin H. Fearon, and Harry E. Cassidy, all of whom agreed with the opinion of Feehan. Hiss' attorneys were successful in locating a Woodstock typewriter, which "may have been the original" owned by the Hiss family in 1938. The grand jury, which was also investigating the case, was given the typewriter evidence, and indicted Hiss for perjury on December 15, 1948.

The first trial for perjury was held in the federal courtroom of Judge Samuel H. Kaufman. Thomas F. Murphy prosecuted and Lloyd P. Stryker represented Hiss. The trial began on May 31, 1949, and a hung jury was declared July 8, 1949. The second trial was held before federal Judge Henry W. Goddard. The prosecutor was again Tom Murphy. Hiss, however, chose a new attorney, Claude Cross. The trial started on November 17, 1949, and Hiss was found guilty on January 21, 1950.

Ramos C. Feehan was the only expert called in the two trials. He testified that, "I reached the conclusion that on government's exhibits 5 through 9 and 11 through 47, that the typing on those specimens was typed by the same machine which typed the four known standards which were submitted to me for comparison purposes.[7] Feehan explained his opinion regarding a defect in the bottom half of the *g*. He also showed that the letter *e* was malformed, the letter *i* had an alignment slightly below the base line, and the letter *o* printed more heavily on the right side. The defense did not cross-examine Feeham.

On January 25, 1950, after being found guilty, Hiss made his statement on "forgery by typewriter." Hiss was then sentenced to five years on each count, with the sentences running concurrently. In November 1954, Hiss was released from the Lewisburg, Pennsylvania, State Prison after serving three years and eight months.

Figure 10–4: Alger Hiss. (*Neil Selkirk*)

In an attempt to prove the forgery by typewriter statement of Alger Hiss, Chester Lane contacted Martin K. Tytell. Tytell was the owner of Tytell Typewriter Company and had spent half his life working with typewriters (today, Tytell and his wife and son are among the country's leading typewriter experts). Lane told Tytell that he would like him to prove that two typewriters could be made to type exactly alike. Lane had a contract which would pay $7,500 for the work and stated, "It is understood that you will work solely from samples without access to, or inspection of, the machine on which the samples are typed."[8] The contract was signed on April 17, 1950.

Tytell determined that the samples from Woodstock N230099 were typed on a Woodstock Pica machine, and set out to build a replica of it. He selected

Figure 10–5: Martin K. Tytell. (*Jacob Lofman*)

model N231195 to rebuild. This was undoubtedly built the same year, if not the same month, as Woodstock N230099. In making the replica, or forged typewriter, he had to be concerned with more than differences in typeface defects and design. To be successful, he would have to create the same regular or irregular alignment patterns. He also would have to get the same regularity of shading, since it is almost impossible to get each typeface to print uniformly by striking dead center. To assist in getting the letters correct, he employed an engraver. After the mechanical adjustments were deemed correct, he adjusted the typewriter to make the spacing between lines exactly like the spacing on the Hiss machine. The next item replicated was the hard–rubber roller. (The hardness of the rubber makes fractional differences between lines. As the rubber wears, variations of the spaces between lines become more apparent.) The typewriter was completed and accepted by Chester Lane on December 28, 1950, eight months after construction began.

Lane then contacted two experts to examine the typewriting of the two machines. Although Elizabeth McCarthy and Evelyn S. Ehrlich found differences, Ehrlich stated that "except for subtle details, I found that microscopic variations on one machine had been duplicated on the other so faithfully that I might not have believed it possible if I had not been informed that two machines were involved."[9] McCarthy's report to Chester Lane included charts that illustrated the progress of Tytell. Chart VI (figure 10–6) shows several characteristics duplicated by Tytell, including vertical alignment of the *a* and horizontal alignment of the *o*.

The building of a forged typewriter by Tytell opened a "can of worms." Some examiners questioned the ethical practice of forging a typewriter. Tytell responded, "I am undertaking a purely scientific experiment. Any knowledge we can gain from it would help, not hinder justice." The authors teach handwriting students to copy another person's handwriting so they can see the defects, and to learn to spot a forgery. Tytell's work was true scientific research, and he should be commended.

Was "forgery by typewriter" used in the Hiss case as Alger Hiss stated? All examinations by the prosecution and defense experts took place before the trials. An attempted forgery of this type is extremely rare, and the experts had little or no knowledge of this type of forgery.

Woodstock N230099, which was located by Hiss's attorneys, became the government's and Prosecutor Tom Murphy's prize exhibit. The typewriter was introduced into evidence as Defense Exhibit UUU on December 15, 1949. Examiner Feehan never referred to the typewriter in his testimony.

Alger Hiss stated that Woodstock N230099 had unusual soldering on the type bars of the machine that was in evidence at the trials. The FBI laboratory studied the soldering on N230099 in 1949 and found it to be normal and similar to other machines. I purchased a Woodstock of the same model, which I examined. My findings showed the same unusual soldering on the type bars that was found on N230099 (the type bar of N230099 was illustrated in Hiss's book[10]).

Since Alger Hiss's statement of January 25, 1950, no one has made a comparison of the "original" Baltimore documents, Hiss standards, and Woodstock N230099 (knowing that an attempted forgery by typewriter is possible). It is hoped that this case will be reexamined, and the questions answered once and for all.

Alistair Cooke, in his book *A Generation on Trial*, stated, "No matter what its outcome through the higher courts may be, this case will, I suspect, offer for some time to come, and perhaps forever, as many puzzles as the celebrated Wallace case." The *United States v. Alger Hiss* case offers a wealth of material to the document examiner. Forgery by typewriter is just one area of controversy. From this case arose several other problems for study in reference to the typewriter, including the comparison examplars of Woodstock N230099; with the Baltimore Documents and the Hiss Standards; the age of Woodstock N230099; and the attempt to identify the typist. There were also problems regarding the documents and microfilm in the envelope, aging of documents while stored, and written notations on the documents. For additional study of the Alger Hiss case, refer to the following sources:

Chambers, Whittaker. 1952. *Witness*. New York: Random House.
Cook, Fred J. 1958. *The Unfinished Story of Alger Hiss*. New York: Morrow.

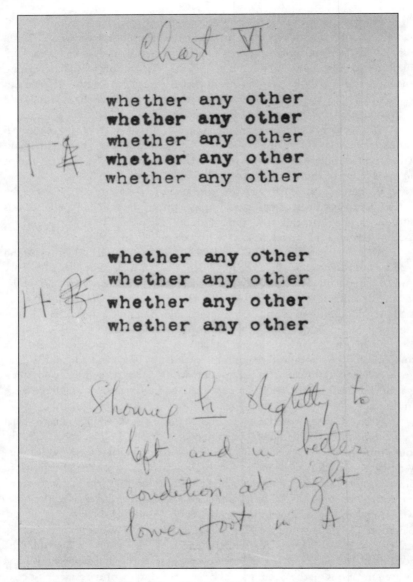

Figure 10–6: McCarthy's Chart VI. The "T" refers to Tytell's typewriter and the "H" to Woodstock N230099. (*Alger Hiss*)

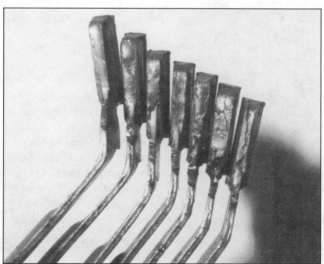

Figure 10–7: (a) Russell Bradford examines the Woodstock soldering. (b) Close-up of the soldering.

Hiss, Alger. 1957. *In the Court of Public Opinion*. New York: Knopf.

Hiss, Alger. 1988. *Recollections of a Lie*. New York: Seaver Books/Henry Holt & Co.

Jowitt, Earl. 1953. *The Strange Case of Alger Hiss*. New York: Doubleday.

Levitt, Morton, and Michael Levitt. 1979. *A Tissue of Lies—Nixon vs. Hiss*. New York: McGraw-Hill.

Reuben, William. 1983. *Footnote on an Historic Case: In Re Alger Hiss, No. 78, Civ. 3433*. New York: National Institute.

Smith, John C. 1976. *Alger Hiss: The True Story*. New York: Holt, Rinehart & Winston.

Tiger, Edith. 1979. *In Re Alger Hiss* (Vols. 1 and 2). New York: Hill and Wang.

Tytell, Martin K. 1952, August. "The $7,500 Typewriter I Built for Alger Hiss." *True Magazine*.

Weinstein, Allen. 1978. *Perjury*. New York: Knopf.

On July 27, 1978, a petition for a *Writ of Error Coram Nobis* was filed to set aside the judgment of conviction dated January 25, 1950. This petition was published as *In Re Alger Hiss*.[11] The petition contained many items, including information obtained under the Freedom of Information Act. On July 15, 1982, Federal Judge Richard Owen, Federal District Court of Manhattan, rejected the petition. The rejection was examined in detail in "Footnote of an Historic Case."[12] On February 16, 1983, the United States Court of Appeals for the Second Circuit said in an unanimous decision, "We find the appeal to be completely without merit." On October 11, 1983, a petition by Hiss for a *Writ of Certiorari* was denied by the United States Supreme Court, without comment.

Forgery by Typewriter Today

Time Magazine (February 10, 1961) reported that in 1958 a Communist forgery factory in East Berlin turned out a rash of eighteen forgeries. One of these—purportedly from the United States Embassy in Bonn, Germany—was planted in a United States diplomatic dispatch.

U.S. News & World Report (March 3, 1980) referred to a CIA report which stated that the Soviets called a halt to these activities for four years in the mid-1970s for unknown reasons. In 1978, the Kremlin streamlined and heavily financed an International Information Department. The agency, working with the KGB, carried out "disinformation" operations that relied heavily on forgery. The CIA believed that as many as fifty KGB technicians were detailed to their squad.

Vocabulary

Some words in this section are particular to typewriter examination. Others also appear in the handwriting vocabulary. You will find most of these words are used in other text books, but two of them have confusing definitions. These are "Exemplar" and "Standards" and are described below.

- *Alignment.* The positioning of characters in relation to each other. If a typewriter is in proper alignment, each character should strike in the center of an imaginary rectangle. If it is out of alignment, it will strike either high, low, to the right, to the left, or in one of the four corners. These defects can be corrected by special adjustments to the type bar and type block by a repairman.
- *Carbon impression.* A typewriting exemplar obtained from a typewriter with the ribbon removed, or with the machine set in the stencil position. A piece of carbon paper placed on top of the exemplar, carbon side down, results in a carbon impression. This type of exemplar is very useful.
- *Character.* A letter, symbol, number, or point of punctuation on a typewriter.
- *Daisy print wheel.* The print element that contains the characters on some electronic typewriters. The design allows one hundred characters on a print wheel. The wheels are interchangeble, allowing one to type at sixteen-plus characters per second.
- *Defects.* Any abnormality or maladjustment in a typewriter which is reflected in its output and which leads to the individualization or identification of its type. Defects can result either from mistreatment of the machine or from ordinary wear and tear.
- *Elite type.* The standard American type providing twelve characters horizontal to the inch and six lines to the vertical inch.
- *Escapement.* The mechanism that controls the horizontal movement of the carriage.
- *Exemplar.* A witnessed document that is typewritten. This differs from a "standard" that is obtained from the manufacturer to show the styles of that company. Some persons use the words exemplar and standard interchangeably.
- *Footing.* The evenness with which a character strikes the paper. A letter may strike heavier to either the left, right, top, or bottom. A letter may also be called "off its feet."
- *Golf ball.* An IBM element containing eighty-eight alphabetic characters, numbers, and punctuation symbols. The characters are arranged in four horizontal rows and twenty-two vertical columns. In 1974, when other manufacturers started producing single-element typewriters, the design of the "golf ball' was changed. Additional characters were added to the eighty-eight which IBM had originally utilized.
- *Horizontal alignment.* The position of characters in relation to each other on the base line. If defective, a character is either too far to the left or to the right.

- *Malalignment.* Defective alignment. *See also* Alignment.
- *Metric system.* A decimal system of weights and measures based on the meter and kilogram. Most countries of the world use this system, and the United States is gradually replacing its customary system of measurements with the Metric System.
- *Micron type.* Space-saving fifteen-letter-to-the-inch type featured on electronic typewriters.
- *Off its feet.* A defect in which a character strikes heavier in one place than in another. *See also* Footing.
- *Pica.* A typewriter that has ten characters to a horizontal inch.
- *Pitch.* The horizontal spacing in a typewriter.
- *Platen.* The roller or cylinder which serves as a backing for the paper. A typewriter may have any one of several degrees of hardness in a roller.
- *Proportional spacing.* Typing that resembles book printing because the letters are of different widths. For example, on the IBM Executive, *f, i, j, l,* and *t* are two unit letters. The *w* is four units, the *m* is five units, and all other small letters are three units. The capital letters are also of different widths—the *I* is two units, *J* is three units, *M* and *W* are five units, and all others letters are four units.
- *Rebound.* A defect in which a second impression is slightly offset to the right or left.
- *Remington Arms Works.* A company that manufactured weapons during the Civil War and reopened in 1873 to manufacture the Sholes typewriter, the first typewriter.
- *Ribbon.* The material that holds the ink that makes the printed impression. Ribbons used on typewriters are made of different materials, and may be on spools or in cassettes. The quality of the ribbon breaks down with repeated use and will leave characteristics in the typing.

  The new carbon-correctable ribbons are valuable to the document examiner. The ribbon is used only once and can be identified with a specific machine. It can be deciphered easily. The search for used ribbons, and the removal of a ribbon from a questioned typewriter, can be of prime importance. Even the new electronic typewriters contain a ribbon that can be deciphered.

  In deciphering a ribbon, remember that it must be examined backwards. A three-line ribbon is examined backwards, but at a left slant. To find a starting point, locate the period. The defects in the type also stand out in this type of ribbon.
- *Serif.* The straight line at a right angle to the straight line of a letter. It is an appendage to square off a letter.
- *Single-element typewriter.* A typewriter on which all eighty-eight elements are on a single (ball) element. The first such typewriter was the Selectric,

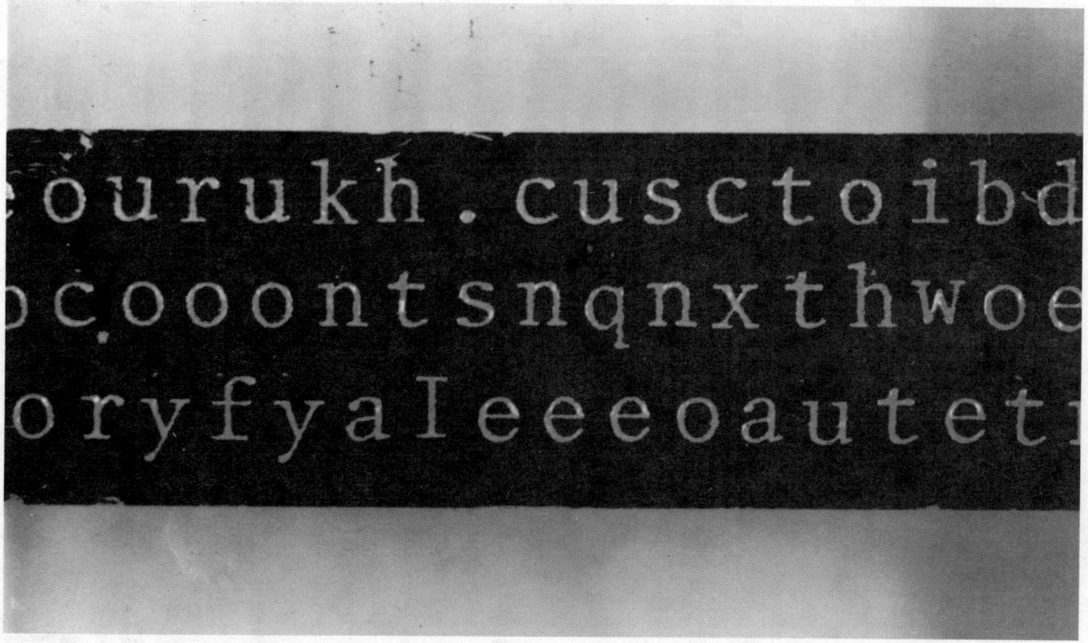

Figure 10–8: Used carbon ribbon, "I thank you."

introduced by IBM in 1961. Prior to 1961, typewriters were made with many keys, each with a character at the end.

- *Slant.* The extent to which a character tilts or leans either to the right or to the left.
- *Standards.* Samples of type of different typewriter models. Each examiner should have a standard file. (*See also* Exemplar.)
- *Stencil setting.* A button on most typewriters that allows one to type without using the ribbon. (*See also* Carbon impression.)
- *Tilt. See* Slant.
- *Type face.* The printing surface of a type block which, when propelled against the ribbon and paper, makes an impression.
- *Typewriter test plate.* A plate of glass, plastic, or photographic film in any size, containing vertical lines for measuring pica, elite, or other type, and also horizontal lines, six per inch. The test plate is designed to be placed on top of a typewriter document to determine if it was typed on an elite or a pica machine. A test plate is also used to check vertical and horizontal misalignment of characters. A large test plate is of great value, as it can assist the examiner in determining if a paragraph or words were added to a document.
- *Typewriter types.* The characters from which an inked print is made on the document. The most popular sizes and styles are elite and pica. Specialized sizes and styles are available for standard makes of typewriters in the following general classifications.
    1. *Microtype, Bank Type,* and *Miniature Gothic.* Very small print for use where space saving is desired, as in statistical work and on stencils. A saving of one-half to one-fourth of the ordinary amount of space and paper used is possible with these small types.
    2. *Primer, Amplitype, Bulletin,* and *Magnatype.* Very large type, for primary schools, photo-offset, show cards, tags, labels, and speech writing.
    3. *Video or Sight-Saver.* Type intended for use by speakers and script writers.
    4, *Medium Roman.* A tall, compact type for legal documents.
    5. *Boldface and Book Type.* Very black type for distance reading, emphasis, or photographing.
    6. *Gothic.* A type that is all capitals and resembles printing. Available in large, small, or condensed sizes, for billing, labeling, card systems, etc. Often combined with pinpoint.
    7. *Pinpoint.* An indenting type for check-protection writing.
    8. *Check validation.* A specialized style for magnetic ink sorting.
    9. *Policy print.* A style that matches the chain printer used by insurance companies.
    10. *Multilith.* Type used for filling in addresses, etc., on multilithed material.

11. *Italic.* Type that resembles italics.

12. *Executive, Art Gothic, Oxford, Royal, Diplomat Artisan, Courier, and Prestige.* Distinctive types for correspondence.

13. *Script, Spencerian, and Corinthian.* Types resembling handwriting for personal use.

14. *Old English.* Type for printing on certificates, diplomas, etc.

15. *Foreign language.* Types including diacritics which can be obtained for almost any language.

16. *Technical.* Special types and keyboards for various kinds of work such as accounting, billing, cartooning, chemistry, communications, dentistry, education, engineering, law, library science, mathematics, medicine, meteorology, music, optics, phonetics, science, shipping, and transportation.

17. *Fractions.* Various type styles, including the split line, italic, and diagonal.

18. *Numerals.* Various type styles, including rounded, italic, and backhand.

- *Vertical line spaces.* Button on side of carriage that allows the platen (roller) to rotate.
- *Vertical alignment.* The up-and-down position of type. A character may be either above or below its proper position because of a defect or a weak shift finger (manual typewriter).

Exemplars

It is important to remember when obtaining exemplars that your opinion will only be as accurate as the exemplars you obtain. Since typewriters are mechanical, some persons believe there is no technique involved in obtaining exemplars. Actually, you must deal with many important items when you examine a questioned typewriter.

The first half of a typewriter exemplar is obtained by typing on the machine in the condition it was found. First, type the entire keyboard twice, then type the message found on the questioned document. The second half of the exemplar should be completed with the stencil setting, so that the ribbon does not come in contact with the paper. If the typewriter does not have a stencil setting, remove the ribbon from the machine. Place a piece of carbon paper on top of your exemplar document, with the carbon side facing the paper. Typing with carbon paper will reveal dirty, defective, or marred type. With the carbon paper in place, type the entire keyboard once more and then type the questioned message. When typing the message, type each word, strikeover, punctuation mark, capital, and lowercase letter as it appears in the document. It is also desirable to change the pressure control and speed in typing the message.

If a type bar is loose, it might hit in one place if struck sharply and another if hit gently. The movement of letters, either horizontally or vertically, is one

LONG BEACH POLICE DEPARTMENT

TYPEWRITING EXEMPLAR

INSTRUCTIONS

Typewriter
Identification

Royal Electric 991 Typewriter, City of Long Beach #45403
Serial Number 01381325

Entire
Keyboard
—Twice

!@#$%¢&*()_+±_:",.?ABCDEFGHIJKLMNOPQRSTUVWXYZ
!@#$%¢&*()_+±_:",.?ABCDEFGHIJKLMNOPQRSTUVWXYZ
1234567890-=½°;',./abcdefghijklmnopqrstuvwxyz
1234567890-=½°;',./abcdefghijklmnopqrstuvwxyz

Message

Christopher Marino	October 15, 1979	197.94
Ronald Skaggs	November 4, 1979	196.73
Robert Hohl	November 15, 1979	197.93
Patrick Smith	November 17, 1979	197.53
Ronald Burbank	January 26, 1980	197.48
Donald Hesslink	February 14, 1980	197.25

Carbon Paper
Impression

Entire
Keyboard
—Twice

!@#$%¢&*()_+±_:",.?ABCDEFGHIJKLMNOPQRSTUVWXYZ
!@#$%¢&*()_+±_:",.?ABCDEFGHIJKLMNOPQRSTUVWXYZ
1234567890-=½°;',./abcdefghijklmnopqrstuvwxyz
1234567890-=½°;',./abcdefghijklmnopqrstuvwxyz

Message

Christopher Marino	October 15, 1979	197.94
Ronald Skaggs	November 4, 1979	196.73
Robert Hohl	November 15, 1979	197.93
Patrick Smith	November 17, 1979	197.53
Ronald Burbank	January 26, 1980	197.48
Donald Hesslink	February 14, 1980	197.25

Typist, Info. &
Signature

Sgt. Deo L. Gernignani

Sgt. Deo L Gernignani, Forgery/Fraud Detail, March 3, 1980,
Typed at Long Beach Public Library (Public typewriter) 10¹
Pacific Ave, Long Beach, Calif.

To obtain carbon paper impression, set machine for stencil (if no stencil, remove ribbon) and
place carbon paper in front of typing paper.

When typing, vary degree of touch; heavy, medium and light.

Figure 10–9: Typewriter exemplar.

of the important elements in examining typewriting. It is, therefore, important to vary the touch and speed when obtaining the exemplar. The final information you should type on the exemplar is the name, model number, and serial number of the typewriter. The date, place, name of person taking the exemplar, and a witness's signature complete the document. If the witness's name is typed with no signature, problems can be raised in court since only a signature can properly personalize a document. After obtaining the exemplar, it is advisable to try to find a piece of paper similar in quality, texture, color, and size to the original on which to duplicate its message.

Standards

An important part of any handwriting examiner's reference material is a typewriter standards file. Ideally, an examiner will have a specimen in this file of every type face manufactured. The FBI reported in the October 1954 *Law Enforcement Bulletin* that "immediately following the establishment of the FBI Laboratory in 1932, contacts with the typewriter manufacturers then in existence resulted in obtaining standards of different styles of type currently on the market. Since then, various manufacturers have furnished standards of newly designed type styles as soon as placed on the market. Contacts with museums and similar sources produced standards of type styles found on machines no longer on the market. Representatives in foreign countries furnished standards of type placed on machines manufactured in their respective countries. As a result, the Typewriter Standards File in the FBI Laboratory is probably the most comprehensive collection of typewriter standards in the world." The San Francisco Postal Inspection Service Laboratory reported in 1970 that their "file of American-made type faces only encompass several thousand specimen sheets representing some seven hundred different type styles, and this collection is undoubtedly far from complete." Joseph Haas of Stuttgart, West Germany, and the Zurich Police Department have two of the best foreign typewriter standard collections.

It is important for each examiner to have a typewriter standards file. For this reason, I started my typewriter file in 1962, shortly after joining the Long Beach Police Department, when Officer (now Commander) Charles Parks asked me to suggest a subject for a college term project. It was suggested that he build a typewriter standards file. Parks contacted local typewriter stores and obtained standards of a few machines. He also obtained the names and addresses of manufacturers, and wrote to them for specimens. The project earned a good grade for Parks, and was of great assistance to me in building my file. The leading typewriters are listed to assist you if you start your own typewriter standards file:

Adler	Olympia
Brother	Remco
Citizen	Royal
Facit	SCM (Smith-Corona)

Hermes	Silver-Reed
IBM	Sperry-Remington
Olivetti	

Addresses of the manufacturing companies are not listed since they are subject to change. Any local typewriter store can give you current addresses, or you can check the *Standard Directory of Advertisers*, published by the National Register Publishing Company, Inc. You can find this book at your local library.

Your typewriter standards file should be placed in order so that an unknown sample of typewriting can be checked against the file. With hundreds or even thousands of standards, this can be very difficult. We did not develop a classification system, or even copy another agency's, because the number of cases did not warrant it. We tied the standards together by manufacturer only. All IBM standards are together, as are all Royal standards. Unknown samples of typewriting can be compared with the "Long Beach Police 21 Typewriters" (figure 10–11). Checking the unknown typed numbers with the 21 Typewriter list usually gives an idea of the kind of machine used to type the unknown sample. A search then can be made of the standards of that machine's manufacturer. This procedure has many faults, but it has been adequate for the relatively few cases reported to the authors.

If you as examiner cannot determine the make and model of a typewriter, you can contact a large law enforcement agency to resource their typewriter file. Another source of help is your local typewriter shop. The employees and repairmen who work with typewriters every day have a great deal of expertise, which they are usually happy to pass on. They can often look at a sample of typewriting and not only identify the make and model, but can also immediately point out defects in the typewriting. The typewriter repairman is a good man to know.

The International Criminal Police Organization (INTERPOL) in Europe uses the "Formule de Classement" as their typewriter classification system.

The initial part of the INTERPOL system is the measurement of one hundred symbols, letters, and spaces in millimeters (this is discussed in detail under the heading Preliminary Examination). The remainder of the first classification is based on the symmetrical balance of certain letters.

There are other Classification Systems besides INTERPOL. Classification systems have been developed by John E. Costain,[13] Linton Godown,[14] David Crown, Donald Doud, Joseph Haas, and the A.S.Q.D.E. All such schemes are based on basic typeface style (Monotone, Gothic, Non-Gothic, Pica); pitch (constant, variable); typeface manufacture; and letter height.[15]

Preliminary Examination

There are three stages of typewriting examination. The first is the preliminary examination to determine the make and model of the typewriter that typed the

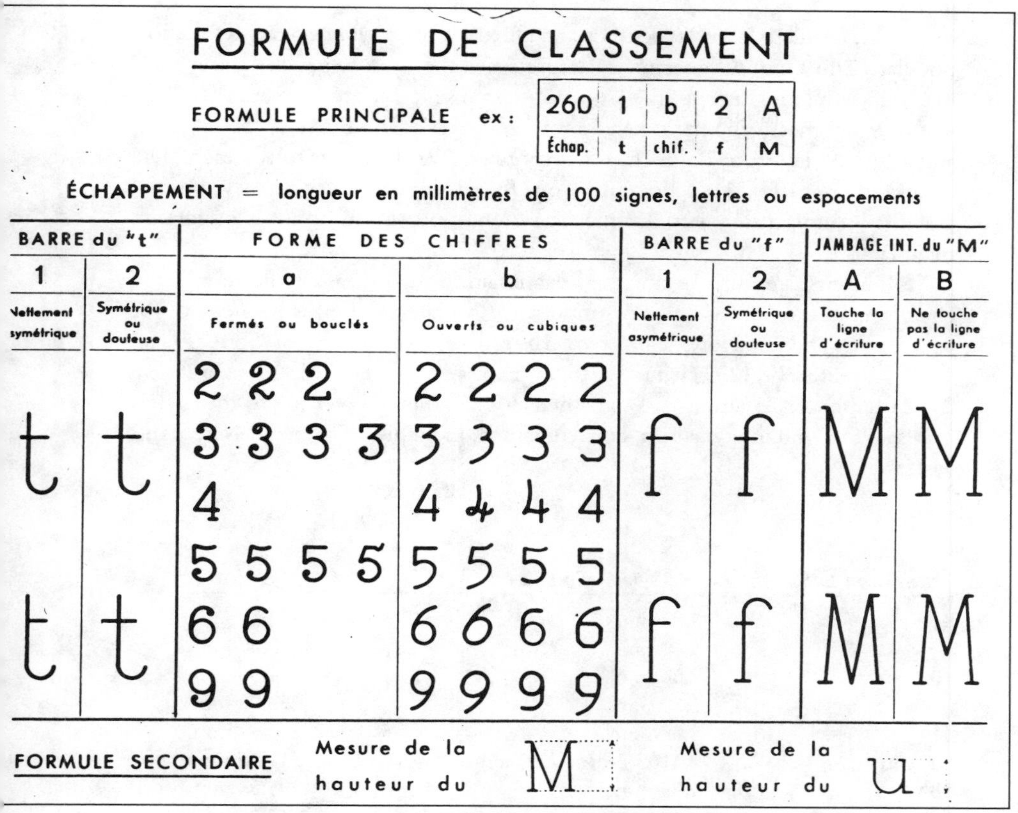

FORMULE DE CLASSEMENT

FORMULE PRINCIPALE   ex :

260	1	b	2	A
Échap.	t	chif.	f	M

ÉCHAPPEMENT = longueur en millimètres de 100 signes, lettres ou espacements

BARRE du "t"		FORME DES CHIFFRES		BARRE du "f"		JAMBAGE INT. du "M"	
1	2	a	b	1	2	A	B
Nettement symétrique	Symétrique ou douteuse	Fermés ou bouclés	Ouverts ou cubiques	Nettement asymétrique	Symétrique ou douteuse	Touche la ligne d'écriture	Ne touche pas la ligne d'écriture

| FORMULE SECONDAIRE | Mesure de la hauteur du M | | | Mesure de la hauteur du u |

Figure 10–10: INTERPOL "Formule de Classement."

questioned document. The second, or identifying, examination is to determine that the questioned document was typed by a specific typewriter. The final or special examination is to solve other types of typewriter problems. Each of the three examinations requires a different set of rules.

Before commencing the preliminary examination, one must understand that all typed characters on a typewriter are one space wide. Therefore, the letters *I* and *M* are the same width as numerals *1* (one) or *4*. (The exception to this is the proportional spacing typewriter, such as the IBM Executive.) Each machine is designed so that a set number of characters occupy a given length. The pitch (horizontal spacing) ranges from 8 to 16 characters per inch. The characters are available in appropriate type styles and sizes. These spacings are controlled by the escapement.

Ten characters (which can be a combination of characters, symbols, or spaces) in an inch of horizontal spacing is called "pica" type, and twelve characters in an inch is called "elite" type. Pica and elite type are well known and the most popular. The United States manufacturers use the inch when designing their machine, while in Europe, the manufacturers use the metric system.

When measuring the type of a foreign typewriter, instead of the 10 (pica) and 12 (elite) letters to the inch, one may find 10½ characters to the inch. The measurements 10½, 11, 12½ and so on, found on a typewriter, may indicate that the manufacturer uses the metric system, and the machine is of foreign manufacture.

The first step in a preliminary examination is to measure the number of characters in an inch of type. A simple and accurate method is to measure for two inches and then divide by two. Instead of a measurement of 10 (pica), 10½, 12 (elite), or 12½ characters to an inch, you are measuring for 20 (pica), 21, 24 (elite), or 25 letters to a two-inch space. When converting to the metric system, 25.40 millimeters (mm) equal one inch. Examples of some measurements are:

Letters in an Inch	Width of a Letter	INTERPOL Measurement Length of 100 characters
9	2.82 mm	282.00 mm
—	2.60 mm	260.00 mm
10 (pica)	2.54 mm	254.00 mm
—	2.50 mm	250.00 mm
11	2.30 mm	230.99 mm
12 (elite)	2.116 mm (or 2.12 mm)	211.66 mm
13	1.95 mm	195.38 mm

When conducting a measurement, each character (letter, number, or symbol) and each space between words is one space wide. Each of these units must be counted to determine the correct measurement.

The next step is to compare a typewriter sample with the questioned document. When making this comparison in the preliminary examination, a negative examination is conducted. This is made in an attempt to find differences in the exemplar and the questioned documents. If one of the documents is typed on a "pica" and the other on an "elite," you will arrive at a negative opinion and say they are not the same (unless it is a machine that types both pica and elite). If the measurement is the same, next examine the characters to find a difference. The manufacturers use letters which are similar to each other, but the numbers used by many of the manufacturers are different. Examine the numbers, again trying to form a negative opinion by attempting to find numbers that are not the same. If they are not the same, you are finished and can positively state the documents are not by the same typewriter.

IBM EXECUTIVE	1 2 3 4 5 6 7 8 9 0
HERMES 2000	1 2 3 4 5 6 7 8 9 0
REMINGTON	1 2 3 4 5 6 7 8 9 0
ROYAL	1 2 3 4 5 6 7 8 9 0
WOODSTOCK	1 2 3 4 5 6 7 8 9 0
I B M ELECTRIC	1 2 3 4 5 6 7 8 9 0
L C SMITH	1 2 3 4 5 6 7 8 9 0
SMITH – CORONA	1 2 3 4 5 6 7 8 9 0
UNDERWOOD	1 2 3 4 5 6 7 8 9 0
REMINGTON 17	1 2 3 4 5 6 7 8 9 0
OLIVETTI	1 2 3 4 5 6 7 8 9 0
HERMES	1 2 3 4 5 6 7 8 9 0
REMINGTON	1 2 3 4 5 6 7 8 9 0
SMITH – CORONA	1 2 3 4 5 6 7 8 9 0
UNDERWOOD	1 2 3 4 5 6 7 8 9 0
ROYAL	1 2 3 4 5 6 7 8 9 0
L C SMITH	1 2 3 4 5 6 7 8 9 0
UNDERWOOD	1 2 3 4 5 6 7 8 9 0
TOWER (Sears)	1 2 3 4 5 6 7 8 9 0
GROMA	1 2 3 4 5 6 7 8 9 0
OLYMPIA	1 2 3 4 5 6 7 8 9 0

Figure 10–11: Long Beach twenty-one typewriters.

On the chart of twenty-one typewriters (figure 10–11), one can easily see the differences in the numbers. On the Remington (third down), the *4* is closed at the top, while the Royal's *4* (fourth down) is open at the top with a slight curve on the first stroke. The Woodstock (fifth down) also has an open *4*, but there is less space between the curved stroke and the second stroke. On the *4* of the Remington 17 (tenth down), the curved stroke starts straight above the second stroke. If two *4*'s are alike, such as in the IBM Electric (sixth down) and Smith-Corona (eighth down), look at another number. The *3* on the IBM curves up in the final stroke, whereas the Smith-Corona curves down. A careful study of the simple construction of a number *1* (one) will often disclose differences. The

With the IBM "Selectric" Typewriter, you
can choose the style of type best for
each production typing application.
1234567890 [ ]@#$%¢&*( )_-+=°!'";:?/,.

With the IBM "Selectric" Typewriter, you
can choose the style of type best for
each production typing application.
1234567890 [ ]@#$%¢&*( )_-+=°!'";:?/,.

With the IBM "Selectric" Typewriter, you
can choose the style of type best for
each production typing application.
1234567890 [ ]@#$%¢&*( )_-+=°!'";:?/,.

Figure 10–12: Similarities in different styles of type.

1 of the IBM Electric, Smith-Corona, and others has a serif at the top that points at an angle to the base line. The serif of the Remington and Royal, however, is parallel to the base line. It can be seen, therefore, that there are great differences in the numbers.

There are also differences in some letters of the different manufacturers. Referring again to the chart of the twenty-one typewriters, the center stroke of the letter *M* in the Remington (third down) rests on the base line, while in the words "L C Smith" (seventh down) the center stroke comes down only halfway. This same center stroke difference can be seen in the letter *W* in the Woodstock (fifth down) and Underwood (ninth down). The final stroke of the letter *R* is different in the Royal (fourth down) and the IBM Electric (sixth down).

A careful examination of figure 10–12 will disclose many differences in the type, especially in the small letters. The letters *y* and *g* are good examples. Despite the fact that the three typewriters in figure 10–12 have different styles of type, many similarities can be found. The letters *c, e, h, i, n, o,* and *u* are the same in all three. In a careful examination of the individual letters, however, differences can be found. Most differences are in the numbers, but differences are also found in the letters.

A negative opinion can be formed during this preliminary examination if horizontal spacing (pica, elite, and so on) are different, or if a difference can be found in the letters and numbers. If the spacing and the characters are the same, you then have a similar make and model of typewriter. This preliminary examination has been an easy mechanical comparison. You must now determine if you have the very same machine that typed the suspect document. The individuality of each machine can be determined by characteristics in the "identifying examination."

Identifying Examination

Once you have identified the make and model of typewriter, you must realize that thousands of typewriters of the same make and model have been made. It is now your job to say that this typewriter, and only this typewriter, typed the questioned document.

Some typewriters have manufacturer-caused problems. Malalignment, both horizontal and vertical, can be seen in some new machines. Once the typewriters are tuned up, the factory precision is altered by the repairmen according to their care of the machines. Type letters later become battered and worn when the type piles up or strikes a staple or solid object. The type may also work loose. It is these defects, which are individual to every typewriter, that make the identifying examination possible.

There are basically nine parts of a typewriter that can cause defects: character, positioning of the character, type bar, ring, type-bar guide, basket misalignment with respect to the platen, mechanism of ribbon, and the escapement.

1. *Character defect*. The manufacture of a character can produce defective letters. A small piece of metal can get in the mold or a bubble can develop in the mold. These and other casting defects can be temporary, or a permanent characteristic.
2. *Positioning of the character defect*. A character is positioned on a type bar electrically by a special apparatus.[16] A slight play of the bar may result in a bad position of the character. A misaligned character can be high, low, off its feet, and so on until resoldered by a repairman.
3. *Type-bar defect*. Each type bar has its own critical shape. The slightly over 3-inch metal bar is made to withstand continual striking without damage. However, if it is bent in a horizontal direction or twisted, a defect can occur. The most frequent reason for this is two letters being struck at the same time. One or more of the keys may be bent or damaged.
4. *Ring defect*. Each type bar has a ring that stops the bar at the proper location and then returns it to its original position. If the ring is defective, the character will strike the platen, remain a second, and then fall back. This slight hesitation causes a second impression called a "rebound" stroke.
5. *Type-bar guide defect*. Every type bar is designed to deliver the character at an exact spot. If the type-bar guide should be moved a fraction of an inch, complete disorder would result. A guide to the right will raise all the characters on the right side of the keyboard, and will lower all the characters on the left. If it is moved to the left, it will cause the opposite effect.[17]
6. *Basket misalignment with respect to the platen*. The "basket" is the location of all key-bars when the machine is not in use. Each key, when pushed, must strike the type-bar guide and platen correctly. If the platen is too high or too low, the defects will show in either the upper or lower half of the character.
7. *Platen defect*. The platen (roller) is rubber, and comes in many degrees of hardness. On striking the paper, the key impresses on the flat surface of the platen. With use, the rubber gets old and hard. Over a period of time, the platen is struck in the same place a great number of times, and this continuous striking causes an unevenness. This irregular surface causes defects throughout the documents. These defects will not be uniform and will appear in different places in the typed documents.
8. *Mechanism of the ribbon assembly*. Defects of the ribbon can be easily detected and are normally corrected before a document is typed. A defect in the ribbon assembly will cause the ribbon to not completely rise. As a result, only a partial impression of the character will be typed.
9. *Escapement defect*. The escapement mechanism on a typewriter consists of three parts, belt, rack and pinion, and the escapement itself. A defect in any of these will cause a horizontal defect. Insufficient carriage movement will also cause incorrect spacing between letters.

The defects in the nine parts of a typewriter listed above can in turn cause defects in typewritten documents. The document examiner normally identifies a combination of "five defects" that were caused by the "defective parts": faulty horizontal alignment, vertical alignment, slant or slope, tilt, "off its feet" or footing, and damaged type.

Faulty horizontal alignment

This is the first defect to check for. When a typist "piles up" type (hitting one key and then another before the first key is out of the way), one key will attempt to move another out of the way, which may cause a slight defect. The horizontal forcing of a key will eventually bend the type arm. This causes the type character to print too far to the right or the left. The escapement mechanism can also malfunction, causing the spacing to be incorrect.

It has been previously stated that pica type is ten letters to the horizontal inch and six lines to the vertical inch. Therefore, each character of a pica type will fit into a square $1/10$ inch by $1/6$ inch. The misalignment of a character can be detected with the assistance of a glass test plate (see Vocabulary). You should remember that each type bar has a slight lateral play to the left and right so it will fit into a type-bar guide. If a character is found too close to another character, check the same character in other locations. If the character is consistent, it is a horizontal defect, and not a "floating key."

The single-element typewriter gives the examiner a new set of problems. On the single-element typewriter there are no keys to pile up, bend, or damage, to create alignment defects. However, the machine does have problems which create an alignment defect. The IBM typewriter ball is positioned with the small letter z in the forward ready position. If the shift key is pressed, the ball rotates with the rear half facing forward and the capital letter Z in the ready position.

Small letter position of the IBM ball:
```
90652z48731
bhkentlcdux
wsi'.1/2oarvm
-yqp=j/,;fg
```
Capital letter position of the IBM ball:
```
()%@Z$*&#
BHKENTLCDUX
WSI'.1/4OARVM
—YQP+J?,;FG
```

When a typing key is pressed, the ball rotates up to five positions to the left or right (there are twenty-two vertical columns, eleven on the small letter side and eleven on the capital letter side). The ball then tilts three additional positions (making a total of four horizontal rows). When the ball is in the proper position, it moves forward, striking the ribbon and impressing a character on the

369

paper. Each of the first two movements of the ball (rotate and tilt) affects the alignment of one or more characters. If there is a rotating misalignment for one letter, it could also affect other letters in the horizontal column. A rotating defect can be found on nearly every machine, and this is the major problem of the single-element typewriter.

Each of the letters in a rotating misalignment will contain a horizontal defect. A ball element misalignment is very slight, and therefore should be carefully examined. Lamar Miller stated, "As would be expected, the more common alignment defects occur at the extreme tilt and rotation positions."[18] The "9bw-" column is the extreme left column, and therefore would contain more defects than the "ztl/2j" column, which is in the center. Miller also said in the summary of his report that "A group of IBM Selectric Model 72 typewriters, with a similar history of use and maintenance, were studied to determine if each of the machines exhibited a unique pattern of alignment defects. It was found that the typewriters could be differentiated on the basis of the lowercase letters alone."

Faulty vertical alignment

In vertical misalignment, the letters (usually the capital letters) print above or below the line of type. If the typist is not pressing down completely on a manual shift key, the capital letter may appear above the line; however, if it is the typist, it will not be consistent in occurrence.

A disorder of the type-bar guide to the right will raise the right letters and lower the left, and vice versa. Examining the letters p and q (letters on opposite ends of the basket) will reveal whether there is a defect. The vertical misalignment should show up in both the upper- and lowercase letters, since both are on the same type bar. This misalignment can also be checked with a typewriter test plate.

In 1961, Buffums Department Store received a series of letters demanding a payment of $3,750. The letters stated that if payment was not made, four surplus incendiary bombs would be exploded in the store. Investigations in the case pointed to two typewriters at the Armed Services YMCA. Exemplars were obtained, and an examination disclosed that every character was of the same style except for the number 8. A defect in the C eliminated one of the typewriters. The second typewriter had several characteristics, including the letter A, which had a vertical misalignment. The letter was also floating with regard to its horizontal alignment. The vertical alignment was one of the characteristics that assisted in the identification of the typewriter.

In the discussion of the problems of the single-element typewriter, you learned that a rotating misalignment for a letter could also affect other letters on the horizontal column. A tilt misalignment will affect the four other letters in the vertical column, and can also affect other letters. The defect affects its vertical alignment, but as with all ball defects, its effect is very slight.

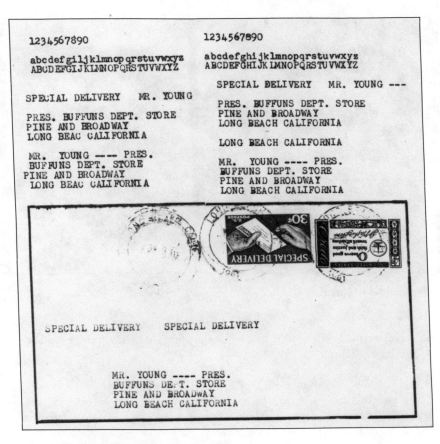

Figure 10–13: Buffuns extortion envelope.

Faulty slant or slope

When a type bar is damaged, the key may become slightly twisted. Sometimes this is found on a new machine, but usually it is seen on a typewriter that has had a lot of hard usage. When this defect occurs, the letter is no longer perpendicular to the line of type. This characteristic therefore becomes an idiosyncrasy of a machine and is very individual. A slant misalignment is more readily detected in the tall letters, and also in capital letters.

An example of slant is displayed in the photograph of the two number 5's (figure 10–14). The left 5 shows the same vertical alignment as the other 5, but is slanted to the left. The slanting can be seen by drawing an imaginary vertical line along the back of the number, or a horizontal line across the top of the number (a typewriter test plate can also assist in this examination). If the slanted

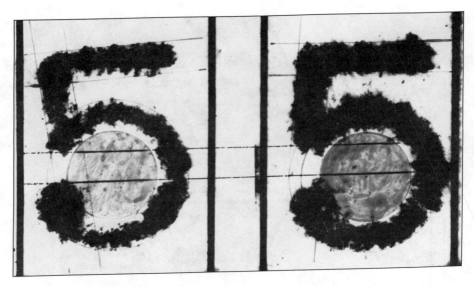

Figure 10–14: Number "5" slant.

character did not have the same base line as the other characters, the individuality would be even greater.

Faulty tilt, "off its feet" or footing

If a character is positioned too high or too low on the key-bar, the character will not type a letter of equal quality. The top or bottom will be darker than the other half. A defect that appears with wear is the typeface striking at a slant rather than flat, with one side of the type printing darker than the other. This fault is more readily observed in the broader letters such as *m* and *w*, and in the capitals.

Damaged type

Defects that occur during manufacture have already been discussed. A more common occurrence is the piling up of letters. One character striking the back of another bends or alters the serif, or parts of the characters. The single-element typewriter eliminates the possibility of keys piling up. There are, however, several ways for the characters on a ball to acquire defects. A ball is interchangeable and can be dropped or damaged in a desk drawer. Even the new daisy wheel, which is made of plastic, may be damaged and produce characters with defects. Typing elements that contain a damaged character should be discarded and new ones obtained. Experience has shown that because of laziness or cost considerations, faulty elements are often retained. The defects may seem minor to the typist, but to the examiner, the defects on a golf ball or daisy wheel are important to an identification.

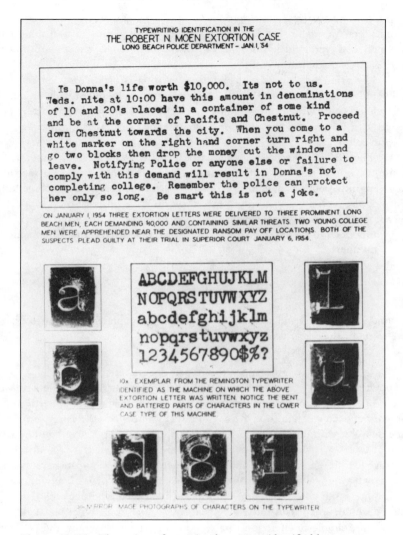

Figure 10–15: The writer of extortion letters was identified by type defects.

A combination of unusual characteristics usually make for a positive opinion. For the sake of analogy, suppose you are hunting a suspect with his left ear completely cut off, his right index finger cut off at the third joint, and the tip of his nose cut off. You can assume that if you find a man with those characteristics, this is the man you are hunting and you can eliminate everyone else. It is similar with typewriters. If an exemplar and the questioned document both have a missing serif on the bottom left side of the small letter *m*, a small letter *a* that is "off its feet," a small *r* that slants to the right, a small *y* with vertical alignment too high, and typing made from the same make and model, you can assume you have a positive identification.

Defects in the type played a part in a California extortion case. Letters were delivered demanding $10,000 each. The letters were subsequently identified, by their defects, as having been typed by the suspect's Remington typewriter. The letters *a, d, i, o, u* and the number 8 all contained defects that assisted in the identification.

The FBI *Law Enforcement Bulletin* of October 1954, stated, "Inasmuch as abuse, wear, and tear are for the most part accidental, each particular machine develops imperfections which are characteristic for the individual machine, thus forming the basis for a typewriting identification. This observation is supported by the fact that no two typewriters have yet been found that have exactly the same imperfection even though made by the same manufacturer with consecutive serial numbers."

Special Examination

With the preliminary and identifying examinations completed, it is time to examine some of the many typewriter problems.

Alterations to a typed document

Typewriters are so manufactured that when a document is typed, the letters of each succeeding line are typed directly under the letters above. A vertical line drawn between the letters of the top line will go between the letters on every line below it without touching a letter. If a horizontal line is drawn under each line of type, each line will be parallel to all the other lines. If a page of type is removed from the typewriter and then reinserted and a new paragraph added, the new typing will not line up with the other type. This new alignment can be seen quite easily with a typewriter test plate, indicating whether each letter on the entire document falls into its $1/10$ inch by $1/6$ inch (pica type) rectangle.

An example of alteration to a typed document is shown in the "Release of All Claims" document (figure 10–16). An examination of the document determined that at least two typewriters typed three different times on the document.

One typewriter typed the upper portion of the document, and the names that were to be signed. A second typewriter typed "LOS ANGELES," "14th June 82," "GREGORY A. YATES," and the word "he" in two places. The document was reinserted in a typewriter at a later time and the following was typed: "ROBERT R. HARRIS, SR.," "KAY HARRIS, AND STEFAN RENEE HARRIS" and then the letter *T* before "he," and a *y* after the words. In the first word ("They"), the *y* was typed in alignment with the *T*, but since it was too

(The undersigned hereby declare(s) and represent(s) that the injuries sustained are or may be permanent and progressive and that recovery therefrom is uncertain and indefinite and in making this Release it is understood and agreed, that the undersigned rely(ies) wholly upon the undersigned's judgment, belief and knowledge of the nature, extent, affect and duration of said injuries and liability therefor and is made without reliance upon any statement or representation of the party or parties hereby released or their representatives or by any physician or surgeon by them employed.

The undersigned further declare(s) and represent(s) that there may be unknown or unanticipated injuries resulting from the above stated accident, casualty or event and in making this Release it is understood and agreed that this Release is intended to include such injuries.

The undersigned further declare(s) and represent(s) that no promise, inducement or agreement not herein expressed has been made to the undersigned, and that this Release contains the entire agreement between the parties hereto, and that the terms of this Release are contractual and not a mere recital.

This Release expressly reserves all rights of the person, or persons, on whose behalf the payment is made and the rights of all persons in privity or connected with them, and reserves to them their right to pursue their legal remedies, if any, including but not limited to claims for contribution, property damage and personal injury against the undersigned or those in privity or connected with the undersigned.

THE UNDERSIGNED HAS READ THE FOREGOING RELEASE AND FULLY UNDERSTANDS IT.

Signed, sealed and delivered this 14 day of JUNE , 19 82

CAUTION: READ BEFORE SIGNING BELOW →

_____ Witness

_____ LS
ROBERT R. HARRIS SR., individually and as
guardian ad litem of MARC E.S. HARRIS, a minor

_____ Witness

_____ LS
KAY HARRIS

_____ Witness

_____ LS
STEFAN RENEE HARRIS

STATE OF CALIFORNIA } ss.

COUNTY OF LOS ANGELES

On the 14th day of June , 19 82 , before me personally appeared

ROBERT R. HARRIS, SR., GREGORY A. YATES, KAY HARRIS, and STEFAN RENEE HARRIS

to me known to be the person(s) named herein and who executed the foregoing Release and They acknowledged to me that they voluntarily executed the same.

My term expires: October 13 , 19 85

_____ Notary Public

OFFICIAL SEAL
JONI M SAND
NOTARY PUBLIC - CALIFORNIA
LOS ANGELES COUNTY
My comm. expires OCT 13, 1985

Form No. L-3851-C

Figure 10-16: Release of All Claims document.

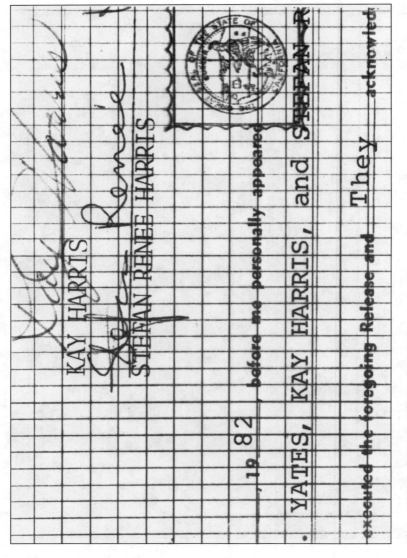

Figure 10–17: Alignment of "Kay Harris" and T

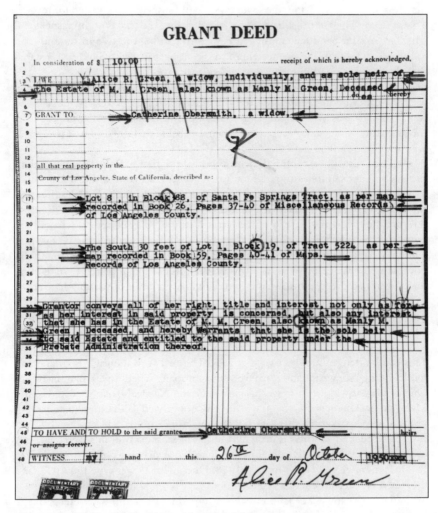

Figure 10–18: Bradford's Obersmith trial exhibit.

close to the letter *e*, the letter was removed, the paper moved, and the letter typed. The typewriter test plate was of great help in solving the above case.

The Obersmith case also concerned an altered document. In 1953, the arrest and trial of Catherine Obersmith held the headlines of the Southern California press. On May 21, 1953, the seventy-year-old suspect was arrested for forging a grant deed. The victim, Mrs. Green, stated during the trial that the suspect and Mrs. Green's husband had an oral agreement regarding the two lots mentioned in the grant deed, so she deeded them to the suspect in 1950. She further stated that she did not deed over the rest of her property.

The defense examiner testified that it would have been nearly impossible for Mrs. Obersmith to have inserted the questioned paragraph. He went on to testify that "It was his best judgment that all portions of the deed were typed at the same time and it was very, extremely improbable that the disputed paragraph was inserted at a later date."

The prosecution rebutted the testimony with that of Ralph Bradford, then the document examiner for the Long Beach Police Department. He testified that he was positive the deed had been replaced in Mrs. Obersmith's typewriter and the disputed paragraph added at a later date. He began his testimony by pointing out that the defect in the serif of the letter *K* assisted him in proving that all the typing, including the questioned paragraph, was typed on the same typewriter. Then, referring to his exhibit, he pointed out that the questioned paragraph did not line up horizontally or vertically with the original paragraphs. He stated that the questioned paragraph slanted downhill while the original paragraphs were at a different level. He also pointed to additional characteristics on the documents. On December 3, 1953, the suspect was found guilty, and later sent to state prison.

Age of document

This can be determined by two methods. The first is to identify the make and model of the typewriter and learn from the company when it was manufactured. One of the early court cases was *Gamble v. Second National Bank* (reported in the *Michigan State Bar Journal*, vol. 4, no. 8). This concerned a document dated 1880, written on a typewriter that was not manufactured until 1911.

The second method is difficult but has been successful in several cases. A hypothetical example is five documents identified as all being typed by typewriter X. Document A was typed first, in 1976. Document B was typed in 1977, and showed a defect in the letter *B*. Document C was typed in 1978 and had defects in the letters *B* and *C*. Document D was typed in 1979 and had defects in the letters *B, C,* and *D*. Finally, document E was typed in 1980 and had defects in the *B, C, D,* and *E*. The questioned document was not dated, but was identified as being typed by typewriter X and as having defects in letters *B, C,* and *D*, but no defect in the *E*. The document was therefore typed in 1979, the same year document D was typed.

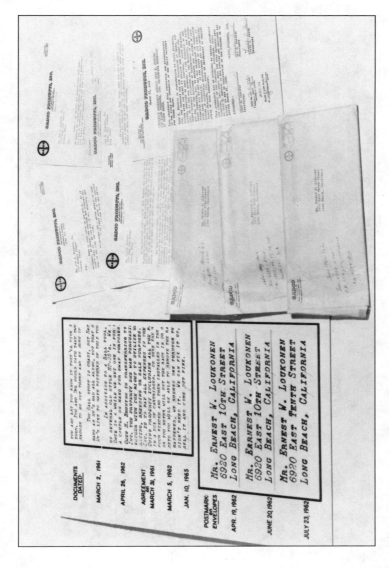

Figure 10–19: Cadco Products Inc. documents.

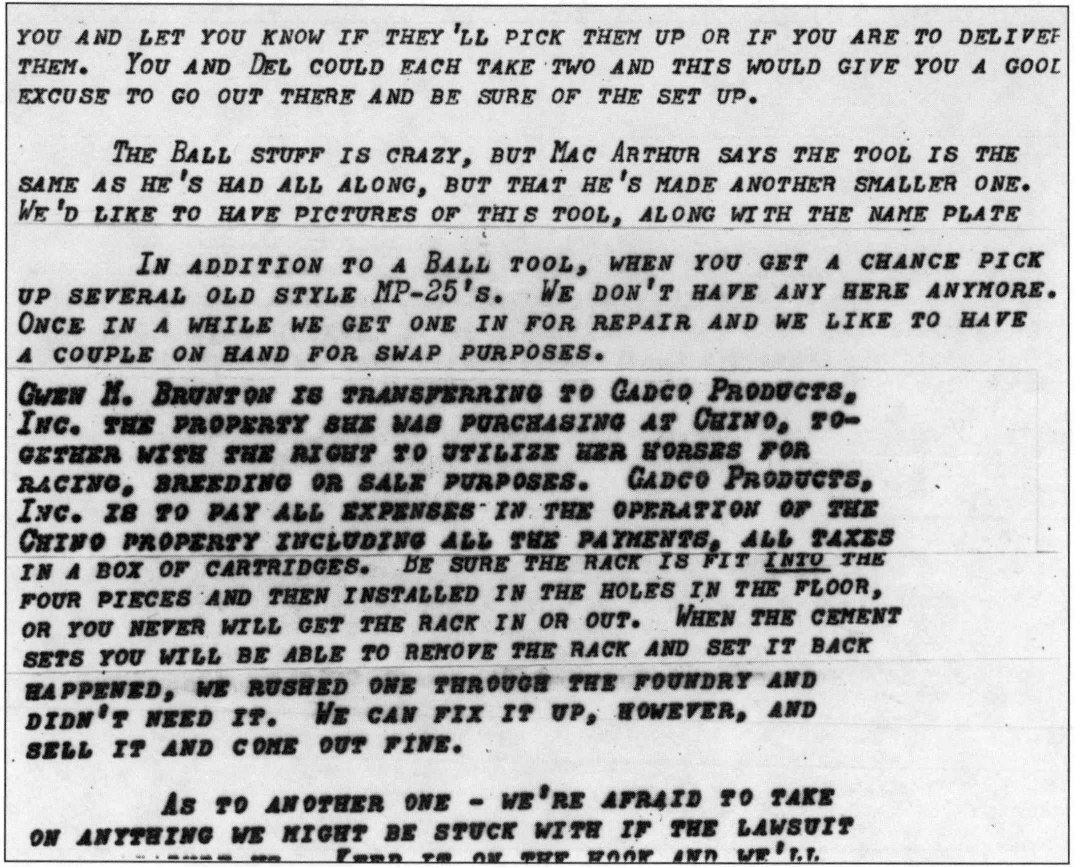

YOU AND LET YOU KNOW IF THEY'LL PICK THEM UP OR IF YOU ARE TO DELIVER
THEM. YOU AND DEL COULD EACH TAKE TWO AND THIS WOULD GIVE YOU A GOOD
EXCUSE TO GO OUT THERE AND BE SURE OF THE SET UP.

THE BALL STUFF IS CRAZY, BUT MAC ARTHUR SAYS THE TOOL IS THE
SAME AS HE'S HAD ALL ALONG, BUT THAT HE'S MADE ANOTHER SMALLER ONE.
WE'D LIKE TO HAVE PICTURES OF THIS TOOL, ALONG WITH THE NAME PLATE

IN ADDITION TO A BALL TOOL, WHEN YOU GET A CHANCE PICK
UP SEVERAL OLD STYLE MP-25'S. WE DON'T HAVE ANY HERE ANYMORE.
ONCE IN A WHILE WE GET ONE IN FOR REPAIR AND WE LIKE TO HAVE
A COUPLE ON HAND FOR SWAP PURPOSES.

GWEN H. BRUNTON IS TRANSFERRING TO GADCO PRODUCTS,
INC. THE PROPERTY SHE WAS PURCHASING AT CHINO, TO-
GETHER WITH THE RIGHT TO UTILIZE HER HORSES FOR
RACING, BREEDING OR SALE PURPOSES. GADCO PRODUCTS,
INC. IS TO PAY ALL EXPENSES IN THE OPERATION OF THE
CHINO PROPERTY INCLUDING ALL THE PAYMENTS, ALL TAXES
IN A BOX OF CARTRIDGES. BE SURE THE RACK IS FIT INTO THE
FOUR PIECES AND THEN INSTALLED IN THE HOLES IN THE FLOOR,
OR YOU NEVER WILL GET THE RACK IN OR OUT. WHEN THE CEMENT
SETS YOU WILL BE ABLE TO REMOVE THE RACK AND SET IT BACK

HAPPENED, WE RUSHED ONE THROUGH THE FOUNDRY AND
DIDN'T NEED IT. WE CAN FIX IT UP, HOWEVER, AND
SELL IT AND COME OUT FINE.

AS TO ANOTHER ONE - WE'RE AFRAID TO TAKE
ON ANYTHING WE MIGHT BE STUCK WITH IF THE LAWSUIT

Figure 10–20: Defects in O and R.

This problem presented itself in the Cadco Products case. An agreement was dated March 31, 1961. The question was given to the examiner: Was the document typed on the date shown on the agreement, and if not, when was it typed? A number of exemplar documents were obtained, dating from March 2, 1961, to January 10, 1965.

The documents were examined and it was determined that some of the documents contained defects in the characters. A chart listed the defects as:

1.	3-2-61	Normal *O*	Defect in the foot of *R*
2.	3-5-62	"	"
3.	4-26-62	"	No defect *R* (letter repaired)
4.	4-19-62	"	"
5.	3-31-61	Questioned defect *O*	No defect *R*
6.	6-20-62	"	"
7.	7-23-62	"	"
8.	1-10-65	"	"

The list of defects and the photograph (figure 10–20) proved the questioned agreement of March 31, 1961, was typed sometime after April 19, 1962.

Identification of typist

Fingerprints can be obtained from a typed question document (see chapter 11). A typist can also be identified by his or her method of typing a document. Some identifying points are:

a. *Date.* The norm states the date is not abbreviated and is in the upper right corner, where it is of value in filing. Variations find the date in the center or on the left side. The Bradford System shows five ways to type dates.

b. *Capitalization.* To type in capitals or lowercase is a question that constantly arises to plague the typist. Two styles of capitalization have evolved: the up-style in which capitals are used freely, as in business writing. The second is the down-style in which capitals are used sparingly, as in newspapers.

c. *Heading.* Main titles are centered and set in capitals. They are not usually underlined, but may be spaced out. They do not include "Re" or "Subject" but some persons include a prefix in the heading. Lt. Col. Oliver North testified before the Iran-Contra committee on July 8, 1987, that he altered and shredded documents. He admitted fabricating documents to cover a home-security system. To make it appear a second letter was typed well after the first, he changed the form and heading. He also used a second typewriter with a distinctive defect in the type ball.[19]

d. *Margins or spacing.* A one-inch margin on all sides, slightly wider to the left, is the norm. Margins vary with most typists. So does the location of the date relative to the top of the paper, the space between the heading and the body, and spacing between paragraphs.

e. *Paragraph.* The amount of horizontal and vertical alignment for each new paragraph is another distinguishing feature.

f. *Punctuation.* Authorities agree that punctuation is a matter of judgment, not of definite rules. Therefore the punctuation or lack of punctuation individualizes a typewritten document. William Schulenberger reported an "unusual typewriter case" that was solved because of an unusual habit when typing an exclamation mark. When examining the questioned document, it was discovered the exclamation mark was one-and-one-half spaces from the preceding character, or a half space out of vertical alignment. This phenomenon was not caused by a defect in the machine but by an unconventional manner of typing the mark. After skipping two spaces, the operator would depress the space bar and back-space key simultaneously and successively hit the apostrophe and period keys while the machine was thus locked. The conventional manner of making the mark, by making one element and back-spacing for the other, would have resulted in normal alignment.[20]

The case of an anonymous letter (figure 10–21) sent to the Culver City (California) Police Department was solved by punctuation marks. The typed anonymous letter was copied, and the copies sent to the various officials. Due to the fact that copies were sent, the typewriter could not be identified. However, the typist was identified by his individual style of typing. Abbreviations, placement of quotation marks around words, ellipse marks (dots) between words, and misspellings, all led to the suspect's identification.

g. *Spelling.* See chapter 7.

h. *Strikeovers or skill.* If the person is an unskilled typist mistakes will be noted in characters in the lower line, such as *Z, X, C,* and *V,* and with letters typed by the little finger. "Hunt and peck" typists have problems with typing *V* instead of *B,* or *I* instead of *O.*

i. *Use of words and grammar.* John O'London said, "My point of view is that, in everyday life, good English follows clear thinking rather than that system of rules called Grammar which youth loathed and maturity forgets.[21] The fifteen most common errors of grammar are: (1) pronouns incorrectly used; (2) singular verbs with plural subjects and vice-versa; (3) tenses of verbs mixed; (4) collective nouns confused; (5) possessives, especially of plural nouns, incorrectly formed; (6) double negatives formed; (7) foreign plurals incorrectly formed; (8) "don't" for "doesn't"; (9) "like" for "as" or "as if"; (10) "set " for "sit"; (11) "lay" for "lie"; (12) "raise" for "rise"; (13) "affect" for "effect"; (14) incorrect placement of "only"; (15) "can" for "may."

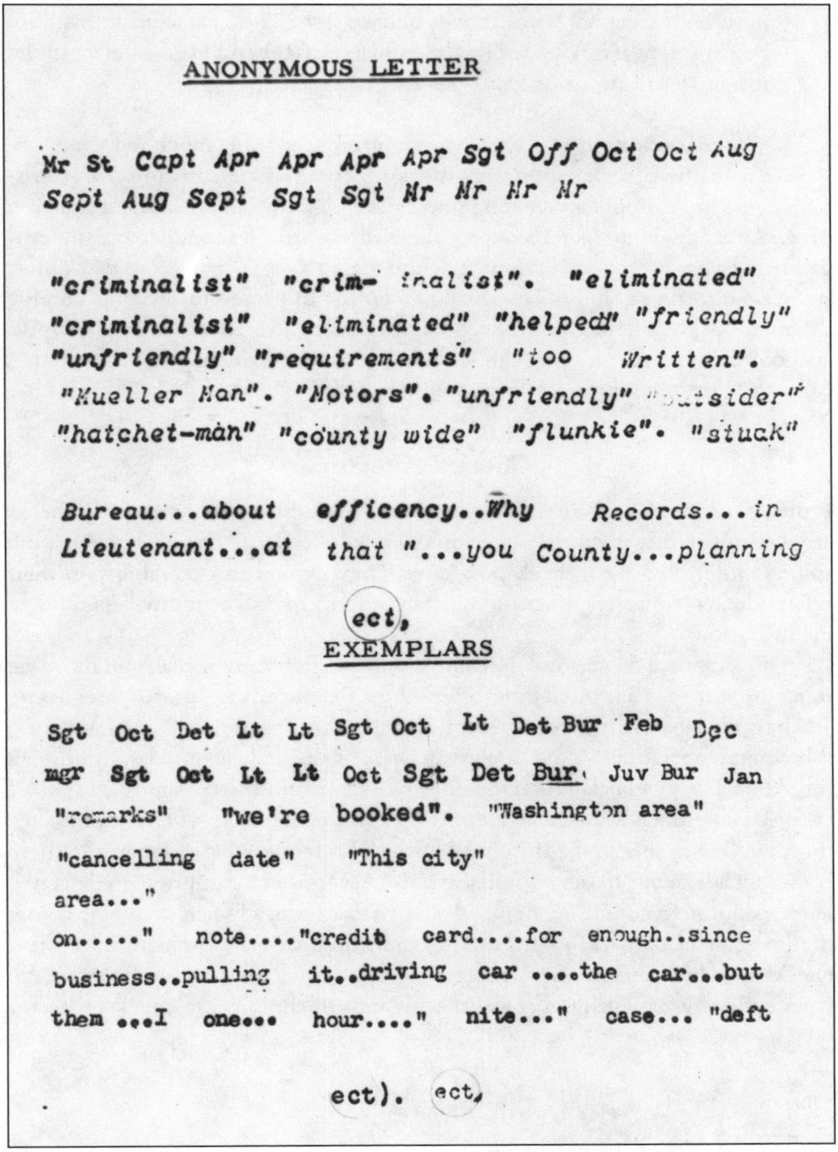

<u>ANONYMOUS LETTER</u>

Mr St Capt Apr Apr Apr Apr Sgt Off Oct Oct Aug
Sept Aug Sept Sgt Sgt Mr Mr Mr Mr

"*criminalist*" "*crim- inalist*". "*eliminated*"
"*criminalist*" "*eliminated*" "*helped*" "*friendly*"
"*unfriendly*" "*requirements*" "*too Written*".
"*Mueller Man*". "*Motors*". "*unfriendly*" "*outsider*"
"*hatchet-man*" "*county wide*" "*flunkie*". "*stuck*"

Bureau....about ***efficency..Why*** *Records...in*
Lieutenant...at that "...you County...planning

(ect),
<u>EXEMPLARS</u>

Sgt Oct Det Lt Lt Sgt Oct Lt Det Bur Feb Dec
mgr Sgt Oct Lt Lt Oct Sgt Det Bur Juv Bur Jan
"remarks" "we're booked". "Washington area"
"cancelling date" "This city"
area..."
on....." note...."credit card....for enough..since
business..pulling it..driving car ....the car...but
them ...I one... hour...." nite..." case... "deft

ect). ect,

Figure 10–21: Exhibit of the anonymous letter.

j. *Vertical alignment.* Alignment problems can be caused by the human element. A weak little finger not pressing all the way down on a shift key will position the capital letter above the base line. This characteristic will not be consistent if it is caused by the human element, whereas a defect in the machine will be consistent.

The identification of a typist can be made using the above ten elements. You have learned that variation from the norm gives individuality to a characteristic. For example, item f above, on punctuation, discusses an unusual exclamation mark. After Schulenberger discovered this characteristic, he conducted an investigation as to how frequently typists type the mark this way. He found that almost no occasional typist, and only a small percentage of professional typists employ this method. He did find business schools that teach the method, but many typists abandon it soon after leaving the school. The strong evidence of this variation from the norm was brought forth and the suspect admitted guilt.

Check Protectors

Professional check forgers specializing in stolen and forged commercial checks are well aware that the average person regards as "official" checks on which the value is imprinted by a check protector. They exploit this credibility in their operation. Fortunately, in so doing, they often provide a positive method of identification.

Professional forgers use the same company, fictitious or real, and the same signatures for only a limited time, after which they begin again with new names and new checks. The check protector used, however, is usually carried over into subsequent operations. This careless practice is utilized in the classification of forged checks by check-protector imprint examination (see chapter 3).

Besides the advantage of identifying the specific make of check protector used, and being able to file the check for ready reference and comparison, there is another advantage to the examination of check-protector imprints. A defective letter, a distinctive "tail," a numeral that characteristically falls above or below the line can all be revealed through examination. Close examination of a few checks for which a single check protector was used will often reveal characteristic flaws sufficient to legally establish the identity of the specific check protector used.

History

The Check Protector has, over the years, been given many names; Checkwriter, Check Punch, Word Writer are just a few. In about 1870, the first of the "protectors" was developed. This consisted of individual punches which perforated figure holes in the paper, similar to the way banks today show the date a check is paid.[22] In 1880, Alvin V. Lane improved on this with his Check Punch, which included a star, dollar mark, or other characters.

Todd–Burroughs

In 1899, George W. and Libanus M. Todd, with the assistance of Charles Tiefel, developed a new protector they called "Protectography." The Todd company started manufacturing this machine, which for the first time forced ink into the

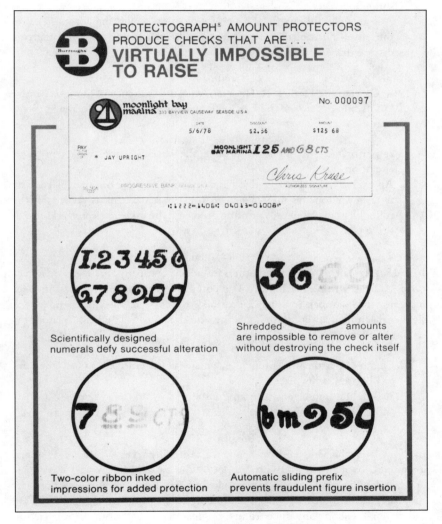

Figure 10–22: Todd–Burroughs check protector. (*Burroughs Corp.*)

385

paper. The amount protector shreds indelible ink into the fibers of the paper under pressure, making it part of the fiber of the document. In the late 1950s, the Todd Company was bought out by the Burroughs Corporation. The Burroughs protector features:

1. Scientifically designed numerals that defy alteration.
2. Shredded amounts (all manufacturers use this element).
3. Two-color ribbon ink. The dye is forced into the paper fiber due to the shredding.
4. Automatic sliding prefix. This prefix slides up against the last numeral on the left, eliminating the possibility of a numeral insertion (most manufacturers use this element).

Hedman

In 1914, Carl M. and Herbert R. Hedman, with the assistance of Douglas Fensler and W.O. Evans, developed the F & E Hedman protector. The Hedman protector features:

1. A perforated "Warranted" through the payee's name, which prevents alteration.
2. An exclusive ink carriage that has no ribbons to wear out or replace. The type never touches ink rollers. With every stroke, ink is picked off the roller like the platen on a printing press, and the ink pad cleans and brushes the type.

Hall-Welter

In 1915, Herman C. Welter and others founded a company and began manufacturing "check writing machines." The company manufactured several models, including the National, Sentinel, Speedrite, Error-No, and the Chexsigno (check signing machine that shreds the signature into the paper). The Hall-Welter protectors feature:

1. Engraved personalized prefix die, which can be removed, and a "The Sum of" bar put in its place.
2. A simplified, inexpensive inking system.
3. Model B-L is equipped for use in any one of twelve world currencies.

Safeguard-REP

In about 1917, the Safeguard Company was started by a Mr. Whittaker, who had invented a "word writer." In the late 1930s, the current slide model was developed, and in the 1950s, a model was made for Sears, Roebuck. A number of years ago, Safeguard Business Systems, Inc. sold the check protector company to REP Industries. The company discontinued the manufacture of both the regular and the Sears models and currently only services and sells parts.

Paymaster

In 1922, Paymaster got its start in the protector business with the "Checkometer Co." In about 1928, the American Check Writer company made the Paymaster protector. In 1939, Paymaster began producing its own check protector. The Paymaster "protective features" include:

1. Change of number styles every four to six years.
2. The word "Registered" perforated through payee name. This feature can be turned off by the use of a lever.
3. A "Gear-O-Matic" inking system that does not depend on friction to provide inking.
4. Two-color ribbon that performs better than liquid ink systems. (Paymaster offers both ribbon and ink machines.)

Speed-O-Print

In about 1960, the Speed-O-Print corporation began a sideline of check protectors. The Speed-O-Print protector features:

1. Manual or electric check protectors.
2. An impression that blends into the paper, making alteration impossible.

Exemplars

Like the typewriter imprint, the check protector imprint on a questioned document can be identified with a known exemplar. The opinion therefore is based in part on the quality of the exemplar. The first step in obtaining an exemplar is to locate paper similar to the questioned document. A piece of paper that is too thin could be overly shredded. A heavier card stock would not print properly, since many protectors are not designed for all thicknesses.

The check protector has several operating arms, each containing the numbers 0 to 9 (and sometimes a "star"). In a ten-number machine, there are ten operating arms. On a typewriter, one can obtain a sample from each key, but on a check protector, one needs a sample of each number on each arm.

Check protectors have a sliding prefix at the left of the amount. The prefix can contain a company name or words such as "Bonded," "Exactly," "Insured," "Pay," "Registered," "The sum" and so on. This mechanism can become so dirty that the prefix will not automatically slide over. Exemplars should be obtained for $1.00, which can check the movement of the prefix.

It is important not to make any adjustments in the check protector or inking system until the initial exemplars have been obtained. After obtaining the initial exemplars, alterations to the machine can be made. One of these could be to remove or add the prefix. Some check protectors use a ribbon instead of ink. The ribbon should be carefully examined, as it may contain valuable information.

Each exemplar should be marked with information, including the make, model, and serial number of the machine. If an alteration to the machine is made, this should be noted on the exemplar. The document should also be dated and witnessed.

Comparison and Identification

The comparison of a check protector can be brought to the attention of an examiner by two methods. The first is by the comparison of a questioned document with an exemplar. The second method is the comparison of two unknown documents that are tied together by a classification system.

Classification for check protectors

Ralph Bradford developed a classification system for check protectors in 1953.[23] The Bradford Classification System did not consider the prefix (company name or "The Sum," etc.) in the original system, since this can be removed on some machines. Numbers were also not considered, since officials of Paymaster stated that they change their number styles every four or five years. The classification of the check protector in the Bradford System contains three parts of the check protector imprint—the "cents" figure, "dollars," and the word "and." When two check protectors classify the same, look for irregularities to prove they were imprinted by the same machine.

Ink and ribbon

The examination of check protectors begins with the first thing an examiner will see: the "ink" that makes the impression. The various manufacturers have patented names for the inking process, but the imprint can be left on the document either by ink or by a ribbon. Todd-Burroughs and Speed-O-Print were the two manufacturers to use ribbons exclusively. Hedman, Hall-Welter, and Safeguard-REP used ink exclusively. Paymaster is the only manufacturer to offer both ink and ribbon check protectors. Some companies use a two-color ribbon and some use two different color inks. Paymaster, with its "Gear-O-Matic" inking system, uses a blue ink for the prefix and a red ink for the amount (this can be changed, depending on the requirements of the user).

You can sometimes determine whether ink or ribbon was used by the bleeding of the ink. This is especially noticeable if the machine has two inks that run together. A ribbon will leave a fine definition at the edge of the color.

Overinking, or defects in the inking, occur frequently in three areas of a check protector: the words "dollars," "and," and "cents." These three parts are used in every impression, whereas the numbers are constantly changed. The constant inking of the three parts may cause the ink to combine with fibers and lint to cake and fill up the letter. If the ink container or ribbon has a defect, it can be very characteristic. The checks of the Chirrick gang were tied together by the Bradford System, identified by the defect in the *s* of the "cts."

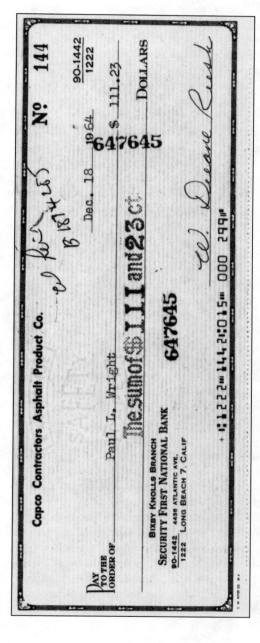

Figure 10–23: The Chirrick gang's defective check protector.

Check-protector defects

Examination of ink defects are for the most part very obvious. The next step in the examination is to look for the less obvious defects. You should examine an imprint not only on the face, but also on the back. Some check protectors perforate the word "Bonded," "Insured," "Registered," or "Warranted," or just a series of indentations on the payee line in order to prevent a payee alteration. The pins that make these perforations become dulled or even broken with use. The examination of these perforations with the use of transmitted light will disclose the degree of perforation, or lack thereof.

Because of the hardness of the type, there is normally not the wear on check-protector characters that there is on typewriter characters. Therefore, the check protector does not change progressively as much, due to defects, as do typewriters.[24] However, during the handling and assembling of the 1,600 to 1,800 parts in a check protector, the typeface may become nicked or marred.[25] The defects on the face of a character are individual and valuable characteristics.

The next very valuable element of comparison is the horizontal and vertical alignment. It has already been stated that the prefix can get dirty and may not move horizontally to the side of the left character. Horizontal misalignment is rare with a check protector. Vertical misalignment, on the other hand, can be sometimes observed. The numbers rotate on the operating arm in a vertical rotation which can become faulty, resulting in misalignment. This misalignment can be seen in figure 10–24 (bottom imprint) in the number 2 which is low.

Other characteristics concern the inking of the characters. When two colors are used, an inking defect can occur. Some protectors use one color for the numbers and another for the words. When the ink is not lined up, the numbers color will bleed into the letters. This can be seen in figure 10–24 (top defect), where the red letters can be seen in the black "6," and the black numbers can be seen on the s. Another inking defect is caused by a character not striking exactly level to the paper. The most common such defect is heavier printing in the lower half. The printed character will appear clear at the top, but will blur or even overink at the bottom. This defect can also be seen in figure 10–24 (center two defects).

The manufacturers of check protectors sell their machines by warning that hand-written checks can be altered. What they fail to say is that check protectors can also be altered and falsified. Many criminals have a great deal of talent, and alterations do appear. Hargett and Dusak reported a case in which a document was placed over a file. Pressure was placed on the paper causing the file to make an impression similar to that of a check protector.[26] I examined one of the most unusual forgeries I have ever seen. Counterfeiters fictitiously printed checks, which had turned out poorly. The counterfeiter then went over the entire check with a ball point pen, inking in what the printing process failed to do. He then used a red ball point pen to draw a check protector imprint. He used a pin to

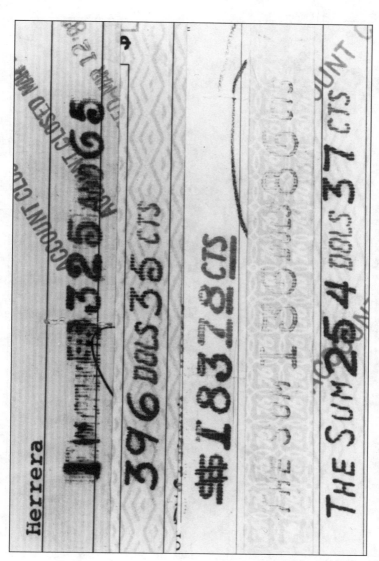

Figure 10-24: Check protector defects.

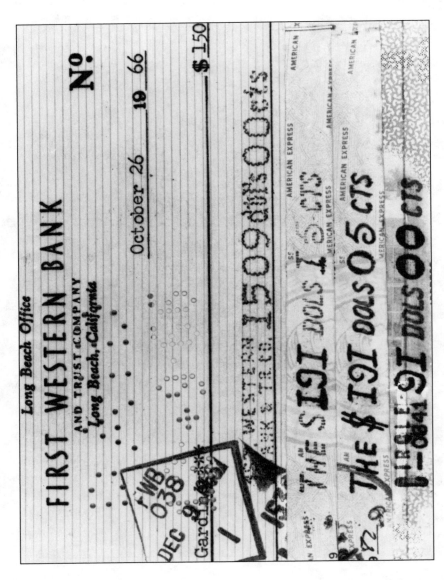

Figure 10–25: Hand-drawn check protector imprints.

simulate the holes of a protector (figure 10–25, top imprint). It is also a common practice of criminals to purchase a $1.00 money order, altering the numbers to raise the amount with an ink pen.

The impression of a check protector can be as individual as the impression of a typewriter, and from it positive opinions can be given. The examiner who compares typewriter and check protector impressions must be very careful. You must be sure to check if the identification is based on individual characteristics or class characteristics of that make of machine. Experience and study of the machines will give you the expertise needed to make the correct positive opinions.[27]

—11—

Fingerprints

Y ou may wonder why a chapter on fingerprints is included in a book on handwriting. With the increasing number of nonsufficient funds and forged checks being passed, fingerprints are being required on some checks as a deterrent. There are also invisible (latent) fingerprints as well as visible prints left on checks and other documents. Many latent prints can be developed and made visible. The fingerprints on the questioned document can then be compared to an exemplar and an identification made.

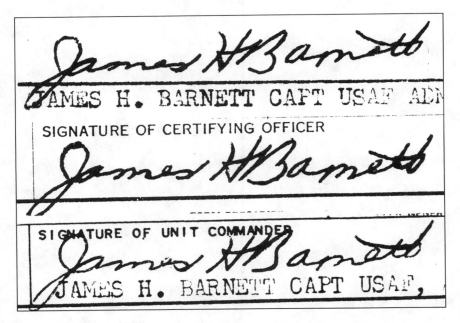

Figure 11–1: James H. Barnett traced forgery.

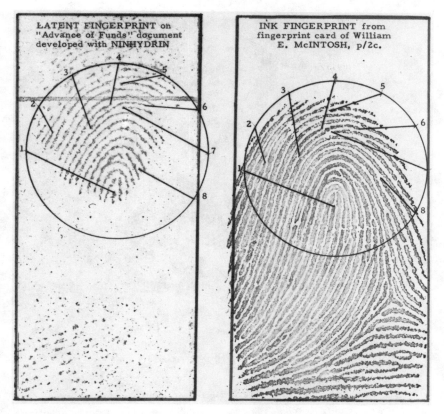

Figure 11–2: Latent and ink fingerprint in Barnett case.

An example of this was a 1960 case at the Boron Air Force Station in California. A military pay order was processed, authorizing three months advance pay. It bore the signature of "James H. Barnett." The document was questioned and submitted for examination. A handwriting examination was conducted, and it was determined that the three signatures were all traced from the same master. The pay order was a forgery.

Since the signatures of Captain Barnett were a tracing, there was no possibility of identifying the author of the forgery. Latent fingerprint development was attempted with ninhydrin to locate fingerprints where fingers would have been used to hold the document in contact with the original when the signature was traced. A left index fingerprint of the suspect was developed in this area.

Handwriting and fingerprints combined to bring the Barnett case to a successful conclusion. A handwriting examiner with a knowledge of fingerprints is able to make a more complete examination.

Figure 11–3: Sir Edward Richard
Henry.

History of Fingerprints

Students of dactyloscopy, the science of fingerprints, have found prehistoric
Indian picture writing of a hand with ridge patterns. Chinese documents from
the eighth century (A.D.) T'ang Dynasty have thumbprints impressed on clay seals
to identify their maker. One of the most interesting documents is a clay tablet
that was a court record from the ancient city of Babylon. Written about 1500
B.C. the tablet is the official report of a deputy sheriff who was ordered by his
brother, a presiding magistrate, to execute a court order in the settlement of a
civil case. A partial translation of the record reads: "Give five and one-half Minae
of silver to Nergaliddin, the creditor of Bel-lumur. Thereafter, you will arrest
Bel-lumur and his son. Prepare a documentary report describing the arrest and
the taking of his house and property, and secure thereon the fingerprints of
Bel-lumur."[1]

The use of fingerprints was commented on in 1684 by Dr. Nehemiah
Grew, in 1686 by Marcello Malpighi, and in 1823 by John E. Purkinje. In 1858,
Sir William Herschel began the official use of fingerprints on a large scale. He
conceived a plan to use them for broad registration as a measure against fraudulent
identities. In 1880, Dr. Henry Faulds discussed the potentialities of identification
of criminals from fingerprints left at the scene of the crime. Faulds demonstrated
the practical application by identifying greasy fingerprints of a person who had
been drinking some rectified spirits from the laboratory supply. In 1892, Sir

Francis Galton, in his book *Fingerprints*, devised the first scientific method of classifying fingerprint patterns. In 1891, Juan Vucetich developed the Vucetich System and installed the first fingerprint files as an official means of criminal identification. This system is still used in most Spanish-speaking countries.

The credit for developing the classification system now in use in most English-speaking countries goes to Sir Edward Richard Henry. While on a leave of absence in London in 1895, Henry visited Sir Francis Galton and was deeply impressed by what he saw and heard. Upon returning to his post in India, he devoted his time to modifying Galton's methods and developed the "Henry System." The British Home Office called together a committee to evaluate the Bertillion system of identification by measurements and the fingerprint systems. Galton and Henry both testified, and in 1901, England adopted the Henry System as the official police identification system. In 1904, during the St. Louis Exposition, one of the speakers was Sgt. John K. Ferrier of Scotland Yard, who was assigned to guard the British Crown Jewels. Ferrier was experienced in fingerprints, and he interested United States and Canadian law enforcement agencies in the system. In 1905, the United States government officially began using the system when the U.S. Army adopted the Henry System.

In June 1923, the Leavenworth Federal Penitentiary files, headed by A. J. Renoe, merged with the National Bureau of Criminal Identification of the IACP under Eugene Van Buskirk. The merging of the two files and the needs of police officials led Congress to establish the Identification Division of the FBI on July 1, 1924. There are now 174 million cards on file.

Herschel and Faulds, working in separate regions of the world, were the first persons to consider fingerprint use in criminal identification. In 1883, Samuel Clemens (Mark Twain) used his genius to write *Life on the Mississippi*, and later, *Pudd'nhead Wilson*. In both books, the science of fingerprints was used, and *Pudd'nhead Wilson* ended with a dramatic identification in court and the proving of the infallibility of fingerprints.[2]

In 1911, in a true-to-life case in New York, fingerprints were used as evidence, very much like the account in *Pudd'nhead Wilson*. The case began when a New York detective lifted latent fingerprints from a windowpane at the scene of a burglary. The detective was called to testify to the identity of the fingerprints. The judge, anxious to establish his expertise in the new field of identification, had each member of the jury impress his fingerprints on a courtroom window. One of the twelve jurors then placed his fingerprints on a separate pane of glass. After returning to the courtroom, the detective identified the correct prints within a few minutes. The case received widespread publicity as the first conviction in New York State on the basis of fingerprint evidence.[3]

Fingerprint Examiner

Fingerprint officers, laboratory technicians, and identification officers have jobs that can be subdivided into seven different and individual classifications. In the complete field of fingerprints, each is dependent on the others; however, the individual jobs may be performed without a thorough knowledge of the others, except for the actual identification of fingerprints. In this chapter we are mainly concerned with numbers four and seven.

1. *Taking ink fingerprints.* This requires only a limited knowledge of pattern identification, but requires care and experience to produce consistently clean, clear, and completely classifiable impressions. Although some operators never master the technique of taking good, complete prints, the majority develop this with persistence and experience. The ability to classify fingerprints and a knowledge of latent fingerprint comparison enforces the importance to the completeness and quality of ink impressions.

2. *Classifying ten-finger ink impressions.* This is not dependent on a knowledge of, or ability to take ink impressions, or even the comparison of fingerprints and latent fingerprint problems. A thorough knowledge of pattern identification and classification, with Renoe or Washington extension, is essential. Speed and ability then develop as experience is acquired.

3. *Searching Henry fingerprint files.* This, as well as the identification of fingerprints, is not dependent on a knowledge or ability to take ink impressions or latent fingerprint comparisons and problems. A thorough knowledge of pattern identification and classification, with Renoe or Washington extensions, is essential. Battley single fingerprint classification, with modifications, is a definite asset and almost a necessity. The problems arising with only a basic background and experience resolve into second-sense technique developed through experience, and a complete understanding of form, proportion, trend, and quality, in addition to a complete education of all fingerprint–identification problems.

4. *Latent fingerprint.* This examination and processing in the field and in the laboratory may be performed without any of the above job-knowledge. However, a thorough knowledge of all possible techniques in fingerprint work aids in the preliminary examination, whether in photographing all or part of an area or in merely making a fingerprint lift of the actual latents. Many unnecessary comparisons could be eliminated if the preliminary examination were more thorough. Practical tests and experience in the absence of supervised instruction are the usual or only education in this area of fingerprinting.

5. *Comparison and identification of fingerprints or comparison and elimination of suspects.* This is the most difficult of all fingerprint problems, and the help most needed by investigators assigned to criminal cases. It carries great responsibility, so an untiring and diligent effort must be honestly made. Greater initiative must be used than in any other area of fingerprint work.

6. *Searching fingerprint files and identification of ink impressions.* This is the best training background preparatory to comparison and identification of latent

fingerprints and partial fingerprints. Also, other comparisons not so routine are:

  a. *The comparison of negative photostat fingerprint cards with ink fingerprints.* The negative photostat will have white ridges with black background to compare with the black ridges on a white background. This type comparison is also made in the old-type driver's licenses.
  b. *The comparison of a subject's fingers with an ink fingerprint card.* This is done by looking at the subject's fingers, either right side up or upside down. The fingers are mirror images if reversed from right to left with the ink impressions on a fingerprint card. Ridges may be highlighted and appear white. Add upside down, and the job becomes more complicated. This type comparison is also made in Identity Recorder photographs of fingers which are photographed with a check in check-cashing operations used in markets and department stores.

7. *The comparison of latent fingerprints and partial latent fingerprints with Henry fingerprint file. Battley single fingerprint file.* This also includes the comparison of latent fingerprints with latent fingerprints (tying cases together).

Each of the above fingerprint comparisons has variations in technique, but the basic principle of comparison is the same. Little information is published on this subject, but there are many books covering all other aspects of fingerprint work. Shortcuts, secrets, and special techniques are developed by individuals through years of practical experience. Like pianists, some investigators develop techniques readily while others go on forever and never get off the ground.

Visible and Invisible Fingerprints

Fingerprints that are examined by examiners are of two types, visible and invisible. With the increasing number of returned checks, merchants are looking for a way to protect themselves against bad-check artists, or, as one author calls them, "vulcanizers" or "short story writers." Commercial manufacturers have produced several types of systems to obtain a visible fingerprint of a check issuer. Comput-A-Print, Identicator (Touch Signature), Identiseal, Signature Guardian, and Signature Security are just a few of these. Most of them use a seal that is affixed to the back of a check. The issuer's finger is placed on the seal after touching it to a specially treated pad. Within a few seconds the print will develop and become visible. Merchants like this method, since the treated pad leaves no ink on the subject's finger.

Identity Recorder Company manufactures a check cashing camera. When a check is to be cashed, the check is placed on the recorder along with the two hands of the subject. A photograph is taken which, when developed, shows a picture of the check and all ten fingers of the check issuer.

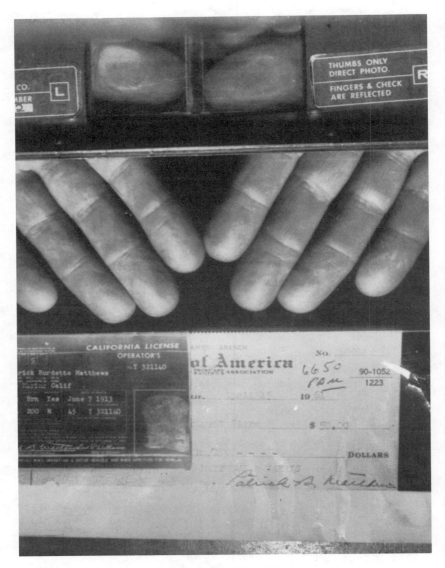

Figure 11–4: Identity recorder photograph. (*Don Fabert*)

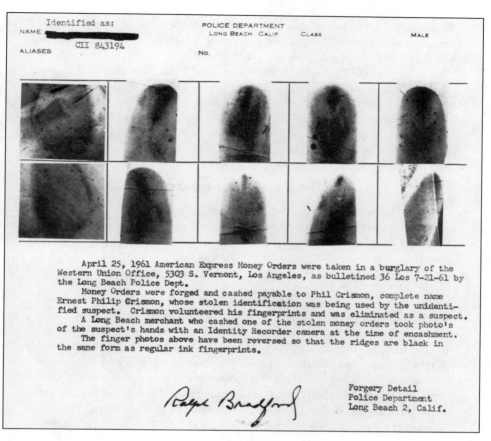

Identified as:
NAME
CII 843194
ALIASES

POLICE DEPARTMENT
LONG BEACH. CALIF   CLASS   MALE
No.

April 25, 1961 American Express Money Orders were taken in a burglary of the Western Union Office, 5303 S. Vermont, Los Angeles, as bulletined 36 Los 7-21-61 by the Long Beach Police Dept.
Money Orders were forged and cashed payable to Phil Crismon, complete name Ernest Philip Crismon, whose stolen identification was being used by the unidentified suspect. Crismon volunteered his fingerprints and was eliminated as a suspect.
A Long Beach merchant who cashed one of the stolen money orders took photo's of the suspect's hands with an Identity Recorder camera at the time of encashment.
The finger photos above have been reversed so that the ridges are black in the same form as regular ink fingerprints.

Ralph Bradford

Forgery Detail
Police Department
Long Beach 2, Calif.

Figure 11–5: Reversal photograph of fingerprints.

There is a slight problem for an examiner with an Identity Recorder photograph because the photograph of the fingers is a mirror image of an inked fingerprint exemplar. The delta on the left in an ink print will be on the right in a photograph. The second problem is that when looking at an ink print, the ridges will ink black and the valleys will appear white. In a photograph, the ridges will appear white and the valleys, being in the shadow and not receiving any light, will appear black.

Photographically, a photograph of a fingerprint can be reversed and placed on a fingerprint exemplar in the proper order, classified, and identified.

The second type of fingerprint to be found on documents is the invisible type which must be developed to be seen. Each ridge on a finger contains pores which excrete sweat from a gland, via the duct, to the surface of the skin. Sweat is about 99 percent water, but the remainder contains minute traces of organic and mineral substances. These combine with oil, grease, and other foreign matter on the body to leave fingerprints. A subject under stress will perspire, leaving latents on the documents he touches. The bank teller who receives a forged check will be under no stress, and in many cases will leave no fingerprints on the check. However, the continued handling of a document by other persons smudges or superimposes latents on the latents (invisible prints) of the suspect. It is for this reason that a questioned document should be placed in a protective container as soon as possible.

Development of Latents

The most important first step in the processing of a document for fingerprints is the photography of that document. The document will be changed to some degree by any of the methods used in the development of latent fingerprints. The four steps most commonly used for the development of prints are:

Powder

Black fingerprint powder is the most popular of the powders. It can be purchased from a manufacturer or made by the formula: ten parts lampblack, four parts powdered rosin, three parts Fuller's earth, mixed together and sieved. The powder is applied with special brushes. Developed latents are then lifted with transparent tape and placed on a clear sheet of celluloid (some agencies place the developed print on a contrasting card). Powder is a common way to obtain prints at scenes of burglaries where latents are found on window sills, glass, desks, etc.[4] The use of powder on paper is a poor choice, the next three methods are far superior.

Iodine (Fuming)

This technique for developing latent fingerprints has been popular for many years. The method is a very easy first step, which can be followed with Ninhydrin and Silver Nitrate. There are two methods of iodine fuming that can be used to develop a latent. The easiest is with the use of an iodine cabinet. Documents are placed in the cabinet with iodine crystals, which vaporize with heat and develop fingerprints.

The second method utilizes an iodine fuming pipe. The materials are placed in the pipe in the following order: glass wool, calcium chloride, glass wool, iodine crystals, and more glass wool.[5] The pipe is held so that the heat from the hand transfers to the iodine crystals. As you blow into the fuming pipe, the moisture from your breath causes the iodine to change to a vapor, which is then blown on the latent area (care must be exercised not to inhale the fumes). Iodine prints are not permanent, and therefore must be photographed soon after they are

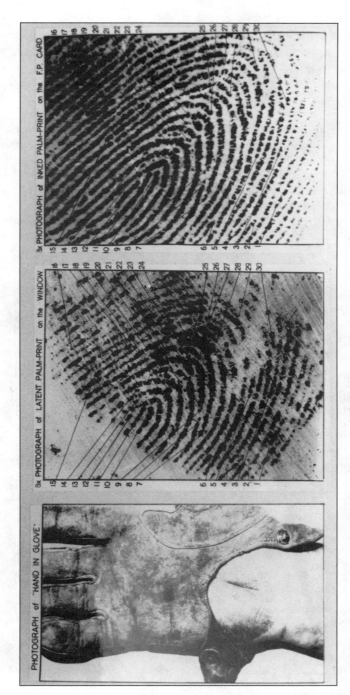

Figure 11-6: Hand in glove, exemplar, and latent fingerprint developed by powder.

developed. The fuming pipe method was very popular with veteran examiners because it was easy to use, developed prints immediately, and the vapor could be directed at any location the examiner desired.

Ninhydrin

This is one of the newest and most popular of the procedures for the development of latents on paper. Ninhydrin (triketohydrindene hydrate) has numerous references dating back to 1910, but the first patent was issued to Oden on August 16, 1955.[6] Ninhydrin, in a solution of ethyl alcohol or acetone, was sprayed on a document; it was then placed in an oven at 176 degrees to 316 degrees. This solution produced excellent fingerprints, but it caused ink to bleed or diffuse.

David Crown of the Postal Inspection laboratory developed a formula using petroleum ether instead of the ethyl alcohol or acetone.[7] This method

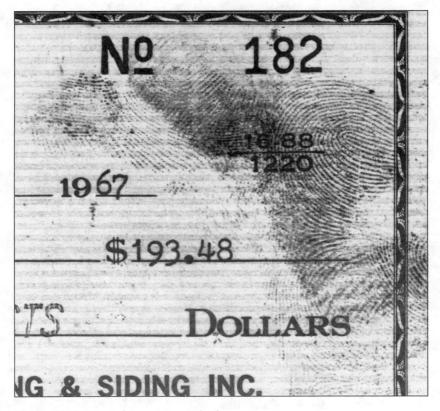

Figure 11–7: Latent fingerprints on checks.

preserved the ink and did not cause the ink to run. The formula used by the authors: Dissolve 3.5 grams ninhydrin in 20 milliliters methanol; add this to 1,000 milliliters petroleum ether. Shake well in a separatory funnel and let stand until the two layers separate. Drain off the bottom layer of methanol and discard. Use the top layer of petroleum ether and ninhydrin.

The solution can be sprayed on the documents. However, we prefer placing the ninhydrin in a porcelain or glass tray (do not use metal) and dipping the entire document in the solution. The document is then laid on a blotter and left to develop at room temperature. The following day prints can be examined. Time is not a factor, as the prints will continue to improve, with the exception of some hard-faced documents, such as U.S. government-issued checks (they can fade and should be photographed).

One should take special safety precautions when you combine ninhydrin and other chemicals. Triketohydrindene hydrate is a white powder that is nine

Figure 11–8: Developing prints on a check using ninhydrin.

parts carbon, four parts hydrogen, three parts oxygen, and water; and *it is toxic.* These chemicals react with amino acids and proteins, essential components of life. Therefore, if ninhydrin is indiscriminately sprayed, the chemical will be in the atmosphere where it can be inhaled.

In 1974, a new reagent for ninhydrin, called Freon, was introduced by Morris and Goode. This new reagent is important because it is nontoxic, nonflammable, and practically odorless, with exceptional non-ink-running properties. A recent study undertaken at the Northeast Regional crime laboratory concluded with the implementation of an improved and efficient method of processing documentary evidence with a freon/ninhydrin solution. Since 1983, the United States Postal Inspection Service laboratory has been processing documents with the new solution and has had excellent results. "The method and the system have proved to be as good or better than any other method we have used for the development of latent fingerprints on porous surfaces," stated Denis J. Tighe in *Identification News.*[8]

Silver Nitrate

If satisfactory latents are not obtained using ninhydrin, try the silver nitrate method. (If silver nitrate is used first, one cannot use ninhydrin.) A 3 to 5 percent solution of silver nitrate is placed in a glass container. The documents are dipped in the solution, then developed by placing them in a strong light, or even sunlight. Caution should be taken that the prints do not overdevelop.

An example of using silver nitrate last was cited by Sebastian F. Latona, testifying before the President's Commission on the Assassination of President Kennedy.[9] Latona, an FBI fingerprint examiner for more than thirty-five years, testified that he received the evidential "brown paper bag" on November 23, 1963. The bag was recovered near a window, on the sixth floor of the Texas school book depository building. (The bag was alleged to have been used by Lee Harvey Oswald to carry the rifle.) Latona examined the bag and determined that someone had dusted it with black powder in an attempt to develop fingerprints—none were found. Latona removed the powder and checked the bag with iodine fuming, failing to obtain any prints. He then processed the bag with a 3 percent solution of silver nitrate and developed a fingerprint and palmprint. The two latent prints were identified as belonging to Oswald.

Vocabulary

The following vocabulary must be thoroughly understood; it is used in this text and in all reference books. To illustrate the vocabulary, a 1946 case that was solved by fingerprint identification, the Webster murder case, will be utilized. (After the fingerprint was identified by Ralph Bradford, the suspect was tried, found guilty, and sent to prison for life. In 1955, the suspect was paroled, and in 1963, he killed again. This time I identified Webster through his handwriting.)

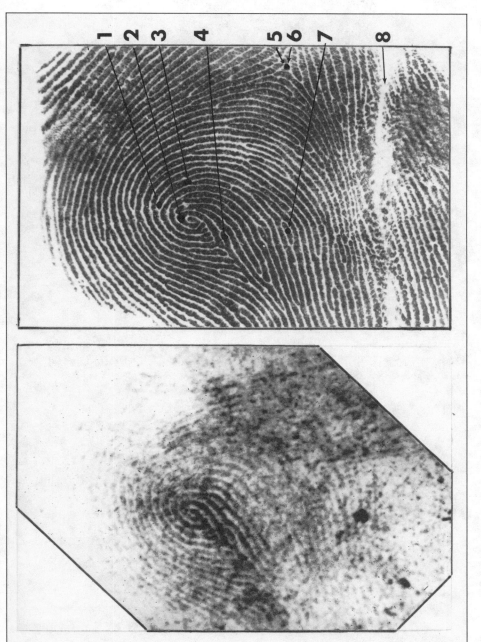

Figure 11–9: Latent print (left) and exemplar in 1946 Webster murder case.

Figure 11–10: Harry Battley.

The Webster fingerprint is classified as a loop (reference as a possible whorl), with a Battley-Bradford core of "JG." In the exemplar (figure 11-9) note: (1) Ridge ending, (2) Core, (3) Bifurcation, (4) Short ridge, (5) Delta, (6) Dot, (7) Island, and (8) Crease.

- *Appendage or Spike.* An upthrust abutting upon a recurve ridge at right angles in the space between the shoulders of a loop on the outside.
- *Bar.* An ending ridge in the center of a staple (innermost recurve ridge) with the end of the bar rising as high as the shoulders of the staple.
- *Bifurcation.* The forking or dividing of one ridge into two or more branches.
- *Classification.* Systematic arrangement of fingerprint types. There are several classification systems, the two major ones being:
  1. The Henry System. Developed by Sir Edward Richard Henry, this is used with Renoe or Washington extensions. This system uses all ten fingerprints in producing the fingerprint classification. With exceptions, all ten fingers are needed to classify and to find the duplicate prints in the file. This is the system used by the FBI and most law enforcement agencies.
  2. The Battley Single Fingerprint System. Developed by Harry Battley, former Chief Inspector in charge of the Fingerprint Bureau at Scotland Yard.

- The Battley System, with Bradford modifications, is discussed in detail in this chapter. Each fingerprint is classified and filed individually from all other fingerprints in a subject's prints file. Only one fingerprint is necessary to classify and to find the duplicate in the file. Latent fingerprints may be individually classified and compared with the fingerprints in the file.
- *Converging of ridges.* In fingerprint patterns the formation of a pocket with a ridge or a pair of ridges running parallel and returning to a bifurcation from a single ridge.
- *Core.* A location on or within the innermost sufficient recurve ridge. When the innermost recurve ridge contains no ending ridge or rod rising as high as the shoulders of the staple, the core is placed on the shoulder of the staple farther from the delta. If the bar rises above the shoulders of the staple, the core is on the end of the center bar, or the end of the farthest bar from the delta if there are two bars.
- *Crease.* It is noted in fingerprint impressions as a white line or streak usually at right angles to the ridges, which end with clear, not puckered, ridges. Flexion creases also occur at junctions of digits; in the palm and on the sole.
- *Dactyloscopy.* The science of fingerprints. Fingerprints may be found on the fingers, palms, and feet. Some books have gone into the examination of fingerprints on various primates, such as the chimpanzee and gorilla.[10]
- *Delta.* That point on a ridge or in front of and nearest the center of the divergence of the type lines. It may be a bifurcation, abrupt ridge ending, dot, short ridge, meeting of two ridges or point on the first recurving ridge located nearest to the center and in front of the divergence of the type lines. When there is a choice between two or more possible deltas, the delta may not be located on a bifurcation which does not open toward the core; when there is a choice between a bifurcation and another type of delta, the bifurcation is selected. When there are two or more possible deltas which conform to the definition, the one nearest the core is chosen, although the delta may not be located in the middle of a ridge running between the type lines toward the core, but at the nearer end only. The delta is the point from which to start ridge counting. In the loop type patterns, the ridges intervening between the delta and core are counted.
- *Divergence.* The spreading apart of two ridges which have been running parallel or nearly parallel.
- *Exemplar.* Known fingerprints of a subject. They are usually obtained by taking an inked impression. Fingers are rolled to get a complete finger impression. On the back of the exemplar a palm impression is also obtained. This document should be dated and witnessed.

The fingerprint is a reproduction of the palm side of the fingertip of a finger onto any surface, showing the pattern of the ridges from which fingerprint

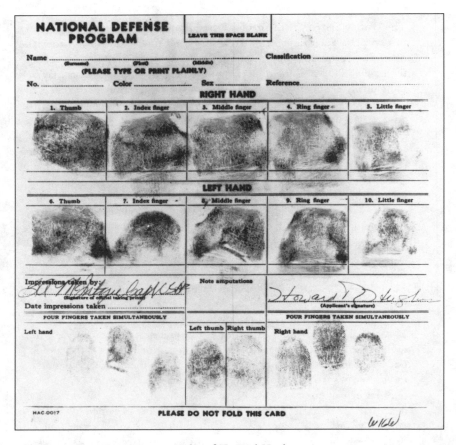

Figure 11–11: Fingerprint exemplar of Howard Hughes.

classification is derived and identification of an individual is determined. Identification may be made on any part of the ridged skin surfaces found on the palms of the hands and fingers, or the soles of the feet and toes, but the latter are not used in fingerprint classification.

- *Island.* The forking or dividing of a ridge into two ridges which, after a short parallel ridge, bifurcate back into one ridge forming the eye or island.
- *Latent.* An invisible or hidden fingerprint which after development by a number of methods becomes visible. These methods include the use of black powder, silver nitrate, and ninhydrin.
- *Pattern area.* The area of loops and whorls on which appear the core, delta, and ridges. It is these with which we are concerned in classifying. Partial

areas may be identified without the core or delta, but are usually more difficult because no fixed point is established.

- *Poroscopy.* The examination of pore openings (found on ridges), which are highly individual and characteristic of the skin area on which they are found. Pores afford additional means of identification.
- *Ridge counting.* The counting of ridges (blacklines on fingerprint card) between the delta and core on a fingerprint.
- *Ridge ending.* The point where the ridge disappears. This is to be considered when the ridges on both sides of a ridge continue, but the center ridge itself stops. A broken ridge with a gap may be an ending ridge, but is considered continuous if it continues after a short break.
- *Scar.* A mark caused by a cut and similar to a crease, except that the edges or ends of the ridges are puckered and irregular.
- *Shavings.* Refers to "thin" ridges and broken fragments between ridges that are not considered in ridge counting because they are too thin. All ridges are equal in width to each other. Anything thinner is considered a shaving or an incipient ridge.
- *Shoulder.* The point on a loop at which the recurving ridge definitely turns inward or curves.
- *Short Ridge.* The ending ridge of each end. May be any length or even as small as a dot.
- *Staple.* The innermost recurving ridge in a loop pattern.
- *Triradii.* The meeting point of three opposing ridge systems. The term "delta" is often used as a synonym for triradius, but triradii may appear where there is no delta.
- *Type lines.* The two innermost ridges which start parallel, then diverge and surround or tend to surround the pattern area.
- *Valley* (Furrows). The area between the ridges. On a fingerprint exemplar, it is the white lines between the black ridges, and on a finger it is the dark lines between the light ridges.
- *Wart.* A defect that usually appears in a fingerprint impression as a white dot, with the ridge or ridges curving around the white area.
- *Whorl tracing.* A tracing that begins at the left delta or the ridge emanating from the lower side or point of the extreme left delta, and is traced until the point nearest or opposite the extreme right delta is reached. The number of ridges intervening between the tracing ridge and the right delta are counted. If the ridge traced passes inside (above) the right delta, and three or more ridges intervene between the tracing ridge and the delta, the tracing is designated as an "inner." If the ridge traced passes outside (below) the right delta, and three or more ridges intervene between the tracing ridge and the right delta, the tracing is designated as an "outer." All other tracings are designated as "meeting."

Classifying Patterns of Fingerprints

Identifying fingerprint patterns is the first step in classifying fingerprints, using either the Battley System and Bradford Modification or the Henry System. A basic piece of equipment needed for the examination and comparison of fingerprints is a precision fingerprint magnifier. A professional magnifier comes with either 4.5x or 5x magnification. Among the most important elements of a magnifier are reticle or classification discs. These discs come with a Henry disc, Battley disc, or combination of the two. The magnification glass and discs are indispensable tools in the examination of fingerprints.

Four types of fingerprint patterns must be identified before moving to step 2. They are:

1. Plain Arch Pattern
2. Tented Arch Pattern
3. Loop Pattern (Radial and Ulnar)
4. Whorl Pattern (includes Plain, Whorls, Central Pocket Loops, Double Loops, and Accidental Whorls)

Plain Arch Pattern

In plain arch patterns, the ridges enter on one side of the impression and flow or tend to flow out the other with a rise or hump in the center.

Tented Arch Pattern

In the tented arch, most of the ridges enter upon one side of the impression and flow or tend to flow out upon the other side, as in the plain arch type. However, the ridge or ridges at the center do not. There are three types of tented arches:

1. The type in which ridges at the center form a definite angle—90 degrees or less.
2. The type in which one or more ridges at the center form an upthrust. An upthrust is an ending ridge of any length rising at a sufficient degree from the horizontal plane at 45 degrees or more.
3. The type approaching the loop type which possesses two of the basic or essential characteristics of the loop, but lacks the third.[11]

Loop Pattern

One or more of the ridges enter on either side of the impression, then recurve to touch or pass an imaginary line drawn from the delta to the core, and terminate or tend to terminate on or toward the same side of the impression from which the ridge entered.

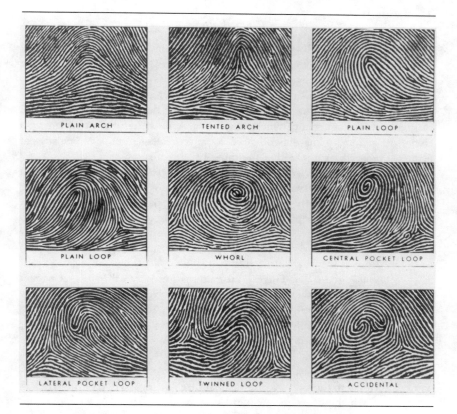

Figure 11–12: Fingerprint patterns.

The essentials of a loop are: a sufficient recurve ridge, a delta, a ridge count between the delta and the core, and a core. A sufficient recurve is defined as that part of a recurving ridge between the shoulders of a loop. It must be free of any appendages abutting upon the outside of the recurve at a right angle as appendages spoil the recurve ridge in loops and whorls.

Ridge counting of loops begins on the delta and counts all ridges on both sides of an imaginary line drawn between the delta and core. Ridges that just touch the imaginary line are also counted.

Radial and ulnar loops derive their names from the radius and ulnar bones of the forearm. Ulnar loops flow in the direction of the ulnar bone (toward the little finger). Radial loops flow toward the thumb or radius bone. In latent fingerprints and Battley single fingerprints, the loops are referred to as Loop Right or Loop Left, depending on the flow of the ridges.

Whorl Pattern

The fourth or numerical group contains all fingerprints that are not arch, tent, or loop patterns, and are therefore grouped into whorl patterns. However, in the Battley single fingerprint system and latent fingerprint comparison and identification the whorl group is subdivided into four patterns:

1. *Plain whorl pattern*. These patterns have two deltas and at least one ridge making a complete circuit, which may be spiral, oval, circular, or variant of a circle. An imaginary line drawn between the two deltas must touch or cross at least one recurving ridge within the inner pattern area.

2. *Central pocket loop*. Similar to a whorl pattern with one exception. An imaginary line drawn between the two deltas must not touch or cross any of the recurving ridges within the inner pattern area. Also, in lieu of a recurve in front of the delta in the inner pattern area, an obstruction or ridge at right angles to the line of flow of ridges is sufficient. The obstruction may be either curved or straight. A dot is not considered an obstruction. The appendage rule also applies to obstruction, as well as recurve ridges.

3. *Double loop whorl*. Fingerprint patterns formerly called lateral pocket loops and twinned loops are now combined and referred to as double loops. They consist of two separate loop formations, with two separate and distinct shoulders and two deltas. This eliminates the s-type core whorl with a common shoulder between the two loop formations. Unlike single loops, the loops of the double loops are not required to have a ridge.

4. *Accidental whorl patterns*. A combination of two different types of fingerprint patterns, with the exception of the plain arch, that have two or more deltas; or, a pattern which possesses some of the requirements for two or more different patterns; or a pattern which conforms to none of the pattern definitions.

Battley Single Fingerprint System with Bradford Modifications

Comparing, eliminating, or identifying fingerprints is the most advanced and difficult part of a fingerprint examiner's job. Very little has been published on the methods, tricks of the trade, shortcuts, and special skills that examiners have gained through years of experience.

In the sections on handwriting, the authors have attempted to teach you the fundamentals, including "parts of letters." Chapter 5 explains how you can break down words into letters and letters into individual parts. This section on fingerprints is organized in the same way. It explains the fundamentals, and then breaks down the fingerprints into four patterns: arch, tent, loop, and whorl. Many examiners stop at this point in their examination. But we want to examine the individual parts of a fingerprint just as we examine the individual parts of handwriting. You can learn to do this by studying the Battley system with Bradford modifications.

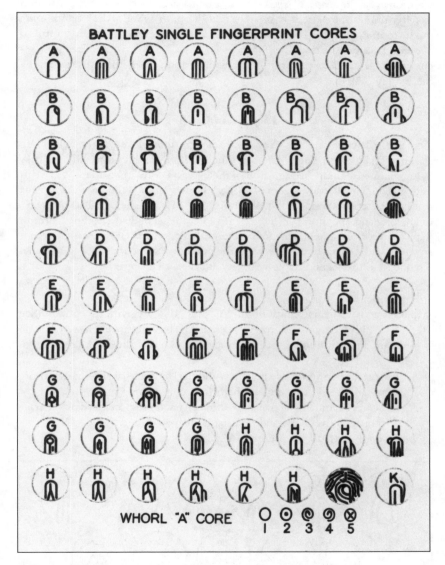

Figure 11–13: Battley classification of loops.

The first step in examining a fingerprint, whether the unknown is a latent-print, ink-print, or photo-print, is to determine the pattern. Do not rely on scars, or even the shape of a pattern, as a target area when searching. Attempt to determine if the pattern is an arch, tent, loop, or whorl. After determining the pattern, *examine* the center of the print to find the core. If the fingerprint is a loop, its innermost ridge will be a "plain staple" (staple is the innermost recurving ridge in a loop pattern). It is these innermost ridges that are classified by the Battley System.[12]

Loop Classification

The Battley System divides the core of a loop into eleven types, which are classified "A" core through "L" core. The Bradford modification of the Battley System comes with the classification of the "second core" the same way the first core was done by Battley (figure 11-13), with a few rules. If the first core is made from characteristics inside the staple, as in "G," "H," or the two-bar "A" core, or are long and one short bar "D" or "E" core, the second core is the innermost staple with or without attached characteristics. If none, then the second core is any unattached characteristics between the innermost staple and the second staple. If none, it is the second staple with any attached characteristics.

A Core

If there is no bar, the core must be an "A" or a "B" core, with exceptions. (See "G," "H," "J," "K," and "L" cores). If a staple is absolutely plain, it is an A core. If there are an even number of bars inside a staple, it is also an A core.

1. 1st core: Innermost staple is plain without a bar inside or any characteristics on either side that are attached. It is an A core.
   2nd core: Second staple is plain without characteristics attached or a characteristic between 1st and 2nd staple. It is an A core.
2. 1st core: A two-bar core is an A core.

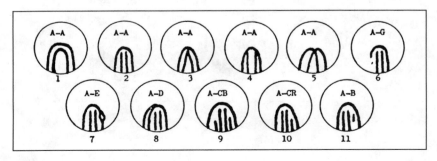

Figure 11–14: "A" core.

2nd core: Innermost staple is plain and is used for the 2nd core. It is an A core.

3. 1st core: Innermost staple is pointed but lacks the point or short rod above the bifurcation that is necessary in an H core. It is an A core.

   2nd core: Second staple is plain without characteristics. It is an A core.

4. 1st core: A two-bar core, both bars attached to the inside of the staple between the shoulders. It is an A core.

   2nd core: First staple is plain without characteristics. It is an A core.

5. 1st core: Interlocking staples are a variation of 3 and 4 above. The innermost staple is pointed but does not have the point necessary in an H core. It is an A core.

   2nd core: The attachments to the staple are between the staple shoulders and, therefore, are not considered as bifurcations characteristics. It is an A core.

6. 1st core: A two-bar core is an A core.

   2nd core: An incomplete staple is a G core.

7. 1st core: A two-bar core is an A core.

   2nd core: The staple has characteristics on the right side. It is an E core.

8. 1st core: Same as 4 above. It is an A core.

   2nd core: Staple has a bifurcation on the left side. It is a D core.

9. 1st core: A two-bar core is an A core.

   2nd core: Two short bars outside of the center of the two center even bars is a CB core.

10. 1st core: A two-bar core is an A core.

    2nd core: One short bar on the right of two even bar cores is a CR core.

11. 1st core: A two-bar core is an A core.

    2nd core: An incomplete bar (not crossing the circle) is a B core.

B Core

If there is no bar inside the staple with characteristics on either or both sides of the staple, it is a "B" core, with exceptions (see "G," "H," "J," "K," and "L").

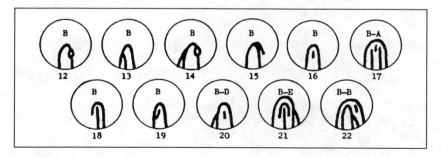

Figure 11–15: "B" core.

12. 1st core: The innermost staple has a characteristic attached without a bar or other unattached characteristic within. It is a B core.

    2nd core: Not illustrated.

13. 1st core: Same as 12.

14. 1st core: Same as 12.

15. 1st core: Same as 12.

16. 1st core: A plain staple with an incomplete bar is a B core.

    2nd core: It is a staple without characteristics. It is an A core.

17. 1st core: An incomplete bar in the staple is a B core.

    2nd core: Two bars are an A core.

18. 1st core: An incomplete staple with a bar is a B core.

    2nd core: Same as 12.

19. 1st core: Same as 12.

20. 1st core: An incomplete bar is a B core.

    2nd core: A characteristic attached on the left side of staple is a D core.

21. 1st core: An incomplete staple with a bar is a B core.

    2nd core: A characteristic attached on right side of staple is an E core.

22. 1st core: Same as 12.

    2nd core: An incomplete bar not attached, between the innermost staple and the 2nd staple, is a B core.

C Core

If there is one bar or an uneven number of bars inside the staple, the core must be "C," "D," "E," or "F" core, with exceptions. (See "G," "H," "J," "K," and "L" cores.) If no characteristics on the staple, it is a "C" core.

23. 1st core: A plain staple with a bar is a C core.

    2nd core: Not illustrated.

24. 1st core: Same as 23.

25. 1st core: Three even bars are a C core.

    2nd core: Innermost staple is plain. It is an A core.

26. 1st core: Same as 25.

    2nd core: Same as 25.

27. 1st core: Same as 25.

    2nd core: The innermost staple has a characteristic on the right side. It is an E core.

28. 1st core: Same as 24. (Connecting point between staple on outside is not considered.)

    2nd core: Second staple is plain. It is an A core.

29. 1st core: Same as 24.

    2nd core: Not illustrated.

30. 1st core: A three-bar core is a C core. The two bars touching the staple between the staple shoulders are not considered attached. It is a C core.

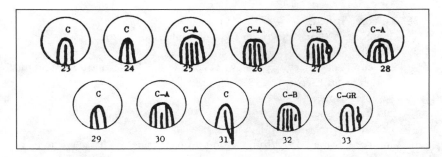

Figure 11–16: "C" core.

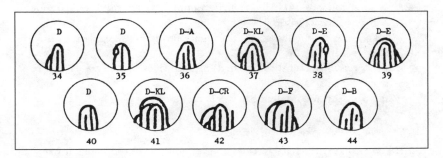

Figure 11–17: "D" core.

31. 1st core: Same as 23. (Bifurcation is outside of a circle.) It is a C core.
32. 1st core: Three bars are a C core.
    2nd core: An incomplete bar is a B core.
33. 1st core: A plain staple with a bar is a C core.
    2nd core: An island on an ending ridge on the right outside of the staple
    is a GR core.

D Core

If there is one bar with characteristics on the left side of the staple, it is a "D" core.

34. 1st core: A plain bar inside of staple with characteristic on left is a D core.
    2nd core: Not illustrated.
35. 1st core: Same as 34.
36. 1st core: Two uneven bars with the shorter bar on the left are a D core.
    2nd core: Innermost staple is plain. It is an A core.
37. 1st core: Bifurcation up from the characteristic on the left side is a KL core.
    (If the bifurcation is up, off the staple proper, the 1st core is a K core.)

38. 1st core: Same as 36.

    2nd core: A characteristic on right of staple is an E core.

39. 1st core: Same as 34.

    2nd core: A connecting point is not considered. The characteristic on the right is an E core.

40. 1st core: Same as 36.

    2nd core: Same as 36.

41. 1st core: Same as 37.

    2nd core: Same as 37. (Bifurcation up on left side of characteristic takes precedence over the outer or 2nd bifurcation down on the left, which is not considered.)

42. 1st core: Same as 34. (All attached multiple characteristics are considered as one characteristic.)

    2nd core: A plain ending ridge on right outside of the staple is a CR core.

43. 1st core: Same as 36.

    2nd core: Characteristics attached on both sides of staple—an F core.

44. 1st core: Same as 36.

    2nd core: An incomplete bar is a B core.

E Core

If there is one bar with characteristics on the right side of the staple, it is an "E" core.

45. 1st core: A plain bar with characteristics attached to the staple on the right side is an E core.

    2nd core: Not illustrated.

46. 1st core: Same as 45.

47. 1st core: Two uneven bars with the shorter bar on the right is an E core.

    2nd core: A plain staple is an A core.

48. 1st core: Same as 45.

49. 1st core: Same as 47.

    2nd core: A characteristic on the right of the staple is an E core.

50. 1st core: Same as 45.

51. 1st core: Same as 45.

52. 1st core: Same as 47.

    2nd core: An incomplete bar is a B core.

53. 1st core: Same as 45.

    2nd core: A plain staple is an A core.

54. 1st core: Same as 47.

    2nd core: Characteristics on both sides of a staple make an F core.

55. 1st core: Same as 45.

    2nd core: A bifurcation UP on the left side of the staple is a KL core.

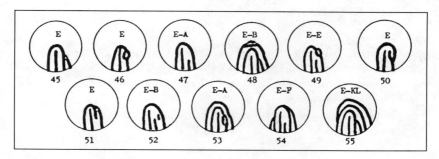

Figure 11–18: "E" core.

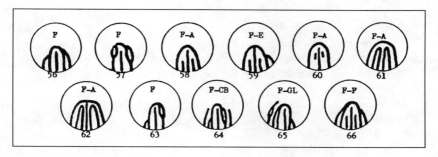

Figure 11–19: "F" core.

F Core

If there is one bar, with characteristics on both sides of the staple, it is an "F" core.

56. 1st core: A plain bar with characteristics attached on both sides of the staple is an F core.

    2nd core: No second core illustrated.

57. 1st core: Same as 56.

58. 1st core: Three uneven bars with a short bar on each side make an F core.

    2nd core: A plain staple is an A core.

59. 1st core: Same as 58.

    2nd core: A staple with characteristics on the right is an E core.

60. 1st core: One bar and two incomplete bars make an F core.

    2nd core: A plain staple is an A core.

61. 1st core: Two plain staples together make an F core.

    2nd core: A plain staple is an A core.

62. 1st core: Two plain staples with a bar between them that touches the staple is an F core.

    2nd core: A plain staple is an A core.

63. 1st core: Same as 56.
64. 1st core: Same as 56.
    2nd core: A bar on each side outside of the staple, is a CB core.
65. 1st core: Same as 56.
    2nd core: A bar with an island on the left outside of the staple is a GL core.
66. 1st core: Same as 58.
    2nd core: A staple with characteristics on both sides is an F core.

G Core

An island on the bar, regardless of the characteristics on the staple, is a "G" core. The order of preference is: "L," "J," "K," "H," "G."

67. 1st core: An island on the bar is a G core.
    2nd core: A plain staple is an A core.
68. 1st core: Same as 67.
    2nd core: A characteristic on the right of the staple is an E core.
69. 1st core: Same as 67.
    2nd core: A characteristic on the left of the staple is a D core.
70. 1st core: Same as 67. (G core takes precedence over C core, so C is the 2nd core if the staple is plain.)
71. 1st core: An incomplete staple without a bar is a G core.
    2nd core: A plain staple is an A core.
72. 1st core: An island, even on an incomplete bar, is a G core.
    2nd core: Same as 67.
73. 1st core: One bar and one incomplete bar make a G core.
    2nd core: Same as 68.
74. 1st core: An incomplete bar and an incomplete staple combined make a G core.
    2nd core: Not illustrated.
75. 1st core: Same as 67.
76. 1st core: An island on the bar is a G core.
    2nd core: A second bar with an island inside the staple is a G core.
77. 1st core: Same as 67.
    2nd core: Characteristics on both sides of a staple is an F core.

H Core

A tuning fork or downward bifurcation on the bar, regardless of characteristics on the staple, is an "H" core.

78. 1st core: A bifurcation down on the bar is an H core.
    2nd core: A plain staple is an A core.

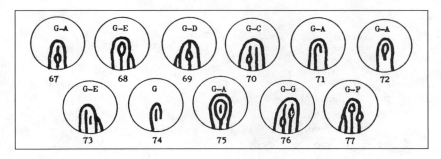

Figure 11–20: "G" core.

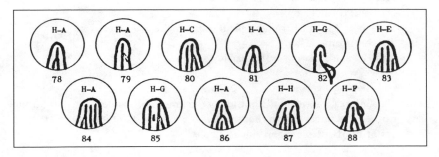

Figure 11–21: "H" core.

79. 1st core: Same as 78.
    2nd core: Same as 78.
80. 1st core: Same as 78 (H takes precedence over C).
    2nd core: Single bar is a C core.
81. 1st core: Same as 78.
    2nd core: Same as 78.
82. 1st core: Same as 78. (Bottom of island is outside of A circle.)
    2nd core: An incomplete is a G core.
83. 1st core: Same as 78. (H takes precedence over E, so that E is the 2nd core.)
84. 1st core: Same as 78. (H takes precedence over A, so A is the 2nd core.)
    2nd core: Two even bars make an A core.
85. 1st core: Same as 78. (H takes precedence over G, so G is the 2nd core.)
86. 1st core: Same as 78. (The bar inside the bifurcation is not considered.)
    2nd core: Same as 78.
87. 1st core: A bifurcation down on the bar is an H core.
    2nd core: A second bar with a bifurcation down is an H core, regardless
        of characteristics on the staple.

88. 1st core: Same as 78.
    2nd core: A staple with characteristics on both sides is an F core.

J Core

Considering the whole impression instead of just the A-circle, if the loop is converging or approximating a central pocket loop, it is a "J" core.

89. 1st core: A converging loop is a J core, and the pattern area is used without restriction to the A circle.
    2nd core: A bifurcation up on the outside of the staple is a K core.
90. 1st core: Same as 89.
    2nd core: An island on the bar is a G core.
91. 1st core: Same as 89.
    2nd core: A plain bar and a plain staple make a C core.
92. 1st core: Same as 89.
    2nd core: An island on the bar is a G core.

K Core

If there is a bifurcation UP on the outside of the innermost staple, with or without bars or other characteristics on the staple, it is a K core. Consider the A, B, and C circles of the Battley Fingerprint Reticule.

93. 1st core: A bifurcation UP on the outside of the staple is a K core and takes precedence over the G core, which is the 2nd core.
94. 1st core: Same as 93.
    2nd core: Two even bars make an A core.
95. 1st core: Same as 93.
    2nd core: A plain staple is an A core.
96. 1st core: Same as 93.
    2nd core: A bifurcation DOWN on the bar is an H core.

L Core

All cores not classifiable in one of the core types, and all scarred and cut patterns, are "L" cores (using the whole print that would be included in a plain impression).

97. 1st core: A scarred core which is not decipherable is an L core.
    2nd core: Same as 1st core.
98. 1st core: A cut pattern is an L core.
    2nd core: The staple without a bar and with a characteristic on the side is a B core.
99. 1st core: A cut pattern is an L core.
    2nd core: A core not classifiable is an L core.

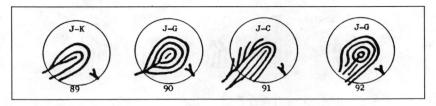

Figure 11–22: "J" core.

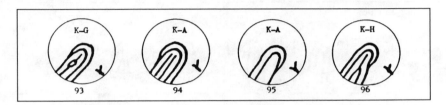

Figure 11–23: "K" core.

Figure 11–24: "L" core.

100. 1st core: A cut pattern is an L core.
     2nd core: A bar inside a plain staple is a C core.

Second Cores of Loops

The second core is the second staple from the core, with the characteristics being between the innermost staple and the second staple, if attached to second staple and unattached to the first staple, with these exceptions: If core is identified by characteristics within the innermost staple, as G or H core, then the first staple with or without attached characteristics is the second core. If the first staple is used for the first core and unattached characteristics are outside the staple, they are the second core.

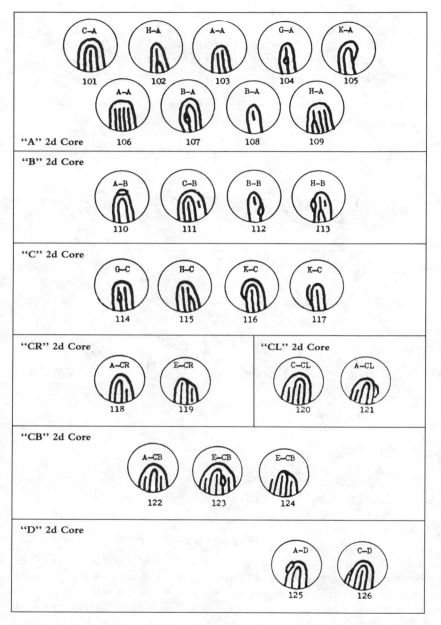

Figure 11–25: Second core of loops.

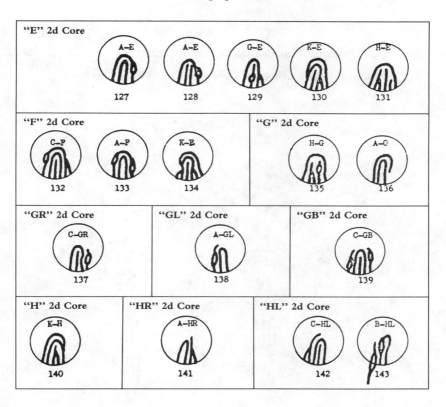

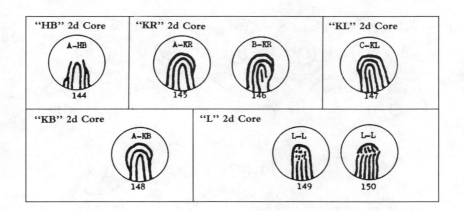

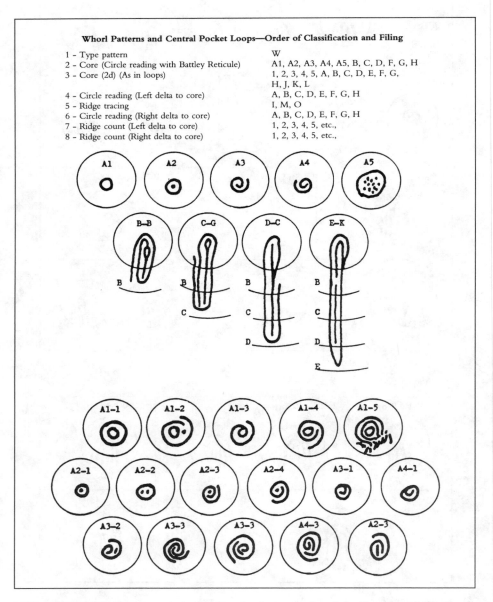

Figure 11–26: Whorl patterns and central pocket loops—order of classification and filing.

Twinned Loop Patterns—Order of Classification and Filing

1 - Type pattern	TL
2 - Trend (Right and Left)	R, L
3 - Circle reading (Between cores)	A, B, C, D, E, F, G, H
4 - Ridge count (Between cores)	1, 2, 3, 4, 5, 6, etc.,
5 - Core (As in loops - ASCENDING LOOP)	A, B, C, D, E, F, G, H, J, K, L
6 - Ridge count (Descending core to delta)	1, 2, 3, 4, 5, 6, etc.,
7 - Circle reading (Left delta to core) Ascending	A, B, C, D, E, F, G, H
8 - Ridge tracing	I, M, O
9 - Circle reading (Right delta to core) Ascending	A, B, C, D, E, F, G, H

  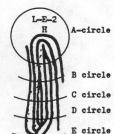

Lateral Pocket Loop Pattern—Order of Classification and Filing

1 - Type pattern	LP
2 - Trend (Right or Left)	R, L
3 - Ridge count (Inner loop)	1, 2, 3, 4, 5, etc.,

Accidental Whorl Patterns—Order of Filing and Classification

1 - Type pattern	Ac
2 - Combination	T-L, T-W, T-TL, L-W, L-TL, W-TL

Figure 11–27: Twined loop patterns—order of classification and filing.

Figure 11–28: Right index fingerprints of Russell Bradford (left) 1936, age five, and (right) 1986, age fifty-five.

Fingerprint Comparison and Identification

The general principles for fingerprint comparison were outlined for the Warren Commission by Sebastian Latona (FBI) and Arthur Mandella (New York Police). Latona stated, "Fingerprints and palmprints are made by the ridges which cover the surface of the fingers and palms. These ridges first appear two or three months before birth, and remain unchanged until death. . . .

"A clear fingerprint impression will contain from 85 to 125 points. While many of the common points appear in almost every print, no two prints have the same points in the same relationship to each other.

"A print taken by a law-enforcement agency is known as 'inked print,' and is carefully taken so that all the characteristics of the print are reproduced on the fingerprint card. A print which is left accidentally, such as a print left at the scene of a crime, is known as a latent print. To make an identification of a latent print, the expert compares the points in the latent print with the points in an inked print. If a point appearing in a latent print does not appear in the inked print, or vice versa, the expert concludes that the two prints were not made by the same finger or palm. An identification is made only if there are no inconsistencies between the inked and latent prints, and the points of similarity and their relative positions are sufficiently distinctive, and sufficient in number, to satisfy the expert that an identity exists."[13]

No two different fingers have ever been found that contain all the same characteristics (with the same relationship to each other), with no unexplained dissimilarities. Research of this has also been extended to identical twins. The fingerprint comparison can now be made in four easy steps:

Step 1: Examination to Determine Pattern

Examine to determine if the print is an arch, tent, loop, or whorl. If the pattern is the same, you can go on to Step 2. If not, you can form a negative opinion and say they are not the same.

Step 2: Examine the Core

Start your examination of the core by drawing a picture of exactly how the core is made and then classify it, using the Battley System. Next, draw a second core using the Bradford modification and classify it. Once you have drawn the double core, then draw in the closest characteristic and memorize it. By giving the latent a classification and drawing it, you make it easy to memorize. It now takes only a few minutes to search each exemplar, looking for a core with the same classification. The classification of the core gives you a big advantage in searching a fingerprint.

Most fingerprint examiners do not classify the core and thus can remember a characteristic for only a few minutes. An examiner who does not break down a pattern into its individual characteristics may make errors in a search. The Battley-Bradford classification assists in that examination. Memorizing a fingerprint core should be taken in easy steps as outlined above.

Step. 3. Search for Characteristics (Points)

The third step in the comparison of fingerprints commences after you determine the pattern and match the latent and exemplar with the same Battley-Bradford core. It is then necessary to search for additional characteristics to make an identification. A forged check on which a fingerprint was developed by ninhydrin illustrates this step (figure 11-30).

An examination of the latent print determined that it was a loop pattern, and classified with the Battley-Bradford classification as an "AA Core." In examining the characteristics to determine if the prints are the same, the core is the preferred starting point. In the latent (figure 11-17) one can see two bars in the center. The top of the bar farthest from the delta is the core (1), and the place to start counting. Start by looking above the core for a characteristic, then go clockwise. Five ridges to the right of the core are two bifurcations (2 and 3) that form an island. Two ridges below the island at 6 o'clock is another bifurcation (4). Seven ridges below this characteristic at 7 o'clock is a ridge ending (5). Three

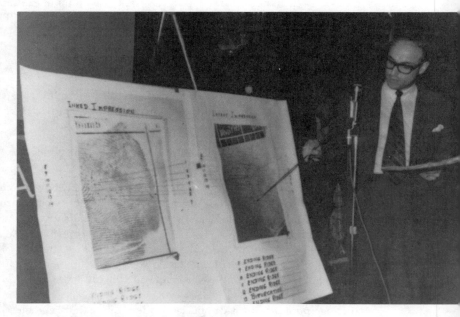

Figure 11–29: Dr. Morfopoulos and exhibit.

A 1967 New York murder case, the Kent case, is an example of what fingerprint examination can accomplish. On June 25, Joseph Murphy, a retired New York City policeman, was murdered in his house in a suburb of Poughkeepskie, New York. Within seven hours, Richard Stanley Kent was arrested for the brutal murder. Since Kent lacked money, the Public Defender's Office defended him. A very important part of the case was a latent fingerprint. The prosecution expert attested to fourteen points of identification in his testimony. The defense contacted Dr. Vassislis C. Morfopoulos, of the American Standards Testing Laboratory, who offered proof to the jury on scientific grounds that the fingerprints were not identical. *People v. Kent* was written under the title "Some Fingerprints Lie," and was published and circulated nationwide.[14]

At the International Association for Identification Conference in Pittsburgh in 1970, Morfopoulos presented exhibits of the Kent case and spoke on how he proved fingerprints lie.[15]

At the conclusion of the speech, a recess was taken to allow the members to examine the exhibit. Following the recess, Morfopoulos agreed to answer questions. Ralph Bradford examined the exhibit from the first row as the doctor spoke. He then classified the two prints using the Battley system with Bradford modifications and memorized both the prints and marks on the exhibit. He also took photographs during the recess to record the event. After the recess, he questioned the doctor without any notes, speaking strictly from memory. The IAI members and the doctor examined the exhibit as Bradford spoke: "Dr. Morfopoulos, I have examined the fingerprint exhibit, and I see your mistake. You are wrong in the comparison of characteristics, but you are right about a comparison of the markings of the identical characteristics. If you will count the ridges to the left of the ridge ending marked 2 toward characteristic 11, five ridges over there is a bifurcation. This bifurcation matches characteristic 11 in the latent print. But, in the ink print characteristic, 11 was marked in the wrong place at the end of a ridge; therefore, there are seven ridges between characteristic 2 and 11. If you will count from characteristic 1 toward characteristic 10, four ridges to the left, this matches characteristic 10 in the latent print. Characteristic 13 in the ink print is the next ridge to the left of characteristic 12, and in the latent print the bifurcation is extended one ridge too far. It should stop on the bifurcation one ridge to the left of the point as marked.

"Unfortunately, the fingerprint expert who marked the latent fingerprint exhibit made two mistakes in marking the characteristics that match with the characteristics in the ink print. The matching characteristics are there, but they are not marked correctly. You made the mistake of comparing marks instead of characteristics.

"It is my opinion you were honest in your belief, or you would not have testified in the case; also, if the exhibits had been marked correctly, you could not have made the mistake. This could only happen to a person who did not understand fingerprint comparison.

"In my opinion, the fingerprint technician who marked the exhibits was very experienced and carelessly marked the characteristics after he had made the identification on the original prints. This would not happen to a less experienced person who is overly careful lest he make a mistake."

This was the first time someone had pointed out that the error was human and that "fingerprints do not lie." T. Dickerson Cooke, Director of the Institute of Applied Science, wrote Bradford, "I am still amazed at your questioning of Dr. Morfopoulos. How you could picture all those ridge details in your mind, I'll never know. It was worth the trip just to listen to you cross-examine the doctor."

Ralph Bradford, in the beginning, attempted only to memorize the double-Battley and one additional characteristic. Later, he added a second characteristic; after thirty-four years of practice, he could almost memorize an entire fingerprint. The modification was developed to assist in memorizing a very small portion of a fingerprint. With a small portion memorized, you can easily search a print in the exemplars.

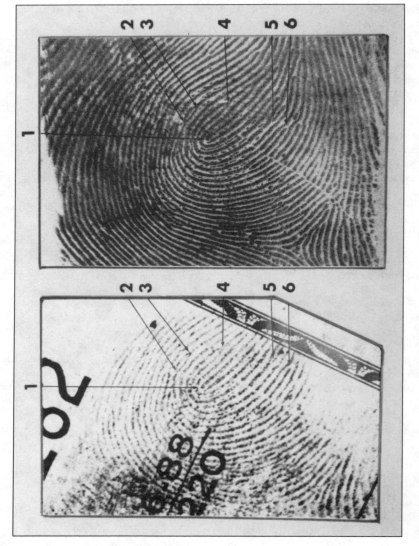

Figure 11–30: Latent print on check (left) and exemplar.

ridges below is another ridge ending (6). Counting the characteristics, we have identified so far:

1. ridge ending (core)
2. bifurcation
3. bifurcation
4. bifurcation
5. ridge ending
6. ridge ending

Each characteristic found in a latent print must be of the same type and at the same location as in the exemplar print. Both the latent and known exemplar must have the characteristics in the same relative position to each other, with no unexplainable differences.

Explainable differences may be caused by foreign matter (dust, lint, etc.) getting in the ink and making a clear ridge on an ink print impossible. Foreign material can also get into a latent print. Some suspects' fingers perspire so much that ridges may appear to bifurcate, due to sweat causing the ridges to "run." Distortion can also appear due to uneven pressure or slippage.

Number of characteristics required

In 1939, the FBI published "Classification of Fingerprints" that stated, "It is well established that twelve or fifteen identical points will suffice." The Federal Bureau of Investigation reiterated in 1963, "Twelve characteristics are ample to illustrate an identification, but it is neither claimed or implied that this number is required."[16]

At the 1970 IAI Conference, a resolution was unanimously adopted to set up a standardization committee. The committee's purpose was: (1) to determine the minimum number of friction ridge characteristics which must be present in two impressions in order to establish positive identification, and (2) to recommend the minimum training and experience a person must have to be considered qualified to give testimony on friction ridge impressions before a grand jury or court of law. Paul D. McCann was named chairman of an eleven-member committee.

McCann reported for the committee that: "The International Association for Identification, assembled in its fifty-eighth Annual Conference at Jackson, Wyoming, this first day of August 1973, based upon a three-year study by its standardization committee, hereby states that no valid basis exists at this time for requiring that a predetermined minimum number of friction ridge characteristics must be present in two impressions in order to establish positive identification. The foregoing reference to friction ridge characteristics applies equally to fingerprints, palm prints, toe prints, and sole prints of the human body."[17] The FBI reported that they were in full accord with the findings of the IAI committee.

The author totally accepts the report of the committee, but recommends to all new examiners that they use at least twelve characteristics as the minimum number for an identification. The author also does not expect fingerprint examin-

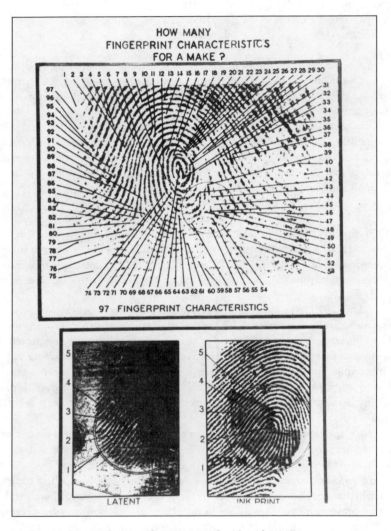

Figure 11–31: Fingerprint characteristics for identification.

ers to memorize a fingerprint as Ralph Bradford did in 1970. It is important to use the Battley System of classification with Bradford modification in examining a latent. You should draw the characteristics, memorize them, and then search the known prints.

Step 4. Consolidate the Information and Make the Identification

For the trainee, this is the last step in the examination of fingerprints. For the examiner wishing to go further in the science of fingerprints, there are many new techniques being developed all the time. Among these advances is the fuming of latents with Super Glue or lasers. Glue with the ingredient cyanoacrylate ester has been used to obtain latents where others have failed. Menzel[18] is working with lasers in fingerprints as well as in handwriting (see chapter 1). Single-fingerprint classification files are now being expanded to contain latents. Utilizing latents in a classified file can tie prints together and identify suspects.

The final step for the advanced fingerprint examiner is testifying in court as an expert. This should not be attempted until the seven different job classifications, listed earlier in this chapter, have all been mastered. Today, there is one more step before testifying in court. The IAI sponsored a certification program for fingerprint examiners in 1977 as a direct result of the Morfopoulas speech in 1970. This program is very important in developing a professional examiner.

When testifying on fingerprints, as with handwriting, you must prepare and present a professional exhibit which will reflect well on you as the examiner. Because the advanced examiner is no longer required to isolate twelve characteristics to make an identification, some departments now use letters instead of numbers to point out characteristics.

As a handwriting trainee, you need not learn these last steps in fingerprints, but the information in this chapter will give you as an examiner the advantage of knowing what is possible. Knowing the possibilities will help you do a better job.

— 12 —

Court Appearance

The conclusion of a handwriting case is achieved with the two parties agreeing to a settlement of the issue, or by a final disposition in a court trial. We are now concerned with this final step. The first eleven chapters have led you to this final step—making a handwriting opinion and an appearance in court. If you have made a full and complete study, you will not arrive at a hasty or "curbstone" opinion. Once you have made a complete examination, a clear report of the opinion can be typed.

Upon receipt of a subpoena, you begin the trial preparation. The construction of a photographic exhibit and the review of your total examination in the case prepares you for a pretrial conference with the District Attorney.

Your name is called and you take the witness stand; this is followed by testimony of your qualifications, which establishes you as an expert. In your direct testimony, you offer your opinion and your reasons for this opinion by presenting your exhibits. Your testimony is followed by cross-examination.

The successful conclusion of a case can depend on your performance in the courtroom, and whether you complete each step correctly before going on to the next. A correct handwriting examination is of no real value if the case is lost in court by an examiner's mistake. Hence, the procedures you will study in this chapter are as important as the material covered in the first eleven chapters of this book.

Handwriting Opinions

Handwriting opinions are divided into two distinct groups: (1) positive opinions, and (2) inconclusive opinions. Hundreds of articles have been written that question whether opinions other than positive should be given. I believe there are only three legitimate opinions: (1) positive—that the writings *are* by the same person; (2) positive—that the writings are *not* by the same person; and (3) no opinion. Many examiners give such opinions as: "Best judgment," "Could be," "Definite determination," "Highly probable," "Possible," "Probable," "Qualified opinion," and "Reasonable certainty," and so on. If your opinion is "highly probable," you are saying there is excellent agreement in all details. BUT you are not sure of your opinion. A few examiners used to use a percentage opinion, as in 70 percent positive and 30 percent uncertain. This type of opinion has no place in handwriting opinions, and can lead to all kinds of problems.

In law enforcement, an opinion such as "best judgment" or "qualified opinion" is of little value to the investigator. He or she needs a positive opinion on which to base an arrest. If an examiner is unable to make a positive opinion, it is not only proper but very important that the examiner explain why he or she is unable to make a positive opinion. There are numerous reasons for being unable to make a definite statement:

1. Limited amount of questioned writing.
2. Span of years between known and unknown writings.
3. Health of the individual has changed between writings.
4. Copied, traced, or drawn writing is involved and no identification may be possible.
5. Copies are involved.
6. Lack of proper known writing. (Unconsciously Written, Normal Consciously Written, and Consciously Written Disguised exemplars were discussed in detail in chapter 6.)

Lack of proper exemplars played a part in an opinion of Joseph P. McNally during the investigation of the assassination of Martin Luther King, Jr. before the Select Committee on Assassinations. In his opinion, McNally stated, "There is sufficient agreement in the 1978 hand-drawn map and the other documents to support a conclusion that James Earl Ray made a map, although the writing on the map was informal, intended for the writer alone, while the other documents were more formal and precise. This informality may explain the deviation in writing style from the more formal documents identified as Ray's writing."[1] Once the investigator understands the reasons for an inconclusive opinion, he or she can attempt to obtain the proper documents so a positive opinion is possible.[2]

The authors therefore believe in only positive opinions, with a verbal explanation of inconclusive opinions. Positive opinions should identify the writer if possible, or exonerate a person if he or she did not write the document.

Maintaining professional integrity is another problem a document examiner must deal with. Outside pressures may emanate from the district attorney's office, department head, investigators, or others, asking for a positive opinion because they "know he did it." An examiner with ten indefinite opinions may begin to wonder if the deficiency rests with him, rather than with the lack of characteristics.

He may now start to press an opinion to show that he is not a could-be examiner. Be sure you don't fall into that trap! It has been said that certain law enforcement examiners almost never exonerate a suspect, but this is a difficult statement to believe. If you can assist the investigator by saying: "This is not the person who wrote the documents, find another person," you have performed a great service to the investigator and to the accused.

A highly important case that gains instant recognition can also cause pressures. An example of this is the 1976 Howard Hughes Mormon Will. Every day, newspapers carried the name of a "handwriting expert" who had an opinion. It was good to see that the legitimate document examiners were named in the paper because they were employed in the case.

Handwriting Reports

There are as many types of reports as there are examiners. No standards for report writing exist, so remember one important element: *Make the report simple.* Use concise terms, and describe only the essential details. The person asking for the report wants to know three things:

1. What questioned material did you examine?
2. What known material did you examine, and who witnessed it?
3. What is your opinion?

An investigator does not want to read a five-page report on the techniques that were used to make the examination. He or she also does not want to be educated in the field of handwriting by reading the reasons for an opinion. An attorney or investigator is not an expert and therefore would not understand the significance of characteristics even if you listed them. In California courts, it is case law that a "discovery motion" may be made by the defense which entails that copies of all reports, including handwriting, must be given to the defense. I examined a handwriting case for the United States Secret Service in 1976 on which I gave a verbal opinion of identification. A discovery motion was made, and since there was no handwriting report to discover, the judge ordered a report written for the attorney to "discover" (*United States v. Raymond Anthony Mitchell*). With a discovery motion, the defense can read your report and use each detail later in court. Your report, therefore, should not go into great detail, but only state the facts.

The report should start with a date, subject, and "Reference: Handwriting Examination" (or type of examination covered in the report). You should also say who is requesting the report. It is preferable to list the individual investigator or attorney, but if that is not possible, an agency may be named. The documents you examined should be numbered, starting with the questioned documents and then the exemplars. Some examiners list the documents as Q1, Q2, and K3. ("Q" stands for "questioned" and "K" for exemplars or "known writing.")

Each item should be described in detail. This need for a full description of a questioned document is illustrated by a case examined by Allyn Cole involving a deed to a highly valuable property.

> The ostensible grantor of the deed said that he learned of its existence long after the deed of execution. [He said that he] did not sign that deed, meaning that he might have signed some deed, but not that deed. The document, then on file with the clerk of the court, was examined by experts employed by the grantor and by some employed by the grantee. All reported that the signature was genuine. All had described the document in their reports as a deed bearing a certain date and bearing a signature in a certain name.
>
> At a later time, signatures of witnesses came into question. This time the document examiner, new to the case, wrote a full description of the deed, which description included information that the document had been divided or separated through the center into a top half carrying a description of the property and a bottom half carrying the signature of the grantor, and alleged signatures of alleged witnesses, and had been rejoined by an almost invisible transparent tape. This newly discovered condition raised a question whether the signature-bearing half had been fraudulently attached to the property-identification half.
>
> The court refused to allow introduction of evidence regarding separation and rejoining of the two halves, and would not hear argument of a theory that the signature-bearing half had been joined to a property-identification half which described property that the grantor did not intend to convey. The court ruled that this separation and joining of the halves should have been discovered during the first examination and that it could not be brought up at the present session which had been designated to receive only testimony about authorship of signatures of witnesses. The final decision at this session of the court went against the ostensible grantor of the deed. Of course, division and rejoining of a document may be innocent if the same halves are involved, and the evidence of what occurred in the case described would have to be considered in relation to the grantor's testimony and the questions about signatures of alleged witnesses (who were never produced). These and several related documents were already in evidence. Testimony about division and rejoining of the document would have given a focus to these other elements, but they seemed not to come to a really sharp focus in the absence of that testimony. For this reason there may have occurred a serious miscarriage of justice. The lesson is clear: the questioned documents must be described fully even though the document examiner has been asked to report upon one element only.[3]

Describing the questioned documents in detail is important so that anyone reading the report will know exactly what documents you are referring to. The district attorney's office will be interested in your detailed description of the exemplars in the case. The description of each exemplar should include the date it was obtained and witnessed, as well as the name of the witness.

Elements of good description need not be lengthy, but should be complete enough to clearly identify each exhibit. Descriptions should include, where applicable, serial numbers, dates, payee names, amounts, firm numbers, and other identifying data. (All items in a report should be assumed to be original unless otherwise stated.) The signatures or questioned writing on the documents are placed in quotes.

Conclude the report with a clearly worded opinion. I use this form:

> From my examination and comparison of the above documents, it is my "opinion" that [describe the questioned writing] were written by the person who filled out the handwriting exemplars in the name _____.

Note that you say "by the person who filled out," since examiners do not know who filled out the exemplar. This final paragraph must state very clearly what your opinion is and no more.

Attorneys often attack the use of the word "opinion"; they ask, "Isn't this merely your opinion?" The answer need never be "Yes." Indeed, if the specialist has made a good demonstration and has presented well-prepared exhibits, the question will appear inappropriate to the jury. They will have already answered this question in their own minds.

The use of an intensifier such as "definite" to strengthen the opinion is also not needed. Alwyn Cole stated, "I suggest it is much better to use the moderate—it might be said, judicial—word 'opinion' and follow with the forceful reasons that will show the substantial nature of the opinion."[4]

There is no more pertinent expression of the status of expert testimony than in the review of the typewriting case of *Lyon v. Oliver*, 316 Ill. 292.[5]

> The opinion of the Supreme Court emphasizes the feature that modern expert testimony no longer can be disparaged by that doubt which hesitates to accept "mere opinion"; because what scientific methods and apparatus has been able to do is reveal FACTS, and these facts can be made, by microscopy and photography, as plain to the tribunal as to the expert so that the observer may form his own opinion adequately from the facts. One arises from perusal of this case with renewed respect for the modern expert.

A report written as described above will suffice for most examinations. There will be times, however, when you must report additional conclusions. A cover letter completely separate from the report not only may be written, but, in some cases, should be written. A professional report should clearly list only the document information and opinion.

Court Exhibits

To Aristotle it seemed that "persuasion is clearly a sort of demonstration, since we are most fully persuaded when we consider a thing to have been demonstrated."

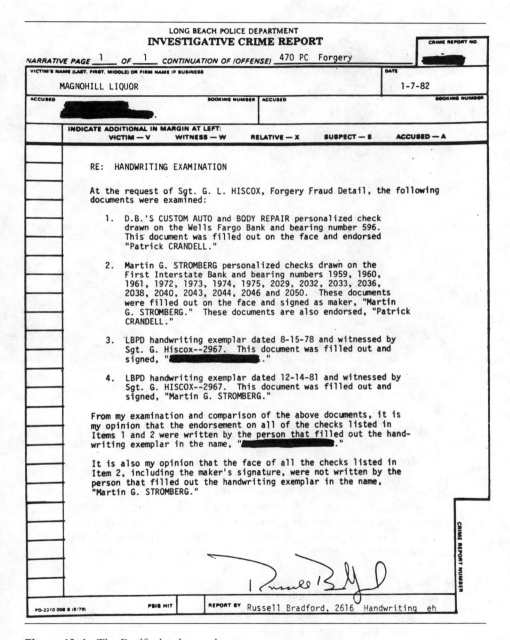

LONG BEACH POLICE DEPARTMENT
INVESTIGATIVE CRIME REPORT

CRIME REPORT NO.

NARRATIVE PAGE ___1___ OF ___1___ CONTINUATION OF (OFFENSE) __470 PC Forgery__

VICTIM'S NAME (LAST, FIRST, MIDDLE) OR FIRM NAME IF BUSINESS

MAGNOHILL LIQUOR

DATE
1-7-82

ACCUSED   BOOKING NUMBER   ACCUSED   BOOKING NUMBER

INDICATE ADDITIONAL IN MARGIN AT LEFT:
VICTIM — V   WITNESS — W   RELATIVE — X   SUSPECT — S   ACCUSED — A

RE: HANDWRITING EXAMINATION

At the request of Sgt. G. L. HISCOX, Forgery Fraud Detail, the following documents were examined:

1. D.B.'S CUSTOM AUTO and BODY REPAIR personalized check drawn on the Wells Fargo Bank and bearing number 596. This document was filled out on the face and endorsed "Patrick CRANDELL."

2. Martin G. STROMBERG personalized checks drawn on the First Interstate Bank and bearing numbers 1959, 1960, 1961, 1972, 1973, 1974, 1975, 2029, 2032, 2033, 2036, 2038, 2040, 2043, 2044, 2046 and 2050. These documents were filled out on the face and signed as maker, "Martin G. STROMBERG." These documents are also endorsed, "Patrick CRANDELL."

3. LBPD handwriting exemplar dated 8-15-78 and witnessed by Sgt. G. Hiscox--2967. This document was filled out and signed, "▓▓▓▓▓▓▓▓▓▓▓▓."

4. LBPD handwriting exemplar dated 12-14-81 and witnessed by Sgt. G. HISCOX--2967. This document was filled out and signed, "Martin G. STROMBERG."

From my examination and comparison of the above documents, it is my opinion that the endorsement on all of the checks listed in Items 1 and 2 were written by the person that filled out the handwriting exemplar in the name, "▓▓▓▓▓▓▓▓▓▓▓▓."

It is also my opinion that the face of all the checks listed in Item 2, including the maker's signature, were not written by the person that filled out the handwriting exemplar in the name, "Martin G. STROMBERG."

PO-2310 008 B (8/79)   PSIS HIT   REPORT BY Russell Bradford, 2616 Handwriting eh

CRIME REPORT NUMBER

Figure 12–1: The Bradford style typed report.

Figure 12–2: "Individual style" exhibit.

Virtually all document examiners agree that cases in court should not be proved with words alone, but by demonstration with exhibits. Your job as examiner is to show the jury exhibits so they can identify the handwriting and not rely solely on your word.

In preparing an exhibit, you must first decide which of the known and questioned documents should be enlarged, so that you will be able to illustrate your opinion. Consideration should also be given to any characteristics that do not match. It is a foregone conclusion that the opposing attorney will ask about them. Therefore, it is preferable for you, the examiner, to point them out first.

There are two ways to construct an exhibit—the "individual style" and the "word style." With the individual style, a row of questioned letters is arranged opposite a row of known letters (figure 12-2). With this style of exhibit, you must guard against overenlarging. Extreme enlargements may overemphasize insignificant details and should only be used in special cases.

In the second method, word style, one compares a questioned word (or several words) with a known word or words (figure 12-2). In many cases, the

Figure 12–3: "Word style" exhibit.

type of case will determine which style should be used. Both styles are acceptable, but we prefer the word style. Proportion, alignment, and other characteristics are more easily pointed out and better illustrated with the word style.

The second problem to tackle is what size to make the exhibit. One method is to prepare a large exhibit that stands on an easel and allows you to point out the characteristics with a pointer. Another method is to make smaller photographs that you can give to every other member of the jury and to other individuals concerned in the case. The individual photograph method has advantages in that each person can clearly see the photographs. With a large exhibit, jurors who have poor distance vision may not be able to see the exhibit clearly. In many of the older courts, the lighting is poor and the examiner is located in a position where he or she is unable to utilize a large exhibit.

Experience has shown that the most serious objection to individual exhibits is the fact that some jurors are unable to follow instructions. Delay is inevitable, if some jurors look at the wrong photograph while others skip ahead. In England, the examiner and the jurors are located at great distance from each other, so individual exhibits are sometimes used. To keep the jurors on track, examiners number the exhibits and also the words on them. The examiner will say, "Refer to photograph #5, and then examine word #4;" and then will discuss the characteristics.

We prefer large exhibits over individual exhibits. A 16 inch by 20 inch exhibit is quite easy to make and can be seen by the jurors. In some cases, a 16 inch by 20 inch exhibit of the questioned document can be hinged together with a same-size exhibit of the exemplar. With a single large exhibit, the examiner commands the attention of those concerned at all times. The use of a pointer directs the attention of the viewer to the exact point the examiner is talking about. The authors believe this is the best method, but each has its advantages.

Ralph Bradford had a Polaroid MP Series Land camera, camera stand, baseboard, and floodlamps for his copy work. The questioned documents were photographed with Polaroid film, which would be later used as his work sheet. After the Polaroid was taken and the exposure corrected, a wet process film was obtained. The latter was then used to make enlargements for court exhibits.

The advance time needed to make an exhibit is one of the problems examiners face. The expense of purchasing photographic equipment and stocking a darkroom is another. One method of preparing instant exhibits has been used by the Arizona Department of Public Safety, Questioned Document laboratory, and other departments. A cutup of the words to be used on an exhibit are attached to a 3 inch by 5 inch card. This card is placed in an opaque projector and shown on the screen in court. The key is to find a method of demonstration that works best for you.

The final decision you need to make about your exhibits has to do with placing "marks" on them. The marks or lines are made on the exhibit prior to court appearance to assist the examiner in explaining the identifying characteristics to a jury.

The authors of leading document books, *Law of Disputed and Forged Documents* (J. Newton Baker),[6] *Scientific Examination of Documents* (Ordway Hilton),[7] and *Suspect Documents* (Wilson Harrison),[8] all object to the placing of marks on an exhibit, and many document examiners agree. These authors point out that (1) marks obstruct visibility—characteristics can be seen better without the marks; (2) marks deface the photograph; and (3) a successful objection may be made to marked photographs on the grounds they are no longer true records of what appears on the document. Another stated that it is inadvisable, if not improper, to offer a marked photograph without an unmarked one.

Ralph Bradford and I began our careers as fingerprint examiners, where it is an accepted practice to mark exhibits. Ralph Bradford started marking fingerprint exhibits in 1923. In 1939, the FBI published *Classification of Fingerprints* and displayed an exhibit with marks.[9] This policy continues to this date.

The examiner makes an "opinion" using the original documents, while an exhibit is made so the examiner can better illustrate the opinion to a jury. An

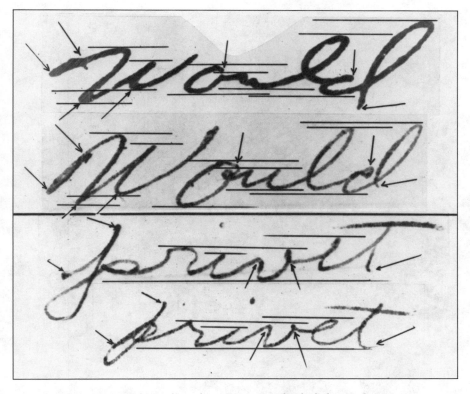

Figure 12–4: An exhibit with marks pointing to individual characteristics.

exhibit is an enlarged reproduction of parts of a questioned document and of an exemplar. Marks and lines are added to the exhibit to assist the examiner in explaining the opinion. A horizontal line can be drawn as a head line to show the irregularity. The marks on a handwriting exhibit, like a fingerprint exhibit, do not damage or deface the exhibit. Albert S. Osborn, in *Questioned Documents*, maintains that "exhibits are made much more effective when certain places and portions are simply designated by small numbers or letters or by small arrows."[10] Osborn also stated that it is proper that "the photographing of the signatures under glass carry uniform ruled squares so that all parts may be compared by inspection" (that would rebut the argument that marked exhibits are no longer true records).

The most important objections were the legal ones, of "dangerous practice" and "improperness." Wigmore's *Evidence* (1979) was researched by the authors, and no legal reason could be found that would object to marks. Osborn's book *Questioned Documents* lists a great number of court decisions. In a Louisiana

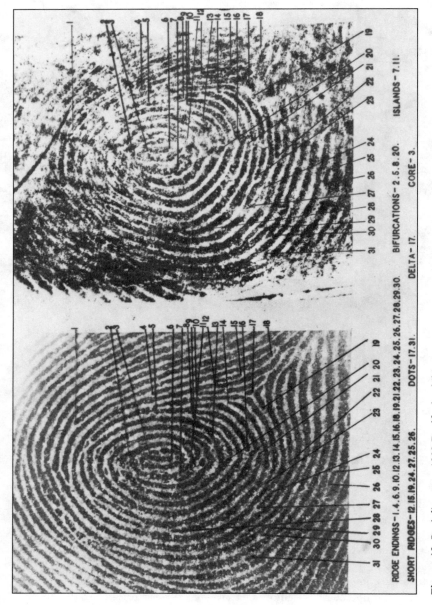

Figure 12–5: A line on a 1938 Bradford exhibit.

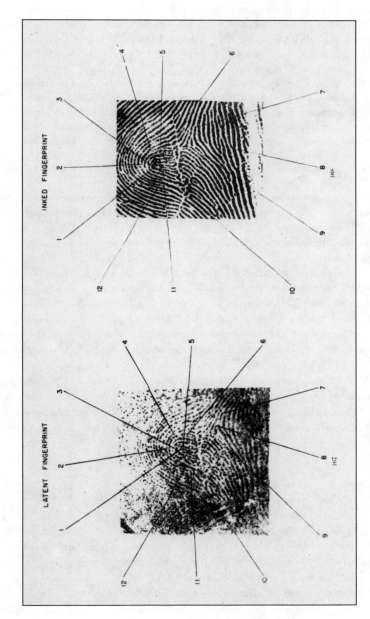

Figure 12–6: Lines on a 1939 FBI exhibit. (U.S. Government Printing Office).

case, *State v. Dunn*, 109 So 56 (1926), defendants objected to the offering on the grounds that the photograph had been tampered with. The objection was overruled because "the marked photograph was necessary to enable the witness to testify in such a manner that the jury could grasp his evidence." A Nevada citation is also listed, *State v. Kuhl*, 42 Nev. 185, 175 Pac 190, 3 A.L.R. (1918).

> These lines, as appears from what record there is before us, were placed on the photographs by the expert for the purpose of more clearly illustrating their testimony. They indicated the points of similarity or identity to which the expert testified. Their existence and significance were fully explained by the witnesses. These markings in no way affected the photographs and we are at a loss to discern any prejudice or injury that could have thus accrued to the appellant.[10]

Charles Scott stated, "It is well settled that a photograph is not rendered inadmissible in evidence by pertinent marks or notations that are properly verified"[11]. A photographic publication agreed: "Since the photographic exhibit is actually a visual aid for the court, it is permissible to use markings to assist the jurors in understanding points of proof."[12]

The marking of an exhibit should be professional, so that it does not defeat the purpose for which it was made. When marking an exhibit, you should: (1) use a ruler and (2) avoid marking every characteristic. Mark only a few characteristics, leaving a few so that if the defense asks, "Are there any more?" you will have some to add. Remember that an exhibit is your way of telling a jury how to find the characteristics. If you leave a few out, they themselves can find them when they examine your exhibit in the jury room.

Fingerprint experts number the characteristics on an exhibit, but this is not recommended for a handwriting exhibit, since in handwriting we do not count characteristics. In handwriting it is the individuality, not the number of characteristics, that is important.

Pretrial Preparation

The former director of the Institute of Applied Science wrote an article with a title that tells the story of a pretrial preparation: "Be Ready in the Morning."[13] It is important to go over your total case, evaluating questioned and known documents, opinions, exhibits, and so on. Your files should be in businesslike order. Complete notes recording dates of examination, reports, and photographs give you confidence and poise as a witness. Presenting yourself as a professional will establish good rapport between lawyer and expert.

One of the items the district attorney will want is a copy of your resume, so that he may qualify you in court. Every document examiner should have a highly detailed resume. It is even more important for the new examiner, thus it should be constantly updated. The resume should contain:

1. *Personal history.* Physical description, address (home and office), phone numbers, etc.
2. *Education.* High school with year of graduation, college attended, listing courses relating to the questioned document profession, with year of graduation. Advanced degrees, if any. Any specialized training including dates and courses of study.
3. *Employment.* Starting with most recent, list names of employers with dates. Specify type of work you performed (if handwriting work involved, put in italics).
4. *Expert testimony.* Agencies testified for and in what courts. List special hearings, depositions, etc.
5. *Special projects.* Articles you have written and also any speeches made. List dates and places.
6. *Honors received.* List with date and reason received. This item is listed on most applications, and the author has never really understood what it means. However, it does remind the author of his favorite Will Rogers quote, written for a weekly newspaper article on March 20, 1933. "Heroes are made every little while, but only one in a million conduct themselves afterwards so that it makes us proud that we honored them at the time."
7. *Associations.* List document examiner associations you belong to and any offices or other positions held. This is important to list, as active participation adds credibility.

With an organized, up-to-date resume, you are ready to be qualified in court. At no time will you be required to use all the information in your resume during testimony, but it will serve as a collective source of your qualifications.

The final step in the preparation for your pretrial conference and the trial itself is obtaining a few essential items. Number one is a quality briefcase that helps you achieve a professional look. You should also obtain an extra-large art portfolio of good quality. The portfolio is a professional way to carry your exhibits into court. Two other items you'll need are a red felt-tip pen (broad point) and an extendable pointer. These items can be carried in the briefcase and should always be handy. The felt-tip pen can be used to draw characteristics during an explanation to the jury. The pointer gives an added professional look.

"It can truly be said that a man's accomplishments are in direct proportion to the amount of intelligent preparation that goes into his endeavors." And, in the words of the late, great General Douglas A. MacArthur, "Preparedness is the key to victory."[14]

Pretrial Conference

The final step of pretrial preparation is meeting with the attorney who will present your case in court. This meeting should be held several days before your testimony is to be given. Go over all points of your testimony with the attorney, as well as any other testimony that relates to yours.

The meeting should include a discussion on how your qualifications will be presented. The attorney might say, "Will you please state to the jury your qualifications as a document examiner," and then let you respond. I prefer this method, but most examiners prefer the question-and-answer method, which breaks up the monotonous qualifying. It also seems more impressive to the jury—an important consideration. If the question method is used, you should go over your resume with the attorney and underline key points.

Point out to the attorney that it is important that a stipulation of qualifications (acceptance of qualifications without testimony) not be allowed. Experience shows that when it appears that the examiner is well qualified, many skilled defense attorneys will try to stipulate that "the examiner is an expert." The jury will then not be able to truly evaluate the expertise. If forewarned, the attorney will not be caught off-guard, will not agree to a stipulation, and can state, "I would like the examiner to state his qualifications and let the jury decide if he is an expert."

Handwriting exemplars are a key target area of opposing attorneys. If they can be kept out, the examiner will have nothing on which to base his or her testimony. Hence, it is crucial to go over them in the pretrial stage and make sure the witnesses have been subpoenaed and can testify as to having witnessed them.

If the person who witnessed the exemplar cannot be found, some exemplars can be introduced under the Official Document section. *Wigmore on Evidence*, Section 2158, says:

> It seems therefore, never to have been doubted that the existence of an official document in the appropriate official custody is sufficient evidence of its genuineness to go to the jury. The forms in which the testimony to this fact may be represented are four, according as the witness is the official custodian himself or some other person, namely:
>
> 1. The official custodian bringing the record into court and identifying it.
> 2. The official custodian certifying a copy from it.
> 3. A private person bringing the record into court and identifying it.
> 4. A private person proving a sworn or examining copy of it . . . .[15]

Special legal problems, or any other type of problem you as examiner can think of, should be discussed at this time. No prosecuting attorney can be expected to know all case law on every subject. The law on court-ordered exemplars is one category that attorneys may not be aware of. Due to their heavy case loads, attorneys cannot do research on all aspects of every case. Examiners, because of their experience, can often inform them of possible problems and their solutions.

It is important to explain your handwriting examination to the attorney. The more he understands, the more professional his questions during the trial will be. A few questions can be written out, for cross-examination. The authors prefer that the attorney be given the freedom to ask an explanation for anything he or she doesn't understand. If an attorney does not understand a part of the examiner's testimony, the jury probably won't understand it either.

If and when you learn that there is another document examiner employed by the defense, you should make this known to your attorney. You should point out that examiners do disagree, particularly when one may have insufficient exemplars. Your attorney can decide if he wishes you and the other examiner to have a meeting. This is often a difficult dilemma. However, if you are both qualified examiners, any differences of opinion may be worked out in a meeting. This would be preferable to two experts testifying against each other.[16]

The district attorney and you should, as a final step in the preparation, visit the courtroom where the trial will be held. Make an on-the-spot check to see if there is a blackboard or easel on which to attach your exhibits. If not, arrangements can be made. Location of the exhibits during testimony should be checked to be sure the jury and the judge can see them. If you plan to use projection equipment, check for electrical plugs and light switches.

The Trial

Before you take your place on the witness stand, there are two extremely important items you must be aware of: confidence and appearance. Very little has been written on these two subjects in the document field. If you do not concern yourself with them, you will not go very far in the business.

Confidence

Every examiner who takes the witness stand is apprehensive. Sweaty palms are normal to each person who must go on the witness stand in front of a judge, attorneys, and members of a jury. No matter how many times you have testified, you will experience this self-consciousness just before testifying. Within a few seconds after the questioning begins, this apprehension will be greatly reduced. With this understanding, you should realize that your feelings are not unusual.

How can you gain confidence and reduce your fears in front of a jury? The number one method is to "be prepared."[17] Know your material forward and backward, the characteristics as well as their variations. When we say "know the writing," we do not mean examine it a few minutes before going on the stand. Ralph Bradford prepared by practically memorizing all the writing. When you are totally prepared, you will carry a confident feeling with you into court.

When does a handwriting trainee become a document examiner? There is no set answer to the question, but it does not happen until an examiner has confidence. Thorough training, coupled with experience, gives an examiner the confidence needed to make positive opinions and back up those opinions.

Figure 12–7: Clark Sellers testifying with an exhibit.

A vital point that will assist you in being confident is the "use of exhibits." An exhibit takes the attention of the people in a courtroom off the examiner, and gives you a crutch to lean on. The exhibit assists you in describing the handwriting characteristics. As your testimony goes smoothly, you will gain confidence. A jury cannot believe an examiner who does not believe in himself. An examiner who is prepared and confident has come a long way toward being a professional.

Appearance

Since your clothes are clearly visible, they will make the first impression on the jury. John T. Molloy spent fifteen years researching 15,000 professional men, developing techniques to gauge the effect of personal appearance on others. His studies were reported in *Newsweek*[18] and in his book *Dress for Success*.[19] Molloy's approach was to recommend that both attorney and defendants dress in a way that the judge and jury will relate to. An examiner should be neatly and conservatively dressed and readily identifiable as being from the upper-middle class. Before grand juries in larger cities, a conservative dark blue suit is recommended.

Because of the possible prejudice of jurors, it is suggested that you do not wear too much jewelry; the one universally acceptable piece of jewelry is the wedding band. Professional emblems and lapel pins should not be worn.

Any good quality attache case or briefcases is all right, but cordovan leather cases are the most acceptable. If you choose an attache case, it should be plain, simple, and functional, with no decorations or obtrusive hardware. You must present a completely professional appearance if you are to be believed in court.

As the role of the examiner is not limited to the courtroom, you must conduct yourself properly in any location where you may be seen. Any conversation with members of the jury should be avoided, as should conversation with the defense attorney, except in the presence of your own attorney. Remember, it is possible to alienate a juror even before you even arrive in the courtroom.[20]

Courtroom Testimony

When your name is called, walk directly to the witness stand, then face the clerk to take the oath. Maintain a serious and businesslike manner while taking the oath. Look at the person administering the oath and keep your hand up until it is fully given. You then will be directed to the witness chair and asked to state your name and to spell your last name for the record.

The attorney will direct questions to you that should be answered clearly, slowly, and loud enough to be heard by all members of the jury. After a question is asked, you should allow a momentary pause before answering. This pause will be especially helpful during cross-examination, where it will serve two purposes: (1) it will allow the attorneys to object to the question, and (2) it will allow you to consider your answer before answering. Your answer should be as brief as possible, unless you are asked to explain. When you are answering questions, direct your answer to the person asking the questions and not to the jury. Later, you will be given a chance to explain your opinion to the jury, and at that point, talk directly to the jury.

After you are sworn in, the questioning will commence. The attorney will ask your profession. Some attorneys then will ask your home address. California has a law (Section #1328.6) that says a specialist (Questioned Document Examiner) employed by law enforcement departments "need not state the place of his residence, but in lieu thereof, state his business address." You will then be asked your qualifications (as per your pretrial conference). When the defense attorney questions you on cross-examination, he or she will ask detailed questions regarding your qualifications. If you have kept a complete resume, you should have no problems answering these questions. The important thing is to be totally honest and not exaggerate any facts. One examiner stated he had testified in over 1,500 cases in his twenty years. If this figure were accurate, he would have testified in court once in every three working days. Obviously, he most likely did not testify this often, as there would be no time for preparation or even examinations. The average for testifying in three large law enforcement agencies is about once in every eight working days.

On December 9, 1981, direct testimony was taken in the Municipal Court of Long Beach Judicial District before Judge Eugene J. Long. Parts of my testimony are included here as examples of typical courtroom testimony.

Q. Mr. Bradford, could you please state your qualifications in the field of handwriting for the court?

A. Approximately thirty-five years ago, I commenced the study of handwriting under the former handwriting expert with the Long Beach Police Department, my father, Ralph Bradford. Under my father, I studied all types of handwriting problems, copied handwriting, traced handwriting on checks, robbery notes, narcotic prescriptions, and all types of documents.

My formal education commenced after graduation from Long Beach City College. I then attended California State University at Los Angeles, where I graduated with a Bachelor of Science Degree, majoring in Police Science. While there, I took a course in Special Police Problems. In that class I researched and wrote a paper, "The Examination of Questioned Documents." I also attended California State University at Long Beach, Orange Coast College, and the University of Southern California, where I took handwriting courses. The Long Beach Police Department held six handwriting courses, of which I attended all six. I have also taught handwriting at California State University at Long Beach.

My on-the-job experience—I worked two years for the Orange County Sheriff's Office and three years for the Santa Monica Police Department. One of my duties at these departments was to assist the handwriting examiner. I was not *the* handwriting examiner, but was merely assisting the examiner as a trainee. In 1961, I was employed by the Long Beach Police Department, as a full-time Document Examiner.

For the past twenty years, it has been my responsibility to examine all handwriting that has come to the attention of the Long Beach Police Department. In that capacity, I have examined more than thirty thousand cases. I have testified in juvenile, municipal, superior, federal, and military courts in more than five hundred cases. I have examined handwriting and testified throughout California and Nevada. I have been called on by the State Bar of California as an impartial expert to examine documents. I also accept private handwriting cases. I have examined handwriting and testified for the Shell Oil Company, Bank of America, Douglas Aircraft Company, and other agencies. I am also a member of several related associations.

The attorney now directed questions that brought out my opinion. When you are shown a document, examine it, and if necessary refer to your notes.

Q. Showing you People's [Exhibits] 5, 6, and 7. Let's start with number 5. Do you recognize that?

A. Yes. That is a California diver's license, and it was examined by myself. It has my initials at the bottom of the document.

Q. What is the source of that document?

A. It was furnished by the State of California, Department of Motor Vehicles. It is a certified document.

Q. Now, People's Exhibit 6. Do you recognize that?

A. Yes. It is a check drawn on the account of Margaret Thomas, and signed Margaret Thomas.

Q. Now, People's Exhibit 7. Do you recognize that document?

A. Yes. That is also a check on the account of Margaret Thomas, and signed Margaret Thomas.

Q. Mr. Bradford, do you have an opinion, based on your examination of the handwriting on the documents listed in People's 5, 6, and 7?

A. From my examination and comparison of the individual characteristics in the writing on these three documents, it is my opinion that the two checks, People's 6 and 7, were signed by the person that signed the driver's license, People's 5.

When testifying regarding a document, identify it as "People's 1," and so on, so there is no confusion as to what you are talking about. It is important to the court reporter, so that the transcript can be properly recorded. Once the documents have been entered into evidence, examined, and an opinion expressed, it is time to mark your exhibits. If you have a combination exhibit with the questioned material on top, that portion will be labeled on the exhibit with the same number as given to the questioned document. The bottom half of the exhibit which contains the exemplar will also be labeled with the same number given that document. The exhibit itself will now be labeled with a number especially assigned to it.

The prosecutor may now ask you to explain to the jury how you arrived at your opinion. It is the job of the examiner to teach handwriting comparison to the jury. It is important to compress a college handwriting course, additional courses, and years of training and experience into five minutes' instruction to a jury. Alwyn Cole's statement on handwriting to the Warren Commission is quoted in chapter 2, and it is an excellent method of explaining handwriting to a lay person. When testifying, I try to teach handwriting to a jury using a method of explaining only three words: characteristics, individual characteristics, and variations.

1. *Characteristics.* Using the exhibit, explain that every line, hook, and curve is a characteristic. If a line starts with a blunt or tapered stroke, that is a characteristic. If the line is then straight or curved, that also is a characteristic. In other words, every part of every line in every word is a characteristic. An examiner must examine every characteristic.

2. *Individual characteristics.* A person is taught in school to write, using the text of a handwriting system. Spencerian, Zaner-Bloser, Palmer, and others are handwriting systems that were taught in the United States. When a person deviates from writing a letter as taught in the system, that letter becomes individual. Hence, a person writing a letter that is different from a known system, is writing an "individual characteristic."

Using your exhibit, first point out a characteristic that is *not* individual. Explain that this method of making a letter is used by most of the systems, and is therefore not individual. Then point out an individual characteristic and explain that this letter is individual because the systems of writing do not teach a letter made in this manner. Now explain how the letter should be made, so the jury can see the difference. If the body of a small *y* is very wide and is written above the base line, that is individual. Students are taught to write bodies of letters the same width, and on the base line. At this point, it might be wise to explain an individual characteristic, using the exemplar and questioned document on your exhibit. Remember to use the exhibits, and remember that you are teaching the jury, so explain in such a way that they can understand what you are talking about. It is this last part that is so important. If you explain class and individual characteristics in proper detail, the jury will be able to find the characteristics that you fail to point out.

3. *Variation.* Explain that no one writes exactly the same every time, and that the reason examiners obtain numerous exemplars is to learn all the variations of a person's writing. Show the jury that variations show up even on the same exemplar. Illustrate variation on the exhibit. If a letter on the questioned document and exemplar are different, check to see if there is a variation on the exemplar. Examiners note all these variations when making an examination.

4. *Forgery or Tracing.* If the case involves a copied signature or a tracing, you must explain how an examination of this type is made. You have already learned that when a person copies a signature, he or she uses one of three methods or a combination of two of them. Method one is to copy a signature "slow" and get all the characteristics correct. When this method is used, you will see heavy, tremorous writing. There will also be patching, breaks, sharp angles, and other defects. Method two is to copy a writing at a faster rate, eliminating the heavy and tremorous writing. When writing at a faster rate, however, the writer will often miss copying the characteristics. Most forgers, however, will attempt Method 3—fast enough to eliminate tremor and slow enough to copy the characteristics.

Using the words from your exhibit that you have explained to the jury, you can now testify to the individual characteristics that helped form your opinion. The amount of questioned writing will determine the amount of detail you will explain to the jury. It is very important to be honest and straightforward, and also to explain any characteristics that do not match. Do not skip over a bad point, or treat it lightly. The defense will hit you with it later, so it is best to go into detail at this time.

It is preferable to testify about the characteristics in the order they appear on your exhibit. Taking the letters in order, you will testify to the nonidentifiable characteristics without putting undue importance on those characteristics. Because the members of the jury aren't trained in your profession, you must explain everything to them several times to make sure they understand your statements. Your expertise is not to be used to impress the jury, but, rather, to lead the jury to see what you see.

Once your testimony directed to the jury is complete, the district attorney will be free to ask questions on anything he or she does not understand. Most experts are so familiar with their subject, that they fail to realize the difficulty it may present to lay persons.

To quote from a speech by one of California's most distinguished judges,

> Testimonial evidence must be fully understood by the triers of fact. This statement is so obvious that it should be superfluous were it not for the fact that experts are not always understandable to the average juror. Experts, being men of learning, often overlook that, what to them is elementary and obvious, may be unknown or difficult to understand by the average lay mind, and that explanations and demonstrations which would be understood and accepted by well-informed persons may be far above the heads of jurors. The questions often asked by attorneys, particularly on cross-examination, pretty clearly indicate that, when we testify, we must do it so clearly that the thought and information in the mind of the witness becomes, as nearly as is humanly possible, implanted in the mind of triers of fact. To do this requires a careful choice of language and such simplicity of expression that the hearers will fully understand everything that is being said, and can devote their entire attention to the information being imparted. If the hearers do not fully understand the words used, we can hardly expect them to understand the subject matter. If a word is used a juror does not understand, it not only does not mean anything to him, but, when he hears it, he mentally wonders what does it mean. In the period of his wondering, he misses the words which follow the word which has bothered him and *they* become mentally lost. When, in testifying, we are compelled to use a word, the meaning of which may not be fully understood, we must then and there stop and explain the term used so that it will be understood.[21]

The counsel is in a good position to judge the understandability of the testimony. He must question the examiner to clear up any complicated point. If the counsel does not understand a point, the jury probably will not understand it either. If the examiner is straightforward and honest, there is no question the district attorney can ask that will embarrass him. A district attorney who asks a question to learn something, or to clarify testimony that has been given, will help the case more than if he or she asked questions prepared by the examiner. The

Figure 12–8: Ralph Bradford (left) and Judge Charles Fricke.

object is to clarify testimony and the prosecutor can best do this with unprepared questions which will attempt to gain the complete answer.

The second phase of testimony concerns cross-examination by defense attorneys. They are of two basic types, the friendly and the "brow beater." The latter is easy to deal with, as long as you keep your cool. If you allow yourself to become angry, you are likely to exaggerate facts and lose the rapport that you have established with the jury. The friendly attorney is the more dangerous, since he will lead you into a feeling of false security with flattery and praise. He is also easy to deal with if you listen intently to the questions, taking time to think through the answer. The examiner should be alert for ambiguous or misleading questions. If you do not understand a question, ask that it be repeated. If the question is still unclear, tell the attorney directly that you do not understand the question. If you have done your homework, you should be prepared to answer any question and feel at ease when doing so.

Albert S. Osborn believed that a court of law was a place for dignity, but he also possessed a keen sense of humor and quick wit. Anybody who attempted to belittle him or his profession did so at their peril. On one occasion, a bumptious cross-examiner remarked, "You know so much about this writing, I presume you could tell me whether or not it was written while the writer was riding on a mule's back?" Osborn replied that he had not had the experience of examining writing performed in this way, but that he had had considerable experience with jackasses. (*Webster's* defines the American vernacular word "jackass" as (1) an ass or donkey, (2) a perverse blockhead.)[22]

Each defense attorney has his or her own trick question to ask in an attempt to fool an "expert." What they do not realize is that the same trick questions have been asked of examiners for years and are no surprise. A few of these stock questions are:

1. "Have you ever made a mistake?" As worded, it is a trick question. Of course, everyone has made hundreds of mistakes. The "mistakes" in this question should be qualified as "handwriting mistakes." If you are questioned regarding handwriting mistakes, answer, "Do you mean in the office opinion or court opinions?" In the office, I make many preliminary opinions that are sometimes wrong. I have also failed to identify many suspects who were guilty, but in case of doubt, I always give the suspect the benefit of doubt. Regarding mistakes in court, I answer, "It has never been brought to my attention that I have made a mistake." With this answer, you are saying you have not made any mistakes and yet do not claim to be God. If you have made a mistake in court, admit it, but add the fact that in the thousands of cases you have examined, you only made one error. Clark Sellers was once asked, "Do you claim to be infallible?" He answered, "No, but I claim to be careful."

2. "Is handwriting examination an exact science or just an opinion?" Handwriting examination like most science, is not an *exact* science. It does, however, use scientific principals and many specialized instruments to form opinions. "Just an opinion" does not in any way describe a handwriting examination. Based on scientific examination, reasoned judgment, and a demonstration and presentation of exhibits, a scientifically backed opinion is given.

3. "Are you being paid to testify?" To this, answer: "I am employed in my profession and paid a salary for my work. This salary is paid just as a salary is paid to a judge, attorney, or member of a jury for their work."

4. "Will you examine these two documents and identify them as being written by the same person?" The documents given the examiner are routine and easy to identify. If the examiner attempts to make any new examination on the stand, the defense attorney will immediately produce additional documents to be examined. All kinds of problems can come up with on-the-spot examinations not conducted in the examiner's laboratory with the proper equipment.

5. "How long did it take to make the examination?" If you answer "ten minutes," that is too short, or if you say "ten hours," you will be asked why it took so long. You could say, "I do not check myself. When I concentrate totally on a handwriting examination, I have no sense of time passing. I have frequently

worked through my lunch hour, not noticing the time. My concentration is on the documents, and not on what time it is."

> **Q.** Do you have any idea how long it took you to make the comparison?
> **A.** No sir.
> **Q.** Would it be true that you spent something less than an hour on this?
> **A.** I would have no idea. Like I said, I have to examine all the characteristics, which means every part of every letter. I am not only looking for individual characteristics to make an identification, but also for the tremor of fraud. While examining all of this, it is hard to tell how long it took to examine the documents.

6. "In this case, you stated the letter *i* contains an individual characteristic. Isn't it a fact that there are only a very few ways the letter *i* can be made?" No, the letter *i* can be made over 5,000 different ways. To further explain, Professor Simon Newcomb's mathematical formula says, "The probability of concurrence of all the events is equal to the continued product of the probabilities of all the separate events. If one thing will occur once in twenty times and another in twenty, the probability of the two occurring in conjunction is represented by the fraction which is the product of one-twentieth and one-twentieth, or one four-hundredth." Some of the over 5,000 ways an *i* can be made[23]:

> a. Pickup. This stroke can be made in three different ways. The initial stroke starts below the base line, on the base line, or above the base line. Pickup 3.
> b. Height. This can also be measured in three different ways. The letter can be taller than the other letters, same height, or smaller than other letters. Pickup 3 × Height 3 = 9.
> c. Width. This can be measured in three ways; wide loop, average, or retrace. Width 3 × 9 = 27.
> d. Body. This can be made four different ways: Curve line up and straight line down, curve up and curve down, straight up and curve down, or straight up and straight down. Body 4 × 27 = 108.
> e. Final stroke. Can be made three ways: straight down, curved right, and curved up. Final stroke 3 × 108 = 324.
> f. *i* = dot. made in four different ways: dot, slash, circle, or omitted. *i* = dot 4 × 324 = 1,296.
> g. Placement of *i* = dot. Placed in four different positions: left of letter, straight above, above at the same slant as the letter, and far right. Placement of dot 4 × 1,296 = 5,184.

There are, therefore, at least 5,184 different ways to make the small letter *i*.

7. "From examining the handwriting, would you describe the subject's character?" Examining character is the type examination completed in the field

of Graphology. In document examinations, we are able to determine if writing was done by the same person, but we cannot determine this person's character. We are also not able to determine sex or personality traits. To the question "Is Graphology a legitimate science?" answer, "I have not completed an in-depth study of Graphology, so I have no way of determining the validity of that field."

8. "Don't scientists place handwriting science at a low level of expert testimony?" When a medical doctor, psychiatrist, or scientist testifies, it is very difficult for a juror to determine the reliability of a witness. In the field of handwriting examination, the examiner presents charts and can demonstrate his opinion to the jury, giving the jury the opportunity to evaluate the examiner. Therefore, I consider a handwriting examiner's testimony of a very high degree of efficiency.

9. "Do experts disagree?" Many articles have been written on this subject, since this is a favorite question of all attorneys. The case of the Howard Hughes Mormon Will, discovered in Mormon headquarters in Salt Lake City on April 27, 1976, elicited many opinions. When the press learned of the will, they went to any and all persons willing to give a handwriting opinion. Not knowing how to determine who was an expert, newspaper and television reporters repeated any opinion given them.

Nine persons' names appeared in the *Long Beach* (Calif.) *Press Telegram* as "having an opinion." Of the nine, four were graphologists who were not trained as document examiners. Two of the persons were autograph collectors, not qualified in any manner. Of the nine so-called experts reported in the media, only two were document examiners. The two qualified document examiners were Jack Harris and Lyndal Shaneyfly, who both stated that the will was a forgery. The graphologists and autograph collectors formed an incorrect opinion and stated the will was genuine. No wonder the public was confused as to the validity of the will, or more important, the validity of the science of handwriting examination.

When you are asked the question about experts disagreeing, you must first rule out an unqualified examiner, if there is one. If all the examiners are qualified, you need to ascertain whether or not they all had the same questioned and known documents to examine. In many cases, the weakness of the exemplars used by one of the examiners will affect the examiner's opinion. In *Howard Hughes v. Maheu* (1970), Ralph Bradford was employed by Howard Hughes' attorneys to examine the handwriting. To compare the questioned document, Bradford needed known writing of Hughes. The attorneys who had been employed by Hughes had a difficult time finding exemplars of his writing. Hughes' secretary signed Hughes' name on many documents, and there were also many forgeries floating around. The attorneys finally located known writing on loan and power-of-attorney documents, as well as a fingerprint exemplar, autographed photographs, and an application for a pilot's license. These and other known documents allowed Bradford to identify the questioned writing and then testify in court. In the Mormon Will case it was very difficult for the many examiners, since they did not know which were the genuine exemplars of Hughes' writing. Examiners contacted me to learn which of the Hughes exemplars had been accepted into evidence in the 1970 case of Ralph Bradford.

One final point on the question "Do experts disagree?" If one examiner arrives at a positive opinion and a second examiner gives a qualified opinion (could be), there may be a very thin line between the two opinions. Two opinions of this type are not in disagreement. The second opinion does not claim the first is incorrect but, rather, not positive. A disagreement exists when one examiner says, "positively yes" and one says "positively no." To the question "Do experts disagree?" the answer is, if the two experts are equal in their qualifications and examined the same documents, a disagreement of opinions is highly unlikely.

10. "When was the last time you attempted to verify your opinion? The appropriate answer to this question is "I don't quite understand what you mean." Then the scenario might proceed somewhat the way it did in a recent case:

Q. Let me give you a hypothetical question. Say you were talking about a radar gun, and you would use the gun on the car. It would then give you a reading. So the person in the car would have a speedometer and could tell you exactly what the reading was. Therefore, the check of the radar would come up to what the speedometer said.

A. Yes.

Q. My question is, when is the last time you examined something now knowing what it was, made an opinion, and then were able to go back and actually question the person who actually did write it, who would tell you whether or not they wrote it—in other words, verify it.

A. In the twenty years I have been in Long Beach, I have made over thirty thousand examinations. I have testified in court more than five hundred and thirty times. Every time I testify in court, I am questioned on the stand. In all of the time I have testified, it has never been proved I have made a mistake. So I am being tested constantly, daily, by every examination I have made. So for the thirty thousand examinations, I have been constantly challenged on every one. If anyone had questioned my opinion, they could have pleaded not guilty, and we would have been in court. After these court appearances, over five hundred times, it has never been brought to my attention I have made an error.

Q. So in other words, in your entire handwriting analysis career, you have never made a mistake?

A. I didn't say that.

Q. My question is, when was the last time you were actually able to check the answers you were giving?

A. Yesterday I identified a person, and later he confessed he did it.

Q. How many times?

A. Hundreds.

Q. In the last year?

A. I examined last year—I can't tell you how many times people have confessed to me. I don't remember. But we have had a great number.

Q. You have had many who didn't; is that right?

A. Yes. And I have gone to court on many of them, and I am here again today.

Q. Thank you.

Usually, at the conclusion of your testimony, you are excused, and you should leave the courtroom. If you remain in the courtroom, the jury may think you are overly interested in the disposition of the case.

Ethics

The ethics or conduct of a document examiner reflects on all the others in this profession. It is, therefore, extremely important that a code of ethics be adhered to by all examiners. We could not improve on the codes of the three leading associations, so here they are:

Code of Ethics
The American Society of Questioned Document Examiners

The American Society of Questioned Document Examiners has for its purpose the promotion of justice through the discovery and proof of the facts relating to questioned documents, and to maintain and advance the technical and ethical standards of the profession of Questioned Document Examination.

Application/In furtherance of these Aims and Ideals, each member of this Society pledges himself to abide by the following rules of conduct:

1. To apply the principles of science and logic in the solution of all document problems and to follow the truth courageously wherever it may lead.
2. To keep informed by constant study and research of all new developments and processes in document examination, with a full realization that accuracy is possible only through competence.
3. To treat information received from a client as confidential; and when a matter has already been undertaken, to refuse to perform any services for any person whose interests are opposed to those of the original client, except by express consent of all concerned, or where required by established administrative procedure or by law.
4. To render an opinion or conclusion strictly in accordance with the physical evidence in the document, and only to the extent justified by the facts. To admit frankly that certain questions cannot be answered because of the nature of the problem, the lack of material, or insufficient opportunity for examination.
5. To act at all times both in and out of court in an absolutely impartial manner and to do nothing that would imply partisanship or any interest in the case except the proof of the facts and their correct interpretation.

6. To give the best possible service in all cases, irrespective of the importance of the matter, and to decline to act in any case in which surrounding circumstances seriously restrict adequate examination.

7. To charge for services, when serving as a consultant, on a basis which considers the extent and character of services rendered, the importance of the matter, and the relationship of the problem submitted to the controversy as a whole. Remuneration shall be fair and equitable considering all of the elements in the case. No engagement shall be undertaken on a contingent fee basis. Members employed by public agencies under an annual salary or contract shall be controlled in respect to monetary matters by policies within their organizations.

8. To make technically correct and conservative statements in all written oral reports, testimony, public addresses, or publications, and avoid any misleading or inaccurate claims.

Code of Ethics
International Association for Identification

As a member of the International Association for Identification and being actively engaged in the Profession of Scientific Identification and Investigation, I dedicate myself to the efficient and scientific administration thereof in the interest of Justice and betterment of Law Enforcement.

To cooperate with other [examiners] of the Profession, promote improvement through research, and disseminate such advancement in my effort to make more effective the analysis of the report.

To employ my technical knowledge factually, with zeal and determination, to protect the ethical standards of the profession of Scientific Identification and Investigation. I humbly accept my responsibilities of Public Trust and seek Divine guidance that I may keep inviolate the Profession of Law Enforcement.

Code of Ethics
American Academy of Forensic Sciences

As a means to promote the highest quality of professional and personal conduct of its members, the following constitutes the Code of Ethics which is endorsed and adhered to by all members of the American Academy of Forensic Sciences.

1. Every member of the American Academy of Forensic Sciences shall avoid any material misrepresentation of training, experience, or area of expertise.

2. Every member of the American Academy of Forensic Sciences shall avoid any material misrepresentation of data upon which an expert opinion or conclusion is based.

Notes

1. A History of Handwriting Examination

1. Albert Osborn, "A New Profession," *Journal of the American Judicative Society* 24 (1940).

2. J. Newton Baker, *Law of Disputed and Forged Documents* (Charlottesville, Va.: Mitchie Co., 1955).

3. Albert S. Osborn, *Questioned Documents*, 2d ed. (Albany, N.Y.: Boyd Printing Co., 1929).

4. J. Clark Sellers, "Sciences Advancements in the Examination of Questioned Documents," no date.

5. Albert W. Somerford, "The Dreyfus Case," *Identification News*, March 1947.

6. Osborn, *Questioned Documents*.

7. Edward D. Radin, *12 Against Crime* (New York: Putnam's, 1950).

8. Claire Carvaino and Boyden Sparks, *Crimes in Ink* (New York: Scribner's, 1929).

9. *New York Times*, Feb. 18, 1902.

10. Elbridge W. Stein, "Ultra-Violet Light and Forgery," *Scientific American,* Oct. 1932.

11. Dan Carter, *Scottsboro* (Baton Rouge: Louisiana State University Press, 1969).

12. J. Vreeland Haring, *Hand of Hauptman* (Plainfield, N.J.: Hamer Publishing Co., 1937).

13. George Waller, *Kidnap* (New York: Dial Press, 1961).

14. *New York Times*, Jan. 15, 1935.

15. J. Clark Sellers, "The Handwriting Evidence Against Hauptman," *Journal of Criminal Law, Criminology & Police Science*, 27 (1973):874.

16. Daniel T. Ames, *Ames on Forgery* (New York: Robinson Co., 1900).

17. George Brereton, "Police Training in College and University," IAI California Conference, 1932.

18. Albert D. Osborn, "Brief History of the American Society of Questioned Document Examiners," *Identification News*.

19. Charles C. Scott, *Photographic Evidence* (St. Paul, Minn.: West Pub. Co., 1969).

20. Wilfred A. Beeching, *Century of the Typewriter* (London, England: William Heinemann Ltd., 1974).

21. Albert W. Somerford, "Comparison of Writing Inks by Paper Chromatography," *Journal of Criminal Law, Criminology & Police Science*, 43 (1952):124.

22. James W. Brackett and Lowell W. Bradford, "Comparison of Ink Writing on Documents by Means of Paper Chromatography," *Journal of Criminal Law, Criminology & Police Science*, 45 (1954):530.

23. Charlotte Brown and Paul L. Kirk, "Paper Electrophoresis in the Identification of Writing Inks," *Journal of Criminal Law, Criminology & Police Science*, 45 (1954): 473.

24. Linton Godown, "New Nondestructive Document Testing Methods," *Journal of Criminal Law. Criminology & Police Science*, 55 (1964):280.

25. Joseph Tholl, "The Eastman Chromogram Sheet for Chromatography," *Police*, July 1966.

26. Daniel Crown, Richard Brunelle and Antonio Cantu, "The Parameters of Ballpen Ink Examination," *Journal of Forensic Science*, 21 (1976):917.

27. Orville B. Livingston, "A Handwriting and Pen-Printing Classification System for Identifying Law Violators," *Journal of Criminal Law, Criminology & Police Science*, 49 (1959):487.

28. Ralph Bradford, *The Bradford System* (Long Beach, Calif.: Dreis Investigation Bureau, 1954).

29. Robert A. Shaw, "Checks & Check Writers," *Law & Order Magazine*, July 1980.

30. David Loth, *Crime Lab* (New York: Julian Messner Inc., 1964).

31. Ordway Hilton, *Scientific Examination of Questioned Documents* (New York: Elsevier/North Holland, 1982).

32. Wilson R. Harrison, *Suspect Documents* (London, England: Sweet & Maxwell Ltd., 1958).

33. President's Commission, *The President's Commission on the Assassination of President John F. Kennedy* (Washington, D.C.: U.S. Government Printing Office, 1964).

34. Joseph P. McNally, "Were There Two Oswalds?" AAFS Conference, 1981.

35. Donald L. Bartlett and James B. Steele, *Empire* (New York: W.W. Norton, 1979).

36. Stanton O'Keefe, *The Real Howard Hughes Story* (New York: American Affairs Press, 1972).

37. Don Dwiggins, *Howard Hughes—The True Story* (Santa Monica, Calif.: Werner Book Corp., 1972).

38. Stephen Foy, Lewis Chester and Magnus Linklater, *Hoax* (New York: Viking Press, 1972).

39. Robert Cabanne, "The Clifford Irving Hoax of the Howard Hughes Autobiography," *Journal of Forensic Science*, 20 (1975):5.

40. James Phalen, *Howard Hughes—The Hidden Years* (New York: Random House, 1976).

41. Charles Hamilton, *Great Forgers and Famous Fakes* (New York: Crown, 1980).

42. Robert A. Jones, "The White Salamanders, Part II," *Los Angeles Times Magazine*, April 5, 1987.

43. Linda Sillitoe and Allen Roberts, *Salamander* (Salt Lake City, Utah: Signature Books, 1988).

44. Anthony Scaduto, *Scapegoat* (New York: Putnam, 1976).

45. Theon Wright, *In Search of the Lindbergh Baby* (New York: Tower Books, 1981).

46. Waller, *Kidnap*.

47. E. Roland Menzel, *Fingerprint Detection with Lasers* (New York: Marcel Dekker, 1980).

48. Inga S. Dubay and Barbara M. Getty, *Italic Handwriting Series* (Portland, Ore.: Portland State University, 1980).

2. Introduction to Document Examination

1. Albert S. Osborn, "The Development of the Document Specialist," *Journal of Criminal Law, Criminology and Police Science*, 33 (1942–43):476.

2. Charles C. Scott, *Photographic Evidence* (St. Paul, Minn. West Pub. Co., 1969).

3. President's Commission, *The President's Commission on the Assassination of President Kennedy* (Washington, D.C.: U.S. Government Printing Office, 1964).

4. Arthur J. Quirke, *Forged, Anonymous, and Suspect Documents* (London, England: George Routledge & Sons, 1930).

5. J. Clark Sellers, "Preparing to Testify," *Journal of Criminal Law. Criminology & Police Science*, 56 (1965):235.

6. Roy Kiser and Barbara Torres, "Reasoning Problems for Trainees," AAFS Conference, 1976.

7. John Wooden, *They Call Me Coach* (Waco, Tex.: Word Books, 1972).

8. Ibid.

9. Albert S. Osborn, *The Problem of Proof* (Albany, N.Y.: Boyd Printing Co., 1926); Albert S. Osborn and Albert D. Osborn, *Questioned Documents Problems* (Albany, N.Y.: Boyd Printing Co., 1944); Albert S. Osborn, *Questioned Documents*, 2d ed. (Albany, N.Y.: Boyd Printing Co., 1929).

10. James J. Horan, "Document Examiners Task Study," AAFS Conference, 1980.

11. David A. Black, "The Microscope in Document Examination," *Journal of Criminal Law, Criminology, & Police Science*, 42 (1951–52):810.

12. Ordway Hilton, "Test Plate for Proportional Spacing Typewriter Examinations," *Journal of Criminal Law, Criminology & Police Science*, 47 (1956):257.

13. Joseph Tholl, "Applied Uses of the 35mm in Document Examinations," *Identification News*, May 1965.

14. Luther M. Dey, "Coming into Focus: A Remarkable New Film for Forensic Photography," *The Police Chief*, Sept. 1979.

15. David S. Moore, "The Electrostatic Detection Apparatus (ESDA) and Its Effects on Latent Prints on Paper," AAFS Conference, 1987.

16. Albert S. Osborn, *Questioned Documents*, 2d ed.

17. Alva Johnson, "Hot Documents," *Saturday Evening Post*, Feb. 8, 1947.

18. Verle Truman, "Spectacular Reflection in Document Examination," AAFS Conference, 1981.

19. Albert S. Osborn, *Questioned Documents*, 2d ed.

3. The Bradford System

1. Rush G. Glick and Robert S. Newsom, *Fraud Investigation* (Springfield, Ill.: Charles C. Thomas, 1974).

2. Ralph Bradford, *The Bradford System* (Long Beach, Calif.: Dreis Investigation Bureau, 1954).

3. Eastman Kodak Co., *Kodak Law & Order Info-Pac* (Rochester, N.Y.: Eastman Kodak Co., 1970).

4. "Fighting Crime with Microfilm," *Photo Methods for Industry*, Dec. 1972; Wayne E. Spiva, "Microfilmed Fingerprints," *Police Chief*, Feb. 1971.

4. Vocabulary

1. Verle R. Truman, "Spectacular Reflection in Document Examination," ASQDE Conference, 1980.

2. Patricia R. Harris, "Disguise, Forgery and Look Alike Writing," ASQDE Conference, 1980.

3. Janet Fenner Masson, "A Study of the Handwriting of Adolescents," AAFS Conference, 1987.

4. Ordway Hilton, *Scientific Examination of Questioned Documents* (New York: Elsevier, North Holland Inc., 1982).

5. Parts of Letters

1. Albert S. Osborn, *Questioned Documents*, 2d ed. (Albany, N.Y.: Boyd Printing Co., 1929).

2. Robert Saudek, *Experiments with Handwriting* (London, England: George Allen & Unwin, 1928).

3. Platt R. Spencer, *Spencerian Key to Practical Penmanship* (New York: Ivison, Phinney, Blakeman & Co., 1866).

4. Walter B. Barbe, *Zaner-Bloser Handwriting Workbook: Cursive* (Columbus, Ohio: Zaner-Bloser, Inc., 1977).

5. Fred M. King, *Palmer Method, Cursive Writing, Grade 4* (Schaumburg, Ill.: A.N. Palmer Co., 1979).

6. Regis Turney, Andrew Maureen, Marijon Binder, Fred Chavez and Philip Mann, *Bowmar/Noble Handwriting, Teacher's Guide Books A–D* (Los Angeles, Calif.:Bowmar/Noble Pub., 1981).

7. *20th Century Handwriting Systems* (Washington, D.C.: Bureau of Chief Post Office Inspector, 1947).

8. Virgil E. Herrick, *Comparison of Practices in Handwriting Advocated by Nineteen Commercial Systems of Handwriting Instruction* (Madison: University of Wisconsin, July 1960).

9. Mary S. Beacon, *Survey of Handwriting Systems by States and Territories in the U.S.A. as of 1965* (Atlanta, Ga.: State Crime Lab, 1965).

10. F. Harley Norwitch, "The 'A', A Research Project," ASQDE Conference, 1981.

6. Exemplars

1. Russell R. Bradford, "Obtaining Handwriting Exemplars from All Arrestees," *Fingerprint & Identification Magazine*, Dec. 1973.
2. Albert S. Osborn, *Questioned Documents*, 2d ed (Albany, N.Y.: Boyd Printing Co., 1929).
3. David J. Purtell, "Handwriting Standard Forms," *Journal of Criminal Law, Criminology & Police Science*, 54 (1963):522.
4. William A. Shulenberger, "The Taking of Handwriting & Handprinting Specimens in the Field," *Identification News*, Dec. 1972.

7. Elements of Comparison

1. Albert S. Osborn, *Questioned Documents*, (Albany, N.Y.: Boyd Printing Co., 1929).
2. C.D. Lee and R.A. Abbey, *Classification and Identification of Handwriting* (New York: D. Appleton & Co., 1922).
3. Ibid.
4. Robert Saudek, *The Psychology of Handwriting* (New York: George H. Doran Co., 1926).
5. Lee and Abbey, *Classification*.
6. Ibid.
7. Ibid.
8. Wilson R. Harrison, *Suspect Documents* (London, England: Sweet & Maxwell Ltd., 1958).
9. Lee and Abbey, *Classification*.

8. Five Types of Handwriting

1. John F. McCarthy, "The Axioms of Handwriting Comparison," IAFS Conference, 1978.
2. James H. Kelly, "Effects of Artificial Aids and Prosthesis on Signatures," ASQDE Conference, 1975.
3. Durley Davis, "Writing after Loss of Favored Hand," ASQDE Conference, 1975.
4. Morton Prince, *The Dissociation of a Personality* (London, England: Longmans, Green, 1930).
5. Corbett Thigpen and Hervey Cleckley, "A Case of Multiple Personality," *Journal of Abnormal and Social Psychology*, 49 (1954):135.
6. David A. Bellomy, "A Case of Forgery by an Alleged Multi-Personality Subject," IAFS Conference, 1978.
7. Michael M. Zanoni and Richard W. Chang, "Handwriting Change and Hypnosis," AAFS Conference, 1985.
8. Albert S. Osborn, *Questioned Documents* (Albany, N.Y.: Boyd Printing Co., 1929).
9. Ibid.
10. Ibid.

11. John J. Harris, "Disguised Handwriting," *Journal of Criminal Law and Criminology*, 43 (1953):685.

12. Osborn, *Questioned Documents*.

13. Ibid.

14. Ibid.

15. Wilson R. Harrison, *Suspect Documents* (London, England: Sweet & Maxwell Ltd., 1958).

16. Osborn, *Questioned Documents*.

17. Harrison, *Suspect Documents*.

9. Hand Printing and Numbers

1. David J. Purtell and Maureen A. Casey, "The Comparison Value of Hand Printing Styles," AAFS Conference, 1981.

2. Ordway Hilton, *Scientific Examination of Questioned Documents* (Albany, N.Y.: Elsevier/North Holland, 1982).

3. James V.P. Conway, *Evidential Documents* (Springfield, Ill.: Charles C Thomas, 1959).

4. Marjorie Wise, *On the Technique of Manuscript Writing* (New York: Charles Scribner's Sons, 1924).

5. Albert S. Osborn, *Questioned Documents*, 2d ed. (Albany, N.Y.: Boyd Printing Co., 1929).

6. Wilson R. Harrison, *Suspect Documents* (London, England: Sweet & Maxwell Ltd., 1958).

7. Wise, *On the Technique of Manuscript Writing*.

8. Alfred Fairbank, *The Study of Handwriting* (London, England: Faber and Faber Limited, 1970).

9. Purtell and Casey, *Comparison Value*.

10. Osborn, *Questioned Documents*.

10. Typewriters and Check Protectors

1. George Herrl, *The Carl R. Dietz Collection of Typewriters* (Milwaukee, Wis.: Milwaukee Public Museum, 1965).

2. Arthur Conan Doyle, *The Original Illustrated Sherlock Holmes* (Secaucus, N.J.: Castle Books, 1980).

3. Arthur H. Gleason, "Scientific Sleuths," *Colliers*, April 27, 1912.

4. H. Montgomery Hyde, *Room 3603* (New York: Farrar, Straus, 1962).

5. David Stafford, *Camp X* (New York: Dodd, Mead, 1987).

6. Hyde, *Room 3603*.

7. Allen Weinstein, *Perjury* (New York: Knopf, 1978).

8. Martin K. Tytell, "The $7,500.00 Typewriter I Built for Alger Hiss," *True*, August 1952.

9. Ibid.

10. Alger Hiss, *In the Court of Public Opinion* (New York: 1957).

11. Edith Tiger, *In Re Alger Hiss*, Vols. 1 & 2 (New York: Hill & Wang, 1979).

12. William A. Reuben, *Footnote on an Historic Case: In Re Alger Hiss, No. 78 Civ. 3433* (New York: National Institute, 1983).

13. John C. Costain, "A Classification and Filing System for American-Made Typewriter Specimens," IAI Conference, 1970.

14. Linton Godown, "Classification, Indexing and Searching Typewriter Specimen Files," *Journal of Forensic Science*, 14 (1969):48.

15. Harold L. Steinberg, *Standard Reference Collection of Forensic Science Materials: Status and Needs* (Washington, D.C.: Government Printing Office, 1977).

16. Jean Gayet and Frank Lundquist, *Methods of Forensic Science*, vol. 2 (New York: Interscience Pub., 1963).

17. Ibid.

18. Lamar Miller, "An Analysis of the Identification Value of Defects in IBM Selectric Typewriters," AAFS Conference, 1983.

19. *The Story of Lieutenant Colonel Oliver North*, U.S. News & World Report, 1987.

20. William A. Schulenberger, "An Unusual Typewriter Case," ISI Conference, 1984.

21. Lois I. Hutchinson, *Standard Handbook for Secretaries* (New York: McGraw-Hill, 1971).

22. E.E. Hoffman, *Billion Dollar Check Racket* (New York: Vantage Press, 1962).

23. Ralph Bradford, *The Bradford System* (Long Beach, Calif.: Dreis Investigations, 1954).

24. J. Clark Sellers, "Check Protector Identification," *Identification News*, Dec. 1952.

25. David J. Purtell, "The Identification of Checkwriters," *Journal of Criminal Law, Criminology & Police Science*, 45 (1954):229.

26. John W. Hargett and Richard A. Dusak, "A Compilation of Research on the Check Writer Industry for the Purpose of Classification and Identification," *Journal of Police Science and Administration*; 4 (1976):404.

27. T.W. Vastrick and E.J. Smith, "Checkwriter Identification-Individuality," *Journal of Forensic Science*, 27 (1982):161.

11. Fingerprints

1. B.C. Bridges, "Pioneers of Finger Print Science," *Fingerprint & Identification Magazine*, Feb. 1954.

2. Samuel Clemens, *Pudd'nhead Wilson* (New York: Harper & Harper, 1899).

3. J. Edgar Hoover, "The Rise of Identification in Law Enforcement," *FBI Law Enforcement Bulletin*, March 1973.

4. James P. Mock, *Basis Latent Print Development: A Guide for the Beginner* (Torrance, Calif.: Police Department, 1987).

5. Andrew J. Brooks, "Technique for Finding Latent Prints, *Fingerprint & Identification Magazine*, Nov. 1972.

6. David Mooney, "Development of Latent Fingerprints & Palmprints by Ninhydrin," *Identification News*, Aug. 1966.

7. David Crown, "Development of Latent Fingerprints," *Journal of Criminal Law, Criminology & Police Science*, 60 (1969):258.

8. Denis J. Tighe, "Freon-Plus Two," *Identification News*, June 1984.

9. *The President's Commission on the Assassination of President Kennedy* (Washington, D.C.: U.S. Government Printing Office, 1964).

10. Harold Cummings and Charles Midlo, *Fingerprints, Palms & Soles* (New York: Dover, 1961).

11. Federal Bureau of Investigation, *The Science of Fingerprints* (Washington, D.C.: U.S. Government Printing Office, 1939; revised, 1963).

12. Harry Battley, *Single Finger Prints* (New Haven, Conn.: Yale University Press, 1931).

13. *The President's Commission.*

14. Ene-Malle Lauritis, "The Legal Aid Briefcase," National Legal Aid & Defenders Association, Oct. 1968.

15. Vassislis C. Morfopoulos, "The Anatomy of Evidence," *Identification News*, Dec. 1970.

16. Federal Bureau of Investigation, 1963.

17. Paul McCann, "Concluding Report IAI Standardization Committee," *Identification News*, Aug. 1973.

18. E. Roland Mengel, *Fingerprint Detection with Lasers* (New York: Marcel Dekker, 1980).

12. Court Appearance

1. Select Committee on Assassinations, *Investigation of the Assassination of Martin Luther King, Jr.,* (Washington, D.C.: U.S. Government Printing Office, 1979).

2. Phillip Schmitz, "Should Experienced Document Examiners Write Inconclusive Reports?" *Journal of Criminal Law, Criminology & Police Science*, 59 (1968):444.

3. Alwyn Cole, "Standards for the Document Examiner," *Canadian Society Forensic Science Journal*, 12 (1979):17.

4. Alwyn Cole, "Opinion v. Demonstrative Evidence," *Identification News*, May 1953.

5. *Illinois Law Review*, November 1926.

6. J. Baker Newton, *Law of Disputed and Forged Documents* (Charlottesville, Va.: Michie Co., 1955).

7. Ordway Hilton, *Scientific Examination of Questioned Documents* (New York: Elsevier/North Holland, 1982).

8. Wilson Harrison, *Suspect Documents* (London, England: Sweet & Maxwell, 1958).

9. Federal Bureau of Investigation, *Classification of Fingerprints* (Washington, D.C.: U.S. Government Printing Office, 1939).

10. Albert S. Osborn, *Questioned Documents* (Albany, N.Y.: Boyd Printing Co., 1929).

11. Charles C. Scott, *Photographic Evidence* (St. Paul, Minn.: West Publishing Co., 1969).

12. *Kodak Law & Order Info-Pac* (Rochester, N.Y.: Eastman Kodak Co., 1970).

13. T. Dickerson Cooke, "Be Ready in the Morning," *Fingerprint & Identification Magazine*, Aug. 1965.

14. J. Clark Sellers, "Preparing to Testify," *Journal of Criminal Law, Criminology & Police Science*, 56 (1965):235.

15. John H. Wigmore, *Wigmore on Evidence* (Boston, Mass.: Little, Brown, 1979).

16. John J. Harris, "Preparation for Trial from a Document Examiner's Viewpoint," *Journal of Forensic Science*, 7 (1962):351.

17. Dale Carnegie, *Public Speaking* (New York: Association Press, 1952).

18. John T. Molloy, "What to Wear in Court," *Newsweek*, Dec. 16, 1974.

19. John T. Molloy, *Dress for Success* (New York: Warner Books, 1976).

20. William A. Schulenberger, "The Document Examiner on the Witness Stand," *Identification News*, Nov. 1967.

21. Charles W. Fricke, "Testimonial Proof of Questioned Documents," California Check Investigators Conference, 1957.

22. Oscar Mendelson, *Liars and Letters Anonymous* (Melbourne, Australia: Lansdowne Press, 1961).

23. Osborn, *Questioned Documents*.

Bibliography

Albert S. Osborn stated, "In every field there are many who never learn that there were those gone before who could have greatly aided them." To unlock the past, the nucleus of a document examiner's library was listed in chapter 2. This bibliography is an expanded version of that nucleus. A few of these books (for example, Bates and Frazer) contain ideas that are impractical or even valueless. But without a broad study, one's education would not be complete. Many of the books listed can be located for study in libraries, either public or university.

Handwriting

Ames, Daniel T. *Ames on Forgery*. Reprint. Littleton, Colo.: Fred B. Rothman, 1981.

Baker, J. Newton. *Law of Disputed and Forged Documents* Charlottesville, Va.: Michie Co., 1955.

Bates, Billy P. *Identification System for Questioned Documents*. Springfield, Ill., Charles C. Thomas, 1970.

Bradford, Ralph. *The Bradford System*. Long Beach, Calif.: Dries Investigations, 1954.

Brunelle, Richard and Robert Reed. *Forensic Examination of Ink and Paper*. Springfield, Ill.: Charles C. Thomas, 1984.

Carvalho, David N. *Forty Centuries of Ink*. New York: Banks Publishing Co., 1904.

Carvalho, Claire and Boyden Sparkes. *Crime in Ink*. New York: Charles Scribner's Sons, 1929.

Conway, James V.P. *Evidential Documents*. Springfield, Ill.: Charles C. Thomas, 1959.

Fairbank, Alfred. *Study of Handwriting*. New York: Watson-Guptill, 1970.

Frazer, Persifor. *Bibliotics or the Study of Documents*. Philadelphia, Penn.: J.B. Lippincott, 1901.

Grant, Julius. Books and Documents. London, England: Grafton & Co., 1937.

Hagan, William E. *Treatise on Disputed Handwriting*. Reprint. New York: AMS Press, 1974.

Hamilton, Charles. *Great Forgers and Famous Fakes*. New York: Crow Publishers, 1980.

Haring, J. Vreeland. *Hand of Hauptman.* Plainfield, N.J.: Hamer, 1937.

Harrison, Wilson R. *Forgery Detection.* New York: Praeger, 1964.

Harrison, Wilson R. *Suspect Documents.* Reprint. Chicago, Ill.: Nelson-Hall, 1981.

Hilton, Ordway. *Scientific Examination of Questioned Documents.* New York: Elsevier/North Holland, 1982.

Jones, Lloyd L. *Valid or Forged.* New York: Funk & Wagnalls, 1938.

Lavoy, Jerome B. *Disputed Handwriting.* Chicago, Ill. Harvard Book Co., 1909.

Lee, D.C. and R.A. Abbey. *Classification of Handwriting.* New York: Appleton, 1922.

Mitchell, C.A. *Documents and Their Scientific Examination.* London, England: Charles Griffin & Co., 1935.

Osborn, Albert S. *Mind of the Juror.* Albany, N.Y.: Boyd Printing Co., 1937.

Osborn, Albert S. *Problems of Proof.* Albany, N.Y.: Boyd Printing Co., 1922.

Osborn, Albert S. *Questioned Documents.* Reprint. Chicago, Ill.: Nelson-Hall, 1981.

Osborn, Albert S., and Albert D. Osborn. *Questioned Document Problems.* Reprint. Chicago, Ill.: Nelson-Hall, 1981.

Quirke, Arthur J. *Forged, Anonymous and Suspect Documents.* London, England: George Routhledge & Sons, 1930.

Sillitoe, Linda, Allen Roberts, and George J. Throckmorton. *Salamander.* Salt Lake City, Utah: Signature Books, 1988.

Saudek, Robert. *Psychology of Handwriting.* New York: George H. Doran Co., 1926.

Smith, Edward J. *Principles of Forensic Handwriting Identification and Testimony.* Springfield, Ill.: Charles C. Thomas, 1984.

Sulner, Hanna F. *Disputed Documents.* New York: Oceana, 1966.

Wigmore, John. *Evidence.* Boston, Mass.: Little Brown, 1924.

Zinnel, George H. *Forgeries.* Minneapolis, Minn.: Bureau of Engraving, 1931.

Typewriting

Bates, Billy P. *Typewriter Identification.* Springfield, Ill.: Charles C. Thomas, 1971.

Beeching, Wilfred. *Century of the Typewriter.* New York: St. Martin's Press, 1974.

Bliven, Bruce. *Wonderful Writing Machine.* New York: Random House, 1954.

Gayet, Jean and Frank Lundquist. *Methods of Forensic Science.* Vol. 2. New York: Interscience, 1963.

Herrl, George. *Carl R. Dietz Collection of Typewriters.* Milwaukee, Wis.: Milwaukee Public Museum, 1965.

Photography

Bureau of Naval Personnel. *Photographer's Mate 3 & 2.* Washington, D.C.: U.S. Government Printing Office, 1971.

Bureau of Naval Personnel. *Photographer's Mate 1 & C.* Washington, D.C.: U.S. Government Printing Office, 1974.

Purves, Frederick. *Focal Encyclopedia of Photography.* New York: Macmillan, 1960.

Sansom, Sam J. *Modern Photography for Police and Firemen.* Cincinnati, Ohio: W.H. Anderson, 1971.

Scott, Charles C. *Photographic Evidence.* St. Paul, Minn.: West Pub. Co., 1969.

Fingerprints

Battley, Harry. *Single Finger Prints.* New Haven, Conn.: Yale University Press, 1931.

Bridges, B.C. *Practical Fingerprinting.* New York: Funk & Wagnalls, 1963.

Clements, Wendell W. *The Study of Latent Fingerprints.* Springfield, Ill.: Charles C. Thomas, 1987.

Cummings, Harold and Charles Midlo. *Fingerprints, Palms and Soles.* New York: Dover, 1961.

Federal Bureau of Investigation. *Science of Fingerprints.* Washington, D.C.: U.S. Government Printing Office, 1984.

Mock, James P. *Basis Latent Print Development, A Guide for the Beginner.* Torrance, Calif.: Department of Police, 1987.

Scott, Walter R. *Fingerprint Mechanics.* Springfield, Ill.: Charles C. Thomas, 1951.

Williams, Richard and Robert Sorenson. *Fingerprint Handbook.* Santa Cruz, Calif.: Davis Co., 1970.

Miscellaneous

Carnegie, Dale. *How to Develop Self-Confidence and Influence People by Public Speaking.* New York: Pocket Books, 1975.

Casey, Maureen. *Syllabus/Bibliography of Selected Books and Articles Relating to Forensic Document Examination.* Colorado Springs, Colo.: American Board of Forensic Document Examiners, 1979.

Lockwood's Directory. New York: Vance Pub. Updated annually.

Molloy, John T. *Dress for Success.* New York: Warner Books, 1975.

Index of Examiners

Index